The Presidency of John Adams

John Adams (*Engraved from the painting by Chappel.*)

The Presidency of John Adams

THE COLLAPSE OF FEDERALISM 1795-1800

by

STEPHEN G. KURTZ

Philadelphia
UNIVERSITY OF PENNSYLVANIA PRESS

Library of Congress Catalogue Card Number: 57-7764

Second Printing, 1969

SBN 8122-7101-7

Printed in the United States of America

to

Francis Godolphin

Preface

WHEN THE EXPERIMENT IN GOVERNMENT FASHIONED BY THE Philadelphia convention of 1787 was presented to the people for ratification few, if any, of its framers were satisfied that it would survive. It was recognized that much would depend upon the wisdom of the men who were to administer this government of laws during its early years. Thus it was that George Washington, greatly against his will, was brought back into public life at the summit of national affairs. There was very little doubt that only Washington, a man whose prestige was as high during his lifetime as any figure in history, could fill the office of first President. His election was unanimous, and if ever the general will existed or was exercised by a political body it was in the choice of Washington to launch this experiment.

It is too often forgotten that there was no modern precedent to guide the first lawmakers, jurists, and administrators of the United States. Central government had to be set over and at times against the governments of thirteen separate and hitherto sovereign states; yet it was demanded that this government must be at the same time integrated with state governments in its functionings. Ancient precedent suggested to a generation steeped in classical history that popular government could not succeed when applied to a widespread geographic area. Opponents of the Federal Constitution were quick to point toward the Roman experience, the gradual withering away of popular institutions, and the degradation of republican virtues as new territories were added and new peoples brought under its dominion.

The geographic immensity of the United States staggered

the imagination of the eighteenth century. It was difficult enough to hold the frontier—western Massachusetts, western Pennsylvania, western Virginia, or western North Carolina—in line with seaboard interests, and every state with the exception of Rhode Island had its frontier expansionist problems, but that New England fishermen and farmers could be united for common reasons with slave-holding Carolina planters took more than ordinary imagination. There was little to help minimize the sense of isolation in a predominantly rural America. Communication by coastal schooner may have been satisfactory for those close to the Atlantic coast, but for those who dwelt inland travel by coach was an ordeal whose rigors could only be borne by the physically hardy. A trip that President Adams made in 1800 from Philadelphia to the new capital site at Washington consumed three full days, and in heavy rain or snow would have been impossible without resorting to horseback. It is hardly surprising to find that most members of Congress, including the Vice-President, were forced to live a bachelor existence or that national politics held little attraction for men living beyond the metropolitan areas surrounding Philadelphia, Baltimore, and New York. Meager salaries discouraged many more, and consequently a major problem during the 1790's was that of inducing men of talent to desert familiar and more comfortable lives for the uncertainties and hardships of Federal service. There was probably not a single national figure from Washington's inauguration to Jefferson's who did not suffer materially as a consequence of service to the national government. It is no wonder that loyalty to state was more prevalent than loyalty to nation among men who made politics or government their avocation.

With these factors in mind it is reasonable to conclude that without Washington's prestige and drawing power the Federal experiment might have floundered. There were many who considered it a failure before it had commenced, and even James Madison could defend the new Federal government as only the best of possible compromises. What would be the result should a man of less popularity undertake the presidency, an office which by 1796 had become the first fruits of violent partisanship rather than unanimity?

Division on a national scale had arisen over the question of defining the scope of Federal and state authority. Those who demanded the use of wider powers by the central government became known as "Federalists," and those who feared the growing power of the national government assumed the name "Republican." Logical words and illogical words did not settle their differences, and it was quickly recognized that a change in personnel was the only solution that the disquieted and the dissatisfied would accept.

In 1795 the first national contest between these two coalitions commenced. A treaty with Great Britain produced an explosion: Republicans claimed that it would not act in the general interests but would only serve the moneyed power that they believed hidden behind Washington's commanding figure. The debate over this measure was more intense than any which had been occasioned by Washington's other controversial measures, and Republicans, rejoicing in the unpopularity of this venture into diplomacy, were determined to agitate the question until the change in personnel that they believed necessary could be engineered. The Constitution happily presented them with the opportunity to do this in 1796 when Washington was expected to step down from the pedestal he had so long occupied.

Historians have in the main agreed as to what happened. We might go so far as to say that there is a standard account, which most textbooks print, how John Adams, President by a three-vote electoral margin, fell into the vacuum created by Washington's departure and crept out of office in the dawn of democracy's birth a broken man, his party, the party of talents, a shattered ruin, his only accomplishment a negative one, that of averting a disastrous war with France, the world's greatest military power. It has likewise been told repeatedly that Hamilton succeeded in breaking this man so devoid of political finesse and in so doing elevated his great antagonist Jefferson to a place where he might reorient American life.

Not long ago Catherine Drinker Bowen in her *John Adams and the American Revolution* reminded us of a man of great vigor and parliamentary talents, an orator who could push the wavering and fearful into defiance of Britain. Gilbert Chinard, in conversations that are remembered with delight, introduced me to John Adams the learned and ambitious New England advocate, who spent a lifetime debating the great problems of man's use of freedom, a man as learned and keen as any of his generation in matters of law and political theory. Roy Franklin Nichols pointed out that there were many problems in the history of the early national period that a study of the Adams administration might help to clarify; problems concerning the management of and creation of national political parties and a national point of view without which a central government in a federal framework might have been impossible. To these three scholars I am indebted for awakening my curiosity.

There was one problem that puzzled me above all others, however: Why was it that Hamilton, so powerful a force in Federalist ranks, could not destroy Adams before he had gained the presidency and why during the ensuing four years was he unable to dominate a party whose leaders looked continually to him for direction? What began as a study of political methodology ended in suggesting answers to some of these questions that the failures of both Hamilton and Adams had left unexplained. John Adams does not emerge a heroic figure; he was not of heroic proportions as was Washington, whose influence often dominated him in life as it continued to do in death. He lacked Washington's ability to override great difficulties with outward equinimity and confidence, he lacked Hamilton's driving enthusiasm and glamour, and he certainly lacked Jefferson's faith in the wisdom of ordinary men and in democracy as a method of government. As time has demonstrated, he lacked the abiding popularity and success of Jefferson as a political figure. Study has proved to my own satisfaction, however, that the Adams record was not as disastrous to the nation or as strong a condemnation of his personal failings as our standard histories would have it. So strongly has the impression of futility been stamped upon the history of the Adams administration that much good and substantial thought and action have been submerged and lost to view. It would be enough to raise these once more to the light of day.

I wish to record my gratitude to Wayne Andrews, whose assistance in the New York Historical Society archives was deeply appreciated, to R. W. Hill and W. L. Leech of the New York Public Library, Alexander P. Clark of the Princeton University Library, Catherine Miller and Mary Townsend of the Historical Society of Pennsylvania, all of whom rendered me interested and fruitful aid. John H. Powell of Philadelphia added to my interest and enthusiasm for this work, and I would add a special word of thanks to Julian P. Boyd, Lyman H. Butterfield, and Mina R. Bryan for taking time from their work on the Jefferson papers project to help me check a reference or discuss an idea.

My gratitude to the Rev. John O. Patterson, Headmaster of Kent School, is in return for allowing me to have time and space for study and writing not ordinarily encouraged in the life of a schoolmaster. Both my wife and our friend Barbara Holly Muller lent me hours of their time in correcting and typing the manuscript. Finally, I am personally indebted in many ways to my father-in-law, Francis R. B. Godolphin. To him this work is affectionately dedicated.

STEPHEN G. KURTZ

Wabash College, Crawfordsville, Indiana

Contents

Illustrations

The Presidency of John Adams

1

Bright Hopes for Mr. Jefferson

THE GROWTH OF POLITICAL PARTIES WAS A SOURCE OF CONstant concern to Washington as his presidential career drew to its close. Although he left a permanent memorial to his hatred of parties in the Farewell Address, his acceptance of John Jay's treaty of amity and commerce in the fall of 1795 did more to solidify party lines than any other action of his presidency. By signing this undistinguished document the President gave up all hopes of retiring from twenty years of public service with the blessings of a united people to comfort him in the wintertime of life. The treaty that Chief Justice Jay concluded with Great Britain proved to administration critics what they had long suspected: that a government dominated by Alexander Hamilton could not be trusted to right America's grievances against England. Mr. Jay's friends considered half a loaf better than none and wondered how a nation with no navy was expected to browbeat a nation that went to work whistling "Britannia Rules the Waves." Their embarrassment could scarcely be concealed, however, and the worst of it was that a national election was in view, Washington was dropping out, and public favor was running in the direction of Monticello.

As 1795 grew old enough for Mr. Jefferson's friends to begin thinking about "next year," it required less and less imagination to see their hero taking the inaugural oath. They were assuming, of course, that General Washington had made up his mind on the retirement question and that the way would at last be open for an honest test of party strength. His immense prestige, so often thrown against them, would no longer stand in the way of ripping Mr. Hamilton's Federalist program open from top to bottom, and the Virginians were already passing from the dreaming to the scheming stage as they prepared to convene the winter session of the House of Delegates in November. They were ready to ride the Jay treaty into the presidential mansion behind Thomas Jefferson.

The opposition leader had retired from Washington's official family at the end of 1793 after a discouraging fight against Alexander Hamilton, who, even out of office, managed to lead the Federalists and to advise the President from his New York law office. Isolated from the world of active politics, Jefferson watched the long struggle over the British treaty from Monticello with interest. He was still politician enough to know that what his partisans called a fight against British influence had not died when Washington signed the treaty that fall. Writing to his friend James Monroe, who was making himself so popular in Paris and so unpopular in Philadelphia that year, Jefferson prophesied that the struggle would continue. "The House of Representatives will oppose it," he wrote in reference to the treaty, "as constitutionally void, and thus bring on an embarrassing and critical state in our government."[1]

The crisis that Jefferson foresaw arising in the House, the one branch of the Federal government that his party could control, arose eight months later in March of the election year, but it took shape first in Richmond in November, 1795.

Leaders of the Republican party in Virginia dropped the problem of co-ordinating their attack with that which would be launched in Congress squarely into James Madison's lap. To condemn the administration meant to condemn Washing-

[1] September 6, 1795, Jefferson, *Writings* (Ford ed.), VIII, 188. The standard work on Jay's diplomacy is S. F. Bemis, *Jay's Treaty* (New York, 1923).

ton, and many men had been known to waver on the brink of what to the revolutionary generation was more a question of morality than politics. Joseph Jones, delegate from the town of Fredericksburg, had talked the matter over carefully with his friends and felt it essential for Madison to spend a night with him on his return trip to Philadelphia. The treaty offered too great an opportunity to be lost through carelessness. What was contemplated, he wrote Madison, was a series of resolutions aimed at a Constitutional amendment giving the House of Representatives an equal voice with the Senate in ratifying treaties. Jones promised to keep Madison's name out of the debates at Richmond.[2]

Ten days later Madison stopped off at Fredericksburg and gave his consent to the plan.[3] By the time he reached Philadelphia assurances that the lower South would support radical changes in the ratifying process were arriving. Senator Jackson of Georgia was as eager as the Virginians to have Madison take the lead. "The people look to you for some amendments which will clip the wings of the executive." Such was the sentiment in his state, according to Jackson.[4]

Federalists were prepared for the worst as they joined their Republican colleagues in Richmond. Colonel Edward Carrington of Richmond took stock of the situation and sent on to the President one of his periodic reports of local politics. As usual, Carrington was unduly optimistic. The Antifederalists, he reported, were talking loudly about chastising the administration and appeared confident that their sister states would support them, but their floor leaders at Richmond were nothing more than a few "hotheads" whose talents in debate would be no match for those of John Marshall and Henry Lee. Marshall, though lacking a national reputation and the popularity of "Lighthorse Harry" Lee, had

[2] October 29, 1795, *Madison Papers,* LC.

[3] Madison to Jefferson, Madison to James Madison, Sr., November 8, 1795, *ibid.*

[4] James Jackson to Madison, November 17, 1795, *ibid.*

already won distinction for his legal talents and forensic powers. Carrington promised strong support from Charles Lee and himself, and he assured Washington that if logic had anything to do with the outcome the Federalists would be more than a match for their opponents.[5]

The Republicans lost no time in demonstrating their power in the legislature and within a week after the opening session had pushed through a resolution commending Virginia's senators for voting against ratification of the Jay treaty by a two-to-one majority. John Marshall's powerful condemnation of the resolve was admired but could not be seen to have won any converts to the administration side. Republicans were convinced after the first test of strength that their numbers would hold.[6]

For their part the minority could not afford to hold back their heaviest weapon. When Delegate Mayo moved that the entire treaty question be placed before the House, Wade Hampton leaped to his feet to throw Washington's prestige at his opponents. The motion implied a criticism of the President, and as far as he was concerned the motion would implicate both Washington's conduct and character. Hampton demanded postponement but was voted down, 110 to 40. As a last resort Charles Lee attempted to give the ensuing debate a completely unofficial character by proposing an amendment to the Mayo motion which stated that it would be both "inexpedient and improper" for the House to express an official opinion. The proper method of criticizing a treaty, through resolutions submitted by the people to their Congressmen, had already failed to change the Executive's position, he maintained, but again Federalist arguments carried little weight. Following the overwhelming defeat of Lee's amendment, John Taylor arose to launch the Repub-

[5] November 10, 1795, Beveridge, *John Marshall*, II, 132; Boyd, *Harry Lee*, 240.

[6] Joseph Jones to Madison, November 22, 1795, *Madison Papers*, LC.

lican attack with the charge that the treaty was unconstitutional.[7]

Over the week end John Marshall labored over his reply to Taylor. His performance at the Richmond hearings in the British debts cases of 1793 pointed to him as the only Virginia Federalist who might be pitted against Taylor on a constitutional question. Realizing that he had no chance of turning the majority from its ultimate objective, Marshall avoided the question of expediency altogether. For more than three hours on November 19 and 20 the tall, relaxed figure held the floor. Again and again he returned to his basic premise that a treaty is as valid when ratified by the President with the consent of the Senate as though approved by the popular branch of the legislature. The Constitution was perfectly clear on the point, and Marshall challenged the Republicans either to accept the Constitution or to change it. He admitted the constitutional right of the House to refuse appropriations after ratification, a far more judicious procedure than to allow the treaty to be "stifled in embryo," but he urged Virginia to avoid the disgrace of giving "an unnecessary affront" to the President, who had acted in good faith throughout.[8]

Carrington and his friends were delighted with Marshall's efforts, but from the final vote on the resolution to uphold the state's senators for their action it was clear that reverence for Washington was melting rapidly. By a vote of 100 to 50 the Executive was chastised. Federalists held to the belief that Washington's character was still their best weapon and succeeded in having an amendment adopted acquitting the President of "evil intention" in signing the British treaty.[9] Public feeling might still be aroused against the Republicans

[7] Jones to Madison, November 22, 1795, *ibid.*

[8] Marshall to Hamilton, April 25, 1796, Hamilton, *Works* (Lodge ed.), VI, 109; T. M. Randolph to Jefferson, November 22, 1795, Jefferson, *Writings* (Ford ed.), VIII, 198.

[9] Jones to Madison, November 22, 1795, *Madison Papers*, LC.

provided Washington's name became the outstanding issue in the treaty question. In the South this was their only chance, and they clung to it.

Jefferson received the news from Richmond with slightly mixed emotions. The tactics of the Federalists were plain to him and might prove embarrassing, but he welcomed the opportunity of opening the question of public participation in the treaty-making process. Marshall's acknowledged talents were causing some embarrassment to "the Republican Party," he commented in writing to Madison, but at least he was out in the open. "He has hitherto been able to do more mischief acting under the mask of republicanism than he will be able to do after throwing it off so plainly. His lax, lounging manners have made him popular with the bulk of the people of Richmond." [10]

Not only did the Virginia Republicans reopen the agonizing treaty question just as it seemed to expire, but they also arose in open rebellion against Washington's leadership. Three weeks after grudgingly acquitting the President of malicious use of his office, the House of Delegates adopted four resolutions that were immediately dispatched to the legislatures of the other states. It was proposed that constitutional amendments be adopted which would ensure that no treaty "containing any stipulations upon the subject of the powers invested in Congress . . ." become law until approved by a majority of the House of Representatives, that a tribunal other than the Senate be set up for impeachment, that the term of Senators be cut to three years, and that no person holding office as a Federal judge be eligible for any other Federal appointment.[11]

There was no doubt that the Virginia resolves would fail to reach the goal of adoption as amendments, but it is equally clear that the avowed purpose of their passage was not the

[10] November 26, 1795, *Jefferson Papers*, LC.
[11] *Maryland Gazette* (Annapolis), December 31, 1795.

true one. Neither two thirds of the state legislatures nor two thirds of the two houses of the Federal legislature could have been expected to accept these radical proposals. Outside the South the Federalist party was too powerful, and only a complete sweep of the elections of 1796 would have changed the complexion of the national legislature sufficiently to realize the Virginia program. In giving their grievances against the administration a national review the Republicans hoped to stir the people to wrath in time to support the promised attack against the treaty in the House of Representatives and successfully to launch the presidential campaign. Having begun the attack the Virginians rested, leaving to Madison and his friends in Philadelphia the final responsibility for the result. The next move depended upon the state Republican organizations.

The first reaction was disheartening. Without waiting for the amendment resolutions to be placed before the legislature, the Maryland Federalists hit back. "Observing with deep concern a series of efforts by indirect insinuations or open invective to detach from the first magistrate of the union, the well earned confidence of his fellow citizens," read a resolution adopted at Annapolis on November 25, "the Legislature of Maryland do hereby declare their unabated reliance on the integrity, judgement, and patriotism of the President of the United States." Washington's old friend Governor Howard lost no time in mailing the declaration to Philadelphia.[12]

So great was the hostility felt in Maryland for the Virginia program that the Republicans made no attempt to bring the proposed amendments officially to the attention of the legislature. When they were introduced it was by Federalist leaders who held back for more than six months until the canvassing for presidential electors had begun. In the

[12] John E. Howard to Washington, December 25, 1795, Washington, *Writings*, XXXIV, 380.

midst of the campaign, a committee of both houses headed by the venerable Charles Carroll, signer of the Declaration of Independence, sent in a damning report on Virginia theories of government.

It was resolved that the first and third resolutions would "endanger the liberty of the people" by granting "too great a preponderancy to the House of Representatives." The second and fourth were simply "inexpedient as not being warranted" from the present organization of the Federal government. The report of the Carroll committee was overwhelmingly endorsed by both houses.[13]

Massachusetts promised to deal more kindly with its powerful sister state to the south. At Boston on January 19 Governor Sam Adams drew attention to the amendment proposals in his annual address to the legislature. While not mentioning the source or openly sanctioning the proposals, the old democrat's well-known radical leanings left little doubt that his blessing went with his recommendation that the assemblymen earnestly consider the need for granting a voice to the House of Representatives in the treaty process. Republicans applauded lustily, but a high-ranking Federalist believed that the Governor's speech had met with "almost universal disgust." Washington's friends hoped to see Sam Adams defeated for re-election on the basis of such foolhardiness.[14] When the lower house returned its answer to the Governor's address several days later the rejection of the Virginia resolutions was clearly forecast.

"In every free republic it is of the highest importance that the Legislature, Executive, and Judiciary powers be preserved as separate and independent of each other," read a reply that John Adams himself might have framed. "The business of making treaties being expressly delegated to the

[13] K. M. Rowland, *Charles Carroll* (New York and London 1898), II, 212.

[14] Christopher Gore to Rufus King, January 21, 1796, *King Papers*, New York Historical Society, Box 6, No. 60.

federal government by the Constitution of the United States, we consider a respectful submission on the part of the people to be the surest means of enjoying and perpetuating the invaluable blessings of our free republican government." [15]

The best that Bay State Republicans could do for their cause was to have the Virginia resolutions tabled for possible review later, a suggestion put forth by Boston's Dr. Jarvis after the Assembly had soundly defeated the motion to debate the proposals in committee of the whole.[16]

The editor of a Connecticut newspaper, taking his cue from Hamilton, who was then producing his "Camillus" letters in defense of the Jay treaty, made certain that his readers were aware of the ultimate issues in the Republican program. He was certain that the treaty itself was but a smoke screen behind which they might maneuver Americans into accepting hated French political doctrines. "Much has been said on the subject of gratitude to France for their aid in the late Revolution," wrote the editor of the New London *Connecticut Gazette*, and quoting a passage from one of Vergennes' letters that Hamilton had lifted from State Department files he concluded, "That France was useful to us is certain: but it is equally certain that the interest of America never entered into their views." [17]

In New England, as in other sections of the country, the Jay treaty, the French Revolution, and the appeal of the Virginians on behalf of the House of Representatives were bound up in one all-embracing political issue. For the moment it suited the purposes of New England Federalists to seek shelter behind the imposing figure of Washington. The entire Southern program, they maintained, was simply an attempt to undermine the President's reputation for honesty.

[15] *Connecticut Gazette*, February 4, 1796.
[16] Gore to King, January 21, 1796, *op. cit.*
[17] *Connecticut Gazette*, *op. cit.*

The Virginia resolves, including that commending her senators, were uncalled-for stabs in the back.

Connecticut acted as expected. Governor Oliver Wolcott's party, firmly buttressed by the Congregationalist clergy and seaboard merchant interests, held the state's offices in an iron grip throughout the 1790's and had no hesitancy in condemning political imports from Virginia. Rhode Island had likewise had little experience with two-party government prior to 1796, and on the fourth of February fell in line with her larger neighbor by voting a resolution in the legislature upholding the President and the administration's policy toward Great Britain.[18]

Vermont and New Hampshire produced enough political opposition to Federalist policies during Washington's second term to suggest the emergence of a strong opposition faction, but in both states the Republican amendment resolutions were defeated. New Hampshire Federalists turned their negative vote sharply back upon the Southerners by charging that the state of Virginia was attempting to "subvert the constitution." Except for the fact that the charge had become a familiar one by 1796, the accusation was serious and showed how little respect among politicians the Republican party had won in the far North.[19]

In the three Middle Atlantic states of New York, New Jersey, and Pennsylvania, Federalist-controlled legislatures debated the Virginia amendment platform and condemned it. The assemblymen of both New York and New Jersey staunchly reaffirmed their faith in Washington,[20] but in Pennsylvania, where the new Republican party organization was strong enough to prevent Federalists from unseating Thomas Mifflin, the commonwealth's fence-sitting governor, Republican leaders found basis for optimism.

[18] *Independent Chronicle* (Boston), February 8, 1796.
[19] Madison to Edmund Pendleton, February 7, 1796, *Madison Papers*, LC.
[20] *Independent Chronicle*, February 8, 1796.

The Federal government had stirred up special attention in Pennsylvania, not only because politics was one of the primary occupations of its metropolis, but also because the recent Whiskey Rebellion had become an important symbol of local opposition to Federal legislation. The upper house was controlled by eastern members of the administration party and passed a resolution declaring "unshaken confidence" in Washington; but in the lower chamber a long debate over the Virginia amendment proposals ensued, ending in a Federalist victory by the margin of 45 to 30. The outcome showed considerable Republican strength in view of the radical nature of the matter under discussion.[21]

In the Republican heartland below the Potomac, South Carolina was the state to watch, as neither party could claim control of the political machinery. Charleston, which dominated the political and economic life of the state, had been up in arms over the Jay treaty. Jay's failure to guarantee compensation for the hundreds of slaves seized by British forces during the Revolution was met with universal anger by the slave-owning aristocracy of South Carolina. Even the powerful Rutledge family had gone over to the antitreaty forces, and a few months later found the family patriarch, John Rutledge, turned down for the Chief Justiceship by a vindicative Federalist majority in the Senate.[22] Senator Pierce Butler of South Carolina was a leading light of the Republican forces in Philadelphia, and even Charles Cotesworth Pinckney, stanch defender of sound government that he was, had found few words with which to defend the administration's acceptance of the treaty. With the balance of party sympathies so even, South Carolina had become a political question mark by 1796.

At the beginning of December a motion requesting South Carolina's Representatives in Congress to vote against appro-

[21] *Aurora* (Philadelphia), February 26, 1796; Hamilton, *Republic*, VI, 327.
[22] Jefferson to William B. Giles, December 31, 1795, *Jefferson Papers*, LC.

priations for the treaty and declaring that the President and Senate had "mistaken their constitutional powers" in ratifying it was introduced in the legislature.

"Gracious heaven," cried one agitated assemblyman, "is this the return which you are about to make to a man who has dedicated his whole life to your service?" Reminders of Washington's revolutionary services were of little avail, however, and by a vote of 9 to 69 the lower house stamped the treaty as "injurious to the general interests of the United States." On the essential point, that of carrying the treaty into effect, South Carolina lined up squarely with Virginia. The legislature instructed its Congressmen to refuse their votes for appropriation, although the majority on this point fell from 60 to 8 votes.[23] Here Virginia scored a tremendous victory, and in Kentucky and Georgia the entire amendment platform was adopted along with recommendations that the House blockade the treaty.[24]

The fate of the Virginia resolutions of 1795 at the hands of state legislatures across the nation demonstrated that in the final analysis, the Jay treaty had failed to cut the sectional line in politics. To Madison's friend Joseph Jones, the man with whom the plan of circulating the resolves in advance of House debate seems to have originated, the outcome was a bewildering disappointment. It was not the failure of the amendment resolutions to gain acceptance that the Virginia Republican found most distressing. This had been anticipated. It was, as he put it to Madison, that Virginia seemed to stand almost alone in its determination to fight administration measures and the philosophy of government that stood behind them. The outcome, he concluded, made Madison's chances of controlling the House of Representatives appear slim indeed.

[23] *Aurora,* January 1, 1796.
[24] Hamilton, *Republic,* VI, 338-339.

In Jones's analysis of the failure two factors weighed most heavily, two that promised little hope for the spring session of Congress. The first was the strength of Federalism in Massachusetts, whose representation in Congress was equal in number to that of Georgia, Kentucky, and South Carolina combined. The second block to Republican success was the steadiness of Washington's popularity, undiminished by the general aversion to the British treaty. Jones pointed out that the President was taking every opportunity that presented itself to further that popularity. His recent speech in praise of the French for their revolutionary aid seemed a case in point. This address, commented Madison's friend, "has had its weight with many who doubted his attachment to France . . . and was well calculated to make impressions with those who do not examine conduct and facts." [25]

Madison was forced to agree on both points. "The name of the President is everywhere used with the most wonderful success by the treaty partisans," he admitted to Edmund Pendleton. Nowhere had the appeal on Washington's behalf met with greater success than in New England, "as is shown by the proceedings of the legislatures of New Hampshire and Massachusetts. The manner in which the latter has treated the proposed amendments of Virginia is as unworthy on the part of Massachusetts as it is unmerited on that of her sister." While the President allowed tensions to mount in Congress by withholding the treaty—on the pretext of waiting for the original copy from England—Madison found his colleagues beginning to hesitate. Time, he admitted, was working against Republican chances.[26]

Federalist politicians viewed the maneuvering of their Virginia rivals with scorn and were quick to conclude that Jefferson's presidential hopes lay behind the façade of Constitu-

[25] Jones to Madison, February 17, 1796, *Madison Papers*, LC.
[26] Madison to Edmund Pendleton, February 17, 1796, *ibid*.

tional reform. "Is it not manifest that the violence of this storm springs from the anticipation of the Election of the Presidency," asked Fisher Ames when the first rumors of the scheme reached him. How industriously the Virginians in Congress had taken up Senator Langdon of New Hampshire, the only New England Senator to vote against ratification of the treaty; and what could their sudden intimacy with anti-Federalists from New York and Massachusetts point to except bargaining for electoral votes? Nothing could be clearer, he confided to his friend Thomas Dwight, than that the followers of Sam Adams and George Clinton were being lined up for Mr. Jefferson. "These little whirlwinds of dry leaves and dirt portend a hurricane." [27]

By late fall Ames had concluded that nothing less than the impeachment of the President was the goal. A month before the Virginia resolves were adopted Ames was making a careful count of the number of antitreaty men returning for the Fourth Congress in anticipation of a Republican attempt to block the treaty's execution. His estimate convinced him that the "anti's" would have a safe majority with which to work but that the impeachment attempt would probably fail. There seemed no doubt to Ames that the radicals would try, nevertheless.[28]

Fearing the worst, Federalists were quick to counteract the effects of the Richmond platform. Edward Carrington reported in December that petitions were already circulating in protest against the assembly's resolutions.[29] The President was able to help his own cause without seeming to meddle in politics by smiling benevolently upon France and by saying nothing about treaties. William Giles, Madison's right-hand man in the House, was forced to admit that Washington had successfully parried the first thrust. In summarizing the news

[27] Ames to Dwight, August 24, 1795, Ames, *Works*, I, 172.

[28] Ames to Dwight, November 18; Dec. 10, 1795, *ibid.*, 178-180.

[29] Carrington to Washington, December 6, 1795, Beveridge, *Marshall*, II, 142.

for Jefferson, Giles complained that Washington had thrown the antitreaty forces completely off balance by adopting a cordial and conciliatory tone with reference to France in his message to Congress of December 7. As far as the President was concerned, the treaty was of absolutely no interest any longer—at least not to Congressmen. In not mentioning the British treaty, wrote Giles, Washington had left the initiative in the matter squarely up to his enemies in the House. Should the attempt be made to prevent the passing of appropriations, the resulting quarrel or war with England would be blamed solely on the Republicans. Giles was beginning to doubt whether the "patriotism" of the House was strong enough to brook the influence of the President and Senate combined. In the face of his own party's growing irresolution, Giles noted the solidarity of eastern Federalists, who had never seemed more united.[30]

While waiting for the Republican attack in the House, some Federalists were busily circulating tales of French intrigue and Republican treason. Edmund Randolph's diplomatic indiscretions were resurrected and the charges of corruption against him were repeated. Even Madison was feeling uncomfortable about the program he had helped to formulate. "An appeal to the popular feeling for the President, and the bugbear of war," he explained to his impatient friend Monroe, were being used over and over again to arouse hostile feelings against the Republicans. Perhaps the combination would be too strong to overcome.[31] Minister to France James Monroe wondered why republicanism at home seemed so hesitant in the face of legislative risks while French republicans stormed the fortresses of Europe.

Meanwhile Washington kept the treaty on his desk, and the recent threats of political war were turning into whis-

[30] December 9, 1795, *Jefferson Papers*, LC.

[31] Giles to Jefferson, December 20, 1795, *ibid.;* Madison to Monroe, December 20, 1795, Madison, *Writings* (Hunt ed.), VI, 260.

pered rumors as the House set itself in order for business. Jonathan Dayton of New Jersey, a political neutral, was chosen Speaker, and Republican handy man John Beckley re-elected Clerk.[32] What had happened to the bravado? Republicans said as little about the treaty in framing their reply to the President's message as he himself had said. They contented themselves for the time being with striking out the words "unequalled prosperity" in describing the nation's economic condition under Washington's administration. The only sign of Mr. Ames's hurricane was a Virginia Congressman's quip that "a late transaction" had diminished his confidence in the President somewhat.[33]

Bills on snuff manufacture, tariffs, and penal codes were introduced, and on January 4 Giles submitted a resolution commending Washington's friendly New Year's Day address to the French Minister. Not to be outdone, a Federalist seconded the motion and asked that one thousand copies of this address be printed at public expense. The latter suggestion was passed over, but the commendation easily passed.[34]

January and February wore on, debates in Congress being as uninspiring as the weather. Routine matters seemed to absorb the politicians and lawmakers. "Where is the treaty?" asked the editor of the New York *Argus*, a violent Republican sheet. "Perhaps Camillus [Hamilton] wished the President to wait until he has gone through the question of constitutionality, not being willing to trust his party with the discussion of this point," was the rhetorical answer.[35] Republican anger against Washington mounted steadily as February passed and no treaty was transmitted to the House. Finally on February 22 resentment burst out in an unprecedented refusal to recess in order to pay respects to the hero of the Revolution on his birthday. Only eighteen anti-Wash-

[32] *Annals*, 4th Congress, 1st Session, 125-150.
[33] Josiah Parker, December 17, 1795, *ibid.*, 144.
[34] Theodore Sedgwick of Massachusetts, January 4, 1796, *ibid.*, 199.
[35] *Argus*, January 7, 1796.

ingtonians had ever voted against it before, but in 1796 the Federalist Congressmen walked out, leaving fifty men to gloat.[36] French Minister Adet described the Republicans as "jubilant" over the affair, but he was less pleased over the inactivity of "nos amis" in a report to his foreign office. He regarded the country as listless toward the cause of France, and the antitreaty party lacking in both sense and vigor. In Adet's opinion, the Republicans seemed far too willing to allow public opinion to decide matters without giving that opinion any direction. This was precisely what Washington was hoping for, he concluded.[37]

The cause of M. Adet's criticism was the hesitancy of James Madison and his partisans, and there was good reason for it. The truth was that a serious split had developed within Republican ranks over the question of opening the debate without further provocation from the Executive. On the one hand, there could be no turning back: the publicity that the Virginia resolutions of November and December had given to the antitreaty fight made dropping it far too awkward, and Federalists would not be slow to publicize the retreat. It would be said, and justly so, that Washington had frightened them into dropping the matter, for the response to the Richmond platform had made it clear that Washington's popularity was the main obstacle to be overcome. On the other hand, it seemed foolhardy to launch an attack without agreement as to the tactics to be used in carrying it out. Extremists, including Jefferson, wished to attack the Constitution itself and to give the popular branch of the Legislature a voice in the treaty-making process. Moderates wished to attack only the expediency of the treaty. Politically considered, one faction thought much was to be gained by attack-

[36] Madison to Jefferson, February 29, 1796, *Madison Papers*, LC.

[37] Pierre A. Adet to the French Foreign Minister, February 23, 1796, F. J. Turner, ed., "Correspondence of French Ministers to the U.S., 1791–1797," American Historical Association, *Report, 1913*, II (Washington, 1904).

ing Washington, while the other thought the President's name best left out of the debate. These questions plagued Madison and Giles through eight indecisive weeks.

The idea of using a congressional debate to touch off the election campaign of 1796 probably occurred to a score of Republican politicians almost simultaneously. Madison and his friend Joseph Jones were the first to co-ordinate action on the state and Federal levels, but the plan to upset the Federalists in the election of 1796 by pushing the treaty question to its furthest extremes can be credited to one of the secondary figures in the Republican party, John Beckley, Clerk of the House.

During the fall and early winter of 1795 Beckley had vigorously expounded his radical viewpoint to his party colleagues at Philadelphia. Some, including Governor Mifflin's advisor, Alexander Dallas, considered attacking both the President and the Constitution far too risky. Within the Republican organization of Pennsylvania a disruptive struggle ensued, ending in Beckley's triumph. Both men had been active leaders in local politics, and both had become outspoken in denouncing the treaty in 1795. Dallas had been mysteriously connected with Fauchet, the former French Minister whose published correspondence had led to the downfall of Secretary of State Randolph. Some persons blamed Dallas for the implication of Randolph in the Whiskey Rebellion. Beckley was involved in just as sensational a scandal, the Hamilton-Mrs. Reynolds affair, which was to break into print in 1797. For several years this insignificant clerk had acted as a trusted lieutenant of the Virginia triumvirate of Jefferson, Madison, and Monroe.[38]

[38] See Philip M. Marsh, "John Beckley, Mystery Man of the Jeffersonian Republicans," *Pennsylvania Magazine of History and Biography*, January, 1948, 54-69. Valuable material concerning Beckley's early career, as well as that of his Federalist counterpart, Edward Carrington of Virginia, is to be found in the *Madison Papers*, New York Public Library. Both the *Madison Papers* and *Jefferson Papers*, LC, contain many of Beckley's letters and political reports of the 1790's. His part in directing the Republican

So serious was the split between the Beckley and Dallas factions that Dallas was finally driven into political exile and took no part in the election of 1796.[39] Beckley condemned him as a political "trimmer" or turncoat, and with all the self-assurance of a successful boss, Beckley took charge just as the much heralded Republican attack seemed to stop in its tracks. Direction of party tactics temporarily fell from Madison's hands into those of the Republican radicals.

As Lord Grenville digested the information that his diplomatic agents sent from America, he was led to caution British military commanders against surrendering the northwestern frontier posts prematurely. The treaty lately concluded between the United States and Great Britain commits His Majesty's government to the surrender of the disputed frontier outposts, he wrote. Before the actual transfer, however, it seemed advisable to make certain that the American government had fulfilled its part of the bargain. "Interesting as this consideration would have been at all times it is rendered peculiarly so at the present moment . . . from the most recent information received from America, there is but too much reason to apprehend that a considerable party exists in the House of Representatives of the United States, which is desirous of disclaiming the validity and binding force of the late treaty." [40]

In the event that Britain refused to surrender the posts on the first of June, many believed that war would ensue, a war that would destroy all that Federalist policy-makers had built in seven years. Washington's neutrality policy would be nothing more than a national joke. Young John Quincy

campaign in Pennsylvania in 1796 can be traced from the *Gallatin Papers*, New York Historical Society and the *Irvine Papers*, Historical Society of Pennsylvania.

39 Raymond Walters, Jr., *Alexander J. Dallas* (University of Pennsylvania Press, 1943), 73.

40 Grenville to Phineas Bond, January 18, 1796, "Instructions to the British Ministers to the U.S., 1791–1812," American Historical Association, *Report*, 1936, III (Washington, 1941), 107.

Adams, who read the dispatches from home with increasing anxiety, correctly estimated what line Grenville would adopt. The Republicans, he wrote in his London diary, were calculating on Britain's refusal as the only foolproof method of winning overwhelming public favor in the ensuing presidential election.[41] Certain it was that they could force such an issue, and men who viewed life as the younger Adams did were convinced that the American Jacobins were that satanical.

[41] John Quincy Adams, *Memoirs of John Quincy Adams*, C. F. Adams, ed., 12 vols. (Philadelphia, 1874–77), I, 483.

2

The Republican Challenge

THE HOUSE HAD NOT BEEN IN SESSION FOR MORE THAN AN hour or two on March 2 when Edward Livingston of New York arose to introduce a resolution requesting that the President lay before the legislature the instructions and correspondence covering Jay's negotiations. It was generally understood, said Livingston, that important constitutional questions would be discussed when the British treaty was officially laid before the chamber by the President. He deemed it essential, therefore, that the members have as much information concerning the diplomacy as possible.[1]

Livingston's unexpected request was the answer of the Republican radicals to Washington's attempt to stop the Virginia movement. In choosing the young New Yorker to open the fight the antitreaty men were obviously trying to give a national rather than a sectional coloring to their campaign. In December it had been rumored that Jonathan Dayton of New Jersey would accept the role of challenging the Executive, but the Speaker was far too cunning a politician to gain notoriety at Washington's expense and had declined the honor.[2] Dayton's record in both the Senate and House shows him to have been unusually adept in divining the course of public opinion. He could usually be found strongly advocating the winning side in public questions. While Dayton had been favorable enough toward most Hamiltonian measures

[1] *Claypoole's American Daily Advertiser* (Philadelphia), March 3, 1796.
[2] W. B. Giles to Madison, December 20, 1795, *Jefferson Papers*, LC.

to be admitted to Federalist ranks, his warm opposition to the Jay treaty had made Republicans hopeful enough about his conversion to support his election as Speaker of the Fourth and Fifth congresses. Despite his friendship with Aaron Burr and risky speculations in western land schemes, Dayton was personally liked by his colleagues in the House. Had he lent his name to the Republican attack on the treaty it would have added much to the hopes of breaking Federalist domination of New Jersey politics. Dayton, however, enjoyed his perch on the fence and found the compensations for remaining there worth the occasional slurs of extreme partisans.[3]

Madison was caught unawares by Livingston's resolution and thought that his colleagues had begun "rather abruptly," a clear indication that the minority floor leader had been left out of last-minute discussions. His comments to Jefferson in the first weeks of House debate show how completely he had come to doubt the wisdom of the approach being taken by Beckley, Livingston, and the rest of the radicals. "A motion has been laid on the table by Mr. Livingston calling for the instructions to Jay, etc. The policy of hazarding it is so questionable that he will probably let it sleep or withdraw it," he wrote three days later.[4] Having lost the direction of affairs to his extremist friends, Madison determined to leave the responsibility of carrying out the threat to others. On the day following his first report to Jefferson, Madison attempted to tone down the resolution by amending it to read, "except so much of said papers as, in his judgement [Washington's], it may not be inconsistent with the interest of the United States at this time to disclose."[5] Not only did his

[3] Material on Dayton is scant, and most information concerning his political career is to be found in widely scattered references to him from among the papers of his contemporaries. See especially the *Hamilton Papers*, LC, and the Dayton *MSS.*, Princeton University Library.

[4] Madison to Jefferson, March 5, 13, 1796, *Madison Papers*, LC.

[5] *Annals*, 4th Congress, 1st Session, 438.

party refuse to support the amendment, but five Southern congressmen, including three of the Virginia delegation, broke with him.[6] Federalists were both amused and puzzled to see the Republican chieftain deserted. Hamilton had been confident that the Republican leadership was determined to avoid a showdown with Washington. He knew both Gallatin of Pennsylvania and Baldwin of Georgia to be in agreement with Madison, but it was becoming evident that leadership had slipped from their control.[7]

On the tenth of March Madison spoke at length on the various positions that might be taken on the Constitution's treaty-making provisions, but Fisher Ames noted that he refused to recommend any one of them. Madison was spinning intellectual cobwebs in his estimation. "Conscience made him a coward. He flinched from an explicit and bold creed of anarchy." [8]

Benjamin Bache, editor of the Republican *Aurora*, allowed one of his editorials to take some highly critical swipes at the Republicans. Their great crusade, he commented, had all the appearances of a last-ditch stand made necessary by the humiliating defeat of the Virginia amendment resolutions in the legislatures of the three powerful states of New York, Pennsylvania, and Massachusetts.[9] The French Minister to the United States was so distressed when Madison attempted to soften Livingston's blow that he wrote home, urging his government to lend its aid to a faltering cause. News of great French victories in Europe would push the wavering into line, he believed. Otherwise defeat seemed inevitable. He had been asked by certain Republican leaders ("les chefs du parti republicain") to make an official statement supporting

6 *Independent Chronicle*, March 17, 1796; Irving Brant, *James Madison, Father of the Constitution, 1787–1800* (New York, 1950), 437-438.

7 Hamilton to King, December 14, 1795, Hamilton, *Works* (Lodge ed.), X, 186.

8 Ames, *Works*, I, 189-190.

9 *Aurora*, March 12, 1796.

their attack on the British treaty—or the British alliance, as they called it. Adet requested permission to intervene.[10]

Business in the upper chamber was neither so pressing nor so fascinating as to prevent the Vice-President's carefully following the activities of the House just a few yards away. "There are bold and daring strides making to demolish the President, the Senate, and all but the House," he declared to his wife after the first week of the debate, but two weeks later Adams began to doubt that the radicals had anything more in mind than electioneering. "It is the general opinion of those I converse with that after they have passed the resolutions which they think will justify them to their constituents, seven or eight of the majority will vote for the appropriations necessary to carry the treaty into execution." [11]

A minor Republican politician from Pennsylvania was only puzzled by the turn of events. "We have serious debates in Congress upon the omnipotency of the President," wrote Andrew Ellicott to his friend General William Irvine. "How it will terminate God knows. I do not like Kings, but if my fellow citizens are determined to have them, my business must be submission." [12]

Hamilton had assumed that his chief antagonist in the House would be Madison and had shaped his strategy accordingly. Writing to William L. Smith of South Carolina, a man who frequently acted as his spokesman in the legislature, he urged that Federalists make every effort to draw Madison into a full-scale debate on the constitutional nature of the question. The Federalist chief was absolutely convinced that the administration's case was watertight. "The Constitution says that the President and Senate shall make treaties, and that these treaties shall be supreme laws. It is a contradiction to call a thing a law which is not binding."

[10] March 7, 1796, *Correspondence of French Ministers, op. cit.*, 836.

[11] March 13, April 1, 1796, Adams, *Works*, I, 488-489.

[12] March 12, 1796, *Irvine Papers*, Historical Society of Pennsylvania, XIII, No. 102.

Smith was assured that Mr. Madison's "sophisms" would be unable to refute the logic of this argument.[13] On the same day Hamilton sent drafts of a refusal message to the Livingston resolution to Washington, who had not asked for one, and another to Senator King of New York for his general edification.

At Monticello, where Republicanism was undaunted by the unkind words of New England legislators, Jefferson felt none of James Madison's hesitancy. He may have noted that Albert Gallatin, rather than Madison, was bearing the brunt of the Federalist counterattack in Congress, but he said nothing about it in writing to Madison at the end of March. If ever there was an occaison for asserting the rights of the House of Representatives to a voice in the treaty-making process, why is it not at this moment, he asked? It was a righteous cause prompted by the acceptance of a treaty that sacrificed "the rights, interests, the honor, and faith of our nation." Jefferson, who was in a position to view principles rather than practical political considerations as the only important consideration, singled Gallatin out for special praise. The Pennsylvania Republican had concluded his March 9 speech with a plea for the adoption of Livingston's resolution as a step that would deliver the deathblow to the aristocratic notion of secret diplomacy. Jefferson was, as he put it, "enchanted" with the address and ranked it as equal in power to the Federalist papers of 1787 and 1788.[14]

With the intention of shaking Madison out of his apparent lethargy, Jefferson gently chided and encouraged him to throw his energies into the fight. For more than two weeks he dug through the mass of papers in his study, attempting to uncover every valuable note he had taken while Secretary of State concerning the President's views on public participa-

[13] March 10, 1796, *Hamilton, Works* (Lodge ed.), X, 147-148.
[14] March 27, 1796, *Madison Papers*, LC.

tion in the treaty process, apparently convinced that Washington could be accused of inconsistency. The results of his labors he mailed to Madison in April, virtually the only part he played in the campaign of 1796.[15]

Throughout the month of March the newspapers gave as much space as possible to the debates in Congress. Most editors printed every major speech in its entirety, and in many cases public interest proved great enough to merit publication of the late speeches weeks after the question had been settled. Every Representative who made any claim to oratorical gifts whatsoever had something to say and usually at great length. Two of the most outstanding men in the House were conspicuously silent, however: Fisher Ames because he was feeble and Speaker Dayton because he evidently could not determine the winning side.

Finally all that could be said had been said, and on March 24 even Dayton, the House being in committee of the whole with Muhlenberg of Pennsylvania in the chair, was forced to take sides. The original resolution stood as Livingston had worded it with the exception of a harmless amendment excluding such papers "as any existing negotiation may render improper to be disclosed." By a vote of 62 to 37 the Livingston resolution was adopted and a committee appointed to deliver it to the President.[16]

The constitutional phase of the antitreaty struggle had ended in an overwhelming Republican victory. If persuasive oratory had anything to do with it, the outcome was a tribute to Albert Gallatin, who had acted as rebuttalist for the Republicans. Those former administration supporters who had

[15] Jefferson to Madison, April 17, 1796, *Madison Papers*, LC. Claude G. Bowers' statement that Jefferson made no effort to influence the outcome of the debate is incorrect. *Jefferson and Hamilton* (Boston and New York, 1925), 307.

[16] *Annals*, 4th Congress, 1st Session, 801.

thrown in their lot with Livingston, Gallatin, and company, may have felt that safety lay in numbers, but Dayton's vote had been given to the minority, and his divining rod rarely failed to point the way to the side of any public question that would ultimately win out. Before adjourning for the day the House heard Robert Harper of South Carolina introduce an omnibus resolution calling for appropriations to execute all treaties lately concluded by the Executive.[17] It was tabled and whether or not it might be useful later was a question that only Washington could answer. The next move was his.

The President's answer to the House request for diplomatic papers showed that he had considered all sides of the controversy, both political and constitutional. His first move was to offset hostility toward his foreign policy by submitting the popular Pinckney treaty with Spain. "This early communication of the Treaty with Spain has become necessary," he wrote, "because it is stipulated in the third article, that Commissioners for running the boundary line between the territory of the United States and the Spanish Colonies of East and West Florida shall meet at the Natchez before the expiration of six months from the ratification. And as that period will undoubtedly arrive before the next session of Congress, the House will see the necessity of making provision, in their present session, for the object here mentioned." [18]

This was the master's touch. By bringing public attention to the fact that a completely acceptable and beneficial treaty had been concluded by the administration, Washington was able to neutralize much of the furor over foreign relations and at the same time remind the House in tactful fashion that it was its responsibility to uphold the good name of the United States in the family of nations. The President said in effect: It is the business of the House of Representatives to

[17] *Ibid.*

[18] *Annals*, 4th Congress, 1st Session, 821.

appropriate the funds necessary to carry treaties into effect, not just popular treaties.

The day after this communication had been received the Clerk of the House, John Beckley, arose and read to an excited gallery and floor the Chief Executive's refusal to release Jay's notes and correspondence. After carefully weighing both the House request and his own responsibilities "to preserve, protect, and defend the Constitution" he found it impossible to comply, said Washington. "The nature of foreign negotiations requires caution; and their success must often depend on secrecy. . . . The necessity of such caution and secrecy was one cogent reason for vesting the power of making Treaties in the President with the advice and consent of the Senate; the principle on which that body was formed confining it to a small number of members. To admit, then, a right in the House of Representatives to demand, and to have, as a matter of course, all the papers respecting a negotiation with a foreign power, would be to establish a dangerous precedent."

Washington turned suddenly and dramatically on his opponents to deliver a challenge that left mouths gaping. "It does not occur that the inspection of the papers asked for can be relative to any purpose under the cognizance of the House of Representatives, except that of an impeachment; which the resolution has not expressed." He supported his stand by three cogent arguments; first, the House had hitherto acquiesced in the construction of the Constitution under which he had conducted foreign relations; second, only by adhering to this construction would the small states retain an equal voice in making laws which would be binding upon all; and third, he pointed out that when the Constitution was under debate a proposal to give the lower house a voice in the treaty-making power had been explicitly rejected. Washington reminded the Congress that he had been a member of that convention and cited as his source the Journals of the General Convention, which had been deposited in State Department archives.[19]

The problem of dealing with this explosive package was one that would determine whether the radicals would be able to hold their leadership of the Republican party. Congressman Blount of North Carolina immediately demanded that the President's message be considered by the entire House and replies to it debated on the floor. Giles of Virginia, who had acted with Madison throughout and who was acting as his spokesman that day, wanted the message treated according to precedent by giving over to a special committee the task of framing a reply. Gallatin's influence was thrown to the radicals however, and by a strictly party vote of 55 to 37 the Blount motion was adopted. Giles voted with his party when he saw that opposition would only deepen the rift.[20]

Madison was deeply shaken by Washington's declaration of war. "The absolute refusal was as unexpected as the tone and tenor of the message was unproper and indelicate," he declared to Jefferson. "There is no doubt in my mind that the message came from New York." [21] Editor Bache was so confident that Hamilton had written the paper that he said so in print. "Thus . . . though his decision could not be influenced by the voice of the people, he could suffer it to be moulded by the opinion of an ex-Secretary." [22]

Both men were correct in assuming that Hamilton had played a part in framing the bombastic reply, but Washington himself had been its principal author. As early as March 3 he had foreseen the necessity of preparing himself to take a stand and had requested Secretary of the Treasury Oliver Wolcott, Jr., to sound out Hamilton, who had had to deal with

[19] *Annals*, 4th Congress, 1st Session, 760-762.
[20] March 31, *ibid.*, 762-769.
[21] April 4, 1796, *Madison Papers*, LC.
[22] *Aurora*, April 1, 1796.

similar situations during his tenure of office.[23] What Hamilton advised Wolcott to tell the President can only be surmised, but that his thinking and Washington's followed parallel lines seems certain.

The actual message began to take shape on March 25, the day after the House had approved Livingston's resolution, when the cabinet was requested to submit opinions in writing on the question of the legislature's rights in foreign affairs. They had unanimously agreed that no such right to confidential information existed under the Constitution, and Attorney General Charles Lee, who had moved up from the Virginia Assembly a few weeks previously, was commissioned to search through the journals of the Constitutional Convention for supporting arguments. The final draft was written by Timothy Pickering with last-minute alterations by Lee, and it was completed before Hamilton's own draft had been received.[24]

Washington explained to Hamilton that changes in his own message had been unnecessary after a comparison between the two showed them to be so similar in tone and content. He apologized for having caused his former aide so great a labor, "much greater than I had any idea of giving," and promised to hold the Hamiltonian arguments in reserve for defense of his action.[25]

The necessity of using Hamilton's weapons against the antitreaty partisans never arose, and Washington's prestige once more proved too great a bulwark to be overthrown. Madison, whose fears of pushing the fight against the President too far had relegated him to a minor role in the Republican campaign, moved into the forefront for the first time after Washington's challenge had paralyzed the resolution of the

[23] Washington to Wolcott, March 3, 1796, Washington, *Writings* (Fitzpatrick ed.), XXXIV, 481-482.

[24] *Ibid.*, XXXIV, 505; XXXV, 3-5.

[25] Washington to Hamilton, March 31, 1796, Washington, *Writings*, XXXV, 6-8.

radicals. Knowing that a mistake had been committed that might jeopardize the success of the approaching campaign, he determined to salvage whatever he could for the party and for Jefferson.

The reaction of public opinion against the House majority for daring to suggest—though they had not actually done so—the impeachment of Washington was almost immediate. It was now an open question, said Giles to Jefferson, whether the majority could stand up under the pressure of "twenty senators, funded gentry, British gentry, land gentry, aristocratic gentry, military gentry, and speculators, particularly when their activity and ingenuity in making divisions amongst the well-meaning part of the community are taken into consideration." Helpful suggestions from Monticello would be welcome, he admitted.[26]

Madison's initial move was to make clear just what the objectives of the Livingston resolution were and on what basis they had been formed. Madison's logical thinking was sorely needed to cut through the maze of confusion. In the form of two face-saving resolutions he attempted to realign the Republican program. Thomas Blount introduced them. "Resolved, that the House of Representatives do not claim any agency in making treaties, but that when a Treaty . . . must depend for its execution . . . on a law or laws to be passed by Congress . . . it is the Constitutional right and duty of the House of Representatives to deliberate on the expediency or inexpediency of carrying such Treaty into effect," and "Resolved, that it is not necessary to the propriety of any applications from this House to the Executive . . . that the purpose for which such information may be wanted . . . should be stated in application." [27]

The day after Blount had put his resolves before the

[26] April 6, 1796, *Jefferson Papers*, LC.

[27] *Annals*, 4th Congress, 1st Session, 771-772. Madison's authorship of the Blount resolutions is certain. See Madison, *Writings* (Hunt ed.), VI, 264.

House Madison took the floor in vigorous defense of them, an action that put considerable strain on the great collaboration between the philosopher at Monticello and the politician at Philadelphia. It was just as much the constitutional responsibility of Congress to make laws as it was for the President with the advice and consent of the Senate to make treaties, declared Madison. No matter how much "veneration might be entertained for the body of men who formed our Constitution," he continued, "the sense of that body could never be regarded as the oracular guide in expounding the Constitution." This instrument "was nothing but a dead letter until life and validity were breathed into it by the voice of the people."

Madison went on to review the amendments that had been proposed in the state conventions as the most valid source book of Constitutional interpretation, and he proved that in those bodies the general view of the treaty power taken by the resolutions under consideration had been most strongly upheld. When he had finished his defense adjournment was called, no one having the inclination or the skill to challenge Madison when he spoke on a matter of Constitutional interpretation.

The happy results of Madison's intervention in the debate were proved on the following afternoon when both resolutions were adopted by a vote of 57 to 35.[28]

No one, including Hamilton and the President, could question the rights of Congress to examine the expediency of Jay's treaty, and though most administration supporters believed the Republican threat to block appropriations on the basis of the national welfare to be an electioneering bluff, there were a few voices raised to warn them against complacency. John Marshall arrived at the capital in February to

[28] *Ibid.*, 772-783. Adrienne Koch, *Jefferson and Madison* (New York, 1950), suggests that much of Madison's material for this speech was supplied by Jefferson in his letter of April 17, 1796.

take part in the Supreme Court hearings of the British debts case of Ware vs. Hylton, and he brought from his experiences with the Virginia Republicans the firm conviction that every effort would be necessary to cram the treaty down the throats of Congress. "I was particularly intimate with Mr. Ames," he wrote to his wife, "and could scarcely gain credit with him when I assured him that the appropriations would be seriously opposed in Congress." [29]

By the beginning of April Federalists had reason to take Marshall's warning seriously. If the House declares France and her worshipers right and our government wrong, wrote one agitated Federalist, the time will have come for the eastern states to separate from a South which constantly attempts to dominate them. He was so infuriated at the course that Southern politics had taken that he thought the rest of the nation would stand idly by should a slave insurrection be the result of the French political heresies so popular in the South.[30]

The passive role that the Federalists had played in the House fight during March gave way suddenly to one of violent counterattack in April. Washington's was the opening salvo. It waked his supporters from their idleness, and gentility gave way to ward heeling so rapidly as to suggest that the traditional picture of Federalist politicians has missed the mark by a wide margin. Robert Harper led off with a blistering condemnation of the entire Republican program. In one of the open letters to his constituents that he was in the habit of mailing home—a practice which explains the steady success of his electioneering canvasses during the 1790's—Harper reduced the enemy propaganda to a single theme. The objective of the anti-Federalist majority in the Congress, he claimed, was to prepare the public for the impeachment of

[29] Beveridge, *John Marshall*, II, 198-199.

[30] Uriah Tracy of Connecticut to Hamilton, April 6, 1796, *Hamilton Papers*, LC.

General Washington. Should they persist in their efforts to discredit the administration, said Harper, the most dire consequences, including war, would result.[31]

On April 13 Sedgwick of Massachusetts took the floor to end more than five days of haggling over Indian affairs and brought three or four Republicans to their feet at once by introducing Harper's omnibus resolution calling for appropriations to carry all treaties into effect at once. In so doing he revealed what was to become the most effective Federalist stratagem. It was improper to hide the British treaty behind the Spanish treaty, cried several men at once. Gallatin, being recognized, wanted the Spanish treaty read separately for several reasons. First, because it was of special interest to his constituents, he said, noting that several petitions favoring its acceptance had already been presented to the Speaker, and second, because there were certain rumors about the treaty with Spain that had to be corrected. He had received reports, said Gallatin, that people in the West believed the Spanish treaty's execution dependent upon that of the Jay treaty.

Giles immediately supported the Pennsylvanian's remarks, and glaring over at Sedgwick declared that "he expected some decent respect for the feelings of gentlemen in conducting this business." He was more sanguine than to expect the House to be bludgeoned into appropriating the accursed British alliance. Sedgwick retorted that other gentlemen besides those from Virginia would be grateful if their honor were recognized throughout the remainder of the debate.[32]

So it began and so it continued all afternoon with personal rancor and sarcasm playing more than their customary role in Congressional debate. One member felt called upon to insist that he had not lost his temper and was not "in a passion" as his opponent charged, and twice the air grew so heavy with

[31] Elizabeth Donnan, ed., "Papers of James A. Bayard," American Historical Association, *Report*, 1913, II (Washington, 1915), 11-21.

[32] *Annals*, 4th Congress, 1st Session, 940-941.

invectives that calls for recess were heard. The only lawmakers who made sense were Gallatin and William Vans Murray of Maryland, who persisted in reminding the House that there was only one matter under formal consideration and only one major consideration: should the British treaty be executed or not, or as Murray insisted, should the valuable frontier posts be accepted from Britain or not. By the end of the ensuing day the Spanish, Algerian, and Indian treaties had been amended out of Harper's resolution until it was finally overthrown by a vote of 55 to 37.[33]

Hamilton followed the debates in the House with growing uneasiness and disgust and reached the conclusion that the time for ground-level political action had arrived. It was time for the "twenty senators and funded gentry" whose influence Giles had feared to bring their pressure to bear upon the situation. He turned first to Senator Rufus King.

Ames writes that a majority against appropriations can be held, he wrote. If so, "great evils may result unless good men play their cards well and with promptitude and decision." Hamilton went on to outline a five-point program, which he thought would turn public opinion strongly against the Republicans. First, the President should be induced to send a solemn protest to the House against such irresponsible action, for the nation was being driven into a most calamitous situation. Second, the Senate must be made to pass a resolution assuring the President of its support and advising him to execute the treaty out of other funds regardless of the line being taken by the House. Third, Hamilton urged King to arouse the merchants of Philadelphia to meet and pass resolutions upholding both the President and the Senate; fourth, to begin the circulation of petitions in favor of appropriating; and fifth, King and his friends must prevent the Senate's adjourning until the term of the House session had ended.[34]

[33] *Ibid.*, 946, 974.

[34] April 15, 1796, Hamilton, *Works* (Lodge ed.), X, 157-158.

Governor John Jay, the third member of the New York Federalist triumvirate, threw himself into the fight, too. Three days after Hamilton wrote King, Jay sent Washington a letter encouraging him in the firm stand that he had already taken with regard to the House. "Your answer to the call for the papers meets with very general approbation here. The prevailing party in the House of Representatives appear to me to be digging their own political graves." A few days later Jay sent Lord Grenville a confidential report on the situation at Philadelphia and urged him to discontinue impressment of American seamen as a measure "prudent" as well as just. Assurances from His Majesty's government, he concluded, would go far "to diminish the credit and influence of those who seize every occasion of impeaching their own wisdom and your sincerity." [35]

British naval policies were relaxed in time to benefit the Federalist party in the late months of the presidential campaign, but Hamilton's strategy had worked so successfully by the time Jay's letter reached Grenville that the assistance of the British navy was unnecessary in putting down the House revolt. Senator King had immediately called a meeting of Philadelphia merchants which overwhelmingly endorsed resolutions demanding the execution of the treaty, and on April 18 Hamilton was able to report a similar demonstration at New York with more to follow.[36] As a consequence of the publicity that the House fight was getting in New York, Hamilton's lieutenants had little trouble in filling petitions as they moved through the city, ward by ward.[37]

In Albany and other parts of upstate New York Senator Philip Schuyler, Hamilton's father-in-law, believed the public to be genuinely alarmed over the possibility of war that

[35] John Jay, *Correspondence and Public Papers of John Jay*, H. P. Johnston, ed. (New York and London, 1890–93), IV, 208.

[36] Hamilton to King, April 18, 1796, Hamilton, *Works* (Lodge ed.), X, 160.

[37] *Ibid.*, 162-163.

Federalist orators and newspapers were assuring them would follow hard on the heels of a House refusal to carry out the treaty. Schuyler had had the New York City petition copied and reported that by sundown of the first day of circulation almost five hundred had been returned fully signed. The fear of a British war was proving the most effective approach in convincing the voters, so effective that "many decided anti-federalists concurred and signed," he wrote.[38]

Back in the national capital John Adams was fuming over the crisis that the adamant radicals in Congress had created. "A few outlandish men in the House have taken the lead, and Madison, Giles, and Baldwin are humble followers," he told his wife. Political philosopher that he was, Adams sought the underlying causes of the disease, and he found it in the deep-rooted jealousy of Congress toward the power and prestige of the Senate. While admitting that the lower house had a right to ask for papers and to express an opinion of the Executive's conduct, he felt that the House had abused these rights out of base motives. Darkly meditating on the possibility of war, both foreign and domestic, the Vice-President gave credence to the rumor that the British Minister had predicted Britain's refusal to turn over the frontier posts unless the House retreated.[39]

Madison was more concerned with his party's program than he had been since the policy of attacking Washington had first been agreed upon. In a despondent mood he unburdened himself to Jefferson in late April. The majority of twenty with which we began this fight has melted away by "changes and absences" to only eight or nine, he said. The insurance companies and banks were exerting a tremendous pressure against the House by refusing loans and discounts to the businessmen who still supported the Republicans, and

[38] Schuyler to Hamilton, April 25, 1796, *Hamilton Papers*, LC.

[39] Adams to his wife, April 16, 1796, Adams, *Letters to his Wife*, II, 220-223.

prices had begun to drop rapidly as a result. "Under such circumstances, a Bank Director soliciting subscriptions [for Federalist petitions] is like a Highwayman with a pistol demanding the purse." [40]

According to a New York merchant, economic conditions were becoming chaotic. "Owing to the resolutions in Congress . . . all insurances and other business is at a stand; nothing doing. The merchants from the country, who come for a supply of goods, all going back without any, as our merchants decline selling at present. Produce has fell [*sic*] amazingly since Saturday. . . . Our banks, I understand, have got alarmed; very little they will do, as they seem to have lost confidence in the government." [41] And in other coastal towns the situation was no different. "The cry is war, war, no insurance to be had, no employment for the people," wrote Senator Langdon of conditions in Portsmouth, New Hampshire; and in New Jersey and Delaware banks and insurance companies were coercing signatures for their anti-House petition with equal zeal.[42] Even in Richmond, where the tide of battle had completely reversed itself in four months, Edmund Randolph reported the Federalists in control of the political situation. Baltimore, as Madison saw it, was worst of all. He explained to Jefferson that Maryland merchants had frozen their assets out of "hopes for indemnities for past losses and fears for their floating speculations which have been arranged on the idea that the Treaty would go into effect." It was a sad commentary on human nature that these men thought only of their own fortunes when the good of the country was at stake, he commented.[43]

Nowhere had the Federalists exerted themselves to do bat-

[40] April 23, 1796, *Madison Papers*, LC.

[41] "Extract from a letter of a Merchant of New York to his friend in Philadelphia," *Maryland Gazette*, April 28, 1796.

[42] Langdon to Madison, April 28, 1796, *Madison Papers*, LC; Madison to Jefferson, April 23, 1796, *ibid.*

[43] Madison to Jefferson, April 18, 1796, *Madison Papers*, LC.

tle for the administration with greater enthusiasm than at the Virginia capital where the Republicans had so hopefully launched their attack five months before. According to Randolph's eyewitness account, John Marshall had taken the lead and was constantly on the speaker's stand "concluding every third sentence with the horrors of war." Two weeks of petitioning and public meetings were climaxed on April 25 with an all-day demonstration ending in the adoption of a series of resolutions condemning the Republican program and demanding the execution of the Jay treaty. Although Randolph described the final result as the victory of three or four hundred British merchants, Marshall declared it the largest protest rally ever seen in eastern Virginia.[44]

Only two of the methods suggested by Hamilton for countering the House blockade were ever put into effect. Washington was not called upon to issue a solemn protest, nor did the Senate pass any British treaty resolutions during April. So suddenly did the crisis pass—the greatest and most prolonged crisis in the youthful nation's history—that Federalists had no occasion for preventing adjournment on its scheduled date. Economic pressure was powerful enough to turn the tide and was probably the key factor in stimulating the flow of petitions that finally broke the back of Republican resistance. A party which proudly claimed to rest upon the broad base of public opinion could scarcely maintain its position in the face of a flood of anti-House petitions that fell upon Philadelphia in the spring of 1796.

At first the Republicans found public petitioning the best of motives for continuing their attacks upon the administration. On March 8 an antitreaty petition signed by more than sixteen hundred men from the Edenton District of North

[44] Randolph to Madison, April 23, 1796, *Madison Papers*, LC; Randolph to Madison, April 25, 1796, Conway, *Randolph*, 362; Marshall to Hamilton, April 25, 1796, Beveridge, *Marshall*, II, 150-153.

Carolina was brought to the attention of the Speaker. Its appearance so early in the month indicated that it had been circulated weeks before reaction to Livingston's resolution could be expected, and it was, therefore, a response to the Virginia resolves of December, 1795. Republican radicals could not be anything but encouraged by it, however. Two weeks later the second major response was received, this time from Congressman Livingston's own constituents. A strong segment of the New York citizenry was behind his call for the Jay negotiation papers, but by the end of March nothing that the Republicans had done had aroused public opinion to the proportions that would be necessary to drive Federalism from power in November.[45] The great ground swell only made its appearance after Washington's call to battle, and if the petition struggle of April, 1796, was a gauge of public opinion, as Federalists claimed it was, the radicals had made a tragic blunder in allowing the sanctity of George Washington's name to become a political football. Federalists were not slow in exploiting the mistake.

[45] *Claypoole's American Daily Advertiser,* March 30, 1796.

3

Popular Federalism

HAMILTON'S DECISION TO ORGANIZE PROTEST MEETINGS AND petition Congress was based upon the assumption that the public might be safely split and dealt with in segments. His primary concern was to move the merchants, brokers, and bankers to protest; the rest would either follow or find their mumblings drowned in the clamor that the stronger and more persuasive voices of nature's elite would raise. His friend Senator Rufus King was a skilled organizer of proper rebellions and moved swiftly to set the machinery of protest in action. He was clever enough to realize the necessity of enlarging the body of active citizenry so as to include those whose interests overlapped those of the business class but whose social standing would link them with "the people," a source of strength that the Republicans were certain to tap.

On April 20 King reported the outcome of his first labors to Hamilton, a lengthy petition signed by the merchants and skilled mechanics of Philadelphia, which was to be laid before the President of the Senate and duly publicized. While admitting that the Republicans were no less zealous than his own agents and no less successful as to numbers, King believed their results less promising. The Republicans were allowing anyone to sign, voters and nonvoters, even aliens, but few of the outstanding businessmen or mechanics would be found among their subscribers. As a follow-up to the anti-House petitions King was prepared to push an amendment through the Senate that would add the Jay treaty to the House appropriations bill covering the Spanish treaty. If this maneuver failed, King was prepared to add both the British and the Spanish treaties to the appropriations bill for the Algerian treaty and, as a last resolve, to lump all pending treaties together in one omnibus bill.[1]

Whether the desperate tactics that King and Hamilton held in abeyance would be necessary or not depended no longer upon their political adversaries but upon the public's reaction to the grave situation. In Virginia, where the paralysis had germinated, the petition–counterpetition struggle was gaining momentum as April wore on. John Marshall was highly optimistic and reported to King that the Republicans were disgruntled over the effectiveness of Federalist rallies and the petitions that resulted from them. His guess was that the results of the battle would be about even as to numbers but that his own party could easily carry the day by stooping to the practice of signing up aliens and nonvoters. The Republicans, apparently, held no such scruples.[2] Hamilton had thrown his New York organization into the fight hopefully but was amazed at the response. His ward lieutenants had secured thirty-two hundred names to their petitions within two or three days, only three hundred less, he reported to King, than "the highest poll we ever had in this city, *on both sides*, at the most controversial election." [3]

While John Marshall was rising to prominence in Federalist ranks for his generalship at Richmond, another young Federalist vaulted into the national limelight at Boston. The Massachusetts Federalists, usually referred to as the "Essex Junto," welcomed Harrison Gray Otis to their select circle after his notorious "Second Shirt" address of April 25.

Taking up the cry of war, which Federalists were using everywhere, Otis painted a lurid picture of a frontier drip-

[1] King to Hamilton, April 20, 1796, *Hamilton Papers*, LC.

[2] Marshall to King, April 25, 1796, *King Papers*, New York Historical Society, Box 6, No. 65.

[3] Hamilton to King, April 24, 1796, *Hamilton Papers*, LC.

ping with the blood of innocent women and children should the willful sinners in Congress persist in turning the savages loose by leaving the outposts in British hands. In singling out Albert Gallatin as the ringleader of the conspiracy Otis cast conscience to the winds. This infidel Jacobin, he cried, had arrived in America without "a second shirt to his back," yet he held in his hand the lives of hundreds of staunch Americans. Gallatin was a foreigner and a French intriguer, he declared, who had already shown his contempt for the law by leading the anarchical Whiskey rebels against George Washington. How long would this be tolerated, he thundered.[4]

Otis, who had been tutored in French by Gallatin at Harvard, later apologized for his heated words, but his diatribe was greatly admired at the time by those whose opinions mattered most to him. A month later he was commissioned United States District Attorney for Massachusetts, and in the fall of 1796 he took Fisher Ames's seat in the House, rather ample compensation for one day's work.[5]

As was to be expected from the hostile response that the Virginia resolutions of 1795 had met in New England, Federalists had little difficulty in swinging public opinion behind them. Fears of war, crippled economic life, and the voice of the clergy contributed to produce what one authority has described as a complete reversal of opinion on the Jay treaty question.[6] But from a quarter where Federalism was hated and the name of Washington least revered came the most persistent demands for the treaty's acceptance and execution. Western Pennsylvania Whiskey Rebels joined forces with Hamilton, King, and Otis all but to ruin the party that had welcomed Albert Gallatin to its ranks.

[4] S. E. Morison, *Life and Letters of Harrison Gray Otis, Federalist* (Boston and New York, 1913), I, 55-56.

[5] *Ibid.*, 57.

[6] *Ibid.* Public opinion on the Jay treaty began its shift during the debate over the Virginia amendment proposals. This phase of the treaty fight has been almost completely overlooked hitherto.

The cause of this strange alliance was explained by the editor of a small-town newspaper when he pointed to a certain "common report" widely circulating at the time of Livingston's opening shot in the party war. According to this rumor, wrote the editor of the *Maryland Gazette*, the Spanish government would withhold ratification of the treaty negotiated by Thomas Pinckney until the British treaty had been put into operation by Congress.[7] Albert Gallatin had referred to the same rumor when he had asked that the House have the Pinckney treaty formally placed before it on April 13, and a few days later he presented to the Speaker the first petition from his frontier district of Pennsylvania calling for House approval of Jay's treaty.[8] William Giles explained the mysterious distortion of frontier politics to Jefferson.

"Among the various arts employed by the treaty making party," he wrote, "a new one has been made to operate upon the Western parts of the United States. The British and Spanish treaties are united and the people told that the execution of the one is essentially dependent upon the execution of the other. To this suggestion is added the importance of the surrender of the posts to the western country. This artifice has so far succeeded that a number of petitions have come forward from the western parts of Pennsylvania praying the concurrence of the House." According to Giles the villain of the piece was Senator James Ross of Pennsylvania, a frontier man who had moved into Federalist circles during the reaction against Republican extremism that the Whiskey Rebellion had produced.[9]

Had Jefferson and Giles known the truth their chagrin would have been far deeper at that moment. Gallatin, whose position had been made untenable by the appearance of the

[7] *Maryland Gazette*, March 10, 1796.

[8] *Connecticut Gazette*, May 5, 1796.

[9] March 26, 1796, *Jefferson Papers*, LC.

petitions from his district favoring the treaty, found to his amazement that the plot had been hatched in the bosom of his own party. He had written to his lieutenant Alexander Addison in April asking why Ross had found it so simple to practice his tricks in hostile territory. Addison's answer was a confession that he and Judge Hugh Henry Brackenridge had engineered it without the aid of Ross or anyone else. They had agreed to give the Spanish treaty as much publicity as possible and allow editors and public to draw the conclusions they wanted to draw. Brackenridge had given Pinckney's treaty to the *Pittsburg Gazette* at a moment when public attention was centered upon the British treaty question, Kentucky papers had picked it up from that source, and the West had drawn its own conclusions about the two. The truth was, said Addison, that he and Brackenridge viewed the Pinckney treaty as worthless without American control of the British-held forts, and, he added, every honest man in the House must know it too.[10]

Brackenridge, who had been Jame Madison's college roommate, was more active than Addison would allow, however. The first petition that Gallatin received from his district was drawn up and signed by the Allegheny County Grand Jury after Judge Brackenridge's eloquent appeal from the bench. He had also taken to the editorial column of the Washington, Pennsylvania, newspaper and according to an unfriendly critic had hopelessly and deliberately confused the public on the provisions of the two treaties.[11]

Among Albert Gallatin's papers may be found a petition from "Sundry Inhabitants of the Western Counties of Pennsylvania in favor of the treaty with Great Britain," dated March 21, 1796. Its contents explain why the Republican

[10] May 4, 1796, *Gallatin Papers,* New York Historical Society, Box 4, No. 13.

[11] Jean Bodollet to Gallatin, May 18, 1796, *Ibid.*, No. 16.

forces in the House broke ranks in the opening phase of the election of 1796.

"The treaties, lately concluded by the United States with Britain and with Spain, open to America a prospect of great prosperity peculiarly interesting to the inhabitants of the western country." The House of Representatives, it continued, threatened to close the Mississippi to Westerners, threatened to prevent the growth of trade with the West Indies, and threatened to prevent frontiersmen from paying their debts by keeping the price of land down and by denying the West an opportunity for rich trade with Europe and the Indies. The petition recorded a deep concern for the good name of the United States in foreign eyes. The British treaty, concluded the petitioners, cannot be of so evil a nature as to justify our presenting "the dreadful spectacle, which we should exhibit to our own citizens and to the world, of a government at war with itself, one branch defeating the purposes and acts of another, the whole deprived of all energy and exertion." [12]

Hamilton or King might have drawn up this petition, which Brackenridge and Addison, along with forty-eight others, signed and sent on to Gallatin. Still another Pennsylvania Republican warned Gallatin that opposition to the British treaty was unpopular at home. "I believe it is the earnest wish of a very great majority here that the treaty should be executed with all Fidelity," wrote David Redick as he prepared to mail another petition from the town of Washington. The idea that the House can set aside a law approved by the President and the Senate "is a doctrine which don't prevail here." [13]

Gallatin's conduct throughout the House fight mirrored the uneasiness he shared with Madison over the approach that their more extreme friends had taken in attacking the

[12] *Gallatin Papers*, New York Historical Society, Box 4, No. 6.
[13] *Ibid.*, Box 4, No. 7.

administration. Both had taken active parts in the House debate over the treaty-making power, but during April Gallatin said little and Madison's tone was markedly conciliatory. The Pennsylvanian did nothing to dramatize his disagreement with the extremists, but his silence was eloquent and to his Western friends he admitted that the protreaty petitions were a welcome excuse for his withdrawal. One of Addison's letters leaves no doubt of this. "Enclosed are some petitions for the execution of the treaty . . . if industry had been used all this country could have been made to support them. The only use they will be of to you will be as an excuse with your friends for pursuing your own wishes." [14]

In desperation the radicals attempted to hold the line by means of a resolution that they hoped would commit the House majority to overthrowing the Jay treaty. Samuel Maclay of Pennsylvania suddenly introduced a resolution that it would be inexpedient at that time to pass laws carrying the treaty into effect, and it was Madison who rose to challenge his colleagues' course of action. Such a resolution, he said, was not to the point: the question before the House was whether or not to pass the appropriations, and anything short of this was superfluous. He went on to suggest that action must be taken on one of three bases: the House was either bound to carry out the treaty by the Constitution, or the treaty ought to be put into operation because it was a good treaty, or on the basis that "there are good extraneous reasons for putting it into effect, although it is in itself a bad treaty." [15]

While a week was spent by the House majority in attempting to prove what had been self-evident from the start —that Mr. Jay had won few prizes in his exchange with British diplomats—Senator King and his business friends were busily protesting. Trade on the Philadelphia market fell off

[14] *Gallatin Papers*, New York Historical Society, Box 4, No. 8.
[15] *Annals*, 4th Congress, 1st Session, 971-976.

sharply, and if Justice Iredell's observations are correct, a few more of the Anglophobes were beginning to turn toward Madison's conciliatory position.[16] From the administration's point of view the week's debate was anything but wasted. As Congress defiantly evaded the final issue, literally hundreds of petitions were presented for consideration, and the pressure of these was great enough to defeat extremism.

A tabulation of the number of petitions and the number of signatures in total is impossible to construct. The *Annals* of Congress note them as presented, but the editors more often than not failed to record the number of signatures or the areas from which they had originated. Those other two guides to early national political events, Bache's *Aurora and General Advertiser* and Fenno's *Gazette of the United States*, made extravagant claims for their respective partisans while failing even to note the public response to their adversaries' successful blandishments. The eighteenth century plainly was not as statistics-minded as our own, and at best we may determine the will of voters in areas sensitive to Federal problems, leaving in doubt the veracity of the politician's claim to speak for the majority of his constituents.

On May 5, 1796, the editor of the *Connecticut Gazette* of New London, a moderate Federalist paper that reflected little of the intense partisanship of the metropolitan sheets, tabulated the petitions presented to the House during the final week of debate. From April 20 to 29 one hundred and four petitions were recorded, sixty-four favoring the treaty and forty urging its destruction. The total number of signatures favoring the Republican side was approximately 7,200 and the total favoring the Federalists about 10,200.[17]

More significant than the figures is the geographical dis-

[16] James Iredell to his wife, April 15, 1796, Griffin J. McRee, *Life and Correspondence of James Iredell* (New York, 1857–58), II, 475.

[17] Figures from *Claypoole's American Daily Advertiser*, May 2, 1796, for the last week of April have been included. The average petition contained fifty signatures.

tribution of the petitions. Philadelphia supplied the greatest number of both petitions and signatures. For example, Representatives Swanwick, Republican, and Hartley, Federalist, turned over petitions numbering 1,500 and 1,400 signatures respectively on April 20 alone. These two men represented the most active districts in the country in this connection, the central and western counties of Pennsylvania following close behind. The areas of New Jersey, New York, Delaware, and Maryland closest to commercial and shipping centers fell in line behind the Pennsylvanians. The New London *Gazette's* summary, noted petitioning from Virginia and Massachusetts but made no mention of completed canvassing from any of the other states in the Union.

Albert Gallatin presented protreaty petitions from the western counties of his own state on April 22 and one from Delaware opposing the treaty three days later. Nothing better illustrates the confusion into which the Republican leadership had fallen.

Madison had already made it plain that he was ready to give up the fight when he had spoken against Maclay's resolution. If the petitions of western Pennsylvania had left any doubts about Gallatin's intentions they were dispelled by his speech concluding the debate of April 26.

"The further detention of the posts, the national stain that would result from receiving no reparation for the spoliations on our trade, and the uncertainty of a final adjustment of our differences with Great Britain," he said, were the three evils that struck him as resulting from the rejection of the treaty. The congressional *Annals* report Gallatin as particularly concerned over the disunion sentiment that the prolonged debate had aroused, a factor far more worthy of consideration in the final analysis than the fact that a repugnant treaty had been signed. Forthrightly, Gallatin deserted his extremist friends. He would vote for full appropriations and would not give assent to any proposition that would either beg the question or defeat the treaty's purposes.[18]

On the day following Gallatin's declaration Federalists Tracy of Connecticut and Gilbert of New York held the floor, the Republicans maintaining strict silence. Even though the two ranking Republicans had capitulated, the division within the party had become clear enough for the outcome still to remain in doubt. A demand for vote on the issue was lost by a narrow margin. Federalists reckoned that the treaty would still fail despite Madison and Gallatin by a vote of 52 to 48.[19] Rumor had it that a showdown would be forced by the radicals on April 28, but when the day passed without decisive action, Federalists breathed more easily. The stage was thus set for the final scene to be acted out by Fisher Ames, dour prophet of Massachusetts Federalism, who brought the struggle to its climactic ending with his great speech of the following day.

Ames's oratorical effort on behalf of the Jay treaty is more famous than the important fight in the House of Representatives itself, and it has been vividly described many times.[20] Gaunt and worn down with sickness, Ames took the floor to lash out against the arrogance, stupidity, and blindness of his opponents. Although Ames had never trekked the wilderness or seen the horrors that he conjured up, he was able to bring his audience to tears as he depicted the murderous onslaught of savages upon innocent frontiersmen and their families. All this, he thundered, would fall upon the

[18] *Annals*, 4th Congress, 1st Session, 1196.

[19] H. C. Lodge, *Life and Letters of George Cabot* (Boston, 1877), 95.

[20] See Claude G. Bowers, *Jefferson and Hamilton* (Boston and New York, 1925), 302-307. This excitingly written account is extremely biased in favor of the Republicans. The description of Ames being carried into the House to give his last efforts for a lost cause is imaginative, to say the least. While noting that Ames arrived in Philadelphia during February, the author leaves the distinct impression that the orator was roused from his sickbed at Dedham just in time to arrive on the floor for the end of the debate. Also, J. B. McMaster, *History of the American People* (New York, 1895), II, 256-286.

consciences of the opponents of the British treaty. They had it within their power to allow the protective arms of the United States to shelter these innocents, yet they held back. Britain would only surrender the Western forts to the Union if the treaty was accepted by the House.

John Adams, a powerful orator in his own right and a man hardened to the emotional style of the day, found tears running down his cheeks when Ames sank back at the conclusion of his speech.[21] Just how important oratory was to the outcome is a matter of speculation. While administration supporters rang out their praises for Fisher Ames, they failed to note the more significant act of New York's Edward Livingston just a few minutes before Ames rose to speak. On behalf of his constituents Livingston presented to the Chairman a protreaty petition with words that spelled out his capitulation. It was his hope, he stated, that the members would act "as they thought best with respect to the British treaty."[22] Livingston had opened the debate in March with his resolution calling upon Washington to account for his actions, he had been hand picked by the Republican radicals, and he had at last deserted them.

Speaker Dayton made his decision clear on the last day. The House of Representatives was about to take upon itself the weightiest decision yet encountered, he solemnly declared. Although he was not the advocate of a British alliance and though he had viewed the high-handed action of Britain upon the seas with ever-increasing anger, he felt it necessary "to sacrifice every resentment, every prejudice, and every personal consideration" to love of country. In the final analysis, concluded Dayton, the evils of rejecting the treaty would be far worse than those resulting from its acceptance. An unmentioned but decisive factor in Dayton's case was a peti-

[21] John Adams, *Letters of John Adams to his Wife*, C. F. Adams, ed. (Boston, 1841), II, 226; *Annals*, 4th Congress, 1st Session, 1239-1263.

[22] *Annals, op. cit.*, 1228.

tion from more than fourteen hundred of his constituents demanding favorable action from the House.[23]

Despite the stand taken by leaders of both parties the final vote showed a deadlock of 49 to 49, a tribute to the independence of mind of our forefathers and a revealing commentary on the state of party development. The chairman of the meeting, Frederick Muhlenberg, Republican of Pennsylvania, shifted uncomfortably and proceeded to cast his vote for the treaty resolution with the explanation that his dissatisfaction might be lessened with proper amendment.

The Federalists had by virtue of Muhlenberg's vote achieved a great moral victory over administration critics. It was clear the next morning that their opponents had spent the night working over a formula that might save face and allow acceptance. Representative Dearborn of Massachusetts was selected to introduce an amendment that described the treaty as "highly objectionable" and called for the passage of the resolution only on the basis of the treaty's supposedly brief duration–until two years after the close of the European war.[24] Since friends of the treaty might be expected to vote against the resolution as amended, the success of the Republican formula rested upon absolute party loyalty. One Virginia Republican, Josiah Parker, broke ranks, however, refusing to accept the treaty no matter how packaged.

Immediately Swanwick of Pennsylvania was on his feet. The antitreaty forces faced a worse situation than before, he admitted, for it would be impossible for honorable men to approve that which they abhorred without clearly stating the overriding considerations in the issue. More than three months of maneuver had brought Madison's party to nought, and for the second time the decision fell to Muhlenberg, whose conscience proved stronger than party loyalty. His vote thrown to the Federalist side carried Washington's for-

[23] *Ibid.*, 1279.
[24] April 30, 1796, *ibid.*, 1282.

eign policy past its final hurdle and brought the Richmond program crashing down.[25]

One of the first post-mortems was conducted by Madison the next day in a letter to Jefferson, who waited anxiously at Monticello for news of the outcome. Without attempting to explain his own tortuous role in the drama, Madison went straight to the immediate causes. Muhlenberg, in siding with the administration, and Josiah Parker, in refusing to accept the crucial Dearborn amendment, were primarily responsible, Madison stated. "The unsteadiness, the follies, and the defection of our friends, rather than the strength of our opponents," he wrote, had caused the defeat.[26]

One notable Republican, for example, had suddenly disappeared when the final roll call had been made. William Findley's Pennsylvania constituents wanted to know why. His explanation, that he had stepped out to express a trunk, was so inadequate that the *Pittsburg Gazette* expressed the wish that the offending trunk had been his casket.[27] The votes of Findley and Muhlenberg might have reversed the decision, and Pennsylvania could thus take credit for having salvaged Mr. Jay's diplomacy.

The Republicans had opened the session of Congress with what their opponents agreed was a safe majority.[28] Between the first of March and the end of April this majority of anti-treaty partisans had disappeared, Madison remarking one week before the final vote that what had been a majority of twenty had become eight or nine. In the last few days the eight or nine had dropped from sight, leaving the two factions exactly equal in numbers during the last three crucial days. Livingston's resolution calling for the diplomatic papers had been adopted by a majority of twenty-four votes in

[25] *Ibid.*, 1291.

[26] May 1, 1796, *Madison Papers*, LC.

[27] July 9, 1796; McMaster, *History, op. cit.*, II, 281.

[28] Fisher Ames to Timothy Dwight, November 18, December 10, 1795, *Works of Fisher Ames*, I, 178-180.

March, and the Blount resolution answering Washington's refusal message by a margin of twenty-two votes. Well into April the bloc of antitreaty votes that Federalists despaired of seemed unbroken. When on April 14 Sedgwick's omnibus resolution failed by a vote of 37 to 55 it was evident that the radicals could still count on the same steady group.

It was during the last two weeks of April that the impact of public meetings, the protests of bankers and merchants, and the petitions began to make themselves felt. During March petitions on both sides of the question had reached Philadelphia, but it was not until the middle of the month, as the seaboard towns were whipped into action, that the full force of the petitioning hit the capital. Robert Harper considered the petitions the principal cause of the withering majority. "Several of its greatest opponents," he wrote in a letter to his constituents, "were induced to vote in favor of it, by a conviction that the people at large wished it to be faithfully executed." [29]

Final proof that the petitions had broken the Republican program can be found in the voting records of those congressmen whose constituencies reacted most violently to the treaty question. Of the twenty Pennsylvania, New York, New Jersey, Delaware, and Maryland congressmen who voted for the Livingston resolution, only eight stood with the antitreaty forces on the final vote. It was in these states that the heaviest petitioning was reported during the last two weeks of debate.

A national breakdown of the voting reveals that New England and the Middle States (New York, New Jersey, and Pennsylvania) contributed 43 votes for the treaty and only 13 against, while the Southern States, including Delaware and Maryland, produced only 11 votes for the treaty

[29] Harper to his constituents, May 2, 1796, Elizabeth Donnan, ed., "The Papers of James A. Bayard," American Historical Association, *Report, 1913*, II (Washington, 1915), 22.

while casting 40 against it. South of the Potomac in the heartland of Jeffersonian Republicanism only 4 votes could be mustered for the treaty, the other 7 Southern votes being border state ballots. All factors point to the conclusion that where mercantile, banking, and real estate interests might hope to profit from the operation of the Jay treaty the response to the Republican program was most damaging.

Perhaps the truth was put most simply by a contributor to Bache's Philadelphia *Aurora*, a self-styled "Maryland Yeoman," when he explained the triumph of the treaty party by singling out the power of "sordid lucre." The frontier had turned the tables, he maintained, out of the desire to open up the fur trade that would follow British evacuation of the Western outposts.[30] Bache himself attributed the radical defeat to the machinations of the merchant class. They had been so zealous in New York, he said, that opponents of the administration had been momentarily stunned. His informants reported that at least eight thousand signatures could have been secured for antitreaty petitions had the counterattack ever begun to roll, and the Republican editor concluded that in no sense had the voice of the people been raised in favor of Hamiltonian policies.[31]

Two days later the Philadelphia editor had begun to concede that public opinion had had something to do with the treaty victory. "Probably some of the members were swayed by the voice of their immediate constituents to a change of opinions; but it is certain that the sense of the people has not been had in favour of carrying the treaty into effect." He took what comfort he could in noting the inconsistency of the Federalists over the matter of the sovereign people. During the preceding summer, Bache pointed out, Washington's partisans had vehemently protested when petitions had arrived asking the President to withhold his signature from the

[30] *Aurora*, May 4, 1796.
[31] *Ibid.*, May 2, 1796.

treaty. This, they had said, was an unwarranted attempt to interfere with a man's private convictions. Now there were loud boasts of popular Federalism.[32]

James Monroe, Minister to France and enthusiast of La Patrie, waited anxiously at Paris for news of democratic advances at home. Madison gave him the unwelcome news of defeat. "Many of the means by which this majority was brought about will occur to you, but it is to be ascribed principally to an appeal to petitions under the mercantile influence and the alarm of war," wrote the Republican leader in what was his most detailed analysis of the defeat. "The people were everywhere called on to chuse between peace and war, and to side with the treaty if they preferred the former. This stratagem produced in many places a fever and in New England a delirium for the Treaty which soon covered the table with petitions. The counter petitions, tho' powerful from Philadelphia, and respectable from other quarters, did not keep pace."

Madison went on to pay tribute to Washington's personal role in the outcome. "Besides the alarm of war, in the smaller states a great excitement was produced by the appeal of the President in his message, to their particular interest in the powers of the Senate. What the effect of this whole business will be on the public mind cannot yet be traced with certainty. For the moment at least it presses hard on the republican interest."[33]

How important was the ruse of tying the Jay and Pinckney treaties together has already been pointed out. Actually, the concessions won by Thomas Pinckney from the Spanish crown had already been won by the frontiersmen themselves. While Spanish officials looked the other way, Americans were making regular use of the Mississippi for transport.[34]

[32] *Ibid.*, May 6, 1796.

[33] Madison to Monroe, May 14, 1796, *Madison Papers*, LC.

[34] Arthur P. Whitaker, *The Mississippi Question, 1795–1803* (New York, 1934), 79.

Nevertheless, the probable effects of both treaties had tremendous appeal in the West. Fur trade, increased land values, and official rights to the great inland waterway, when added to the promise of peace with the Indians, proved irresistible. Widespread suspicion of the Federal authority had dropped suddenly in Kentucky when in 1791 the administration had announced plans for raising an army for frontier defense and for securing navigation rights on the Ohio and Mississippi waterway.[35] Even though he was intensely Republican and pro-French, the Westerner had the best reasons for embracing the administration's foreign policy achievements of any man in the Union.

Just what the struggle over diplomacy signified to ordinary Americans, it is impossible to say. To those who identified themselves with the Federalists it may have seemed as it did to a contemporary Pennsylvanian who could see no great principles at stake. To Alexander Graydon it was merely electioneering and a struggle for public favor. The House, he recorded in his diary, has spent weeks in debate "upon every point but the one really in issue, namely, whether any treaty, whatever might be its stipulations or advantages, was admissible with Great Britain." [36]

Vice-President John Adams, on the other hand, saw more than politics-as-usual in the long fight. "Five months have been wasted upon a question whether national faith is binding on a nation," he commented tersely to his wife.[37]

To Republicans the outcome was more damaging than the chagrin that they felt, for they had been beaten in the sphere of national politics with the first party struggle for the presidency but six months distant. "A crisis which ought to have been so managed as to fortify the Republican cause has left it in a very crippled condition," wrote Madison to Thomas

[35] Harry Innes to Jefferson, May, 1791, *Jefferson Papers*, LC.

[36] Alexander Graydon, *Memoirs of a Life Chiefly Passed in Pennsylvania* (Harrisburg, 1811), 395.

[37] Adams to his wife, May 3, 1796, *Letters to his Wife*, *op. cit.*, II, 228.

Jefferson, who had viewed the battle as one between democracy and Federalist authoritarianism. "Elections in New York, Massachusetts, and other states where the prospects were favorable have taken a wrong turn under the impressions of the moment." The only solution for the problem of growing British influence in the United States, he admitted to James Monroe, was peace in Europe since Britain must be placated so long as she had an excuse for preying upon American shipping. Monroe was urged to warn French officials against rash changes in their American policy, as harshness could have no other effect than to play into the hands of the Federalist Anglophiles.[38]

French Minister Pierre Adet, disgusted with the ineptitude shown by his Republican friends, had reached the conclusion that only his own personal direction of American political warfare could salvage the cause of worldwide republicanism and prevent the further increase of British prestige in the New World. Rumors of his recall, he notified his superiors, had already hurt the Republican party, and he urged that he be kept on at Philadelphia. His presence would be absolutely essential during the coming months, he assured the Directory, if "a man devoted to France" were to be elected at the next election.[39]

Official reaction in Paris was angry and shortsighted, for the acceptance of Jay's treaty by all branches of the American government was viewed as nothing less than the completion of an Anglo-American alliance directed against republicanism in general and against France in particular. Monroe's first report on French opinion was a portent of the stormy diplomatic history of the administration that was to succeed Washington's. At Paris, Monroe said, the United States was regarded as "a perfidious friend." Washington's

[38] To Jefferson, May 22, 1796; to Monroe, May 14, 1796; *Madison Papers*, LC.

[39] Adet to the French foreign office, April 23, 1796, *Correspondence of French Ministers*, 897.

proclamation of neutrality had been bad enough, but the Jay treaty sealed the fate of the Franco-American alliance of 1778. Talk of war was common.[40]

For Republicans the optimism of December, 1795, was but a dim memory; hopes of using the treaty issue for political profit had died; the issue had boomeranged, leaving the party torn by doubt and recriminations. Jefferson himself came to recognize that no issue had been so beneficial for the Federalists in uniting them just as disunity over the presidential campaign seemed a certain prospect.[41] Nevertheless, Madison and Jefferson had learned a valuable lesson about party leadership—never again did they fail to take the lead in political warfare.

[40] Reported by Madison to Jefferson, May 22, 1796, *Madison Papers*, LC.
[41] Jefferson to Aaron Burr, June 17, 1797, *Jefferson Papers*, LC.

4

The Candidates of 1796

HAVING SETTLED THE GREAT FOREIGN POLICY ISSUE OF WASHington's second administration, the politicians turned with what must have been a sense of profound relief to the more familiar arguments and devices of electioneering. The third presidential contest in the history of the United States, while it was fought out by party organizations that had arisen in response to the administration program, was nevertheless decided by what were primarily local or regional issues. The President would be chosen only indirectly by the people, and whether Federalists or Republicans would prove victorious in state contests for the electoral college often rested on nothing more than the popularity of local politicians. Regional loyalties were stronger than devotion to the new Federal compact, the sense of nationality was yet undeveloped, and the isolation of most communities such that momentous national issues roused far less interest than the seaboard and urban newspapers of the time imply. Perhaps the most important single factor in the contest (if newspaper sources may be trusted at all) was the personal popularity of the candidates for high office.

The election of 1796 was vigorously contested, because for the first time opponents of the administration saw a chance to win. Washington was expected to retire from public life, and as the new year opened one of the men most vitally concerned with that eventuality was already contemplating its consequences.

"In perfect secrecy between you and me," wrote John Adams to his wife, "I must tell you that I now believe the President will retire. The consequence to me is very serious, and I am not able, as yet, to see what my duty will demand of me." Adams concluded that he could only wait, watching the events of the next few moments with close scrutiny, in the hope that Providence would show the way. Adams viewed the nomination as a matter of honor, and while he was frank to admit that he was one of the few to whom the honor logically might be tendered, he apparently saw no means of winning the prize. No thought of lining up local machines entered his mind, and the modern dilemma of how and when to announce availability was no part of the eighteenth-century political code.

"It is no light thing to resolve upon retirement," he went on. "My country has claims, my children have claims, and my own character has claims upon me; but all these claims forbid me to serve the public in disgrace . . . if I have reason to think that I have either a want of abilities or of public confidence to such a degree as to be unable to support the government in a higher station, I ought to decline it." His thoughts passed on to the possibility that men of opposite viewpoints might be elected to the two highest offices, and he concluded, "It will be a dangerous crisis in public affairs if the President and Vice President should be in opposite boxes." [1]

Two weeks later Mr. Adams was writing with less caution. "I am, as you say, quite a favorite. I am to dine again today. I am heir apparent you know, and a succession is soon to take place," he told his admiring wife in words that Benjamin Bache would have delighted to spread across his Republican sheet. "Whatever may be the wish or the judgement of the present occupant, the French party and the demagogues in-

[1] January 7, 1796, Adams, *Works*, I, 483-484.

tend, I presume, to set aside the descent. . . . I have no very ardent desire to be the butt of party malevolence." [2]

A few days after receiving this report Mrs. Adams read that the Southern politicians were talking of the coming election in terms not so flattering to her husband. The line being taken, wrote Adams, was that the Vice-President was not so dangerous to republicanism as was often said; a bit inclined towards monarchial experiments perhaps, but all in all, a good man for Vice-President. He might be re-elected provided that Northern men supported Mr. Jefferson for the presidency. Adams, who was listening to the tavern and coffee house talk with excited interest, also testified to the popularity of John Jay among Federalists, and but for the unexpected notoriety that his diplomatic handiwork brought to him, Jay might well have been the choice to succeed Washington.[3]

The basic assumption upon which all the early campaign talk was founded was, of course, the retirement of General Washington. John Adams testified to the fact that no one expected anything else of Washington but that it was considered diplomatic not to speak of the question except in confidence.[4] James Madison was so certain of the President's withdrawal and so convinced that Jefferson was the only possible Republican choice that he notified Monroe of their friend's candidacy in February. "The Republicans, knowing that Jefferson alone can be started with hope of success, mean to push him. I fear much that he will mar the project and insure the adverse election by a peremptory and public protest. The candidate for the Vice President is not yet designated." [5]

[2] Adams to his wife, January 20, 1796, *ibid.*, 485.

[3] Adams to his wife, January 23, February 15, 1796, C. F. Adams, ed., *Letters of John Adams to his Wife*, 2 vols. (Boston, 1841), II, 192, 200-201.

[4] *Ibid.*, February 15, 1796.

[5] February 26, 1796, Irving Brant, *James Madison, Father of the Constitution, 1787 to 1800* (New York, 1950), 433.

Thus, on the surface at least, politics seemed a simple matter; there would be no great struggle for honors, Washington would retire, and Adams or Jefferson would take his place. Vice-President Adams simply assumed that the nomination would be his by virtue of meritorious past conduct, and Madison revealed that early in the election year his party had gone so far as to agree that Jefferson was the only possible candidate. All that was left for Republicans to do in completing the nominating process was to secure Jefferson's acceptance and find a second candidate. Madison was absolutely confident that Washington would resign. He had written the President's farewell message four years before and knew with what reluctance Washington had accepted a second term of office.[6]

Widespread complacency over the retirement question faded away as the result of rumors that began to circulate during the battle over the Jay treaty question. On March 1, a day before Representative Livingston presented his famous resolution, John Adams wrote his wife that strong pressures were being exerted upon the President in favor of a third term. Despite the fact that Washington himself took Adams aside and assured him of the absurdity of such rumors, the "heir apparent" was doubtful.[7] He enjoyed the austere President's unusual display of intimacy and could not doubt his sincerity, but the situation created by Republicans in the House threatened a major crisis, and Washington had been held against his will once before.

Furthermore, one important result of the House fight against the treaty was an increase in Washington's personal popularity. The twenty-second of February was marked by extravagant displays of loyalty and affection. The Virginia amendment resolutions of December, 1795, so critical of Washington's administration, were the chief political topic at

[6] *Ibid.;* see also Washington, *Writings* (Fitzpatrick ed.), XXXII, 45-48.
[7] Adams to his wife, March 1, 1796, *Works*, I, 486-487.

the time (the time lag must constantly be born in mind in dealing with eighteenth-century politics), and the President profited by the comparisons drawn between the two brands of Southern political philosophy. "Boston with every other considerable town in this state, has marked the revolution of the last birthday with uncommon demonstrations of glee," wrote a Boston man. "It appears that our beloved President still reigns in every breast where genius, virtue, and patriotism are implanted—he still continues *the man of the people. . . .*"[8]

From Portsmouth to Savannah, Federalist orators were extolling the virtues, the wisdom and strength, of Washington. There is no doubt that he could have had a third term of office had he followed the wishes of Federalist leaders, but Washington took advantage of the momentary calm that followed the treaty debate to inform Hamilton and his friends that his desires remained unchanged. His first letter on the subject was addressed to Governor Jay of New York.

The diplomatic crisis had passed without seriously damaging either his policy of peace with foreign states or the stability of the federal experiment, he said. The constant burdens of office were clearly destroying his physical and mental vigor, and the never-ending cry that his administration sought to undermine the liberties of the people had so weighed upon his spirits as to make retirement a necessity. "It would be uncandid," he concluded, "and would discover a want of friendly confidence (as you have expressed a solicitude for my riding out the storm) not to add, that nothing short of events . . . as might render a retreat dishonorable, will prevent the public annunciation of it in time to obviate waste or misapplied votes at the Election of the President and Vice-President upon myself."[9]

[8] "Extract of a letter from Boston," *Connecticut Gazette*, March 17, 1796.

[9] May 8, 1796, Washington, *Writings*, XXXV, 35-37; John Jay, *Correspondence and Public Papers of John Jay*, H. P. Johnston, ed., 4 vols., (New York and London, 1890–1893), IV, 212.

The one conceivable situation that Washington had in mind in refusing Jay's appeal to stay on was that of a war with France, and both James Monroe and the President's special emissary, Gouverneur Morris, had sounded an alarm from the continent that winter. Washington had been warned that the Directory was bent upon a bellicose American policy, and as disheartening as this was for Washington, it was precisely what the New York Federalist chiefs saw as their best hope.

At the same time that Washington asked Hamilton for the draft of a valedictory message, he admitted his concern over French relations in submitting for Hamilton's answers a questionnaire covering the problem. Above all, he asked, what is to be done if a new French Minister arrives demanding that the United States live up to the 1778 alliance by defending French possessions in the West Indies, for this would entail conflict with Great Britain? [10]

In appealing again to Hamilton the President gave his former aide an opening that might be used to pry him loose from his retirement decision. Fortunately, for Washington's sake, Pierre Adet was as alive to the American political situation as Hamilton was, and he knew full well that the pro-French Republicans would stand no chance of defeating Washington. He suggested to his superiors that temporary silence from Paris would best aid the Republicans and that his recall would be a serious blow to their prestige. Adet would do nothing to bring on the crisis that might keep Washington on the Federalist ticket.[11]

In June Washington left the capital for Mt. Vernon, Congress adjourned, and Bache's *Aurora* launched a misguided campaign intended to prepare the public for French retaliation against the new Anglo-American alignment. Re-

[10] Washington to Hamilton, May 10, 1796, *Hamilton Papers*, New York Public Library.

[11] *Supra*, p. 76. Adet to the French foreign office, April 23, 1796, *Correspondence of French Ministers*, 897, *supra*, p. 50.

peatedly, Bache hammered home the theme that the administration had proved unfaithful to its republican mission in the world and that French action against American commerce must be the logical consequence of Jay's diplomacy.[12]

Washington, in a fury over Bache's editorials and evidently convinced that the Republican editor had sources of inside information, immediately thought of dispatching a special envoy to Paris to salvage both his peace of mind and the fruits of his foreign policy. Turning again to Hamilton, he asked whether he had the constitutional authority to make such an appointment during the Senate's recess. Why, he asked, had he not published his retirement announcement before leaving Philadelphia? The canvass for electors had already begun in Virginia and his name was being used freely on both sides. If Bache was correct, a situation was about to take shape that would prevent an honorable withdrawal. "I desire to be buffeted no longer in the public prints by a set of infamous scribblers," he fumed.[13]

Hamilton, speaking for the President's secretaries who had received similar letters and requests for advice, told the President to wait and to say nothing. It was true, he lamented, events might take a turn that would make retirement impossible.[14]

The Republican press was responsible for a chain of rumors regarding the retirement question that were not laid until the Farewell Address was released at the end of September. Secretary of State Timothy Pickering, who was expected to be a reliable source, openly stated that he expected Washington to quit office, and it was noted that Mrs. Washington had packed more than the usual number of trunks for the journey to Mt. Vernon that summer. The Secretary of the Senate, Samuel A. Otis, told Mr. Adams, who was as much

12 *Aurora*, June-July, 1796; Washington, *Writings*, XXXV, 95-96.
13 June 26, 1796, Washington, *Writings*, XXXV, 101-104.
14 *Ibid.*, 104.

in the dark as anyone, that the President would wait until electors had been chosen before making his decision known. Hardly a compliment to the expectant heir.[15]

Jefferson, on the other hand, assumed that Washington would remain simply because he alone could save the Federalists from a well-earned defeat, "the colossus of the President's merits with the people," as he put it in a letter to Monroe, being more than the Republicans could hope to overcome; but Wade Hampton told Charleston friends in confidence that Hamilton himself had admitted the President to be unmoved by appeals to remain. He would, said Hampton, announce Jefferson's candidacy the moment Washington made a public statement. Still, no one knew for certain, not even Washington.[16]

By the end of June Thomas Greenleaf, editor of the New York *Argus*, had reached the conclusion that the President viewed his services as indispensable, and though there was no truth in such an assertion, there were a good many Federalist bigwigs who were doing their utmost to convince Washington of it. Governor Oliver Wolcott of Connecticut, one of those public figures of great influence who never appear in history texts, voiced the hope that Washington might be persuaded to remain in office until the war in Europe had ended. The newspapers he read that summer were filled with the exploits of a new French general on the Italian front, but no prophet arose to foretell the future of Napoleon Bonaparte. To many Federalist chiefs such a suggestion seemed reasonable, in fact essential to good government. The younger Wolcott, Washington's Secretary of the Treasury, echoing the line of his demigod, Hamilton, informed his father that the President would probably stay on. The possibility of war, forcing itself upon the United States in the

[15] Adams, *Works*, III, 417.

[16] Jefferson to Monroe, July 10, 1796, *Jefferson Papers*, LC; Edward Rutledge to Henry M. Rutledge, July 21, 1796, *Rutledge Papers*, Historical Society of Pennsylvania, No. 1.

shape of French privateers, he wrote, made retirement now appear impossible.[17]

By the end of summer the fears and hopes of the two parties seemed confirmed. No announcement from Mt. Vernon had relieved Mr. Jefferson's admirers of their anxiety, and as the states began to move toward the crucial contest for presidential electors it was impossible to rule Washington out of the contest. Jonathan Dayton had banked his political reputation upon the prestige of Washington when he had voted against Livington's resolution (an unpopular step at the time), and it was with relief that he concluded that Washington would again dominate the field. Early in September he informed Wolcott, Jr., that New Jersey voters were enthusiastic for a third term. He asked for final confirmation on the question, however, since a last-minute withdrawal could throw the political situation in New Jersey into utter confusion.[18]

The evidence overwhelmingly testifies to the importance of the third term issue in 1796 and points up the fact that local politicians in standing as Federalist electors were thinking in terms of Washington rather than John Adams. A Virginian, for example, in announcing his views as candidate for the electoral college from Loudoun and Fauquier counties, declared himself ready to support Jefferson provided General Washington was not a candidate. He pointedly mentioned Mr. Adams as a candidate he would not vote for.[19] A Savannah editor, utterly disgusted with the theme that Washington was the only man big enough to hold the Union together, descended to sarcasm in what he labeled "A Republican Prayer."

[17] August 9, 1796, George Gibbs, *Memoirs of the Administrations of Washington and John Adams, edited from the Papers of Oliver Wolcott*, 2 vols. (New York, 1846), I, 375.

[18] Dayton to Wolcott, Jr., September 4, 1796, Gibbs, *Memoirs*, I, 381.

[19] Albert Russell to the Freeholders of Loudoun and Fauquier Counties, Virginia, *Columbian Mirror*, Alexandria, Va., September 20, 1796.

"Our President which art in office, illustrious be thy name; thy election come, our will be done, resign for none on earth, until thou art called to heaven—Vouchsafe us our peaceful bread; but forget not the trespasses against us, lead Jay not into temptation and deliver us from the evil which we suffer under the British treaty, for in thee is vested all constitutional power and glory. Amen." [20]

As the convassing entered the homestretch, editor Bache warned his readers of the great Hamiltonian hoax. "It is important that all should know that George Washington will not run again," he declared six days in advance of the Farewell's appearance. "It requires no talent at divination to decide who will be candidates for the chair. Thomas Jefferson and John Adams will be be the men." [21]

Pennsylvania Republican leader John Beckley, who knew Bache well and presumably the source of this information, was careful to follow up the announcement with a personal word to his Republican cohorts. "The President has at last concluded to decline," he informed county chairman, General William Irvine. "You will readily perceive that this short notice is designed to prevent a fair election, and the consequent choice of Mr. Jefferson." [22]

Washington's public farewell to the American people was printed in David Claypoole's *American Daily Advertiser* on September 19 and was reprinted in papers all over the nation through the first week in October. The address included his original notes, a portion of the draft prepared by Madison in 1792, and some very lofty sentiments on the evils of political parties that Hamilton had polished up.[23] While the President's words concerning foreign relations have become

[20] *Columbian Museum,* September 27, 1796.

[21] *Independent Chronicle,* September 22, 1796, reprint from *Aurora.*

[22] September 15, 1796, *Irvine Papers,* Historical Society of Pennsylvania, XIII, No. 112.

[23] Washington to Hamilton, August 10, 1796, Washington, *Writings,* XXXV, 178-179.

proverbial, if frequently misunderstood, his sound advice has been happily overlooked on the subject of political conduct. He warned his fellow citizens that parties could only tend to divide the nation and that division of a lasting nature could become the foundations of sectional antagonism of the worst kind. Most significant for his contemporaries was his warning against parties as the instruments of foreign influence.

"Against the insidious wiles of foreign influence . . . the jealousy of a free people ought to be constantly awake; since history and experience prove that foreign influence is one of the most baneful foes of Republican Government. . . . Excessive partiality for one foreign nation, and excessive dislike of another, cause those whom they actuate to see danger only on one side, and serve to veil and even second the arts of influence on the other. Real patriots, who may resist the intrigues of the favorite, are liable to become suspected and odious; while its tools and dupes usurp the applause and confidence of the people, to surrender their interests." [24]

The charge that his administration had devoted its foreign policy to serve British interests, a charge associated with the Jay treaty, we know to have been slanderous in Washington's eyes. French partisans accused the Federalists of selling out to Great Britain in signing the treaty, and Washington pointedly remarked upon the "foreign influence and corruption which find a facilitated access to the government itself through the channels of party passions." [25]

There is no doubt that Washington's words were widely read, and that their effect upon the election of 1796 was considerable.[26] In the first place, the timing of the announcement was carefully and cleverly arranged. For reasons that Wash-

[24] *Ibid.*

[25] *Ibid.*

[26] Editors throughout the Union printed the Address in its entirety and usually without editorial comment, whether friends or foes of the administration. Commentary ultimately followed after a few days. Unlike a

ington and Hamilton could not gauge the crisis with France had not materialized; in fact it gave every appearance of having been dismissed by the Directory as an unprofitable gamble. The domestic squabble that was bound to arise over the recall of Republican favorite James Monroe—a step that Washington, after consultation with Hamilton and his secretaries, had decided upon in August—had not yet arisen to give grounds for the charge that the President was retreating in the face of sharp attack. The rumors and uncertainty surrounding the question of his retirement could have had no other effect than to serve the Federalist party well. Candidates for electoral colleges had been able to stand upon Washington's popularity and possible future, rather than upon his past. In holding back the announcement Washington and Hamilton, who, when he had first received the outline of a draft in May, had replied, "A thing of this kind should be done with great care and much at leisure," had been able to fuse the immense prestige of the President with the election.[27]

Even the remote possibility that Washington might be the opposition candidiate forced Jeffersonians to scatter their fire. Instead of concentrating solely on the unfortunate weaknesses of Mr. Adams as a political candidate, they found themselves driven against the obvious merits of Washington as a candidate. The universally accepted belief that new candidates would be involved had begun to evaporate as the summer passed without the expected dictum from Mt. Vernon. Instead many had reached the conclusion that a third term had been reluctantly forced upon the President, a belief that Bache, in following a mistaken editorial policy, had done as much as anyone to instill. The Republican press had just

similar presidential statement today, this address was all the news of the day or week that the paper carried. It could not easily, therefore, be passed over by an unfriendly reader.

[27] Hamilton to Washington, May 10, 1796, *Hamilton Papers*, LC.

had time to reorient itself when the final word was released. To attribute such strategy to Hamilton alone would be to rob Washington of the political sagacity of which his second term of office bears abundant witness and further to perpetuate a myth of the great man's political ineptness that the facts simply do not bear out.

Through his intimate connection with the President Hamilton was given an advantage over rival political bosses that was considerable. While leaders of the Adams factions in Congress and in New England were forced to curtail their activities out of respect for Washington, Hamilton, who knew in August that the die was cast, could press forward freely as he saw fit. The actions he took that summer were of crucial importance in the history of the Federalist party, for it was at this time that the seeds of its dissolution were sown; behind the secret of Washington's ultimate decision the New York Federalist had maneuvered the vice-presidential nomination to his personal tastes. In neither party was there an open struggle for the first nomination.

Republicans had settled upon Jefferson as their standard bearer as early as 1794. The French Minister had notified his government at the time Jefferson left the Department of State that the "republicans" or "patriots" had no leader who could rival Mr. Jefferson or anyone else who would be a satisfactory successor to Washington.[28]

Jefferson himself drew attention to the continuous talk of his presidential hopes in the public papers in April, 1796, and it seemed of the utmost importance, he wrote Madison, to let it be known that he held no such hopes. His retirement from public life was permanent, the issue was "forever closed," and who but Madison more deserved the nomination of all true republicans? It was imperative for Republican chances, said Jefferson, that this be understood in

[28] C. W. Upham and O. Pickering, *The Life and Times of Timothy Pickering*, 4 vols. (Boston, 1867–73), III, 227.

order that there be no "division or loss of votes, which might be fatal to the Southern interests." [29]

Madison, of course, paid no attention to the wishes of his friend, and by September there was no doubt in anyone's mind, including Jefferson's, that only one man in Republican ranks could draw votes enough to unseat the Federalists. Yet despite his popularity among the politicos and the widespread admiration that was his south of the Potomac, his name was little discussed in Northern newspapers until the last two or three weeks of the convassing. For example, let us look as the toasts offered at antiadministration dinners and meetings as described by the reporters of the day.

In March, 1796, the enthusiastic sons of Hibernia met for their annual Society dinner at a large Philadelphia tavern, but while toasts were drunk to a whole series of institutions and men favored by Republicans—the French Republic, the new Batavian Republic, the Rights of Man, Edward Livingston, and many others—Jefferson was unmentioned.[30] Members of "The Mechanical Relief Society" of Alexandria, Virginia, showing strong antiadministration feelings, drank to the House of Representatives, Representative Livingston of New York, and the revolutionary services of George Washington, but the supposed leader of the Republican party was overlooked.[31]

A month later The Tammany Society of Philadelphia toasted the people of the United States, the people of France, and left out Jefferson.[32] Even on the Fourth of July, when Jefferson might have been remembered without an election to add interest to his name, Boston Republicans drank a total of twenty-six toasts to every imaginable antiadministration symbol except Jefferson—Sam Adams, patriots of '75, Lafayette, the French Republic, the militia of the United States,

[29] Jefferson to Madison, April 27, 1796, *Jefferson Papers*, LC.
[30] *Claypoole's American Daily Advertiser*, March 26, 1796.
[31] *Aurora*, May 11, 1796, reporting an April gathering.
[32] *Ibid.*

etc., but nothing of the party's candidate for the presidency. Likewise, in a Morristown, New Jersey, Independence Day celebration boisterous defenders of Mr. Jefferson's ideas staggered through glasses to "the virtuous minority of the House of Representatives," and even to George Washington, "may the virtues that inspired him in 1776 direct his future conduct," but no voice was raised in honor of the author of the Declaration.[33]

Further examples could be produced and doubtless examples to prove that Jefferson was remembered, but the fact of his omission from the thoughts of obvious partisans on public occasions as reported in pro-Republican newspapers is of significance. The fact is that the public was very poorly informed about the candidates until very late in the campaign, they could not decide the election directly and showed more apathy than might be expected, and the absence of campaigns by the candidates themselves did nothing to whip up enthusiasms. Neither Adams nor Jefferson lifted a finger to influence the election one way or the other. Whatever pressures might have been exerted by Jefferson were handled by his close friend and political guardian, James Madison, while Mr. Adams appears to have had no such alter ego and sailed on his merits alone. Hamilton, who cared very little for the "crown prince," was playing his own tune and attempting to persuade as many local Federalist chiefs to join him as possible. Jefferson was more fortunate than Adams in having the man who was closer to being a party boss than anyone else, James Madison, as a personal friend; in contrast Vice-President Adams could count on nothing but ridicule and enmity from Alexander Hamilton.

On the whole, Madison was wiser than Hamilton, too, for he was careful to eliminate as many points of confusion as possible by calling a caucus of Republican politicians to dis-

[33] *Independent Chronicle* (Boston), July 7, 1796; *Argus* (New York), July 15, 1796.

cuss candidates. It was characteristic of Hamilton and the faction devoted to him that no such open meeting was held before Congress adjourned. Under the system of national elections observed in 1796 the choice of a vice-presidential candidate was as important as that of a presidential candidate. Electors, lacking telephone and telegraph contact with other states, cast their ballots for the two men who should fill the nation's top offices. They did not cast one ballot for a President and a second and separate ballot for a Vice-President. Thus, the two men receiving the highest and second highest number of votes were elected regardless of party or anticipated rank. In this way Mr. Jefferson was to become Vice-President despite the fact that no one had voted for him as anything but President.

With hopes of preventing their second candidate from receiving more votes than their first, Republican Senators met together to agree upon a running mate for Jefferson, sometime during the first two weeks of May. From fragmentary sources it is apparent that the meeting was angry and turbulent. Burr of New York was mistrusted by Southern Republicans, yet they knew an Eastern man would add great weight to the ticket and increase Jefferson's chances of securing electoral votes north of the Potomac. His nomination was strongly objected to by Senator Pierce Butler of South Carolina. The vote was a deadlock, and it was not until New Hampshire's John Langdon arrived to break it that a decision could be reached. Even men on the outside heard rumors of the tempest. Butler had worked mightily to stop the Jay treaty, alienating many conservative Charleston friends. He reasoned that his own nomination would at least guarantee South Carolina's vote, that Northern votes were a remote possibility at best, and that Burr was liable to lose Republican votes in the otherwise solid Southern states.

The decision finally went to Burr, nevertheless. His influence and future strength in New York were considered promising, and no one doubted that Burr might easily throw his weight toward Federalism without inducements to the contrary. "Burr they think unsettled in his politics," wrote Federalist eavesdropper William Smith of South Carolina, "and they are afraid he will go over to the other side." [34] The results proved the gamble expensive. Robert R. Livingston of New York and Pierce Butler both disappeared from active Republican ranks after 1796, so great was their fear and disgust over such a bargain.

Jefferson had nothing to do with Burr's nomination by his party, and unless a substantial body of evidence on the subject is totally misleading, he was almost indifferent to his own chances for office. Certainly he did nothing to promote his cause, and his supporters found it necessary throughout the campaign to assure one another that he would accept the office if and when it was tendered. When Tennessee's Senator William Cocke informed Jefferson of the frontier's enthusiasm for his candidacy in August, he received no answer until October 21; and the reply was that Mr. Jefferson had no desire for office and would rather be thought worthy of it than to hold it.[35]

John Beckley, who was directing the Republican strategy in the key state of Pennsylvania, felt called upon to assure co-workers that their candidate would accept the presidency as the campaign went into its final month. In doing so he admitted that he had received no definite confirmation of this from Monticello, however.[36] Late in September Madison wrote James Monroe, "I have not seen Jefferson and have

[34] William Smith to Ralph Izard, May 18, 1796, "South Carolina Federalist Correspondence," *American Historical Review*, XIV (July, 1909), 780; recorded notes of a conversation between John Adams and the Secretary of the Senate of the United States, July 17, 1796, Adams, "Diary," *Works*, III, 417.

[35] William Cocke to Jefferson, August 17, 1796, note in Jefferson's handwriting summarizing his reply dated October 21, 1796, *Jefferson Papers*, LC.

[36] Beckley to William Irvine, October 4, 1796, *Irvine Papers*, Historical Society of Pennsylvania, XIII, 115.

thought it wise to present him no opportunity of protesting to his friends against being embarked in the contest."[37]

Jefferson's personal feelings about the matter were explained frankly to his son-in-law. If public office were thrust upon him, he commented, he would much prefer that it be in the form of the vice-presidency. "The considerations which induce this preference are solid, whether viewed with relation to interest, happiness, or reputation. Ambition is long since dead in my mind. Yet even a well weighed ambition would take the same side." His reaction to the news that John Adams had defeated him was one of relief. Writing to Edward Rutledge of Charleston he said, "On principles of public interest I should not have refused [the presidency]; but I protest before my God that I shall . . . rejoice at escaping. I know well that no man will ever bring out of that office the reputation which carries him into it."[38]

When strong doubts arose over the validity of Vermont election returns and it seemed that the House of Representatives might be called upon to choose the second President, Jefferson turned immediately to Madison, urging him to throw his influence toward his opponent, Mr. Adams. "I pray you to declare it on every occasion foreseen or not foreseen by me, in favor of the choice of the people substantially expressed, and to prevent the phenomenon of a Pseudo-president at so early a day."[39]

There is no doubt of it. The party of Jefferson was not led by Jefferson in its first national campaign. Whatever his motives, it is clear that he did not want office in 1796, did not aid in the campaign, and did nothing to secure the nomination. The relative tranquillity within Republican ranks stands in marked contrast to the machinations of Federalist hopefuls.

[37] September 29, 1796, Irving Brant, *James Madison, 1787–1800*, 444.

[38] Jefferson to T. M. Randolph, November 28, 1796; to Rutledge, December 27, 1796, *Jefferson Papers*, LC.

[39] January 17, 1797, *Madison Papers*, LC.

5

Adams and Hamilton

NO CAUCUS OF FEDERALIST LEADERS CHOSE JOHN ADAMS TO succeed Washington, and he never had the united following within his party that Jefferson enjoyed in Republican ranks. On the other hand Adams had twice been elected Vice-President, and this meant more in 1796 than it would today. In the first election Washington had received a unanimous first ballot of sixty-nine electoral votes. Adams, who was second, received thirty-four, but his nearest competitor, John Jay, had received only nine. Even when an opposition had gathered behind George Clinton in 1792 Adams had taken second place by a twenty-seven-vote margin over the New York governor. Mr. Adams was not just the man who would step into Washington's shoes in the event of death, he was the man who had twice received the second largest electoral vote.

It was already apparent by 1796 that the electoral balloting system was at odds with the development of political parties, but nothing was done to change it until the election of 1800 dramatized the ease with which the public will might be subverted. Hamilton and his powerful friends were as tempted to thwart the will of the Federalist rank and file in 1796 as many of them were to bargain Aaron Burr into the presidency four years later. Disliking and fearing Mr. Adams, they could not take the nomination—if it may be called that —by an open test of strength. The United States was not far enough removed from British custom for Adams to have been deluding himself when he viewed the coming election as a "succession" to power. Though he clearly recognized that a large segment of the population did not think in such terms, his party had attracted most of the men who did.

There was also a sense in which a republic still led by the men who had directed its independence movement owed the highest public trust to the few who remained in the front ranks of national politics. Adams believed that he was expected to play a major role in public life and spoke of the many "claims" upon himself to do so. Adams may have been vain, but he was neither insincere nor unintelligent. Americans chose to celebrate the announcement of the Declaration of Independence rather than the acceptance of the Constitution as a memorial day; and Washington, Adams, and Jefferson alone remained national figures from that group which had led the independence movement. Patrick Henry still stirred memories, but he was old and chose obscurity rather than publicity. The outstanding services that Adams had rendered in 1775 and 1776 when he had teamed up with Sam Adams and Richard Henry Lee to push and persuade wavering men into an open break with England were not easily forgotten; no one had been a more powerful debator, orator, or strategist than the John Adams of 1776.[1] He had represented the Confederation during and just after the Revolution at Paris, London, and The Hague. His championship of New England fishing rights on the treaty commission had not been forgotten in Massachusetts, and his successful negotiation of a Dutch loan at a time when the Continental Congress had reached the end of its resources was a contribution of large proportions to the survival of independence.[2]

1 Catherine Drinker Bowen has done full justice to the work of Adams in relation to the declaration of American independence. *John Adams and the American Revolution* (Boston, 1950), 488-599.

2 The most complete account of Adams' European experience and his diplomatic career is to be found in Gilbert Chinard, *Honest John Adams* (Boston, 1939), 107-218.

Despite past services and great talents there were serious drawbacks to Adams as a presidential candidate. Unlike Jefferson, he had turned towards conservatism in the years immediately following the Declaration of Independence. He had come to see that property rights might seriously be endangered by the spirit born of the Declaration and the writings of Paine. When the French Revolution began Adams welcomed it and hailed its limited monarchy phase. He could not view post-Louis XVI developments in France as either beneficial or constructive. Along with Washington, Hamilton, and Gouverneur Morris, John Adams had taken the side of Edmund Burke in evaluating the effects of the French Revolution. Still, his strongly conservative beliefs and intellectual idiosyncrasies would have made little difference had he not been so determined to publicize them.

The Defense of the Constitutions of the United States and *Discourses on Davilla*, published in America between 1787 and 1793, presented Adams' views on human nature and government openly. Unlike Madison and Hamilton, who published their "Federalist" articles under the pseudonym "Publius," Adams signed what he wrote. He was too honest to do otherwise and far too convinced that he was right to think it necessary. His words could easily be taken out of context to prove that he preferred British to American, aristocratic to republican, ways of thinking and acting. His best defense against such charges was the fact that he lived and dressed simply, fashionable eighteenth-century proofs of republican virtue. Furthermore, his views had long been known, and the public had grown accustomed to the oddities of "The Duke of Braintree."

The other major defect in John Adams as a presidential candidate, perhaps the more important of the two, was that Hamilton disliked him. To be mistrusted or disliked by the powerful Federalist leader was to be haltingly supported in many circles where Hamilton's most ardent disciples reigned supreme. Adams returned the mistrust measure for measure, which did not help matters greatly. The belief that Hamilton had twice attempted to deflect votes from him rankled in Adams' mind. There is no record even to suggest that they corresponded or spoke through intermediaries during the months of the 1796 campaign. The few interviews that they had had during Hamilton's tenure as Secretary of the Treasury had been strained and uncomfortable. Jefferson recorded his impressions of one in his diary of those years.

After a ceremonial dinner at the President's mansion one evening conversation turned to the topic of government. Adams brusquely commented that were the British government purged of corruption in high places it would be the most perfect ever devised by man. Hamilton immediately countered with the remark that to purge the British government of official corruption would be to strip it of its virtue.[3]

Adams liked to lead, and Hamilton liked to lead. Compromise between the two was rendered unlikely where viewpoints clashed, owing to mutual jealousy and suspicion. Nevertheless Hamilton accepted Adams as the Federalist party's candidate for President, and there is no better explanation for his acceptance than that the vast majority of Federalists, those who had stood behind Adams in 1792 and those who remained loyal during the great crisis of Federalism of 1799 and 1800, wanted and expected Adams to be the party's candidate. Many of them were men of local influence politically but whose party sense was not strong, Elbridge Gerry of Massachusetts being one of the most notable. So strong was pro-Adams sentiment in Massachusetts that Hamilton made no effort to prevent endorsement of Mr. Adams, and without the strength of Massachusetts Federalism would have remained a point of view rather than a party.

[3] Jefferson, *Writings* (Ford ed.), I, 179-180.

According to a letter that William Smith of South Carolina wrote to Rufus King in midsummer the Federalists had left Philadelphia with the clear understanding that Adams and Thomas Pinckney of South Carolina would be supported. Smith, who was close to the inner circle of Hamiltonians, mentioned no formal agreement and no party conclave.[4] The testimony of Secretary of the Treasury Wolcott was to the effect that Adams' candidacy was inevitable owing to his popularity among the rank and file, a popularity arising from what he termed "official station and other circumstances." Near the close of Adams' turbulent administration Wolcott exclaimed to Fisher Ames, "It was not your fault, nor that of any other Federal character, that in 1797 we had no other choice than between Mr. Adams and Mr. Jefferson."[5]

Clearly, however, there was another choice, and for several months the men closest to Hamilton saw it as the best choice. The fact that Thomas Pinckney was put forth as a candidate for the vice-presidency and privately promoted by leading Hamiltonians as presidential material goes far to explain both Jefferson's election and the eventual collapse of the Federalist party. When he landed at Charleston in December, 1796, the former envoy to Spain found himself a contender for the presidency.

Just as the Republicans were attempting to break the hold of their opponents in the North, by nominating Burr, so the Federalists were driven by sectional considerations to find a second candidate from the South. There were border states in 1796 as there were in 1860. Massachusetts, Connecticut, and Rhode Island were as solidly Federalist as Virginia, Kentucky, and Georgia were Republican. North of the Mason-Dixon Line New York and Pennsylvania were doubtful and

[4] July 23, 1796, C. R. King, *Life and Correspondence of Rufus King*, 6 vols. (New York, 1894–1900), II, 66.

[5] Gibbs, *Memoirs of the Administrations of Washington and Adams*, I, 378; to Ames, August 10, 1800, II, 400.

powerful. Even though John Jay had been elected Governor of New York in 1795 there was little to indicate that a fundamental change in public sentiment had at last broken the dominant Clintonian spell of suspicion towards the central government. Pennsylvania likewise hung in the balance. Her administrative machinery rested in the hands of Governor Thomas Mifflin, who had yet to cast his not inconsiderable weight to either of the new parties. Although he kept Jeffersonian Alexander Dallas on his payroll no one could be sure that Mifflin might not move suddenly in either direction. Republican hopes ran high that Federalist control of the legislature might be ended by a strenuous effort. Burr was expected to cut into Hamiltonian strength in New York, and his intimate connections with New Jersey's Senator Dayton held out hopes in the third of the so-called Middle States.

Below the sectional dividing line three states suffered strong pockets of proadministration sentiment to exist. Maryland and Delaware sent both Republicans and Federalists to Congress, but in both cases state machinery was controlled by administration supporters. Commerce and banking both played important roles in economic life, and Baltimore remained a stronghold of Federalism during the 1790's despite the rising tide of militant Jeffersonianism in the section as a whole. While not all merchants and bankers were Hamiltonians and not all planters Jeffersonians, most of them lined up as history has traditionally presented the picture. Washington's personal popularity was tremendous in these border states, a factor that helps to explain still further the existence of Federalist strength in these areas of the upper South.

The one Southern state that Federalist leaders saw a chance of capturing in the election of 1796 was South Carolina, and in anticipating a close contest it was natural that the alignment of political forces in Charleston should have been a source of intense interest to them. The metropolis of Charleston was the key to eight electoral votes that could swing the election, and the personal leanings of a few distinguished tyros in the legislature could be counted on to influence the outcome decisively.

Had John Jay not made his foray into diplomacy Hamilton might well have contested Mr. Adams' endorsement, but as it was Jay had become the substance of the evil spirits in American economic life to every artisan and farmer baffled by the rising cost of living. Hamilton accepted John Adams without enthusiasm, but he was anything but passive when it came to the selection of the party's second candidate. He may have been flattered by the report that Rhode Island leaders were intending to push him for the vice-presidency, but he was not tempted by such thoughts and turned instead to mapping out a new political career for Patrick Henry of Virginia as the election year opened.[6]

It would have been an extraordinary test of party development had Hamilton and his friends persuaded the old orator of the Revolution to come out of his retirement in 1796. Next to Washington, and possibly Jefferson, there was no one in the South who could match Henry for popularity. He had gradually let it be known that his violent anticentralism had died since 1788, and Washington had taken such reports seriously enough to offer Henry the State Department in the moment of Edmund Randolph's sudden exit.[7] The President was as well aware of the need for driving a wedge into the solid framework of Republicanism in Virginia as Hamilton was, and Henry's support for his achievements was eagerly solicited. By splitting Virginia's block of twenty-one electoral votes a vital blow at Republican prestige might be struck, especially since the Constitution provided that electors could cast their ballots for only one man from a given state.

Early in April Hamilton entrusted the task of sounding

[6] Adams, *Works*, III, 423, Diary entry for August 11, 1796.

[7] See pp. 249-250.

out Henry to John Marshall, who had just won the confidence and admiration of Federalists in the Jay treaty fight. Senator Rufus King followed up Hamilton's suggestion and in doing so urged that no Northern names be mentioned. Marshall approached his work with tact, using Henry Lee to make the original overture as if it were all the brainchild of local patriots. Henry proved unenthusiastic at the outset but promised to meet with Federalist leaders in Richmond at the end of May.

Before this interview Marshall, Lee, and Edward Carrington carefully considered the approach to be taken. (These three together with Hamilton and King were apparently the only Federalist politicians drawn into the secret.) Hints were dropped that his candidacy would be well received in Eastern quarters, but Henry was too old. "Mr. Henry has at length been sounded on the subject you committed to my charge," reported Marshall to Senator King. "Governor Lee and myself have conversed with him on it tho' without informing him particularly of the persons who authorized the communication. . . . His unwillingness, I think, proceeds from an apprehension of the difficulties to be encountered by those who shall fill high executive offices." [8]

Despite the precautions taken there were suspicions in enemy quarters. Jefferson, never surprised at Hamilton's dark wanderings, considered the reports a smoke screen, an insincere political trick, and in July told Monroe that the "monocrats" were paying court to the old man in the firm belief that he would accept nothing. "He has been offered everything which they knew he would not accept. Some impression is thought to be made, but we do not believe it is radical." It was quite obvious, he concluded, that New York

[8] Marshall to Hamilton, April 10, 1796, *Hamilton Papers*, LC; Marshall to King, May 24, 1796, *King Papers*, New York Historical Society, Box 6, No. 66.

quarters would stoop to anything in order to cause a split in Virginia ranks.[9]

Actually Hamilton and King had lost little and gained considerably in wooing Patrick Henry; he had been brought one step closer to making an avowal of political leanings, and later he was to express them openly. Jefferson was undoubtedly correct as shown by the fact that before the Henry negotiations were completed the New York Federalists were already in pursuit of a more promising candidate from the South.

One of Rufus King's last services to the party of talents before accepting the Ministry to England was his suggestion to Hamilton that they take a serious look at the pretensions of the Honorable Thomas Pinckney. From his vantage point in the Senate during the Jay treaty fight King had been able to see clearly that the fruits of Pinckney's Madrid negotiations were the stuff of which good politicking is made. He had been impressed with the high regard that Southern congressmen expressed for Mr. Pinckney's talents, and he was able to see that the Spanish treaty was the first administration measure to win the unanimous applause of both the South and West. Three weeks before Marshall and Henry Lee drew Patrick Henry aside in earnest conversation, King turned Hamilton's gaze upon the homecoming diplomat.

"To his former popularity," he pointed out, "he will now add the good will of those who have been particularly gratified with the Spanish treaty; should we concur in him will he not receive as great, if not greater, southern and western support than any other man?" Hamilton wasted no time in useless debate. "I am entirely of the opinion that P. H. declining, Mr. Pinckney ought to be our man," he replied.[10]

[9] July 10, 1796, *Jefferson Papers*, LC.

[10] King to Hamilton, May 2, 1796; Hamilton to King, May 4, 1796, *Hamilton Papers*, LC. Hamilton's attempts to prevent King's resigning his Senate seat for a diplomatic appointment were unavailing. King maintained a keen interest in domestic politics, his correspondence providing a candid

Much has been surmised about the "Pinckney Plot" that grew out of this Hamilton-King exchange. The usual account, taken from the diary of John Adams, is essentially correct: the Hamiltonians supported Pinckney for the second office while privately urging his qualifications for President. Knowing that Adams would receive little, if any, Southern support because of Jefferson's popularity in that section, Northern and Southern electors, in casting their second ballots for Pinckney, would unwittingly make him President. The problem was that of instilling party regularity as a necessity in the minds of New Englanders who could not be expected to look the other way while so obvious a steal was carried off. This part of the story has never been told.

The idea of supporting Pinckney was spread by word of mouth among the Federalists at Philadelphia during the spring of 1796. On the testimony of Robert Harper and William Smith, it is clear that Congress broke up with a clear understanding among administration supporters that Washington and Adams would again be the candidates unless and until the President made a public statement. Smith and Harper were to return to Charleston to build up Mr. Pinckney's case among friends in the event that Washington retired, but they were careful to make no public statements that might embarrass the party.[11]

By July the powerful Rutledge faction at Charleston had come over to the idea of pushing Pinckney for the vice-presidency while hoping for even higher things. At the end of the month Edward Rutledge, in a letter to his nephew, reported that Wade Hampton's announcement of Washington's final determination to withdraw had touched off

---

picture of Hamiltonian adventures from 1797 to 1800. King, *Life and Correspondence*, Volume II.

[11] Smith to King, Charleston, July 23, 1796, King, *Life and Correspondence*, II, 66.

enthusiastic talk about Major Pinckney. Most men in Charleston, he declared, were agreed that Jefferson's chances were best, but that Pinckney might come in first if supported by the electors of Kentucky and Tennessee, the area where his popularity was assumed to be greatest. Rutledge, who was both friend to Jefferson and father-in-law to Thomas Pinckney, was torn. "Should it be so, I shall have cause to be pleased and to regret it, in the same moment." [12]

Early in the autumn the first word from the homecoming envoy was heard, and his response to well-wishers at Charleston was all that could be desired. Pinckney wrote wistfully of his desire to retire from public duties, but in the gentlemanly political tradition he demurred a rejection of public trust. This was enough for Edward Rutledge. "His countrymen are opposed to his plan of retirement, and I believe he will fill the President's chair," he announced to his nephew. "The eastern states, it is said, and said by the influential men of that country, will vote for him and Mr. Adams. The Southern States will vote for him and Mr. Jefferson, and when each department agrees in that manner, he must be the person." [13]

When Thomas Pinckney docked at Charleston a few weeks later crowds lined the waterfront to cheer him. The horses of his carriage were unhitched by enthusiastic neighbors, who drew him home in triumph through the streets of Charleston.[14] Hamilton could have achieved no more complete a victory. Pinckney had become a presidential candidate through the inconspicuous efforts of Harper and Smith, Jefferson's friends found themselves unable to deny a favorite son, and Adams and Burr had been forgotten.

Had sectional feeling not run as high in New England as

[12] To Henry M. Rutledge, July 21, 1796, *Rutledge Papers*, Historical Society of Pennsylvania, No. 1. Henry de Sausure to H. M. Rutledge, n.d., *ibid.*, No. 5.

[13] To Henry M. Rutledge, October 20, 1796, *ibid.*, No. 4.

[14] *Maryland Gazette* (Annapolis), January 26, 1797.

in the deep South, Thomas Pinckney might well have been Washington's successor, but Federalist leaders in the Eastern states were not going to surrender to the South or to Hamilton without good cause. The New York chiefs were intelligent enough to know that Massachusetts and Connecticut sentiment ran counter to their desires, and they made no attempt to sell Pinckney in that area as a presidential candidate. Oliver Wolcott of Connecticut, as secure a politician as the period affords and one who enjoyed being master in his own house, balked at the thought of slipping an unknown Southern diplomat into the presidency. Though his son constantly repeated the Hamiltonian plea for party unity, Wolcott saw as quickly as Rutledge did that equal votes for Adams and Pinckney in New England would defeat Adams. Who was Thomas Pinckney, they asked; after all, there were rumors that this South Carolinian had been sympathetic to the French Revolution as a result of social experiences in England. He might be no more sound in his political views than Jefferson.[15]

Hamilton answered their objections through his alter ego, Oliver Wolcott, Jr., who was picked to hold Connecticut in line. His arguments were clever. The anti-federalists have no intention of delivering votes to Colonel Burr, Wolcott told his father, because it is far more to their purposes to re-elect Adams Vice-President. Should this result, they confidently expect Mr. Adams to decline the honor of serving under Jefferson, he reasoned. This would ruin Mr. Adams' career for good, and a man more amenable to Jefferson's leveling philosophy would be found. He assured his father that Pinckney was to be depended on and warned that the failure of New England to give him equal support with Adams would result in a serious split among the friends to good government.[16]

[15] Gibbs, *Memoirs, op. cit.*, I, 402.
[16] October 17, 1796, *ibid.*, 387.

Threats of a secession among a handful of Southern Federalists failed to impress New Englanders, however, and a new line was adopted to frighten them. The information that Adams had fewer electors than had been anticipated was spread. The need of keeping Jefferson from the presidency was greater than that of protecting Adams out of sentiment. "There are still *hopes* that Mr. Adams will be elected," reported Wolcott, Jr., to Hamilton. "I hope Mr. Pinckney will be supported as the next best thing which can be done. Pray write to your eastern friends." [17]

Hamilton's answer was that he had already sent out one round of letters on the subject and that a second had immediately been dispatched.[18]

Theodore Sedgwick was one of the men who could be trusted. He was told that there was one and only one issue in the election and that was to defeat Jefferson rather than to elect Adams. An understanding had been reached months before that friends to good government would stand by Adams and Pinckney. To falter at the last minute was to give the administrative power over to Jefferson. Talk of a plot deliberately to bring Pinckney in ahead of Adams was pure slander, he asserted. There was no assurance whatsoever that Pinckney would garner Southern electoral votes, and, concluded Hamilton, even if Jefferson should fail the presidency we will have at best a divided administration with the enemy in a position to render great harm to the Federal structure.[19]

From outward appearances it is possible to believe that the Hamiltonians had never wanted their hand-picked candidate to run ahead of Adams, that they sincerely believed Adams weaker than Jefferson, and that they saw Pinckney as the only answer. While the French Minister, Pierre Adet, in reporting the election to his superiors said simply of the

[17] November 6, 1796, *Hamilton Papers,* LC.

[18] Hamilton to Wolcott, Jr., November 9, 1796, *ibid.*

[19] Hamilton to Sedgwick, November, 1796, Hamilton, *Works* (Lodge ed.), X, 195-196.

Hamiltonians, "Pinckney was the man of their choice," Speaker of the House Jonathan Dayton said nothing of a scheme to rob Adams of the presidency when he wrote in October to his friend and partner in western land speculation, John Symmes. "General Washington, having declined a re-election, a new President will be presented to us on the 4th of March—either Mr. Adams, Mr. Jefferson, or Mr. Pinckney will be the man." [20]

Senator William Bingham of Pennsylvania, a man on the inside, expressed no knowledge of secret maneuverings when he summarized the political news for an amused Rufus King, now safely ensconced in the American Ministry at London. "The friends of Mr. Adams may calculate on a majority in his favor, but so small, that on so momentous an occasion, it would be risking too much to trust entirely thereto. It is therefore deemed expedient to recommend to the federal electors to give an uniform vote for Mr. Pinckney, which with those he will obtain to the southward, detached from Mr. Adams, will give him a decided majority over other candidates." [21]

Likewise, the testimony of Elias Boudinot of New Jersey is against any sort of plot to cheat Adams. He viewed it as entirely possible that New Hampshire and Massachusetts Federalists might refuse to scatter their second votes for fear of electing Jefferson to office, but from his correspondence with friends in those states he surmised nothing more devious than this. And if the letters of William Vans Murray of Maryland are any indication of political thinking among Federalists in the upper South, there was not only no plot, there was total confusion. Writing in October to his intimate friend the Secretary of War, James McHenry, he commented that both Adams and Jefferson would receive Mary-

[20] December 15, 1796, *Correspondence of French Ministers, op. cit.*, 978; October 15, 1796, B. W. Bond, ed., *The Correspondence of John Cleves Symmes* (New York, 1926), 276.

[21] November 29, 1796, King, *Life and Correspondence*, II, 113

land electoral votes. "No Vice is yet mentioned here," he declared. "Who is thought of for Vice President?"

McHenry, who followed worshipfully behind Hamilton in all political matters, replied that Adams and Pinckney were to be equally supported; and this only a few days before the voters went to the polls to select electors, was the first that Murray had heard of the matter.[22]

The Hamiltonian line, whether sincere or not, was notably unsuccessful where it counted most—among his closest friends in Massachusetts. Fisher Ames spoke constantly of Adams as the party's candidate in the late weeks of the campaign, and in characteristic language he condemned the thought of allowing the power of numbers to outweigh principle. Although he admitted to Christopher Gore that Pinckney stood the best chance if equally supported and that Pinckney was to be preferred to Jefferson, he would not subscribe to rumors which hinted that Adams' chances were hopeless. It was possible, he admitted, that some Republican electors might cast their second ballots for the South Carolinian with hopes of winning him over later; still, Pinckney was not presidential material. "On the one hand, he is a good man," concluded Ames, "on the other, even a good President thus made by luck or sheer dexterity of play, would stand badly with parties and with the country." [23]

Another high-ranking Massachusetts Federalist, George Cabot, refused to swerve in his loyalties or to believe that a plot was under way to cheat Adams. Writing to Oliver Wolcott, Jr., after the election he declared that he and his friends had had but two objectives throughout the cam-

[22] Boudinot to Samuel Bayard, December 14, 1796, J. J. Boudinot, ed., *The Life, Public Services, Addresses, and Letters of Elias Boudinot*, 2 vols. (Boston and New York, 1896), II, 118-119; Murray to McHenry, October 3, November 2, 1796, McHenry to Murray, November, 1796, B. C. Steiner, *Life and Correspondence of James McHenry* (Cleveland, 1907), 198, 201-202.

[23] December 3, 1796, Ames, *Works*, I, 206; see also 195-206.

paign; first, to defeat Jefferson or what he termed "a French President," and second, to elect John Adams.[24]

Election day in Massachusetts showed the Adams men in complete control. While an anxious Madison believed New Englanders to be playing a hypocritical game in talking Adams while secretly urging Pinckney ("It is even suspected that this turn has been secretly indicated from the beginning in a quarter where the *leading* zeal for Adams has been affected"), his friend John Beckley more accurately described the situation as one that would result in a Federalist schism. The enthusiasm for Adams he believed to be real and the Hamilton maneuvering for Pinckney just as real.[25]

Even though few Federalist leaders saw through the Hamiltonian argument that Adams strength was dwindling and that in Pinckney lay the only hope of defeating Jefferson, the truth is that such reasoning was pure subterfuge. Robert Harper unfolded the complete plot as King and Hamilton had originally worked it out in a letter to his friend Senator Ralph Izard of South Carolina.

Harper pointed out that a Republican victory in Pennsylvania would certainly defeat Adams but that Major Pinckney could be certain of support from the Eastern states, Georgia, the Carolinas, and Virginia. "It is not Adams or Pinckney with us, but Pinckney or Jefferson," he admitted. Reports that Pinckney had been chosen in order to split the Southern vote for Jefferson were erroneous. "Major Pinckney may be assured, and I speak from the most certain knowledge, that the intention of bringing him forward was to make him President, and that he will be supported with that view." [26]

[24] Lodge, *Cabot, op. cit.*, 119; Cabot to Wolcott, Jr., April 13, 1797, Gibbs, *Memoirs*, I, 492.

[25] Madison to Jefferson, December 5, 1796, *Madison Papers*, LC; Beckley to Wm. Irvine, *Irvine Papers*, Historical Society of Pennsylvania, XIII, 115.

[26] Dec. 1, 1796, U. B. Phillips, "South Carolina Federalists," *American Historical Review*, XIV (July, 1909), 782-783.

Robert Harper and his colleague, William Smith, were the most ardent Hamiltonians in the South. There seems little reason to doubt that Harper knew what he was talking about.

Pinckney's nomination as Vice-President had been an excellent idea, but there was too much talk about his candidacy in the final month of the campaign. Hamilton's letters as well as those of his lieutenant, Oliver Wolcott, Jr., succeeded only in arousing the suspicions of New Englanders whose loyalty to John Adams proved far deeper than Hamilton had gauged. Had it not been for their interference Pinckney would probably have been President or, as Vice-President, a powerful figure in 1800. After a brief term in the United States Senate during which he showed great promise, he dropped from sight as a national influence. New England fears rather than Jeffersonian electors were primarily responsible for his defeat.

Hamilton must be condemned as a strategist, because he failed to estimate the pro-Adams sentiment in New England correctly. There is no record of his even attempting to do so, though it would have been a simple matter for him to have gotten accurate reports of electoral sentiment from intimates such as Ames, Gore, Cabot, and Higginson. These men had followed his lead before, but Hamilton did not take into account the popularity of Adams with the rank and file, and even the most powerful political factions must bow to public sentiment occasionally.

No one loved or admired Hamilton more than his law-school roommate and lifelong friend Robert Troup of New York, yet even Troup balked at the idea of pushing Pinckney openly. Two years later in writing to Rufus King he mentioned an occasion during the election when Hamilton had publicly expressed his desire for Pinckney's election over Adams despite the warnings of his friends. Yet, at the time, Troup had followed the fear line exactly as Hamilton had laid it down. He had described to King how Adams would fail by a narrow margin and then declared, "but we have Mr. Pinckney completely in our power if our Eastern friends do not refuse him some of their votes. . . . Upon this subject we are writing to our Eastern friends and trying to make them accord with us in voting unanimously for Mr. Adams and Mr. Pinckney." [27]

There was sufficient doubt about Adams' strength for the fear campaign to have worked efficiently. Doubtless many Federalists sincerely believed that Pinckney was their only bulwark against Jeffersonian victory. Had Hamilton not pushed the idea of a straight party ticket so often and so early honest doubts might easily have worked against Adams. Brilliantly conceived, the project of electing a dark horse candidate was miserably carried out and must take rank with Hamilton's great failure of 1800 as a major cause of the Federalist party's collapse.

[27] November 16, 1798, November 16, 1796, King, *Life and Correspondence*, II, 466, 110.

6

Imported and Domestic Designs for Victory

WHILE POLITICIANS IN FIFTEEN STATES SCRAMBLED FOR PUBLIC favor the ambitious French Minister, Pierre Adet, was attempting to size up the situation as a whole. The picture he created was not one that gave him much pleasure. It was important both to his government and to his own career that the drift toward Great Britain that had marked the past three years be ended. The new Secretary of State, Mr. Pickering, was the most violent Anglophile, and if the stories about Mr. Adams were true Franco-American relations would reach even lower depths on his assumption of office. It was clear to Adet that Jefferson stood no chance of being elected unless the Potomac barrier were broken, and as he pondered this fact he reached a definite conclusion—his own intervention on behalf of the Republicans could tip the scale and lead to the promotion of Pierre Adet to more promising diplomatic posts.

Adet's decision to revert to the high-handed methods of his famous predecessor, Edmund Genêt, turned the election of 1796 into a unique comedy of errors: never before or since has a foreign power acted so openly in an American election. Until the publication of his diplomatic notes in November the campaign had centered around the personalities of Adams and Jefferson, the principal though passive contenders, and around the concept of government that Hamilton had stamped upon Federalism. Adet added a live issue that transcended the provincial outlook of the average voter.

There were very few Americans in or out of office who frankly advocated close ties with the government of George III, but in contrast there were thousands of Americans who looked upon France through a sentimental fog, remembering Yorktown with gratitude and seeing the revolution of 1789 as but an extension of their own fight against kings and privilege. Through Jefferson, Monroe, Genêt, and the unfortunate Edmund Randolph the Republican party had become the recognized champion of French republicanism. Adet knew this, and he also sensed that Washington's policy of neutrality and the Jay treaty had seemed like slaps in the face of a struggling sister republic to many American citizens who would welcome a chance to square the record.

Knowing of the tenor of Adet's relations with Timothy Pickering, Republicans leaned over backward in their assurances that the people were with France and would show it as soon as Washington could be dropped. Within a few months of his arrival at Philadelphia the French Minister had become as intimate with what he termed "the chiefs of the Republican Party" as his British counterpart, George Hammond, had long been with the Hamiltonians. Early in March Republican leaders in Congress had conferred with Adet, urging him to add the weight of French approval to their fight against the Jay treaty in the House of Representatives. Being a wiser and more cautious man than his predecessors, however, Adet had given his sympathy freely and had cleared with his foreign office before moving into the open. Before instructions from Paris could cross the Atlantic the House had capitulated to the President.[1]

The Directory took up other means of displaying its resentment over administration policy: American merchant-

[1] *Correspondence of French Ministers, op. cit.*, 836.

men were seized in Mediterranean and Caribbean waters without warning.

Early in January Hamilton responded to the distress calls of his New York mercantile friends in a letter to Washington. "We seem to be where we were with Great Britain when Mr. Jay was sent there. I cannot but discern that the spirit of the policy then pursued with regard to England will be the proper one now with respect to France." It would be best to appeal to the self-interest of France and failing in that to arm in self-defense, he counseled, adding that France had already gone farther in her insults than England had.[2] Washington's views on the matter were in accord with Hamilton's. Repeated complaints were made to Adet, and James Monroe was instructed to do his utmost to alleviate the distress through his good offices at Paris. No drastic action was taken, however, and nearly three years passed before American merchant vessels were allowed to arm. Not until the Jay treaty had been put to rest was French policy given primary attention. Throughout that memorable struggle England showed little interest in encouraging her American partisans. Her attacks upon United States commerce decreased so slightly after the signing of the Jay treaty that Hamilton was led to exclaim in April, "The British Ministry are as great fools, or as great rascals, as our Jacobins." [3] Benjamin Bache ran a regular feature in the *Aurora* all year long listing those American ships boarded or seized by British men-of-war, sarcastically entitling the column "Further Evidence of British Amity."

Had Great Britain not let up in her preying upon neutral shipping during the summer and fall of 1796, whether out of regard for Federalist political interests or not it is impossible to say, the Republicans might easily have won over considerable Eastern seaboard support in 1796. As it was French

[2] January 19, 1796, *Hamilton Papers*, LC.

[3] Hamilton to Wolcott, Jr., April 20, 1796, *ibid.*

attacks increased while British seizures diminished somewhat, and Francophiles did their utmost to place the blame at the feet of John Jay and the President, while their opponents played up the possibility that France was attempting to frighten the nation out of its neutrality.

It was no secret to men in official position that France, England, and Spain had not dropped their designs upon the trans-Appalachian territory of North America after the inauguration of the Federal government. The Pinckney treaty promised to act as a catalyst to the process of populating and binding the frontier to the rest of the Union; but while hoping for the best, those charged with the responsibility of preserving that Western empire for Americans could do little more than keep close vigilance and hope that the army along the Spanish borderland would remain loyal.

At the end of May, 1796, the President received from the Secretary of the Treasury, Oliver Wolcott, Jr., a detailed report on the activities of two French agents named Collot and Warin then operating in the Western states. According to the account that Wolcott received ("on best authority") Adet had furnished them with instructions for a trip through western Pennsylvania, Kentucky, and down the Mississippi to New Orleans. Collot and Warin were to record the names of the outstanding leaders in each of the villages they passed through, to sound out local sentiment with regard to "a political connection with France," and to persuade the inhabitants that in the event of a political separation from the United States they ought to look toward France as "their natural ally and protector."

All this was typical of the reports of intrigues that Washington and Jefferson, while Secretary of State, had been accustomed to receiving from government agents since 1790. The one startling departure from this formula that Wolcott's notes disclosed was that these agents were to act as the champions of an American political party: "The Frenchmen before mentioned were moreover instructed to use all means in their power to promote the election of Mr. Jefferson." What seemed most outrageous, if it was true, was that the spokesman for the Republican party in the House of Representatives, Alber Gallatin, had aided Minister Adet in drawing up the instructions for Collot and Warin.[4]

In view of the fact that Wolcott was no friend to Gallatin, Jefferson, and the Republicans in general, and considering the mysteriousness of his sources of information, it would seem unwise to pay more than passing attention to this memorandum. Washington seems to have done nothing to diminish the effectiveness of the French propaganda. Fortunately, there is a check against the veracity of the Wolcott report, and it shows that every detail except that concerning Gallatin was correct.

General Collot was provided with instructions from the French Minister, who had gotten authorization directly from Paris on every point. The orders from the French foreign office were dated November 2, 1795, and they actually asked that Mr. Jefferson's election be promoted by every available means.[5] Whether Gallatin was one of those with whom Adet was in the habit of conferring cannot be proved. His name was not mentioned by Paris authorities.

The shipping seizures, the Wolcott memorandum, the letters of James Monroe and Gouverneur Morris, and finally the attitude adopted by the *Aurora* toward French policy convinced the President that a crisis fully as great as that which had just passed with England was approaching. Hamilton had advised that the same lines be followed in dealing with the Directory as had been pursued during the British crisis of 1794–95.

Back at Mount Vernon after the adjournment of Congress, Washington gave his attention to the problem of diplomacy.

[4] Gibbs, *Memoirs*, I, 350-351.

[5] *Correspondence of French Ministers*, 928-929.

So far as the President and his advisors were concerned the weakest link in American diplomacy was the quality of American representation at Paris. Senator Monroe had shown himself sympathetic with France before his appointment, but at Paris he had embraced with fervor the work of atoning for the coolness of his predecessor, the aristocratic Gouverneur Morris. He proved to be extremely popular with French leaders and with the people of Paris.

When Monroe arrived at Paris he had begun by assuring the Directory that the United States would give England no rights incommensurate with prior treaty obligations to France. Pickering complained that Monroe had misrepresented American intentions, that the Jay treaty was in no way an infraction of promises to France, and that Monroe's excessive partiality to France was an embarrassing fact to the administration. With equal righteousness the American Minister maintained that he had been purposefully left in the dark on the vitally important matter of Jay's instructions. The President's advisors were convinced that Monroe was not defending administration policy, and they succeeded in persuading the President that they were correct in this viewpoint. In June Washington decided that Monroe must be replaced.

The two considerations that made the task difficult were those of finding a suitable successor and of dropping the former Virginia Senator gracefully. The obvious solution to the second problem was to name a minister extraordinary with special powers to deal with a specific situation. Such had been the policy of 1795, and it was generally accepted diplomatic practice; but in response to Washington's question concerning his constitutional power to make such an appointment during the recess of the Senate the Secretary of State had declared that the President had no such power. Washington then addressed the same question to his Attorney General, Charles Lee.[6] Before Lee could answer, the three Hamiltonian secretaries, Pickering, Wolcott, and McHenry, had drawn up a long report on the entire question and submitted to the President what appeared to be a completely incriminating letter concerning Monroe's political loyalties.

The heads of departments agreed that the President had no power to dispatch a special diplomatic agent without the consent of the Senate. Therefore, the only means of superseding Monroe was to name a new minister. Monroe, they agreed, had not used the documents furnished him to explain American policy correctly and had thereby exposed the United States to undeserved attack. "Whether this dangerous omission arose from such an attachment to the cause of France as rendered him too little mindful of the interests of his own country, or from mistaken views of the latter, . . . the evil is the same." They suggested as Monroe's successor one of four Southerners: Patrick Henry, John Marshall, William Smith, or Charles Cotesworth Pinckney. The report concluded with a damning allegation of Monroe's political activities. "A minister who has thus made the notorious enemies of the whole system of the government his confidential correspondents in matters which affect that government, cannot be relied upon to do his duty to the latter." [7]

Since it was well known that Monroe's closest political associates before his selection had been Jefferson, Madison, Pierce Butler, Aaron Burr, and the other outspoken critics of the administration in Congress, the statement was one that Washington could have accepted without serious doubt. What clinched the indictment, however, was the disclosure of a letter that Monroe had written a year before to his friend Dr. George Logan of Philadelphia. It unfortunately

[6] Washington to Pickering, June 24, 1796; to Charles Lee, July 6, 1796; Washington, *Writings*, XXXV, 122-123.

[7] Washington, *Writings*, XXXV, 123-124, Note 47.

suggested that Monroe was one of the sources for the very well-informed pieces that Benjamin Bache frequently printed in his attacks upon the administration.

Monroe sent Logan a short sketch of political affairs at Paris and announced that he had sent a copy to John Beckley. If Logan and Beckley considered it worthwhile they should have the piece printed in Bache's paper. Monroe promised to send similar reports from time to time, and he added that by this means the "public may be more correctly informed of the progress of the revolution than they can be from the English (administration) prints." [8]

The disclosure of Monroe's intercepted letter settled the matter with the President. John Marshall was invited to take the Paris mission, and upon his refusal the offer was tendered to General Pinckney, who accepted.[9] So suspicious had Washington become of Monroe that a week after receiving the report from Philadelphia he notified Pickering of the departure of former congressman John Dawson of Virginia, known to be a severe critic of the administration and a friend of Monroe's, for Paris. "As every day brings forth matter to view, vigilance with caution becomes more and more necessary." [10] When in August it became necessary to inform Pinckney of the true causes for Monroe's recall the President cautioned the cabinet to speak carefully about the matter with even the most trusted friends. The Republicans were certain to make a martyr of the discredited diplomat, and the President wanted as little information to leak out as possible.[11]

With the dismissal of Monroe the last anti-Federalist in high position under Washington was dropped: the nonpartisan character of the administration was a thing of the past, and this was made abundantly clear only a month before

[8] June 24, 1795; Washington, *Writings*, XXXV, 128, Note 56.
[9] *Ibid.*, 128-129.
[10] *Ibid.*, 138-139.
[11] *Ibid.*, 174.

the publication of the Farewell Address, which contained some very fine-sounding phrases to express Washington's abhorrence of partisanship. State canvasses for presidential electors had commenced at the same time.

The reaction in Paris to Monroe's recall was an angry one. Monroe himself sensed that war was not beyond the realm of possibility and before his departure attempted to convince the Directory that hostilities with the United States would only injure France in the long run. "War with France will force the American government to throw itself into the arms of England . . . aristocracy will gain supreme control in the United States, and liberty will be compromised. By patiently enduring, on the contrary, the wrongs of the present President, you will leave him without excuse, you will enlighten the American people, and decide a contrary choice at the next election. All the wrongs of which France may have to complain will then be repaired." [12]

In Monroe's eyes the Republican party would suffer infinite harm, if not collapse, in the event of a French war. The assertion seems a logical one. Probably a majority of Americans sympathized with France, and many certainly believed that the administration had given France cause for anger. The people might vote for the opposition to the administration so long as the threat of war remained, but opinion would tend to shift the moment the threat became reality. The advice that Monroe left with the French government was to avoid war, and in the two years that followed it was constantly reinforced by other Republican leaders.

Hamilton saw as clearly from New York as Monroe did from Paris that an important distinction was to be made between the threat of war and war itself. He was convinced that the pro-French sympathies of the public could be effectively used to promote the election of Jefferson should the

[12] A. Thiers, *Histoire de la Revolution Français,* 10 vols., 5th ed. (Paris, 1836), IX, 41.

administration in any obvious way lay itself open to the charge that it was not trying to avert a showdown. Upon this conviction he acted and continued to act so long as France left any room whatsoever for the American government to initiate hostilities. His policy changed only when he became convinced that France had pushed too far and had leaned too heavily upon the fact that she had many republican sympathizers in America. As far as the election of 1796 was concerned, Hamiltonians were the strongest advocates of a soft French policy. This point must be emphasized, because the Federalist party has become closely associated with ardent nationalism and warm ties with Great Britain. In 1796 when France was commencing those attacks which led to the so-called undeclared naval war of 1798–1799, the Federalists had everything to gain by advocating appeasement. This consideration was fundamental to Hamiltonian campaign strategy.

In May the French government made complaints concerning the activities of an obscure American consul named Parish at Hamburg, Germany. When Hamilton learned of it he carefully used his influence to remove the offensive official, drawing the matter to the President's attention through his warm admirer, the Secretary of War, James McHenry. Though Mr. Parish was probably a perfectly satisfactory civil servant, wrote Hamilton, he ought to be superseded as consul for reasons of a more important nature. "We must not quarrel with France for *pins and needles*. I hope you will attend to this matter, even if at the expense of being a little officious." The Federalist leader knew that both Washington and Pickering could become sensitive about unofficial and unsolicited advice, and since he was not supposed to know of the affair McHenry could make a more diplomatic approach.[13]

On the same day Rufus King, Hamilton's confidant,

[13] June 1, 1796, *Hamilton Papers*, LC.

brought the same matter to the attention of Timothy Pickering. Parish ought to be removed, wrote King, on the grounds that he is at fault. "A compliance with the desires of those who complain will be politic—the point is not of sufficient importance to be made a serious and solemn question between the two nations." [14] The fact that both letters were postmarked "New York" makes the dispatch of them on the same day more than coincidental.

A week later Pierre Adet informed his government that Hamilton was in Philadelphia bent upon political business. Adet explained that Hamilton was openly speaking of the possibility of war between the two nations as a calamity to be averted at almost any price. The Southern Federalists in particular seemed most bellicose, and Hamilton was privately urging them to avoid war and to fall in line with administration policy. It seemed ironical, commented Adet, that only a few weeks before Hamilton had been equally fervent in his desire to avoid the horrors of a British war.[15]

The official demands of the French government that were expected during the summer of 1796 were held back while privateers and naval vessels continued to pick away at American commerce. The aspect of the situation that was causing the President most concern was that engineered by Benjamin Bache of the *Aurora.* In mid-July Washington wrote Pickering that the Republican editor's "indecent" charges of British influence and administration favoritism were based upon "misrepresentation and mutilated sources." He wished that the public might be presented with a complete review of the commercial policy of his administration, but he could see no way of presenting it unless France made the diplomatic moves so long anticipated. In the meantime he urged silence and caution upon his Secretary of State. By the end of the month Washington concluded that the crisis

[14] June 1, 1796, *King Papers*, New York Historical Society, Box 6, No. 69.
[15] June 9, 1796, *Correspondence of French Ministers*, 920.

would go no further: it was perfectly possible that the warnings were but "a contrivance of the opposers of the Government to see what effect such threats would work . . ." [16]

Whether the threats were unfounded or not, Bache's newspaper campaign was working with telling effect. George Cabot, a Federalist stalwart from Massachusetts, testified that during the summer a neighbor had seriously insisted that Jefferson's election was a necessity if war was to be averted, and rumor had it that Hamilton himself had reluctantly expressed the same opinion.[17]

In the fall New England Republicans were assuring themselves that news of French victories in Italy would arrive in time to ensure Jefferson's election, and it was widely reported that a powerful French fleet lay off Halifax, for what purpose no one was quite sure. The *Connecticut Gazette* told its readers that the huge armada could be used to attack American coastal towns.[18]

By late summer no official announcement of French policy had been made, and Hamilton continued to wear a smile for the French Minister. When Adet stopped at New York on his way to New England for a sight-seeing tour the Federalist chief politely invited him to dinner. The French diplomat, claiming a previous engagement, refused, but paid a formal call before moving on to Boston.[19] By personal example Hamilton was attempting to emphasize the need for caution in dealing with the French situation.

Adet's New England jaunt convinced him that the time had come for France to play its hand openly if the Republicans were to succeed in the forthcoming election. His letter to the French foreign office of September 24 is the most re-

16 Washington to Pickering, July 18 and July 25, 1796; *Writings*, XXXV, 144, 153-154.

17 Cabot to Oliver Wolcott, April 13, 1797; Lodge, *Cabot*, 122.

18 Cabot to Wolcott, October 11, 1796, Gibbs, *Memoirs*, I, 386; *Connecticut Gazette* (New London), October 20, 1796.

19 Memorandum in Hamilton's handwriting, *Hamilton Papers*, LC.

vealing document concerning his political connections with the Republicans that has been discovered. Because it clearly demonstrates how influential the representative of a foreign power had become in the inner councils of an American political party, and because it testifies to the widespread influence of the French Revolution in contemporary American political life, this letter is worthy of close attention.

At Boston Pierre Adet found "nos amis" extremely cool at first. They had interpreted the silence of the French government over the administration's acceptance of the Jay treaty as a token of disinterestedness. Having given up hope of French support they had almost abandoned the elections in Massachusetts to the Adams supporters. He had told them, wrote Adet, that France had by no means forgotten their needs and pledged his support in the very near future. Their hopes rose, and "they promised me to act industriously in dropping John Adams and electing Jefferson."

The most influential men from both Massachusetts and New Hampshire had impressed upon their foreign ally the strength of the Adams faction in New England and at the same time the necessity of electing a man who could act as "a mediator between it [France] and the United States." Adet's conclusion was that the merchants of New England, like those at New York and Philadelphia, could only "be led by fear." [20]

The French government had come to understand the psychology of fear by 1796, and by embroidering its policy of imperialism with the ideals of equality and fraternity France had succeeded in becoming the greatest military power of the revolutionary era. When it was learned that the House of Representatives had failed to block the Jay treaty the French Directory granted Pierre Adet permission to intervene in the American election. He was ordered to announce the suspension of full-scale diplomatic relationships and to

[20] *Correspondence of French Ministers*, 948-949.

announce that France would henceforth treat American shipping precisely as the United States government permitted Great Britain to.[21]

Allowing from six to eight weeks for the exchange of letters across the Atlantic, the undated order from Paris was probably received by Adet at the end of August. The timing of the announcements was left for the Minister himself to decide upon, and it was Adet's idea to act on the eve of the Pennsylvania electoral contest. He chose Monday, November 2, to publish the decree. It was not too difficult for Federalists to trace a connection between his threat and the outcome of Friday's balloting. The citizens of Pennsylvania chose an electoral ticket that was pledged to cast every vote but one for the Republican candidate in December.

It was not only the timing of Adet's four proclamations that showed how openly the French Minister was attempting to influence the electorate, it was the manner in which he presented them. As a prominent authority on the influence of the French Revolution upon America has put it, "There was a momentary revival of methods that had for some time been left in abeyance. The French minister, Adet, like his more famous predecessor, Genêt, resorted to rhetoric and opened direct communication with the people." [22]

Pierre Adet was a far more intelligent French agent than either of his two predecessors, and he plainly took a calculated risk in doing what he did. Both Genêt and Fauchet had been rebuffed for meddling with the American people during the neutrality debate in the case of the former and during the Whiskey Rebellion in the latter's case. Adet would have been totally blind had he not seen that his attack must either succeed or his own career be ruined. He was persuaded by his own observations and by his friends in Republican party

[21] *Ibid.*, 969.

[22] Charles D. Hazen, *Contemporary American Opinion of the French Revolution* (Johns Hopkins University Press, 1897), 285-286.

circles that the prize was worth the risk, and he threw himself into the campaign with Gallic vigor.

In rapid succession from November 2 to 21 Adet published four diplomatic notes in Bache's *Aurora,* notes which have been characterized as "campaign documents." [23]

The first was the decree applying the new French naval policy to her ally, the United States; the second, an address to all French citizens in the United States, ordering them to wear the tricolor cockade; the third, the announcement of the suspension of full diplomatic intercourse; and the fourth, a review of French policy toward America in which Jefferson was openly praised for his devotion to genuine republican principles.

When the President and the Secretary of State read Adet's first broadside in the Monday afternoon papers, both acted quickly and in the case of Pickering, whom the British Minister, Robert Liston, described as "one of the most violent anti-Gallicans I have ever met with," [24] the reaction was explosive. The angular New Englander saw the implications of Adet's sudden move at once, for the decree had been printed so as to allow just enough time for circulation throughout Pennsylvania before election day. If a reply was to be read in the far western counties before the end of the week it would have to be sent to the newspapers at once.

Apparently without consulting Washington, Pickering struck off an answer matching the challenging tone of the French decree in every respect. There was no doubt that Pickering's temper was up. The public had read the French announcement before Adet had formally notified the President of it.[25]

[23] H. J. Ford, "Timothy Pickering," *American Secretaries of State and Their Diplomacy*, S. F. Bemis, ed. (New York, 1927), II, 204.

[24] Brant, *Madison,* 449.

[25] William Smith to Ralph Izard, November 3, 1796, U. B. Phillips, "South Carolina Federalists," *American Historical Review,* XIV (July, 1909), 781.

John Jay (*Engraved from the painting by Stuart and Trumbull.*)

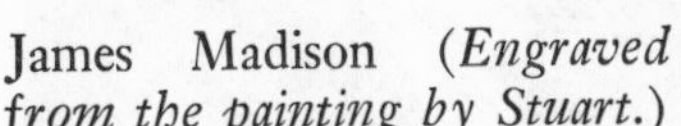

James Madison (*Engraved from the painting by Stuart.*)

Thomas Jefferson (*Engraved from the painting by Stuart.*)

Timothy Pickering (*Engraved from the painting by Stuart.*)

Alexander Hamilton as an officer of the Continental Army (*From the painting by Charles Willson Peale.*)

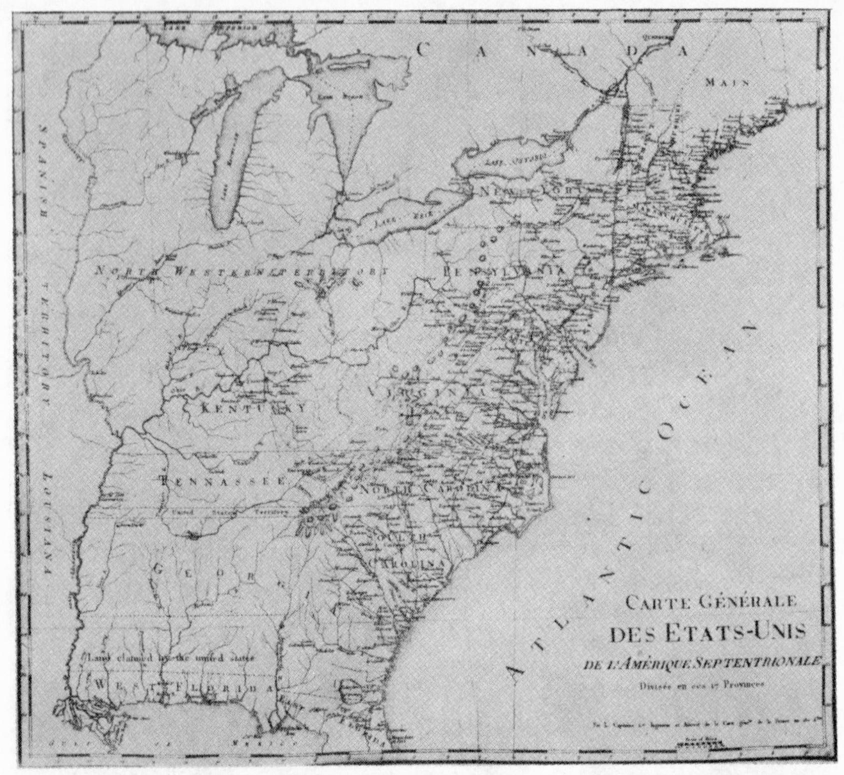

A French cartographer's view of the United States in 1796. Note that "Main" and the two Floridas are included among the seventeen provinces, although Maine was a part of Massachusetts until statehood was granted in 1820, while East and West Florida were Spanish colonies.

The following morning the President met with the cabinet, approved Pickering's reply, and agreed that to delay would be to allow public anger to mount unbridled.[26] It was thought best to keep Congress out of the affair.

Washington's concern over the new development was great. His term of office was drawing to a close, and to leave the nation at peace with the world when he retired was one of his fondest hopes. Furthermore, the administration's long months of cautious and guarded planning with regard to the Pinckney mission could be scrapped in a hurried attempt to neutralize what Federalists recognized as an ill-gotten political advantage for their opponents.

Washington's first reaction was to turn to Hamilton for advice, and those who doubt Washington's dependence upon Hamilton would do well to review this episode carefully. In a letter written just after reading Adet's announcement, the President asked for detailed answers to three specific questions. The first was that of dealing with Adet personally. What attitude should he take toward Adet at the public reception of the following week? Second, did Hamilton think that the administration would gain more or lose more in replying to Adet through the press? Washington was apparently reluctant to approve Pickering's reply during the cabinet meeting of the following morning. Third, how could the charge be met that "we can bear everything from one of the Belligerent powers, but nothing from another of them?"[27]

Hamilton's reply to these questions was written two days later: in the meantime Pickering's open letter had already been approved and published. The President was advised to receive the French minister "with dignified reserve, holding an exact medium between an offensive coldness and cordiality. The point is a nice one to be hit, but no one will

26 Washington to Hamilton, November 3, 1796; Washington, *Writings*, XXXV, 256.

27 November 2, 1796; Washington, *Writings*, XXXV, 251-252.

know better how to do it than the President," wrote Hamilton honestly. So far as the newspaper reply was concerned he thought there were points both for and against it. "But whatever be the mode adopted, it is certain that the reply will be one of the most delicate papers that has proceeded from our Government; in which it will require much care and nicety . . . and will at the same time save a great political interest which this step of the French Government opens to us." The question of bearing much from England and nothing from France could be answered only in the future. That the time had come to forbear and not to arm was his final admonition.[28]

The President noted to Hamilton after the cabinet meeting of November 3 that the decision to deal openly with the French Minister had been thought best. When Hamilton replied on the fifth, he showed anxiety for the over-all strategy of passive resistance that had been tacitly agreed upon since early spring. It was essential, he thought, to avoid a rupture with France at almost any cost, but if it could not be sidestepped the public must be convinced that the administration had done everything to avoid it. Without saying that Pickering's reply had lacked the necessary delicacy, Hamilton let his sentiments be known. Keep a careful check on Pickering's temper, he urged.[29]

William Smith of South Carolina, close to the inner circle of Federalist leaders, thought that Pickering's reply was an essential measure and well timed "lest it might not operate enough before the election; by publishing it on Monday (*sic:* Tuesday) it was just in time to influence the Election in this state (Pennsylvania)." [30] Unlike Hamilton, Smith considered the need of offsetting the effect of the decree in Pennsylvania more pressing than that of waiting silently for

[28] *Hamilton Papers,* LC.

[29] *Ibid.*

[30] To Senator Ralph Izard, November 3, 1796; U. B. Phillips, "South Carolina Federalists," *American Historical Review,* XIV (July, 1909), 781.

the public to react against it. Few Federalists, in fact, seem to have felt that French intervention would serve them and not their opponents.

Perhaps the observations and exhortation appearing in the *Gazette of the United States* the day following Adet's pronouncement was what Hamilton was banking on. Wrote "Brutus," "The *Aurora* threatens us with war if we elect John Adams president . . . will the real and independent Americans be so crouching as to have a President forced upon them by such daring manoeuvers?"

Pickering explained to the new American Minister at London, Rufus King, that he had been forced "reluctantly" to make a reply by the closeness of the Pennsylvania election, and he noted with satisfaction how the newspapers were making pointed conjectures as to French motives.[31]

The more Hamilton studied the effects of the controversy upon the public the more convinced he became that it would be a mistake for official sources to contribute further. "I regret extremely the publication of the reply to Adet otherwise than through the channel of Congress," he complained to Wolcott. "The sooner the Executive gets out of the newspapers the better." [32]

On November 16 Adet publicly announced the suspension of full-scale diplomatic intercourse ". . . as a mark of just discontent . . . to last until the government of the United States returns to sentiments and measures more conformable . . . to the sworn friendship between the two nations." [33] Adet let it be known that the Secretary of State had been most curt in his reception of this news.

A few days later the *American Daily Advertiser* printed the long-awaited answer of Adet to Pickering's open letter of November 3. In it he made an open appeal for Jefferson's

[31] November 14, 1796; King, *Life and Correspondence,* II, 109.
[32] November 9, 1796; *Hamilton Papers,* LC.
[33] *Aurora,* November 16, 1796.

election by contrasting the cordiality of relations between the two states during Jefferson's administration of the State Department with the strained relations existing since. Pickering again protested, and Hamilton once more chose Wolcott to speak for him at Philadelphia. Pickering's handling of the entire affair displeased him. The Federalist boss re-emphasized that it was essential to keep the quarrel going but to keep the tone of it "smooth, even friendly, yet solemn and dignified." He told Wolcott that the best answer to Adet's outrageous attacks would be the publication of a formal review of the nation's foreign policy since April, 1793, along the lines of a paper that he enclosed.[34]

Just how effective Adet's maneuvers were in determining the outcome of the election is a difficult question to answer. Madison and Jefferson knew very little, if anything, about the French Minister's plan and undoubtedly would have disapproved his emergence as a party worker had they known of it in advance. The more extreme Republicans in the Middle and New England states felt that it would benefit their chances and did not scruple to consider the ethics of foreign intervention.

Hamilton was convinced that Adet had made a serious blunder, but he was probably thinking as much of the administration that was to follow as of the effect it would have upon the national election. He was meticulous in his own approach to the situation and constantly advised the administration to adopt and maintain an injured silence. He was, therefore, distressed that the President, who seemed to accept the idea, had allowed Timothy Pickering so free a hand in dealing with the crisis.

In December Hamilton wrote a lengthy article reviewing Franco-American relations since 1776 in which he attempted

[34] Hamilton, *Works* (Lodge ed.), X, 210-213. Hamilton consistently refused to deal directly with Pickering, preferring to use Wolcott as his representative in cabinet discussions.

to prove that France had never acted except in her own best interests. He carefully allowed that up to 1793 the interests of the American states coincided with those of France, but that since Genêt's arrival in the United States American and French interests had been at variance. The plan of publishing the article in Wester's New York *Minerva* for some reason appeared unwise after he had completed it, and the piece remains among his unpublished papers in the Library of Congress archives.

In his message of December 7 the President pointedly passed over French affairs with a promise of taking the subject up in a separate message later (January 5, 1797). Washington said only that relations were strained owing to French attacks upon American commerce.[35] Pickering had preferred fighting it out with Adet, and most of the Federalists agreed. A Maryland politician wrote James McHenry that the note of November 2 together with Pickering's reply were being circulated as Federalist campaign literature in the South and West. A spirited answer to Adet's suspension notification would be welcomed, he thought.[36]

William Cobbett of *Porcupine's Gazette* compared Adet's actions to those of a highwayman and published all his notes in an electioneering pamphlet called "A Diplomatic Blunderbuss," while his counterpart, Benjamin Bache, printed and sold "Notes addressed by Citizen Adet . . . to the Secretary of State" as Republican propaganda.

From the reports that he got from friends in the Southern states Elias Boudinot of New Jersey concluded that Adet's notes "to the people rather than the government of the Union . . ." had hurt the Republican cause. "Even Virginia has taken fire and a great conversion is working there on the

[35] Washington, *Writings*, XXXV, 318-319.

[36] Hugh Williamson to James McHenry, Baltimore, November 21, 1796, Steiner, *McHenry*, 190-191.

subject," he wrote.[37] If there was a conversion taking place in the Republican heartland south of the Potomac it began too late to influence the election results. In Pennsylvania alone French threats and electoral returns seem to have tied in together.

Politically speaking, the French bid for Jefferson's election was but one of several campaign techniques; though it was undoubtedly the most extreme of them. For the most part the political orators and writers confined themselves to mudslinging. Federalist propaganda stated that Jefferson was a radical democrat who would undermine the economic well-being of the nation as well as the morality of the American people. He had opposed the adoption of the Constitution and preferred French irresponsibility and license to American respect for the rights of property. In his defense, Republicans widely circulated the Declaration of Independence and the Virginia Bill of Rights, while proudly extolling his services as Secretary of State as proof of his respect for the Constitution. His Southern residence and origins were used to offset his popularity north of the Delaware: sectional antagonisms were widely used for smear purposes.[38]

John Adams, who drew less fire from his opponents than Mr. Jefferson because he was less easily identified with Federalist economic policies than either Washington or Hamilton, was most effectively besmirched with the labels of monarchist and aristocrat, labels that have been associated with

[37] Boudinot to Samuel Bayard, December 14, 1796, Boudinot, *Life and . . . Letters*, II, 120.

[38] For a résumé of campaign techniques covering both parties see J. B. McMaster, *History*, II, 289-307. Claude G. Bowers has treated the election of 1800 in some detail in his *Jefferson and Hamilton*. The charges thrown at Jefferson in 1796 changed little over four years. Both accounts are based almost entirely upon newspaper sources and therefore fail to present anything like a complete picture of how an election was managed. Jefferson's famous Mazzei letter with its insinuations about Washington was not printed until the campaign ended. Bowers (*Jefferson and Hamilton*, 307) mistakenly claims that it plagued Jefferson throughout the campaign. Jefferson wrote that his letter was first published in April, 1797.

his name ever since. "It was generally reported that he never appeared in public except with a coach and six horses, evidently a monarchical institution. It was useless to assert that two were the real number, the six and titles remained for political purposes." [39] As Charles A. Beard put it, "In an age when most of the political writings exalted popular sovereignty and flattered the people, Adams had the courage of his convictions and wrote out with great labor and pains his disbelief in simple direct popular rule. What many other statesmen before and since have said privately, Adams published in a laborious systematic form. Only one other man of the period expressed similar political doctrines with equal clarity . . . James Madison, author of Number Ten of *The Federalist*, but Madison announced his views anonymously." [40]

In his *Defense of the Constitutions of Government of the United States of America*, first published in 1786, Adams frankly recognized the fact that all societies tend to divide into two distinct groups, "gentlemen" and "common people," caused by the unequal distribution of wealth and recognized outwardly by disparities of culture. He stoutly maintained that the true purpose of government was to protect the rights of the common people in a popular assembly and the rights of the wealthy in an upper house or senate. The executive's main responsibility was to decide between the two when they became deadlocked.[41] Adams was, therefore, vulnerable to charges of being antirepublican; a monarchist, since he emphasized a strong executive; and a tool of British influence. One concrete example will suffice.

A prominent anti-Federalist newspaper ran a series of

[39] W. C. Ford, *Washington*, II, 158-159.

[40] C. A. Beard, *The Economic Origins of Jeffersonian Democracy* (New York, 1915), 319. Hamilton, perhaps the most voluminous political writer of his generation, used pen names continuously. It is extremely unlikely, however, that his opponents ever failed to recognize his style.

[41] Adams, *Works*, VI, 516 ff. See also Correa M. Walsh, *The Political Theory of John Adams* (New York, 1915).

articles signed by "Sidney" during the last week of October that attempted to demonstrate by quoting from the *Defense* that the Federalist candidate favored limited monarchy for America, opposed the United States Constitution, and could scarcely uphold it with sincerity if elected President.[42]

Though the Federalists preferred the party label "Federal Republican," their opponents unsparingly spoke of them in print as the "Monarchists." John Ward Fenno, editor of the most influential proadministration sheet, complained bitterly during the campaign that the "Jacobins" were unfairly printing the electoral ticket of the Federal Republicans under the heading of "Monarchist Party," and the same was true in most of their newspaper letters, pamphlets, and handbills.[43] Perhaps Fenno had a better sense of humor than he allowed his paper to exhibit.

It is possible to trace the growing strength of political parties and the parallel awakening of the public to their importance by studying the amount of space given to domestic political news in the newspapers. While it is a distinct disappointment to the student of American political history to find that our early news sheets paid far greater attention to British and French politics than to American, it is of course an important reminder that the Revolution did not put an end to colonial outlook and habits of thinking. We must constantly remind ourselves that the Atlantic Ocean and the Western frontier were hardly equal influences upon American life up to the period ending roughly in 1820, or perhaps with the War of 1812.

While most newspaper editors seem to have regarded news from Philadelphia as of secondary importance and filled the first two pages of their scant newspapers with the happenings reported from London or the continental war fronts, the outstanding papers at the capital, Bache's *Aurora* and

[42] New York, *Argus*, October 24-31, 1796; reprinted from the *Aurora*.
[43] *Gazette of the United States*, November 4, 1796.

Fenno's *Gazette of the United States*, led the way in giving to American politics a place of primary importance in their news reporting. The *Aurora* set the tone of Republican propaganda more than any other paper of the 1790's and was widely circulated both in actual copy and in reprint through other antiadministration papers. From the Federalist side Fenno's *Gazette* shared its leadership with William Cobbett's *Porcupine's Gazette*, which was a match for the *Aurora* in diatribe and libel. All three were highly partisan, though Fenno maintained a dignity in his reports that both Bache and Cobbett were willing to sacrifice for readability and shock appeal.

Too often, however, accounts of early American political life are taken from the principal party organs of the large towns. A survey of local papers such as the *Maryland Gazette* of Annapolis, the *Connecticut Gazette* of New London, and the *Columbian Museum* of Savannah perhaps reveal little that may be directly tied in with a national election; but they do show us that Americans were far less interested in national politics than the big party papers lead us to expect. The very fact that local editors printed virtually nothing about candidates and how they were chosen and did little to publicize the issues of 1796 beyond printing the state electoral lists is of course of profound importance. It goes far to explain why early American politics were controlled so easily by the upper classes and why the Federalists could win and hold office for so long without flattering or responding to the vanity of the average man. It helps to explain also why Hamiltonianism made an indelible imprint upon American political and economic life. The politically active citizens, as the French recognized in their constitutions of the revolutionary era, were drawn for the most part from the middle and upper classes—the merchants, bankers, and businessmen from industrial areas, the larger independent farmers or planters from rural areas.

It would be erroneous to say that the common man was insensitive to national issues, but he was certainly less alarmed over the growth of national banks, treaties, and congressional debates than over poor crops and adverse weather conditions. Political life, like economic life, was still a matter of local circumstances for the most part, and the average man's horizons seemed confined to the valley and the township rather than the state or nation.

Eighteenth-century newspapers reflect little interest in national political events, because they had not created much. The cheap private letter, rapid transportation, and the radio did not exist to rival the newspaper in stirring up political consciousness. Not until Washington's Farewell Address was printed did most papers, including the most violently partisan, begin to speculate on or advocate candidates. The *Maryland Gazette*, for example, did not print a single election story until the election was over. On February 16, 1797, it was reported in its pages that the President of the Senate had officially counted the electoral votes and had announced his own election to the presidency. Bonaparte's decrees took the front page and held it from the summer of 1796 to the early months of 1797.

There was probably greater public interest in the election of 1800 than in that of 1796, yet Representative John Dawson of Virginia, a lieutenant of Madison and Jefferson, wrote less than two weeks before electors met to cast their ballots, "The choice of the President seems to engage the attention of every person *already*." [44]

Although the period during which political writers appealed directly to the voters was far shorter than it is in modern times (most editorials, pamphlets, and broad-sides appeared in November), campaigning was intensive. In keeping with its principles, the Republican party was the more

[44] To Madison, New Brunswick, N. J., November 28, 1800, *Madison Papers*, LC. Italics my own.

active of the two in its efforts to influence the general public. Washington and Hamilton were as frequent targets as Mr. Adams himself, while one of the virtues of Thomas Pinckney was that he escaped vilification almost entirely. If little was said about him during the canvassing, he at least had the virtue of being undefiled.

Probably the most undeserved accusation of all was that leveled at Washington by a writer calling himself "A Calm Observor" and recently identified as John Beckley.[45] The writer charged that Washington had stolen public funds and deserved impeachment, though he cited no authority to back up the charge.

Tom Paine's notorious public letter to the President charging him with being devoid of any principles whatsoever was circulated widely by the Republicans to add to the bitterness of Washington's last weeks of public life. When Cobbett answered him with "A Letter to the Infamous Tom Paine," a Federalist pamphlet, the President was forced to concede that it was "not a bad thing," though he often professed to a violent aversion for the "political scribblers." [46]

Private correspondence was made to serve political purposes; and so far as the organization and co-ordination of the campaign were concerned, the private letter was by all odds a more important instrument than either the press or political conference. Through forgeries and through the seizure of private letters much information and misinformation were circulated. In August Washington complained to General Pinckney that their correspondence was being tampered with, and a few weeks later he cautioned Hamilton of the same.[47]

During the last month of the campaign several of Washington's letters of The Revolutionary War were sold by a New York printer as Republican pamphlets. A few were

[45] Raymond Walters, *Alexander J. Dallas* (University of Pennsylvania Press, 1943), 74.

[46] Washington, *Writings,* XXXV, 360.

[47] *Ibid.,* 176, 198.

genuine, but the majority were forged.[48] Bache of the *Aurora* printed and sold Washington forgeries in Philadelphia as the campaign reached its climax,[49] but the most involved forgery story to come out of the election was that concerning Hamilton and the third term question.

Robert Patton, Philadelphia postmaster, noticed a suspicious-looking letter addressed by Alexander Hamilton to a certain William Cooper of Suffolk, Virginia. Knowing that Hamilton was not in the capital at the time, Patton held the letter and made inquiries that led him to a laboring man who had recently arrived from Virginia. Patton interviewed the man, found that he had been paid to carry the letter to Philadelphia, and promptly wrote to the addressee as to the authenticity of his correspondence with Hamilton. Cooper replied that he was not acquainted with Hamilton and forwarded another letter written to a neighbor of his that intimately concerned the Federalist chief.

The Cooper letter, dated March 3, 1796, said that Washington was certain to announce his resignation during the summer and that he, Hamilton, was being urged to stand for the presidency. He wished to know what his chances of support might be in the South. According to the fictitious Hamilton it was necessary to convince the people that he had constantly worked for the public good despite his belief in the use of repressive methods.

The second letter, supposedly written by State Representative William Van Allen of New York, was even more crude than the first. Van Allen related that he had walked into Hamilton's law office one day to find the Federalist boss pacing nervously up and down. Suddenly he wheeled about and blurted out that Washington's resignation announcement was to be the signal for a Jeffersonian *coup d'état*. Hamilton was supposed to have outlined a counterplot for which he

48 Washington, *Writings,* XXXV, 363-364.
49 Washington to Jeremiah Wadsworth, March 7, 1797, *ibid.*, 421.

would pay his followers liberally from the Treasury funds he had embezzled while serving in the cabinet.

These two letters never reached print and nothing was heard of the affair outside of the small circle of top-ranking Federalists. Cooper and Graham notified Hamilton that they had instituted libel proceedings against a local resident, Dr. Richard H. Bradford, whom they were certain had forged both.[50]

The entire episode is too involved to draw worthwhile conclusions from. Perhaps the hope was to get Cooper and Graham to circulate the letters in their bewilderment or perhaps to seize them before they were picked up at the Suffolk post-office.

Federalist campaign strategy was not as well organized as that of the Republicans. Their outstanding party organs, the *Gazette of the United States* and *Porcupine's Gazette*, played a smaller role in carrying the issues to the people than did Bache's *Aurora.* The reason for this is simple: neither Cobbet nor Fenno was intimate with Federalist bigwigs, whereas Benjamin Bache was in constant touch with high-ranking local and national Republican leaders. The private papers of Hamilton, Jay, Wolcott, Pickering, and Rufus King reveal no correspondence or reference to the men who ardently defended the policies that they pursued.

Besides heaping calumny upon Jefferson's head, the Federalists held up Genêt, Randolph, and the original foes of the Constitution as the men who stood behind Jefferson's candidacy. Who are the men who support Thomas Jefferson, asked editor Fenno: men who objected to the adoption of sound government, men who opposed neutrality and favored war, men who supported Citizen Genêt and opposed Washington, and men who encouraged the Pennsylvania insur-

[50] The letters and explanatory notes in Hamilton's hand are to be found among Hamilton's papers for 1796 in the Library of Congress. Patton first notified Oliver Wolcott, Jr., who then relayed the Postmaster's report to Hamilton at New York.

rection of 1794.[51] James Monroe was charged with implicating himself in French speculative schemes of a fraudulent nature.[52]

There is no record of any of the candidates taking an open part in the electioneering. No speeches or articles were issued by Adams, Jefferson, Pinckney, or Burr in behalf of their parties or themselves. Only once during the year did Jefferson appear to take any step toward aiding his supporters. Early in March he wrote Madison that it had become increasingly evident that Hamilton had left the nation's finances in a hopeless mess of perpetual and mounting debt. He suggested that Albert Gallatin be commissioned to condense the financial situation into pamphlet or speech form, a service, said Jefferson, for which "he will merit immortal honor." [53] Gallatin's critical review of treasury policy in the House that autumn seems to have been an outgrowth of Jefferson's suggestion. Otherwise Jefferson did nothing, and the other candidates apparently remained silent.

On the national level each party made one important mistake in the course of the campaign. In the long run Adet's intervention hurt the Republicans by adding one more link to the chain of events that had gradually bound the fate of France and the Republican party so closely together. If French threats, which Wolcott labeled the "boldest attempt to govern this country which has been made," [54] caused the sweep of Pennsylvania electoral votes to Jefferson, there came a time when the Republicans were tremendously weakened by their dependence upon the destiny of France. Nothing showed this more clearly than the fact that during the years 1798–99 Jefferson seriously tried to change the name of the party to "Whig."

There is no evidence whatsoever to show that Jefferson,

[51] November 3, 1796.

[52] Monroe to Jefferson, July 30, 1796, *Jefferson Papers*, LC.

[53] Jefferson to Madison, March 6, 1796, *Jefferson Papers*, LC.

[54] Wolcott to Hamilton, November 17, 1796, Gibbs, *Memoirs*, I, 395-396.

Madison, Gallatin, or any other primary leader in the party considered Adet's intervention advisable. The logical assumption is that the same group of radicals who engineered the House fight against the Jay treaty backed Adet's entry into the campaign. Had the French Minister been as careless as his two predecessors his letters might positively have identified them. We know only that local political leaders at Boston and Philadelphia—perhaps Beckley, Leib, McClenachan at the capital and Jarvis, Varnum, and Freeman at Boston—definitely requested that France administer the rebuke that they felt their campaign against the administration needed.

The Federalists for their part had in the Pinckney treaty and in Randolph's supposed treason a formula for political success in the Republican strongholds of the South and West. Paul L. Ford, after editing Jefferson's papers, came to the conclusion that its championship of free inland navigation was "the true unifying influence politically throughout the South which gave the Democratic Party its consistent support from that quarter," [55] and Eugene Link in his study of the Democratic-Republican Societies considered the Pinckney treaty a primary cause of the rapid decline of the organizations after 1795.[56]

Undoubtedly the Federalists lacked the organizational means with which to campaign widely in the South and along the frontier, but even at Richmond and Charleston, isolated centers of Federalist political strength, the implications of Randolph's conduct, as well as that of Genêt and Fauchet, were not pushed; and the Pinckney treaty was strangely neglected after the House had dropped its blockade of the British treaty in the spring.

While the election of 1796 exhibits unmistakable signs of

[55] The wording is that of S. F. Bemis, who paraphrases Ford's statement in his article, "Thomas Jefferson," *American Secretaries of State and Their Diplomacy*, II, 45.

[56] Eugene P. Link, *The Democratic-Republican Societies*, (Columbia University Press), 1942, 200.

growing national political parties in the form of two major alliances of local organizations, eighteenth-century political life was still predominantly local in both outlook and operation. On the state level only can an accurate portrayal of early American political action be made. It is to this important story that we must turn our attention if we are to learn how it was that Adams and Jefferson came together at Philadelphia in March, 1797.

7

The States and the Presidency

THE PATTERN OF ELECTIONEERING AND PUBLIC RESPONSE throughout the Union was far from uniform. Ten of the states, casting more than half the electoral vote, were strangely tranquil throughtout the campaign, their voters impervious to the issues and personalities that were creating divisions among neighbors across otherwise imperceptible boundaries. In New York and New Jersey, for example, there was far less interest in the national election than there was in nearby Pennsylvania. Wherever electors were chosen directly by the citizenry excitement ran high, the newspapers reflected a high degree of political development, and political machines could be seen in operation; where the choice of electors rested with the state legislature, interest in the presidential contest appears to have been far less keen than in the progress of the European war.

If there was one issue that might be called a national issue it was the British treaty and the administration's stand with relation to it. The votes of many had been determined long in advance of the electoral canvasses by the stand the Republicans had forced them to take in openly attacking the President's policy. Perhaps John Adams was only speaking the truth when he described his inauguration as Washington's triumph rather than his own. In a very real sense the second President was forced to recognize the binding force of both Washington's policies and his appointments, because the tremendous popularity of the first President had been largely responsible for his own election. Few Presidents, if any, have entered office under so heavy an obligation to their predecessors, and if to Mr. Adams' name those of James Madison and William Howard Taft are added, we are reminded that personal success in the undertaking is not likely to follow. Knowing how strong a hold Washington had on the public mind, the radicals in the Republican camp did their utmost to undermine his reputation for wisdom and moderation. This onslaught, beginning with the resolutions of the Virginia legislature of December, 1795, and culminating in the attempt to block the Jay treaty's execution at Philadelphia, had been timed to coincide with state elections; the men chosen for the state legislatures would choose presidential electors in the fall of 1796. It was the success of Aaron Burr in capturing control of the New York state legislature in 1800 that spelled disaster for the Federalists and brought Jefferson to power, but if Madison's estimate of the situation created by his more daring colleagues in 1796 was correct, the public had been roused to Washington's defense once more. The attack had been carried too far.

"Our politics assume a pacific and insipid face," wrote Fisher Ames a few days after the British treaty fight had ended. "Who shall be President and Vice President, are questions which will put an end to the armed neutrality of parties." He acknowledged that Jefferson and Adams would undoubtedly be the principal candidates and showed little interest in the second candidates.[1]

The lull in public agitation over political events that set in after the capitulation of the Republicans lasted until September, when Washington's Farewell Message again fomented it. No broadsides, speeches, or publications of a political nature jarred the tranquillity of summer. For the political strategists it was a time for inventory, and even the most careless of these was sufficient to show how evenly matched

[1] Ames to Thomas Dwight, May 19, 1796, Ames, *Works*, I, 193.

the political forces were and why it was that in November the hopes of both parties hung largely upon the outcome in Pennsylvania, the one state where a complete upset was possible.*

From the Republican point of view prospects in New England looked bleak. The state legislatures controlled twenty-eight of New England's thirty-nine electoral votes, and not one of these assemblies, meeting in joint session, was commanded by Jeffersonians. The administration had been uniformly supported by the five state organizations throughout the Jay treaty agitation despite the fact that Governor Sam Adams of Massachusetts was known to be friendly to the Republican cause.

Both Vermont and New Hampshire passed resolutions praising Washington for his leadership of eight years when the Farewell Address appeared in the autumn.[2] No Federalists of note appeared in Philadelphia from these two border states, and the two Jeffersonians whose names we remember, Matthew Lyon and Senator John Langdon, were without influence at home. Langdon had changed sides during the treaty fight and was politically adrift. There was no doubt in anyone's mind that New Hampshire and Vermont would support Mr. Adams.[3]

The political life of both Rhode Island and Connecticut during the 1790's was equally one-sided so far as national parties are concerned. The Wolcott faction in Connecticut had survived a land speculation scandal in 1795, and remained strong enough to deliver the vote intact when Governor Wolcott demanded it. As in most states, there was considerable speculation in frontier lands throughout the revolutionary and early national periods in Connecticut, and

* See Appendixes A and B, pp. 409-411 for details of electoral choice and list of 1796 electors.

[2] Washington, *Writings*, XXXV, 333.

[3] W. A. Robinson, *Jeffersonian Democracy in New England* (Yale University Press, 1916), 13-16.

when a report on land sales came up for review in the legislature the deep-seated resentment felt by rural representatives for Eastern economic and political domination broke out into a fierce intraparty quarrel.[4] Here was grist for the Jeffersonian mill, but Republicans lacked both leaders and organization. If the Hamiltonian election scheme was to succeed anywhere it would be in Connecticut, the line between Hartford and the office of the Treasury Department being direct and very much a family matter. Wolcott, Sr., was on cordial terms with leading Hamiltonians, and his son was a zealot for the Pinckney scheme. In November the Governor's name headed the electoral ticket, which a well-disciplined legislature selected. Had the Republicans possessed an organization in Rhode Island four electoral votes might be said to have been at stake, but the direct system of electoral voting (through a system of town meetings) resulted in the selection of four men who cast their votes for Adams.[5]

In Massachusetts a two-party struggle developed over the choice of the seven popularly elected presidential electors provided for by the state constitution. The friends of John Adams would have walked away with these seven plus the nine chosen by the legislature had Jeffersonians at Boston been less determined and active. The promise made by Boston's Republican leaders to Pierre Adet was carried out, and only in Massachusetts was New England Federalism seriously challenged.

Republicans were able to make effective use of two political weapons they lacked elsewhere in New England; one was the popularity of the aging revolutionary patriot, Sam Adams, and the other was newspaper influence in the Boston *Independent Chronicle*. At the height of the campaigning in November Fisher Ames noted the importance of the Republican press as having a most pernicious influence. "Many

[4] *Ibid.*, 12.
[5] *Ibid.*

of my plain neighbors who read the Chronicle," he said, "will not commend the President. Their reasoning is from what they know, and they take facts from that paper." [6]

Throughout the campaign in Massachusetts Republicans assaulted Washington and the administration's controversial measures rather than the works of Mr. Adams. In September Ames had been entirely optimistic about Federalist chances of making a clean sweep of all sixteen electoral votes. He wrote Oliver Wolcott, Jr., that the publication of the President's Farewell Message had worked wonders, reviving memories of Washington's great services; loyalty to the President, he thought, seemed unquestionably more important to most voters than dissatisfaction over the British treaty.[7] By November, however, he had lost confidence in killing off the "democrats," as Ames sneeringly labeled his opponents. The *Chronicle* had no rival that could match it for public appeal.

The political dividing line in Massachusetts ran north and south, along a line separating the western agrarian way of life from the seaboard commercial complex. In 1796 the voting pattern showed Federalism strongest in the western countries and Republicans strongest in coastal towns and villages surrounding the metropolis of Boston. In the period separating the adoption of the Constitution and the election of 1796 the Bay State's political alignments had exactly reversed themselves. In 1788 the farmers of the interior had been strongly anticentralist, while the urban coastal area had returned men to the convention favoring ratification.[8]

[6] Ames to Oliver Wolcott, Jr., November 14, 1796, Gibbs, *Memoirs,* I, 393.

[7] September 26, 1796, *Ibid.*, 384.

[8] A. E. Morse, *Federalist Party in Massachusetts to 1800* (Princeton University Press, 1909), 179-183. Morse suggests that Shays's Rebellion left an indelible impression upon the generation that experienced it and that their fear of demagoguery bound them to conservative politics. See also R. J. Taylor, *Western Massachusetts in the Revolution* (Brown University Press, 1954), 103-178.

Until 1793 the faction headed by Governor John Hancock had managed to rule the political realm without organized opposition, but with his death and the elevation of Sam Adams to the governorship the era of personality factions may be said to have ended. Adams, though he cannot be called a Jeffersonian Republican, lined up on national issues much as the Virginians did. He was never to be an important figure in the party councils of the Republicans, but his radicalism, his democratic sympathies, and his lifelong rule of appealing to public opinion wherever possible, link him with the party that Madison and Jefferson brought to life.[9]

Governor Adams' popularity with the people was immense, and in 1796 he was returned to office by a large majority. It is significant that the Boston press paid far greater attention to this gubernatorial campaign than to the presidential contest. In the light of Adams' five-thousand-vote margin of victory over Increase Sumner, candidate of the Essex Junto, out of a total vote of twenty-three thousand, it was not surprising that Republicans should run the Governor in a popular election for the electoral seat of the First Middle District. Running against the otherwise unknown Thomas Dawes, the Governor was given what his biographer has described as a "drubbing," the votes being 975 for Adams and 1,428 for Dawes, whose outstanding virtue was simply that he had declared his intention of voting for John Adams if elected.[10]

Further evidence of the Vice-President's popularity among the voters of his native state is afforded by the outcome of the canvass in the Second Middle District where Sam Adams' associate of revolutionary days, Elbridge Gerry, proved the principle attraction. While the Governor was being routed

[9] *Ibid.*, Morse, 140.

[10] Figures for the Adams-Sumner election from the *Independent Chronicle*, May 9, 1796. Morse reports the figures as 15,194 and 10,184, *Federalist Party in Massachusetts*, 179. John C. Miller, *Sam Adams, Pioneer in Propaganda* (Boston, 1939), 398. *Claypoole's American Daily Advertiser*, November 17, 1796.

by a political unknown, Gerry, who could boast neither wide personal following nor the backing of the district's powerful Federalist chiefs, was winning by a decisive margin. His pledge to vote for his long-time friend John Adams won him the electoral college place and launched him on one of the most tortuous political careers in American annals.[11]

In November all seven men pledged to vote for Adams were chosen in direct elections. George Cabot reported the outcome to Oliver Wolcott, Jr., noting at the same time that no one could be sure how the college would vote on the second ballot even though only two weeks remained before its convocation.[12] Thus despite the popular appeal of the commonwealth's governor and the existence of a strong opposition newspaper, favorite son sentiment dictated that Virginia had held the presidency long enough.

Political conditions in the states of New York, New Jersey, and Pennsylvania were in marked contrast to those of New England. Personal factions there were, such as those headed by George Clinton, Robert R. Livingston, Aaron Burr, and Thomas Mifflin, but in both New York and Pennsylvania ties between local organizations and national political leaders were strong, political contests were sharply contested, and the one-sided political development of New England was lacking. New York and Philadelphia were the leading maritime-commercial centers of the nation, and each was the center of highly developed party organizations that set policy for smaller machines throughout the Union. From his law office Hamilton, working closely with Governor Jay at Albany and with congressional leaders in the capital, sent out the score of letters by means of which Federalist battles were directed. At Philadelphia a less famous organization was being perfected by local Republican leaders, foremost among them the almost mythical John Beckley, whose pres-

[11] *Claypoole's American Daily Advertiser*, November 17, 1796, no figures.
[12] November 30, 1796, H. C. Lodge, *George Cabot*, 112.

ence in Philadelphia throughout the 1790's lent a unity to Republican campaign activities that they would otherwise have lacked. The fact that most leading lights of the Republican party were Southerners presented administrative and organizational problems that Federalists never faced.

The national capital was a notoriously unhealthy place for summer residence; the yellow fever frequently drove those who could afford it into the hinterland, while those who could not were left helpless in its wake. Politicians could usually afford the relief, and the fact that Jefferson, Monroe, Giles, and Tazewell were farmers as well as politicians meant that Philadelphia was vacated by high-ranking Republicans from June until Congress reconvened in the late fall. The direction of national policy was therefore left in the hands of secondary leaders living in the city, and the events of 1796 were scarcely to commend this arrangement.

The dominant politician in New York State from 1787 to 1795 was George Clinton, popular champion of antipatroonism and antifederalism, and a man of such vigor that six consecutive terms at Albany were demanded and granted. In 1795 the old revolutionary hero was forced to retire because of ill health and failing mental powers but not before he had stamped his antiadministration point of view upon the many who were later recruited by the indefatigable Burr. The great disadvantage in Clinton's system of personal government was that it tended to shunt men of outstanding abilities directly into national politics and kept them from developing the solid ties with state machinery that so marked the Virginians. Robert R. Livingston and his younger brother Edward were highly regarded by anti-Federalists in all parts of the United States, yet neither made the impression upon state political life that their talents warranted, and even Burr, who genuinely desired the governorship, never took his chances seriously until Clinton had retired.

As a result Republicans were hard pressed to find a candidate who could be confidently pitted against John Jay when he returned from England in 1795, supposedly a successful negotiator at the time of his selection. The best that anti-administration forces could agree upon was Justice Robert Yates of the state supreme court, a man whose only claim upon posterity was his withdrawal from the Constitutional Convention in the summer of 1787. Nevertheless, Jay was able to defeat his opponent by only 1,589 votes out of a total of well over 25,000, evidence of evenly matched political forces.[13]

Within the Empire State the city of New York was of mercurial political temperament, parties rising and falling with frequency. Until the summer of 1795 the city had been "nearly unanimously federal" according to J. B. Hammond, whose researches into New York political history are a landmark in local historiography, but in December of that year its voters returned Edward Livingston to Congress on the basis of his name and antitreaty protests. The protracted struggle over the Jay treaty promised to keep New York in the antiadministration column until the crucial state elections of March, 1796, but once more the tide shifted. Federalists made an almost complete sweep of state offices in the spring and assured themselves of twelve electoral votes for the party's presidential candidate, or more correctly, candidates.

Although Governor Jay may have added considerably to his party's chances through skillful use of patronage, there is little doubt that the fight in Congress and the entire Republican program of opposition to the administration's foreign policy was the determining factor. Livingston had launched the attack upon Washington, and the indications are that the public reacted violently against the attack. Federalists, already geared to bring every possible economic and political pressure to bear upon the situation in Congress, were excel-

[13] M. L. Davis to Albert Gallatin, May 14, 1798, *Gallatin Papers,* New York Historical Society, Box 4, No. 798, No. 21.

lently prepared to fight a strenuous battle for state officers. There is abundant evidence to suggest that they campaigned more vigorously than ever before.[14]

"Never General, have we had so great a stake as at the next Election," wrote State Senator Ambrose Spencer to General Samuel Webb in March, 1796. "The electors for President and Vice President are to be chosen, and a Senator also. Cautious then indeed ought we to be, and none but the most popular should be taken up."

Spencer went on to urge Webb's good offices in persuading General Van Renssalaer to drop his plans for procuring the seat in the Senate left vacant by Rufus King. Many of the Federalists considered the old patroon too unpopular to make a showing that promised success in a heated election. Hoping to take advantage of the confusion in anti-Federalists ranks occasioned by Clinton's sudden retirement, the Federalists proposed to unite behind one of the more conservative Republicans.[15]

Although this particular plan failed to carry with respect to the Senate vacancy, the group associated with Spencer managed to get its strategy adopted in the party's attempt to unseat Edward Livingston when he ran for his second term in December, 1796. Indeed, Hamilton lamented the policy of borrowing candidates from the popular party and explained Livingston's success in the ensuing campaign by pointing to the loss of regular Federalist voters that resulted. In backing a candidate because of his familiarity with the artisans and mechanics of the city the Federalists had lost the conservative influence that they regularly counted on, he told King.[16]

With this single exception 1796 was a Federalist year in

[14] J. B. Hammond, *History of Political Parties in the State of New York from 1788–1840*, 2 vols. (Albany, 1842), I, 95-96, 98-101.

[15] March 13, 1796, S. B. Webb, *Correspondence and Journals of Samuel Blachley Webb*, W. C. Ford, ed., 3 vols. (New York, 1894), III, 200.

[16] December 16, 1796, Hamilton, *Works* (Lodge ed.), X, 216-217.

New York. The story was completed so far as the presidential election was concerned when the Republicans failed to calculate the results of the House fight against Washington correctly. The state legislature controlled the electoral vote, and in losing control of the state government through its national political strategy New York Republican leaders must be accorded a considerable share of the blame.

The existence of a working agreement between the leading Republicans of New York and Virginia during the 1790's has long been accepted and often referred to as a New York-Virginia alliance. The basis for such a belief appears to be the fact that the voting records of men from these states often tallied and the fact that it was the New York vote in 1800 that sent Federalism to its grave. The origin of this alliance has never been uncovered, but Irving Brant has proved that it cannot be traced to the famous "botanical" expedition that Jefferson and Madison took through New York in the summer of 1792. Through careful examination of the itinerary of this trip Brant has demonstrated that the two men could have had neither time nor physical energy enough to have brought the Clinton, Burr, and Livingston factions together and into harness with their powerful Southern organization. The trip was merely a botanical expedition after all.[17]

The overtures for such a co-operative venture, one that was the cornerstone of the national Republican party, were made by Robert R. Livingston in the winter of 1795 to James Madison, who, as House minority leader, was preparing the last attack upon the Jay treaty. Livingston enclosed what he considered to be confidential information on Jay's London negotiations when he wrote, "You will probably think when you read this that I avail myself of slight circumstances to open a correspondence with you, and perhaps it

[17] Irving Brant, *James Madison, Father of the Constitution, 1787–1800* (New York, 1950), 339-340.

will be candid to own that that desire had no little influence upon my pen." [18]

Burr's young Tammany organization was worked in later, doubtless through the agency of Burr himself while in the Senate, and Clinton's closest connection with what has been mistakenly considered a triple entente between the three men was his reluctant acquiescence in having his name placed at the head of Burr's electoral ticket of 1800. In 1796 Clinton let it be known that he would prefer Jefferson to Adams, but he engendered no enthusiasm. Perhaps he still held hopes of national leadership for himself or perhaps he was too tired to care.[19]

All things considered, it is no wonder that Hamilton showed little concern over local politics after March, 1796, and equally clear why Republicans in New York made so little stir over Mr. Jefferson when November came; the die had been cast eight months before. The miracle that could have given Jefferson New York's twelve electoral votes in 1796 did not occur until 1800, and in that year the miracle-worker had a personal stake in the matter.[20]

Outside New England there was no state more uniformly Federalist in political matters than New Jersey. From the early days of the Revolution to the year 1790 the state was run by a faction dominated by Governor William Livingston, who was succeeded in the latter year by William Paterson. The change in governor brought no new social or economic group to the fore, since Paterson was one of that aristocracy of wealth and talent that had held matters in its own hands from the beginning. Few royal governors and councils could have boasted the governmental prerogatives that the New Jersey land-owning hierarchy possessed. Paterson, being a man of marked legal talent, resigned the state office

[18] January 30, 1795, *Madison Papers*, LC.

[19] E. W. Spaulding, *His Excellency George Clinton, Critic of the Constitution* (New York, 1938), 218.

[20] Hammond, *Political Parties in New York*, I, 102.

to become a Justice of the United States Supreme Court in 1793.

During the next three years the governing faction moved steadily closer toward the Federalist party, and it was a marked feature of Richard Howell's administration that New Jersey militia were among the first to respond to Washington's call for an army to put down the Pennsylvania "Whiskey Rebellion." Hamilton considered the state a stronghold of administration support and wrote of Governor Howell and his friends as "all zeal" in their desire to display the strength of the new Federal government.[21] In the spring of 1796 New Jersey Federalists found little difficulty in raising petitions among the citizenry protesting the House blockade of the British treaty.

The foremost New Jersey politician on the national stage in the year of Washington's retirement was Speaker Jonathan Dayton. A maverick in the Jersey fold, Dayton had shown independence of mind sufficient to throw him into opposition to both the Excise Tax and the administration's handling of the Pennsylvania crisis, but his fraternizing with southern politicians during the Jay treaty fight was cut short when the final test came. When forced to take sides Dayton cast his vote as those at home would have willed it. His conduct left him outside the state's inner circle, suspiciously watched as the time approached for the New Jersey legislature to select its seven-man electoral slate. Though the matter of Dayton's relationship with Aaron Burr remains a mystery, there is sufficient evidence to suggest that a connection between the two existed. With Dayton apparently popular with members of the legislature there was uneasiness in high Federalist circles over his role in the state canvass.[22]

[21] Hamilton to Rufus King, September 27, 1794, Hamilton, *Works* (Lodge ed.), X, 69-70.

[22] For a summary of early New Jersey history see F. B. Lee, *New Jersey, Colony and State*, volume IV (New York, 1902); W. R. Fee, *Transition from Aristocracy to Democracy in New Jersey, 1789-1829* (Somerville, New Jersey, 1933).

"How are your election prospects," wrote Hamilton to Elias Boudinot in July. "Do not let the discontent with Dayton hazard the main point. T'is better by a coalition with him to secure that, though you make some sacrifice of opinion, than to produce a dangerous schism." [23]

Whether or not the New Jersey junto had under consideration means of chastising the offending Speaker, the record does not disclose; Hamilton's letter put an end to anything but the most cordial dealings with Dayton, who once more was able to maintain his precarious position as a powerful independent. Madison had suspected the year before that as the popular drift moved so would Dayton, writing to Jefferson at the time that New Jersey had "changed all her members except Dayton, whose zeal against Great Britain saved him." [24] In the fall of 1796 the Pennsylvania Republican leader, John Beckley, placed false hopes on Dayton's recent conversion to antifederalism. "We have great hopes in New Jersey," he exclaimed to one of his party workers.[25]

Against hopes the Hamiltonians threw well-contrived plans for committing the Speaker well in advance of election day. As soon as Oliver Wolcott, Jr., received word of Washington's decision to retire he wrote Dayton that Republicans in Philadelphia were openly boasting of their chances of splitting the New Jersey electoral vote. He asked Dayton to comment on the possibility and in evident reference to Burr, inquired whether there was any chance of a Republican gaining votes on the second ballot.[26]

In reply to Wolcott, Dayton covered himself with innocence when he reported that Robert Livingston of New York had been mentioned by some but that it seemed more logical that Republicans might drop him for a man from the

[23] July 7, 1796, Hamilton, *Works* (Lodge ed.), X, 183.
[24] January 26, 1795, *Madison Papers*, LC.
[25] Beckley to Gen. William Irvine, October 4, 1796, *Irvine Papers*, Historical Society of Pennsylvania, XIII, No. 115.
[26] September 7, 1796, Gibbs, *Memoirs*, I, 382.

Middle States with greater popularity. His words were reassuring, however; "the man from Monticello" would get no electoral support from New Jersey.[27]

In this last Dayton proved correct; the seven electors chosen a few weeks later cast their ballots in accordance with the Hamiltonian scheme, Adams and Pinckney each receiving seven votes. Whatever tendencies toward schism had been discernible in the Federalist camp during July had been healed over by November.

Leaving the situation in Pennsylvania for closer attention later, our survey takes us beyond the Delaware into the upper South. So tranquil was the political scene in the state of Delaware that it might almost suffice to dismiss the territories that had once comprised Penn's lower counties with the statement that Federalist domination was virtually complete. Throughout the House fight against the Jay treaty Delaware citizens had contributed more than their numerical share of proadministration petitions, and the legislature was so overwhelmingly dominated by Federalists that no Republican strategist gave more than a passing glance at the electoral story there.

Young Thomas Rodney has left us a journal that describes with disgust how little enthusiasm the name of Jefferson excited in 1796. "Court party carried by large majority, the country party all left and run over, as the wits say. Their ticket was badly composed and the few people who wanted a change would not trust them." [28]

In Maryland and Virginia thirty-one electoral seats were at stake, and the campaigning was correspondingly heavy since all these votes were directly determined by the people. So strong were sentiments among the voters that Madison had pointed to Baltimore as the scene of the worst Federalist

[27] September 15, 1796, *ibid.*, 383.

[28] Thomas Rodney, *Journal, 1796–1797*, Historical Society of Pennsylvania.

economic blackmail along the coast during the House debate.[29]

The Livingston resolution may be taken as a party measure, and when it was introduced in March three of Maryland's five Representatives voted for its adoption. Six weeks later and, as Madison saw it, as a result of economic pressures exerted at Baltimore, not one of the Maryland Republicans stood with the party leaders. Two Jeffersonians, Dent and Christie, had made an about-face, and Representative Gabriel Duvall, who was to reappear as a Republican electoral candidate in the fall, had found it either necessary or expedient to resign.[30]

As a result of the Republican challenge Maryland Federalists, already in control of both the state administration and the upper house of the legislature, were drawn closely together. The President had done his utmost to hold Maryland in line with the administration by offering cabinet posts to Marylanders with unusual persistence. James McHenry of Baltimore took the War Department folio after Henry Knox's resignation even though, as everyone recognized, his talents were in no wise outstanding. C. C. Pinckney of South Carolina, the only other Southern state besides Maryland where the Federalist party had even the least semblance of power, had previously turned the appointment down as had former Governor John E. Howard, also of Maryland. Another native of Maryland, ex-Governor Thomas Johnson, was tendered the State Department at the time of Randolph's resignation and before either Patrick Henry or Timothy Pickering were asked.[31] When the Navy Department was created in 1798 President Adams likewise turned toward Baltimore, selecting a businessman of that city, Benjamin Stoddert, as the first Secretary.

[29] Madison to Jefferson, April 18, 1796, *Madison Papers*, LC.

[30] See below, p. 162.

[31] Bernard C. Steiner, *Life and Correspondence of James McHenry* (Cleveland, 1907), 161.

The canvassing in Maryland, where electors were chosen in district elections, was apparently directed entirely by local politicians, William Vans Murray being the most active of the Federalist leaders, and former Congressman Duvall being Jefferson's most ardent disciple. Murray constantly sought information from national headquarters, if Hamilton's office may be so designated, but he received no help from that direction. His services included the authorship of a series of newspaper articles loudly praising the revolutionary services of Mr. Adams, and it is not surprising that he was later to be appointed by that gentleman to a diplomatic post. Murray was one of the first to recognize the need for national direction of political campaigns. "The timing of the exertions of the Fed party seems to me very important," he told his friend McHenry in September. He went on to suggest that cabinet members take upon themselves this responsibility, but Murray's sensible idea received scant notice. His own optimistic reports of Federalist strength in Maryland may have suggested to this Hamiltonian club (for there was nothing of a political nature that McHenry did not immediately pass on to New York) that their aid was unnecessary, for Murray declared it as certain that Adams would receive nine of the state's eleven votes as the campaigning began.[32]

The nature of the campaigns waged by Republicans and Federalists in Maryland and Virginia was similar. Federalists on both sides of the Potomac, for example, insisted that Jefferson's conduct as a revolutionary governor had been cowardly and that James Madison was a political turncoat. At Annapolis Federalist agitators kept the Jay treaty issue alive by carefully analyzing Madison's views on the treaty-making power as he had expressed them in the Constitutional Convention and as he had expressed them in 1796 on the floor of the House. It was charged, not without some justification, that he had altered his opinions. One Maryland legis-

[32] Murray to McHenry, September 9, 1796, *ibid.*, 197.

lator was so disturbed by this charge that he wrote in confidence to Jefferson asking for help in meeting it.[33]

Republicans, on the other hand, found great delight in clipping embarrassing excerpts from the voluminous writings of candidate John Adams. "A Republican Citizen," writing for the *Gazette* at Annapolis, proved conclusively that a Jeffersonian orator had deliberately put the words of Plato's *Republic* into Mr. Adams' mouth as his own.[34] Whether all this had much influence upon the outcome it may be seriously doubted; one gathers the impression that a stringent libel law would have put an end to most of the press campaigning and that writers and orators regarded slandering opponents as sort of a game not to be taken too seriously by anyone.

In what was undoubtedly the outstanding contest for a single seat in the upper South the Jeffersonian candidate won by a wide margin. Gabriel Duvall, who had declared himself a candidate for the electoral college by stating that he was "decidedly in favor of Mr. Jefferson as President of the United States," was regarded as an outspoken Republican despite his resignation from Congress in the midst of the Jay Treaty debate. Against him Federalists of Anne Arundel County pitted the venerable Charles Carroll, a figure of national reputation. Duvall won handily with 170 of the 210 votes cast.[35]

In November seven men pledged to John Adams were elected and four pledged to Jefferson, but the returns of the electoral college showed that five men had voted for Jefferson. It is a wonder that this situation was not repeated more often; no elector was forced to pledge himself beyond the first ballot.

[33] Peregrine Fitzhugh to Jefferson, March 25, 1797, *Jefferson Papers*, LC.

[34] *Maryland Gazette*, November 17, 1796.

[35] *Maryland Gazette*, October 27, 1796. Duvall's pledge made up the entire news item from that area and was relegated to the third page. *Claypoole's American Daily Advertiser*, November 16, 1796.

From Virginia, controlling the largest block of electoral votes in the Union, Federalists could expect little, if any, support. Jefferson was the Republican candidate, the legislature was in the hands of his ardent supporters, the state administration was never out of the control of his immediate friends, and consequently the possibility of Federalist victory in any of the twenty-one electoral districts was regarded as unlikely. There were centers of Federalist strength in Richmond, the Northern Neck comprising Fauquier and Loudoun counties, and in the Shenandoah Valley area around Winchester. In these three districts Federalists campaigned strenuously, and their success in one contributed mightily to the defeat of Jefferson in the presidential race.

Knowing that Jefferson's great virtue as a candidate was his claim to pure republicanism and leadership against central government strength, Federalists left no avenue unexplored in their attempts to impugn the sincerity of Jefferson's convictions. Scandal, rumor, and half-truths were employed without regard to conscience and with sufficient effectiveness as to cause their opponents to take the defensive.

It was charged that Jefferson had stooped to making a corrupt political bargain with Senator Burr of New York at the time of Burr's visit to Monticello in October, 1795. The visit had not been public and the exposure of this incident, undoubtedly a second link in the establishment of the political alliance that helped to create the national Republican organization, caused consternation in Jefferson's circle. It was contrary to the political ethics of the time for a candidate to high office to be overly zealous in his own cause, and when the morally indignant Federalists protested that a monstrous bartering for national office had taken place they touched upon a tender spot. The charge gained enough credence for Jeffersonian lieutenants to gather eyewitness accounts of what they maintained had been surely a social gathering. Several of these sworn statements are to be found among Mr.

Jefferson's papers; they say that politics were not even mentioned.[36]

In a political speech delivered at Dumfries, Virginia, in September Colonel Charles Simms, Federalist electoral candidate in the Stafford County District, accused Jefferson of cowardly conduct as Governor during Arnold's invasion of Virginia. In contrast, he pointed out, Mr. Adams had exhibited manly courage in defying Great Britain during the early months of the Revolution. Colonel Simms went on to cast doubts upon the sincerity of Virginia republicanism; there was unequal representation in the legislature that could not be overlooked, the western counties being virtually powerless and in bondage to the area east of the Blue Ridge. Mr. Adams had objected to this sort of thing in the British House of Commons, yet he was branded an aristocrat, said the Colonel, and he quoted from his candidate's writings to prove it.

These two charges were difficult to meet and were constantly reiterated throughout the campaign. Daniel C. Brent, who opposed Simms, wrote to John Taylor for answers and published Taylor's reply as the most effective way of meeting the accusations. In this particular case the voters paid little heed, however, and in November the returns from Stafford County gave Brent the victory, "almost unanimous."[37]

So widespread was the cowardice charge against Jefferson that Taylor went to great pains in collecting eyewitness accounts of Jefferson's movements during the British invasion of January, 1781. These, needless to say, fully attested the Governor's courage and competence throughout the crisis. Taylor, himself a candidate for the electoral college, revealed that these letters were being printed as a campaign

[36] Affidavit dated October 17, 1796, bearing the signature of J. J. Monroe, *Jefferson Papers*, LC.

[37] John Taylor to Simms, October 7, 1796, *Jefferson Papers*, LC; *Claypoole's American Daily Advertiser*, November 16, 1796.

pamphlet.[38] No sooner had this Federalist attack been met than Jefferson was accused of having sordid economic motives for his revolutionary enthusiasm. It was claimed by opponents in the Northern Neck that John Marshall had evidence to show that the Republican candidate had been in debt to British merchants in amount greater than the value of his entire estate at the outbreak of the Revolution and that he had been sued by these merchants in Virginia courts immediately after the war. When confronted with the claim that he had conducted such a suit against Jefferson, John Marshall denied it, disclaiming any knowledge of Mr. Jefferson's financial standing or of the sources from which this rumor had originated. False as the charge apparently was, it had caused commotion enough to set candidate Brent at the task of tracing it down. He labored manfully for the privilege of casting a ballot for Jefferson.[39]

The most honest and effective campaign charge that Federalists in Virginia leveled against their powerful opponents was that which concerned the apportionment of seats in the legislature. "A Mechanic of Alexandria," for example, was scornful of Jeffersonian Republicans who levied heavy taxes and passed laws forcing western men into the militia while at the same time denying them representation in either the state or national legislature. Here, he declared, were the "dregs of Monarchy and British influence" that were so often charged to Federalism.[40] In the vicinity of Winchester petitions were circulated, which mark the first seeds of the

[38] Taylor to Simms, *op. cit.* A resolution of the House of Delegates dated 1781 and signed by Clerk John Beckley was printed in the *Columbian Mirror*, Alexandria, October 18, 1796.

[39] Senator Stevens T. Mason to D. C. Brent, October 25, 1796, *Jefferson Papers*, LC.

[40] *Columbian Mirror*, Alexandria, September 27, 1796. See F. S. Hart, *The Valley of Virginia in the American Revolution, 1763–1789* (University of North Carolina Press, 1942) for the beginnings of the separate statehood movement in Western Virginia. Resentment against the established church during the colonial era and the absence of slavery on a large scale set the western farmers in opposition to the seaboard ruling classes.

separatist movement that culminated in West Virginia statehood. These petitions maintained that since representation in the Richmond legislature was denied the people of the Shenandoah Valley, separation and secession were in order. "The great contrariety of sentiment respecting the measures of the General Government which prevail between the citizens of the lower and upper counties has produced a strong desire for separation among inhabitants of the Northern Neck and the territory westward of the Blue Ridge," wrote a contributor to the *Winchester Gazette.*[41]

Opponents of the Republican state regime also pointed to the value of a strong central government in upholding minorities' rights. No man who had opposed administration measures, or who had approved the rash program of the House of Representatives in opposition to both the President and the Senate, said "A Farmer" writing to the voters of the Northern Neck, was deserving of support for the electoral college. And in nearby Richmond John Marshall and his friends had turned the city into what Edmund Randolph described for Madison as "little more than a colony of Philadelphia." "Whatever is said in favor of the government is circulated under franks from the Treasury, but not a Virginia eye here has seen Gallatin's pamphlet or Dwight's address to the President."[42]

Despite spirited campaigning on behalf of the President and Mr. Adams, and despite optimistic reports such as those sent by Fisher Ames, who in his travels through the state in November could see little but enthusiasm for administration policies, the Republican machine was never in danger of losing its almost complete hold upon Virginia politics. In fact the confidence of Jefferson's supporters in one district was such that two Jeffersonian electoral candidates were put up,

[41] Reprinted in the *Connecticut Gazette*, May 26, 1796.

[42] *Columbian Mirror*, September 27, 1796; Randolph to Madison, January 8, 1797, *Madison Papers*, LC.

and in the three-way contest the Adams elector drew only 84 votes of more than 700 cast.[43]

When the canvass ended one candidate pledged to Adams was elected, though Ames had made the mistake of identifying the zealous Daniel Brent as an Adams man. The lone Federalist was Leven Powell from the district comprising Loudoun and Fauquier counties. On record is a short speech of Powell's, which proves that there was no last-minute switch or slip-up in the Virginia situation: he had stood as an Adams elector from the beginning and was elected as such. In the address he criticized the bargain that Burr had made with Jefferson as foul play, attacked what he maintained was Jefferson's expedient acceptance of the Constitution of the United States, and praised the steady republican conduct of John Adams.[44] He was elected in a district where the desire for separate statehood was strong and where resentment against the planter aristocracy had become traditional. His victory by a comfortable margin is not surprising.

If John Marshall was correct in his report on another district contest a second Adams candidate narrowly missed election. In Princess Anne County Republicans had been so lethargic that no one had bothered to campaign against the Federalist candidate, and by noon of election day it was seen that few voters were taking the trouble to make the trip to the polling station. Strenuous action by Republican leaders collected enough dubious voters, as Marshall saw it, to defeat the honest campaigner.[45]

Feeling that little campaigning was necessary to secure a Jefferson ticket in Virginia, Republican leaders seem to have

[43] Ames to Wolcott, Jr., Martinsburg, Va., November 16, 1796, Gibbs, *Memoirs*, I, 373; *Claypoole's American Daily Advertiser*, November 16, 1796.

[44] *Columbian Mirror*, October 1, 1796; *Claypoole's American Daily Advertiser*, December 12, 1796; Ames to Jeremiah Smith, September 4, 1796, Ames, *Works*, I, 198.

[45] Marshall to James Iredell, December 15, 1796, G. J. McRee, *Life and Correspondence of James Iredell*, 2 vols. (New York, 1857–58), II, 482.

spent most of their time and energy in Richmond thrashing out one last insult for the President. Marshall had introduced a resolution of commendation to Washington just after the publication of the Farewell Address, but by the time Republicans had finished amending it the tone had been so changed as to leave Attorney General Charles Lee with the impression that it was a studied insult. "Nothing beyond mere civility should be found in the answer," he advised the President, who had referred the matter to him.[46]

Such was Virginia's last legislative act of the year. If nothing else, the Republican organization had been consistent throughout the campaign.

Looking southward from Virginia, Federalists could hope for little support unless South Carolina provided it. The most complete survey of political conditions in the Carolinas on record is one that Federalist Robert Goodloe Harper prepared for Hamilton in early November. He was a politician of note in that he had completely altered his party standing from the time he had entered Congress, yet he continued to be re-elected throughout the 1790's. When he arrived in Philadelphia for the opening of the Fourth Congress he had paid homage to both Madison and Jefferson, but within a few months Harper had become the most partisan of Federalists. Along with William Smith, Thomas Pinckney, and Charles C. Pinckney he contributed much to the maintenance of Federalism's one stronghold in the deep South.

In 1796, Harper returned to Charleston to see what could be done for Thomas Pinckney's cause. It was on his return trip to the capital that he paused at Raleigh, North Carolina, to sum up his impressions of political prospects for his New York friends. "I do not believe the states east of the Hudson are more decidedly correct in all the great points than these

[46] A. J. Beveridge, *Life of John Marshall*, 4 vols. (Boston and New York, 1916–19), II, 159; Lee to Washington, December 28, 1796, Washington, *Writings*, XXXV, 350.

two," he confidently began. He noted that Republicans had gained little sympathy in their desperate bid to stop the Jay treaty; "on the treaty-making power, Ames himself is not more orthodox than these people." Toward France little of the enthusiasm that kept Virginia political life in ferment could be seen: Harper felt that the administration's neutrality policy was overwhelmingly favored. Furthermore, he had not heard of a single elector in either state who would not vote for Washington again. As for Mr. Adams, he had to admit that there was little enthusiasm. Most of the talk concerned Jefferson and Pinckney, and on that vital point Harper was reassuring. The Charleston diplomat would receive all the second ballots from both the Carolinas and from Georgia. "Jefferson's friends would infinitely rather see Pinckney President than Adams, and many will support him with that view." [47]

The electoral results a month later proved Harper's optimism unfounded. In the three states that he claimed to have surveyed, Adams received one vote, Pinckney only nine, and Jefferson twenty-three. Harper undoubtedly based his report on letters and interviews with local Federalist leaders, and there is nothing in the conduct of these men to suggest that they had developed the art of sampling public opinion to any great degree. During the legislative year 1795–96 North Carolina politics had focused round the question of administration foreign policy, and in the fall, as a result of the revulsion felt for the terms of the Jay treaty, an ardent Republican, Judge Samuel Ashe, had ousted the Federalist incumbent in the gubernatorial contest. Simultaneously, only one Federalist was elected to the House of Representatives. By the spring of 1796, however, the same phenomenon observed elsewhere along the coast, a countercurrent created by the fight against the President in the House, had taken place in North Carolina. Republican strength in the legislature fell

[47] Harper to Hamilton, November 4, 1796, *Hamilton Papers*, LC.

off sharply, a Republican, Timothy Bloodworth, was sent to the Senate by only one vote, and in the fall a leading Jeffersonian was defeated in a bitterly fought campaign for a seat in the House of Representatives.[48]

Both Harper and Ames were substantially correct in reporting a swing toward Federalism in the coastal areas of the South, but any change in sentiment where elections are indirect is deceptive. The men who were to choose electors in November had taken their seats prior to the shift in public opinion, and only the strongest kind of pressure from the electorate could have forced their hands. Ames noted that one of the electors chosen by the legislature of North Carolina had gone on record for Adams, but the rest were friends to Jefferson.[49]

In South Carolina the outcome of electoral balloting depended upon circumstances lacking in other states; Pinckney's home was in Charleston, and the Rutledges were personal friends of Jefferson. Just as in Calhoun's day, it was debatable during the 1790's which party the South Carolina planters supported on the national scene. Thomas Pinckney had been governor before undertaking his diplomatic appointment, and his political affiliations at the time were entirely vague as were those of his successor, William Moultrie. It was not until Charles Pinckney took office in 1796 that a definite partisan headed the state administration, and he, in contrast to Thomas and Charles C. Pinckney, was a determined Jeffersonian supporter. His success indicated that the state politicians would choose Jefferson electors in the fall.[50]

There were other signs, however, that Pinckney's election as governor was evidence of his personal following rather than evidence of a Republican upswing. Many planters had

[48] W. E. Dodd, *Life of Nathaniel Macon* (Raleigh, N. C., 1903), 90-91; J. E. Moore, *History of North Carolina* (Raleigh, 1880), I, 417-421.

[49] Ames to Christopher Gore, Dec. 3, 1796, Ames, *Works*, I, 205.

[50] Yates Snowden *et al.*, *History of South Carolina*, 5 vols. (New York and Chicago, 1920), I, 503, 524.

solid economic reasons for feeling grateful for the acts of the administration at Philadelphia. Protectionism was favorably regarded by the depressed indigo planters, while others had profited substantially from the assumption of state debts. Furthermore, the republicanism of Mr. Jefferson's friends was not viewed as safe doctrine by the slave-owning oligarchy; it was widely reported that radical political doctrine had been responsible for the bloody Haitian slave revolt of 1793. Motives other than personal preference dictated Harper's dramatic conversion to Federalism, and these forces were still strong in 1796.[51] Democratic doctrine logically demanded a reapportionment of seats in the state legislature, and this would have deprived the tidewater of a control over state affairs that they had come to regard as hereditary. In 1790 the state constitution had been adopted without giving the concessions to the upland counties that their men demanded—representation according to population and a more centrally located capital. To the discomfiture of a good many Charleston politicians, Jeffersonianism was popular in the western counties.[52]

Finally, the position of the powerful Rutledge family was ambiguous. They had opposed the adoption of the Jay treaty, had been chastised by the Federalist Senate for doing so when John Rutledge's nomination as Chief Justice had been defeated in 1795, and the head of the family was a long-time friend of Thomas Jefferson's. Thomas Pinckney's sudden candidacy upset expectations.[53]

Oliver Wolcott, Jr., in summing up the election reports for his father at the end of November, pointed to the Rutledge faction as holding the presidency within its hands; the

[51] U. B. Phillips, "South Carolina Federalists," *American Historical Review*, XIV (July, 1909), 731-732, 734.

[52] Phillips, *op. cit.;* Snowden, *History of South Carolina*, I, 512-513.

[53] Phillips declares that Federalists had on several occasions been unable to break Rutledge's control of state politics, inferring that his leanings were definitely Republican.

result would turn upon the balloting of the South Carolina electoral college, he stated, and Edward Rutledge was believed to command its decision. His reports from all over the Union indicated that Adams lacked but three votes for a majority. His fear was that Rutledge's disgust with the Jay treaty would give the decision to Jefferson.[54]

Rutledge, whatever his predilections toward the Republican party at the time, was not what can be called a party man. In the fall of 1796 his nephew John had been sent to the House of Representatives as an independent, apparently instructed to bide his time and watch developments. A letter that the young congressman wrote to Edward Rutledge in July before he had taken his seat clearly indicates that the Charleston leader was a neutral and not strongly in favor of the Republican program. John Rutledge, knowing nothing of the plan then under way to make Thomas Pinckney a presidential candidate, suggested the home coming diplomat as a logical choice to succeed William Smith in the House and then wrote, "For God's sake, do not send Charles Pinckney or any of that class." [55]

Even allowing for the frankness that family connection made possible, it seems certain that a fledgling politician would hardly dare speak so scornfully of the leading Jeffersonian in South Carolina had he not been certain that his views would be received sympathetically. Edward Rutledge's friendship for both Jefferson and Thomas Pinckney decided a delicate personal choice: each received the state's full electoral vote in December.

So far as the states of Georgia, Kentucky, and Tennessee were concerned there was little doubt in anyone's mind that Jefferson and Burr would garner the entire electoral vote. There were lingering hopes among Federalists that Pinckney

[54] November 27, 1796, Gibbs, *Memoirs*, I, 401-402.

[55] S. E. Morison, *Life and Letters of Harrison Gray Otis, Federalist*, 2 vols. (Boston and New York, 1913), I, 61; Rutledge to Edward Rutledge, July 7, 1796, *Rutledge Papers*, Historical Society of Pennsylvania, No. 13.

might be granted one or two votes on the basis of his treaty's popularity in the two western states, but these did not materialize. Georgia's four electors were chosen by voters in twenty-one counties voting directly for a party ticket. The four counties that gave the Federalist ticket a majority, all of them western counties, may be said to have cast a protest vote against tidewater domination, precisely as was the case in both South Carolina and Virginia.[56]

The westward colonizing movement in Georgia had produced the same sectional tensions as in most states, and the frontiersmen were loud in their demands for reapportionment of seats almost as soon as county boundaries had been determined. Nothing indicates that these isolated voters in the deep South were concerned with political events in Philadelphia or with Mr. Jay's famous negotiations. Surveying the pages of the Savannah *Columbian Museum* for 1796 one is impressed with the lack of news from the North and the absence of presidential campaign talk. It was not until the election was over that the editor printed Adet's bombastic diplomatic notes, for example.[57]

While Washington's second administration had done much to commend the new Federal government to the people of Kentucky and Tennessee, political ties were with Virginia. The Jay and Pinckney treaties promised immense benefits to the frontier, and the prestige of the central government was higher in 1796 than it would be again until 1801, for Wayne's military victories on the Ohio and the long-awaited surrender of the British posts were the outcome of Washington's work. In brief, Kentucky and Tennessee were grateful for what fell their way, but their political leaders remained in opposition, and there was no Federalist organization or press to challenge them. Whatever the administration ac-

[56] U. B. Phillips, "Georgia and States Rights," *Report of the American Historical Association, 1901*, II (Washington, 1902), 91.

[57] Adet's notes of November were printed in the *Columbian Museum*, December 27, 1796.

complished was credited to Washington personally. "We now have a real peace with the Indians, which is the only time we could have said as much since the American Revolution commenced," wrote Madison's Kentucky land agent, Hubbard Taylor, in midsummer. "The time is now drawing near that electors are to be chosen. . . . The minds of the people in this part of the country seem a great deal agitated. If the old president still inclines to serve it will possibly split our votes, otherwise the vote will be unanimous for Mr. Jefferson . . . the vice president is not so much spoken of." [58]

The fact that Burr's name was not mentioned by Madison's friend is noteworthy, because it is certain that his name was being used by the voters in their political speculations. Taylor probably knew where the Virginia leadership stood with regard to Burr, and nothing stands out more dramatically in the 1796 election returns than the deliberate rejection of Burr by the Jeffersonian organization in Virginia. Burr had worked hard to win the friendship and gratitude of Tennessee politicians, and his success in this enterprise was no small part of his bargaining power in winning the nomination. It was Burr who had insisted on pushing Tennessee statehood to the test in 1796 and Burr who was among the first to befriend Andrew Jackson, who had arrived in Philadelphia as Senator-elect in May. To Federalist observers Burr's strange anxiety over Tennessee's admission was pure electioneering. "One more twig of the electioneering cabal for Jefferson," commented Connecticut's Chauncey Goodrich. "It probably originated from that quarter where so much mischief is brewed," he wrote, at the same time noting that Burr had introduced a bill for Tennessee statehood in the Senate.[59] While Federalists did their utmost to block passage of such recognition—contending that the first census was inaccurate and a new one necessary before action could

[58] July 16, 1796, *Madison Papers*, LC.

[59] Goodrich to Wolcott, Sr., May 13, 1796, Gibbs, *Memoirs*, I, 338.

be taken—their maneuvering proved indefensible when Burr and his associates in the Senate reverted to precedent, demonstrating that Tennessee had followed precisely the same procedure that had been accepted as the basis for the admission of Vermont in 1791 and of Kentucky in 1792.[60]

Angry Federalists grumbled that the three electoral votes of Tennessee had been thrown into the scales of battle owing to the stupidity of New Hampshire's Senator Livermore, who, as President *pro tempore*, had cast the decisive vote. "It must be left for him to account for his conduct; his friends are chagrined," barked Goodrich of Connecticut to his political mentor at Hartford.[61]

A survey of political conditions in the states on the eve of the election of 1796 demonstrates that Federalists had every reason to anticipate success, provided Pennsylvania is eliminated from the reckoning. All thirty-nine New England votes were safe; Federalist-dominated legislatures in New York, New Jersey, and Delaware could be counted upon to deliver twenty-two; Maryland was expected to contribute seven or eight; and the Carolinas were looked to for four or five votes. When Oliver Wolcott, Jr., sat down to make a final report for his father on the national situation in November, his own tabulation must have been essentially the same. His figure was seventy-six electoral votes for Adams, and he was already aware of the revolution that had occurred in Pennsylvania.[62]

In Pennsylvania the two parties seemed evenly matched, and had the two tickets been supported proportionately to their supposed strength, the outcome would have been of a totally different complexion, for a reasonable guess would have allotted Adams seven of the fifteen Pennsylvania bal-

60 *Claypoole's American Daily Advertiser*, May 31, 1796; William Smith to Ralph Izard, May 18, 1796; U. B. Phillips, "South Carolina Federalists," *American Historical Review*, XIV, July 1909, 780.

61 To Wolcott, Sr., June 1, 1796, Gibbs, *Memoirs*, I, 343.

62 November 12, 1796, Gibbs, *Memoirs*, I, 357.

lots. This would have made the final outcome eighty-two votes for Adams and sixty for Jefferson. Three important considerations made the predictions of the best-informed experts of doubtful merit, however. First, no elector was forced to pledge his second or vice-presidential ballot, and there is no indication that anyone did so. There was nothing to prevent isolated electors casting one vote for Jefferson and a second for Adams, or vice versa. It is a tribute to the discipline that party organization had already achieved that such an accident occurred only in the Maryland electoral college.

Secondly, the situation at Charleston was clouded owing to Edward Rutledge's unique position, and all the experts agreed that as he decided so would the balloting at Charleston go. No one seems to have guessed that he would split the vote evenly, overlooking completely the rise of political parties.

Finally, it was impossible to rule out a unanimous victory by either of the parties in Pennsylvania; allowing for the inevitable miscalculations as to other states, fifteen votes for Jefferson from Pennsylvania would have brought the Republicans to power. The Pennsylvania clash was the most closely followed and skillfully fought campaign of the year. Its startling conclusion left Republicans jubilant, Federalists disconcerted, and the few who had been quietly urging Thomas Pinckney's pretensions wondering if the plot might not be hatched after all.

8

A Political Revolution in Pennsylvania

JOHN BECKLEY WAS BY PROFESSION A CLERK. BORN A VIRGINian, he had settled in Philadelphia when the Federal government was brought there from New York in 1792. Whether it was at the suggestion of Madison and the other Virginia lawmakers that he had made his home in the new capital cannot be said with certainty. The abilities he had shown as clerk for the Virginia House of Delegates during the 1780's made him an eligible candidate for that position in the House of Representatives, and he was re-elected by each new Congress until the Federalists suddenly threw him out in 1798. If no other gauge of party strength could be found we might see in the unceremonious rejection of John Beckley that the Republicans had been brought low by the XYZ revelations of 1798. Beckley was kept on, not just because he was a skilled clerk, but because he proved extremely useful to James Madison and Thomas Jefferson. As an observer and liaison man with the local politicians of Pennsylvania Beckley was valued. Perhaps he was not so powerful as to rightfully be labeled Republican party chairman,[1] but he certainly was more than a clerk. He had been taken with Madison and Jefferson on the first lap of their famous summer excursion of 1792, wrote occasional political letters to them during their absences from Philadelphia, and in the winter of

[1] Phillip M. Marsh, "John Beckley, Mystery Man of the Early Jeffersonians," *Pennsylvania Magazine of History and Biography* (January, 1948), LXXII, 54-69.

1795–96 had been one of the originators of the plan to win the presidential election by means of the House appropriations fight. That master strategy had come to grief, ending in several states in a recognizable swing toward federalism.

We suspect that Beckley was one of the Philadelphia Republicans who urged Pierre Adet to take definite action against the administration, action that might atone for the Livingston resolution debacle. The wisdom of this measure is open to question, but if by early November Jefferson and Madison were beginning to have doubts about Mr. Beckley as anything more than a clerk, December 7, 1796, was to reassure them. On that day Pennsylvania's electoral vote was delivered intact, with the exception of one unavoidable ballot, to Mr. Jefferson. Beckley deserved most of the credit. His skillful direction of the Pennsylvania campaign in the fall of 1796 marks him as one of the outstanding political tacticians of his generation. In strategy mistaken, in tactics a master, John Beckley ended his public career in an obscure Philadelphia clerkship secured for him by powerful friends at Harrisburg whose high offices Beckley had done so much to deliver to them.

By the middle of September, 1796, Beckley was excitedly speculating on November's possibilities. Republicans could expect unanimous support from Georgia, the Carolinas, Virginia, Kentucky, and Tennessee, he wrote to his friend General William Irvine of Cumberland County. Other reports he had received indicated at least half the electoral votes of Delaware and Maryland, "some from New Jersey," and a few for Jefferson from New York and New England. It was almost possible to imagine Pickering, Wolcott, and company packing up their bags. "If Pennsylvania does well, the election is safe," was his confident conclusion.

Beckley then went on to unfold the simple plan by which Pennsylvania might be won for Jefferson. Federalists controlled county returns by their dominance of the political life of the small towns, "the rotten towns," as he phrased it, and in concentrating on the urban voters they left untapped a vast reservoir of potential Republican strength. A Republican electoral slate would be drawn up secretly and circulated "through the proper hands" to the most trustworthy farmers in each county. "No ticket must be printed," he cautioned. Voters must become acquainted with the Federalist ticket through the newspapers, but they were to have personal attention in familiarizing themselves with the Republican ticket. The last and most important detail was to get the vote out on election day, this being done by the county party workers.[2]

For at least two years before the presidential election the Pennsylvania Republicans had been directed through a committee of correspondence. Among the names appearing on a paper dated 1794 and found among Albert Gallatin's papers are such prominent local and national figures as Frederick and Peter Muhlenberg, Daniel Heister, John W. Kittera, William Maclay, William Findley, John Smilie, Albert Gallatin, and William Irvine. All were distinguished in some line of public service, six having served in the House of Representatives, one as United States Senator from Pennsylvania, Irvine and the Muhlenbergs prominent in the Revolutionary War, and Heister a favorite among the German population.[3] Several of these names were selected by the state Republican caucus which met at Carlisle to choose electors a few days before Beckley wrote Irvine. Even this meeting was held in secrecy, for the ostensible reason for the Carlisle gathering was to purchase state-held lands being sold for taxes. John Montgomery, delegate from Northumberland County, asked Irvine to send his nominations on to him because he had been

[2] September 15, 1796, *Irvine Papers,* Historical Society of Pennsylvania, XIII, No. 112.

[3] *Gallatin Papers,* New York Historical Society, Box 3, 1794, No. 64.

unable to attend. The Carlisle ticket was to be official,[4] Irvine was told.

A week after his initial letter of instructions to Irvine, Beckley mailed the electoral slate to party workers; it was headed by the names of Governor Thomas Mifflin and Judge Thomas McKean. "The Governor is as fully eligible as Judge McKean, and it is believed his name will greatly assist the ticket." He advised Irvine to make copies of the list and to send them on to the most popular Republican leaders in western Pennsylvania. As he wrote word reached him that the Governor had at the last minute withdrawn his name. He had been too long an independent, and perhaps his decision was influenced by the fact that he had taken an active part, albeit reluctantly, in suppressing the Whiskey Rebellion in western Pennsylvania. The electoral ticket was to be spread minus one name. Beckley wrote that he was also shipping a number of pamphlets "by way of address to the people of Pennsylvania, showing the strong reasons there are for this state's having a Southern, rather than an Eastern President." [5] The enclosed electoral ticket, containing the names of six men who had served on the 1794 committee of correspondence, included: Thomas McKean, chief justice of the state supreme court from Philadelphia, Jacob Morgan from Philadelphia County, Jonas Hartsell of Northampton, Peter Muhlenberg of Montgomery, Joseph Heister of Berks, William Maclay of Dauphin, Joseph Hanna of Bucks, John Whitehill of Lancaster, Abraham Smith of Franklin, William Brown of Mifflin County, John Piper of Bedford, John Smilie of Fayette, James Edgar of Washington, and William Irvine of Cumberland County. The one notable name not appearing was that of former Congressman Frederick A. Muhlenberg who, for his decisive vote in favor of carrying the Jay treaty, had been cast out of the party. Here was a ticket that Beckley could present with

[4] September 15, 1796, *Irvine Papers*, XIII, 111.

[5] Philadelphia, September 22, 1796; *ibid.*, XIII, No. 113.

confidence, far stronger than the Federalists could anticipate, and one that could win if kept secret long enough to prevent the opposing party from adding prominent figures to their own.

Part of Beckley's plan was purely psychological. In his original letter to Irvine, and presumably to other key men across the state, he included an estimate of Jeffersonian strength in other states far beyond anything that could have reasonably been expected at that date or at any other during the campaign. On September 30 after another week's interval, Beckley again sent his county workers misleading information: the latest reports, he wrote, give Jefferson even better chances in New England—all of Rhode Island, two in New Hampshire, three or four in Massachusetts, and one or two in both Vermont and Connecticut—plus all the Southern vote except half of Maryland's.[6] A few days later he sent information which again demonstrates that he was deliberately building up false hopes in order to produce more zeal in his confederates. Jefferson's popularity was catching on like a prairie fire, the band wagon was beginning to roll, no one is working for a lost cause, he said in effect. On October 4 he reported that news had just arrived from New York which stated that Hamilton had made an about-face and was advising the election of Jefferson as the one man who could prevent the outbreak of war with France. "Will it not be desirable to throw this paragraph into the Carlisle paper?" he asked Irvine.

At the same time the resourceful state committee, headed by Beckley and Dr. Michael Leib of Philadelphia,[7] was sending to Irvine and other county leaders one hundred handbills, promising a thousand more, and asking that they be distributed beyond the Alleghenies before local distribution

[6] Beckley to Irvine, *ibid.*, XIII, No. 114.

[7] Raymond Walters, Jr., *Alexander James Dallas* (University of Pennsylvania Press, 1943), 74.

so that they would be given state-wide attention before the Federalists had a chance to print up a counteraddress.[8] Nothing seems to have been left out of Beckley's calculations, and he himself was confident that the die had been cast. The identity of the Republican ticket had leaked out by the first week in October, but Beckley was either anticipating the disappointment of his workers or merely telling the truth when he said that it was too late for the Federalists to change their ticket. "The aristocrats themselves say that the Republican ticket is best, and believe it will carry," he wrote.[9]

"The Federal and Republican Ticket," framed by the Federalists just before the Pennsylvania Assembly rose in July and released in late September, was singularly lacking in significant names. Most were undoubtedly locally prominent, and three were selected with an eye to catching the German vote;[10] but not a single Federalist elector had the state-wide or national prominence of Peter Muhlenberg, William Irvine, William Maclay, or Justice McKean. Federalist editor John Ward Fenno might curse his opponents for their unfair and unsportsmanlike behavior in labeling the Federalist ticket "Monarchist" while calling themselves "Republican," and he might truthfully question the democratic character of Thomas McKean—"Who is the plain, simple republican and who the haughty, imperious monarchist—Israel Whelen or Thomas McKean?"[11] But there was no denying the fact that the Federalists had been outsmarted or that McKean's name would be better known to the voter than Whelen's. The tactics used successfully by Burr in defeating the New York Hamiltonian ticket in 1800 were exactly those used by John Beckley in 1796, secrecy and famous names, and the Federalists of Pennsylvania were con-

[8] Beckley to Irvine, October 4, 1796; *Irvine Papers,* XIII, No. 115.

[9] *Ibid.*

[10] Henry Wynkoop, John Arndt, and Valentine Eckhart. See Appendix B. *Claypoole's American Daily Advertiser,* November 4, 1796.

[11] *Gazette of the United States,* November 4, 1796.

fronted with the same problem that suddenly faced Hamilton in the spring of 1800. They were forced to fight with swords of wood while their opponents fought with iron.

By late October the Republican campaign workers were ready for the final push. Word came from party headquarters that "select republican friends" from Philadelphia were to be sent out bearing parcels of six to eight thousand tickets for distribution in each county. County leaders were asked to aid. Lest the voters have short memories or be unable to write, it was thought advisable to have the ballots filled out before election day. Beckley added one last bit of encouragement, in keeping with what he had been using as an inducement to labor all fall. Returns from the recent elections for House seats show Republican gains, he said. Frederick Muhlenberg had been defeated and Representative Swanwicke reelected despite spirited Federalist opposition.[12]

County Republicans responded in grand style. From W. H. Beaumont of Washington, Pennsylvania, Albert Gallatin received word that Judge Hugh Henry Brackenridge, early American novelist and college classmate of Madison, Giles, and Burr, was doing everything possible at Pittsburg to defeat the Federalists, who had been in power there ever since the revulsion against the Whiskey Rebellion. In other quarters in the west, William Findley was campaigning actively for Jefferson in an effort to make up for his sudden disappearance when the final vote came on the Jay treaty. The address to the people mentioned by Beckley to Irvine had found its way across the Alleghenies and was to be printed with the electoral ticket just a week before election day. "Washington County will do its duty on the approaching occasion," promised Beaumont.[13]

In accordance with Republican campaign needs Pierre

[12] Beckley to Irvine, Philadelphia, October 17, 1796; *Irvine Papers*, XIII, No. 116.

[13] October 24, 1796; *Gallatin Papers*, New York Historical Society, Box 4, 1796, No. 20.

Adet came through with his belligerent demands for a return to justice. Chauncey Goodrich noted with disgust that many voters were wearing red, white, and blue French cockades in their caps as they marched to the polls.[14] Two days before election, Beckley sent Irvine his last-minute estimate of the situation as he saw it in Philadelphia. Both parties were equally active and sanguine, he admitted. Republican hopes rested finally on returns from the western counties. We anticipate victory in the city and county of Philadelphia, some losses in the middle counties, wrote Beckley, and if all goes well the victory in the west which will tip the scale.[15]

Pennsylvania voters were confronted with two tickets of fifteen names each. Only one name appeared on both ballots, that of Samuel Miles, who had been settled on finally by the Republicans as the substitute for Governor Mifflin, even though his name had already appeared on the Federalist ticket.[16] At the polls voters were expected to choose fifteen men regardless of party. This was theory, but the returns show that the straight ticket vote was generally preferred. In the city of Philadelphia each of the fifteen men on the Republican ticket won by about 650 votes over the Federalist electoral candidates, and in Philadelphia County, where there was even less deviation from the average figure of Republicans over Federalists, the margin was approximately 1,430 votes.[17] The same amazing uniformity may be seen in the Chester County returns, where the Federalist ticket was victorious. No Federalist, including Thomas Bull who lived in Chester County, won by a margin of more than 415 or less than 408 votes.[18] Here is conclusive evidence of

[14] To Governor Wolcott, November 15, 1796; Gibbs, I, 394.

[15] November 2, 1796; *Irvine Papers,* XIII, No. 117. See H. M. Tinkcom, "Political Behavior in Pennsylvania, 1790–1801," (University of Pennsylvania doctoral dissertation, 1948), 320-322.

[16] *Claypoole's American Daily Advertiser,* November 25, 1796. See Appendix C.

[17] *Ibid.,* November 7, 1796.

[18] *Ibid.,* November 9, 1796.

the high point of development that these two parties had reached in Pennsylvania and equally conclusive evidence that the voters were choosing between parties and not between individuals on the ticket.

On November 18 Governor Mifflin was supposed to announce the official results and proclaim the fifteen men receiving the highest votes as the electors who would meet at Harrisburg on December 7. When the day for the announcement arrived, results from three western counties had not been delivered. Greene, Fayette, and Westmoreland County returns were in utter confusion, and it was known that the outcome would be close. If Mifflin proclaimed the electors without the results of these three counties included, the Federalists would have had the majority.[19] To delay meant charges of trickery, for it was probable that the western counties would tip the scale. Mifflin was in a ticklish spot and finally turned the matter over to the state supreme court, which decided after a week's delay to announce the winners without the figures from Greene County. Thirteen Republicans, Samuel Miles, and one Federalist, Robert Coleman of Lancaster, were named.[20] Miles and Coleman had received the smallest number of votes of the fifteen, but the margin of victory in each case was astoundingly close. Judge McKean, who headed the list, had but 235 votes more than his nearest competitor, and the average margin was but 85 votes.[21]

The charges of conspiracy that Mifflin must have feared were numerous. Oliver Wolcott, Jr., was certain that Alexander Dallas, "the real Governor," was deliberately holding back the returns, "hoping to rise to power by bringing on a disputed election." [22] Dallas as Secretary of State of the commonwealth received the official results from each county to be certified and handed on to the Governor. He was known

[19] Tinkcom, "Political Behavior in Pennsylvania," 315-316.

[20] *Claypoole's American Daily Advertiser*, November 25, 1796.

[21] Tinkcom, *op. cit.*, 318.

[22] To Governor Wolcott, November 27, 1796; Gibbs, *Memoirs*, I, 400.

to be a strong partisan of Jefferson, had been implicated in Randolph's supposed treason, and had taken a leading part in Republican politics in Pennsylvania until the election of 1796. He had opposed Beckley's plan for using the Jay treaty as an issue in the election and had wiped his hands of all responsibility for the outcome in Pennsylvania. The angry Beckley had called him politically suspect as a result.[23] Whether Wolcott's charges were reasonable is doubtful. Uriah Tracy, also of Connecticut, thought Mifflin himself was playing a dishonest game in an attempt to give Jefferson the entire fifteen votes.[24]

The final results in Pennsylvania showed that the Republican ticket had been carried in fourteen counties and the Federalist in the remaining ten.[25] As Beckley had surmised, it was Philadelphia and the surrounding counties plus the western vote that spelled victory. The Adams ticket had been preferred in Chester, Delaware, York, Bucks, Montgomery, Lancaster, Dauphin, Luzerne, Huntingdon, and Somerset counties. Official returns printed on November 15 gave the Federalists a margin of 927 votes over their opponents, but when the votes from two of the missing three western counties were added in, the Republicans were found to have picked up enough ground to pass their rivals on the popular vote. On the basis of electoral strength the victory for Jefferson looked decisive and seemed to be the neatest coup of 1796. In popular vote it was anything but decisive.

The citizens of Pennsylvania had given Jefferson a popular margin equal to half of 1 per cent of the total vote cast: the Republican ticket 12,306 and the Federalist ticket 12,181.[26] Despite the exertions of both parties and the proximity of the halls of Congress where so many bitter debates had taken

[23] Tinkcom, "Political Behavior in Pennsylvania," 313; Raymond Walters, *Alexander J. Dallas*, 72-75.

[24] To Governor Wolcott, December 6, 1796; Gibbs, *Memoirs*, I, 407.

[25] *Claypoole's American Daily Advertiser*, November 12, 15, 25, 1796.

[26] *Claypoole's American Daily Advertiser*, November 25, 1796.

place that year, in spite of the Whiskey Rebellion, the Jay treaty, and the first chance to vote for a candidate opposed to the principles of Federalism with some chance of success, the citizenry were comparatively lethargic in getting to the polls. More than thirty-one thousand votes had been cast for gubernatorial candidates in 1796, even though there was almost no opposition to Mifflin.[27] In fact, the average turnout for Mr. Mifflin's re-election in the years 1790 to 1796 was thirty-two thousand, but for the two presidential contests of 1792 and 1796 an average of only 24,420 had taken the trouble to vote.[28] Despite the fact that the newspapers had shown far more interest in the Adams-Jefferson election than in Washington's second contest, the people showed little more. It is impossible to view the results as evidence of rising democratic sympathies among the people. Why such apathy? Mr. Tinkcom in his analysis of the Pennsylvania story suggests that the indirect method of election and the fact that the voters were kept in the dark as to candidates until the last few days before election accounts for the low vote.[29] Both reasons seem valid, though the second is open to question in the light of Beckley's work in circulating his slate. Is it possible that the men who held the information neglected to tell their neighbors who the presidential candidates were? Republicans began to spread their propaganda in early October so that even a far western committeeman could write Gallatin two weeks before election day that campaigners were already at work in the most far-flung corners of the state.

The answer to this question, vital to the understanding of politics in the early days of the Republic, is that the colonial legacy was far more important than the influence of the French Revolution. The average voter was still thinking in provincial terms: about Virginia, or Massachusetts, or Penn-

[27] Figures among Gallatin's private papers, New York Historical Society, Box 4, 1796, No. 23.

[28] Tinkcom, "Political Behavior in Pennsylvania," 324.

[29] *Ibid.*, 325.

sylvania, and not about the Union and its management. In setting up the electoral machinery in most states the politicians realized this. Men were called upon to vote for their neighbors and not for Washington, Adams, or Jefferson. Beckley himself was delighted with the strong ticket he and his friends had been able to assemble, just as Burr was when he topped off his own slate with Clinton and Gates in 1800. Why were they so delighted with their handiwork if not out of the realization that the voters would support the locally prominent? These were outstanding local figures who would vote for Jefferson and not the Rights of Man personified.

Finally, there is this consideration. For twelve straight years the supposedly aristocratic, monarchical, and overbearing Federalists controlled the Federal government. When the means were at hand to end their domination the public did not rise up and do so. The men who took an active part in the political life of the 1790's were not all rich or all poor. They were probably more wealthy on the average than men in public life since Jackson's day, but what leads us to set down as a cardinal tenet of historical faith that the Federalists were a group of wealthy men serving in politics? Again, was Jefferson less an aristocrat than Washington? Hamilton more of an aristocrat in the eyes of the public than Madison? John Adams more so than Aaron Burr? In matters of theory there were differences, and the theories were and still are important, but the man on the street or in the field in 1796 could see for himself. In matters of houses, slaves, clothing, and wines for the table there was no great difference. Well might John Fenno ask, "Who is the simple republican and who the haughty aristocrat, Israel Whelen or Thomas McKean?" When it seemed expedient the Republicans could champion a McKean or a John Taylor just as under trying circumstances New York Federalists could back a friend of the artisans and mechanics in order to defeat young Edward

Livingston or thunder against unequal representation in the Virginia legislature. Perhaps to the voters of 1796 there was not so much difference between Republicans and Federalists after all. They had to be educated to these differences in theory and rights. The educational process had not yet made its impression; perhaps it never has. It seems a simple answer to the question of political feelings to scan the wrinkled pages of eighteenth-century newspapers. According to certain prominent histories of the 1790's men were wildly angry over the Jay treaty, the Livingston resolution fight, the Alien and Sedition Acts, and the election of Jefferson. But what men? And what newspapers are we looking at when we describe the "marching mobs" and the burnings of Mr. Jay in effigy? Bache's *Aurora* and the *Independent Chronicle* suggest public fury, but the New London *Gazette* and Annapolis *Gazette* suggest public apathy.

The results in Pennsylvania came as a distinct shock to Federalists everywhere, while Republicans were jubilant. Oliver Wolcott, Jr., all but gave up the ghost even before Mifflin had officially announced the results. "The election of Mr. Jefferson I consider as fatal to our independence now that the interference of a foreign power in our affairs is no longer disguised," he wrote on November 19.[30] He considered the defeat due to "too much Toryism on the one hand, and too much democracy on the other," but it had been that infernal French Minister who was most responsible. "If Mr. Jefferson is elected it will be owing entirely to the influence of his [Adet's] paper." Wolcott was inclined to easy pessimism, however. When the official electors were announced he wrote his father gloomily that one of the two Federalists was of doubtful loyalty. He could not blame the western counties for going Republican—they were at least consistent—but the silly Quakers had been bought off. Many influential men, he testified, had changed their votes when Adet's

[30] To Governor Wolcott, November 19, 1796; Gibbs, *Memoirs*, I, 396.

notes pointed to Jefferson as the man who could save us from war. Philadelphia had been bullied.[31]

Fisher Ames was equally disconcerted: "I have supposed that Pennsylvania held the balance, and I am sorry to infer from the votes of Philadelphia that it will be wrongly inclined." [32] Chauncey Goodrich, on the other hand, was defiant. "This government yet rests on New England prudence and firmness; it is a tower that hitherto has abode in strength under the smiles of a good Providence, and I confidently believe that it will not hereafter disappoint the wishes and hopes of the virtuous." He wondered what Providence had in store for Pennsylvania. The yellow fever, he remarked, had struck the last two times Pennsylvania had gone wrong, during the Genêt alarm and during the Whiskey Rebellion.[33] John Adams declared at the end of his administration that Pennsylvania, along with New York and South Carolina, had "much guilt to answer for." [34] In 1796 he dismissed the Pennsylvania upset with one terse statement to his wife; "Adet's note had some effect in Pennsylvania and proved a terror to some Quakers; and that is all the ill effect it has had." [35]

If the testimonies of Wolcott and Adams are correct, the Adet notes may be said to have produced precisely the results that were intended for them. James Madison, who had no connection with the maneuvering that brought the French Minister into the political battle, was both alarmed and indignant over Adet's action when he first heard of it. "Adet's note . . . is working all the evil with which it is pregnant," he wrote Jefferson on December 5. "Those who rejoice at its indiscretions and are taking advantage of them have the im-

[31] November 27, 1796; *ibid.*, 401.

[32] Ames to Wolcott, Jr., November 14, 1796; *ibid.*, 393.

[33] Goodrich to Governor Wolcott, November 15, 1796; Gibbs, *Memoirs*, I, 394-395.

[34] Adams to Francis Van der Kemp, July 26, 1802; Adams, *Letters*, Historical Society of Pennsylvania, No. 31.

[35] December 12, 1796; Adams, *Works*, I, 495.

pudence to pretend that it is an electioneering maneuver, and that the French Government have been led into it by the opponents of the British treaty." [36]

In this case Madison's opponents had better sources of information about the movements of his political allies than he did. The Republican party's friendship for France would one day prove a dangerous liability, but in December, 1796, it had rewarded a resourceful and unscrupulous political captain with the necessary means for political revolution. Beckley's victory all but disrupted the Federalist party, already wracked by internal fevers.

[36] December 5, 1796, *Madison Papers*, LC.

9

Discontent with Hamilton

THE OUTCOME OF THE PENNSYLVANIA ELECTION SEEMED TO confirm what Hamilton and his friends had been warning the New Englanders of from the beginning—Pinckney would have to be supported on the second ballot for fear that Adams would fail on the first. After Beckley's coup it indeed seemed that there was no other safe way of keeping Jefferson in private life.

As soon as Hamilton received the news from Philadelphia he dispatched one last appeal to his friends in Massachusetts and Connecticut, urging them to support the straight ticket and to waste no votes.[1] It soon appeared that there was need for disciplining the New Jersey camp as well.

Jonathan Dayton was deeply disturbed by the results in his neighboring state and was wondering whether there might not still be a chance for Burr. His desperate letters to Representative Theodore Sedgwick of Massachusetts reveal how little cohesion existed between the various branches of the Federalist party as late as three weeks before election day. If he was only playing a game with the New Englanders it is still significant that he should have thought it worthwhile to make advances so late.

[1] Stephen Higginson to Hamilton, December 9, 1796, *Hamilton Papers*, LC. Higginson, Customs Collector for the Port of Boston and a man who owed his Treasury Department appointment to Hamilton and Wolcott, Jr., served as a valuable link between Hamilton's New York circle and the Essex Junto. In writing to Hamilton he mentioned Hamilton's circular letter of November 28, 1796.

We all agree that Jefferson is the man to beat and Adams the man to beat him with, he wrote. Unfortunately, it appeared that Mr. Adams' chances were slipping. Jefferson and Pinckney would certainly take the entire Southern vote, and Pennsylvania would cancel out whatever Massachusetts and New Jersey might produce. It also appeared that Senator Burr would have some support in each section of the country. Dayton asked Sedgwick to relay the observations of his Massachusetts friends at once and to suggest some plan whereby Jefferson might still be kept from office. The New Jersey Congressman appeared to be in deadly earnest. He was growing so perturbed that on the next day he dispatched a second letter to Sedgwick, with whom he seems to have been particularly intimate. "Every moment's reflection serves to impress on me the importance of fixing upon some plan of co-operation. . . . If Mr. Adams cannot succeed, is it not desirable to have at the helm a man who is personally known to, as well as esteemed by us both," Dayton asked.[2]

Sedgwick posted a reply a week later. His advice was to adhere to the original plan of supporting Adams and Pinckney equally. Pennsylvania, he wrote, had turned out badly but might not be entirely lost. The greatest danger was that a tie might result that would throw the election into the House of Representatives, where Jefferson would be certain of victory. As he saw the situation, Federalists could be confident of the entire New England vote, of New York, and of at least twelve more electors south of the Delaware. With apparent sincerity Sedgwick added, "If Pinckney is elected over Adams, it will be a constitutional mischief." Concerning Dayton's obvious references to Burr, Sedgwick was blunt. Burr would not receive the support of his party, because they did not trust him. Recall, he said, how the Republicans had fought for Monroe's nomination as Minister to France when

[2] November 12, 13, 1796, *Hamilton Papers*, LC.

it became known that Senator Burr wanted the post. "They dread his independence of them." [3]

There were no secrets between Theodore Sedgwick and Alexander Hamilton, nor can there be any reasonable doubt that Sedgwick was insincere in his expressed desire to see Adams elected. On the same day that he replied to Dayton, Sedgwick mailed both of Dayton's letters to Hamilton. "I need not say," he cautioned, "that this information must be kept secret. . . . Dayton would doubtless deem it a breach of confidence." [4]

By election day the existence of a plot within the Federalist party to elect Thomas Pinckney was generally accepted by leading political figures. Joseph Jones of Virginia wrote to Madison of the prevelant belief that Jay and Hamilton were deliberately attempting to keep Adams from the presidency. He assured Madison that the electors had all been instructed as to the dangers of giving their second votes to Pinckney and "to turn their attention to some other person." Pinckney, he thought, would lack the independence of mind that both Jefferson and Adams possessed.[5]

John Adams was likewise convinced that there were powerful forces within his party that were determined to keep him from the presidency, and he had no doubts as to the man responsible for the intrigue. "If Colonel Hamilton's personal dislike of Jefferson does not obtain too much influence with Massachusetts electors, neither Jefferson will be President, nor Pinckney Vice President," he wrote his wife just after the electoral vote had been cast. "I am not enough of an Englishman, nor little enough of a Frenchman to please some people. These would be very willing that Pinckney should become chief. But they will be disappointed. I find nobody here intimidated. . . . The southern gentlemen with whom I have

[3] November 19, 1796, *ibid.*
[4] Dayton to Hamilton, November 19, 1796, *ibid.*
[5] Jones to Madison, December 9, 1796, *Madison Papers*, LC.

conversed have expressed more affection for me than they ever did before since 1774. They certainly wish Adams elected rather than Pinckney. Perhaps it is because Hamilton and Jay are said to be for Pinckney." [6]

In New England where Hamilton's and Wolcott's exertions had steadfastly been aimed at uniformity on the two ballots, the Pinckney scheme met its end. Sectional pride, loyalty to Adams, and mistrust of Hamilton on the part of the secondary leaders of the party denied Thomas Pinckney the eighteen votes that would have made him President. While John Adams was confidently supported by the entire electoral college strength of New England, the South Carolina diplomat was hesitantly supported by only twenty-one.

The fears of the electors caused the defeat, according to Boston's Stephen Higginson. Hamilton's letter of the previous week had prevented many from throwing their votes away, he told Hamilton two days after the election, but three Massachusetts electors had refused to be kept in line. Many of us, he admitted, were worried lest Pinckney come too close. In that case the Adams men would certainly have weeded the Pinckney supporters out of the patronage lists, Higginson himself being collector of the port of Boston. "Should Adams fail, as I expect, some attempt should be made to appease him." Higginson suggested that Hamilton, Jay, and Washington give this matter serious consideration. Higginson was apparently trying to soften the blow when he concluded by pointing out that Burr had met with no success in Massachusetts whatsoever. Even Elbridge Gerry, who had been singled out for special attention from the Burr campaign workers, refused to throw his vote to the New York Senator.[7]

The returns from New Hampshire were the worst disappointment of all for the Hamiltonians. The entire second vote

[6] December 12, 1796; Adams, *Works,* I, 495-496.

[7] Higginson to Hamilton, December 9, 1796, *Hamilton Papers,* LC.

had been thrown to Connecticut's favorite son, Chief Justice Oliver Ellsworth. Vermont stayed in line, but the electors of Connecticut matched those from Virginia in their purposeful desertion of party discipline. Governor Wolcott explained to his son how it came about, but he made no apologies for dropping Pinckney and showed no indication that anyone had even hoped to support Hamilton's favorite.

We met in great confusion, said Wolcott, because no one had heard last-minute returns from the Southern states. With the hope that news might arrive during the day, the electors had decided to put off the vote until late evening. By afternoon it was thought best to vote according to what Massachusetts had done, for it was probable that enough second votes had been scattered by the Massachusetts electors to put Jefferson in office. Unfortunately, no word came through from Boston or anywhere else, and the electors at Hartford concluded that the risk of electing Jefferson Vice-President was less than that of allowing Pinckney to supplant Adams. The result was that Connecticut scattered five second votes and added its sin of omission to those which denied a respectable man the vice-presidency.[8]

The story was much the same in Rhode Island, and the entire vote of the Southern states that had been so confidently spoken of in the fall amounted to three from Delaware, four from Maryland, one from Virginia, one from North Carolina, and the eight of South Carolina. Georgia and the frontier contributed nothing to Pinckney's chances. In the same area Jefferson had collected fifty-four votes and Aaron Burr seventeen. Oddly enough, the only state that gave the Hamiltonian favorite more votes than anticipated was Pennsylvania. There Samuel Miles attempted to keep a foot in each camp by casting his first ballot for Jefferson and his second for Pinckney.

[8] Wolcott, Sr., to Wolcott, Jr., December 9, 1796, Gibbs, *Memoirs*, I, 408.

If Pinckney suffered at the hands of his party, Burr was even more roughly handled. His campaign was covered in secrecy and probably was not extensive. Higginson mentioned that Judge Melancthon Smith of New York had attempted to stir up interest for Burr in Massachusetts, but aside from this sole reference to his campaign in New England, no one seems to have given him much hope in that quarter.[9] Pennsylvania Republicans showed surprising independence in giving him all thirteen of their votes, and in Maryland Burr received only one less vote than Jefferson when an Adams elector dropped Pinckney for Jefferson on the second ballot.

That Virginia's powerful Republican organization feared Burr far more than they did Adams is demonstrated by their neglect of his fortunes to the tune of nineteen electoral votes. One Republican in the electoral college stood by the alleged party candidate, while fifteen were wasted upon Sam Adams, three on George Clinton, and one on Washington. It is beyond question that this design was prearranged.

There was no exchange of letters between Burr and Jefferson or Madison during the summer and early fall, and so completely in the dark was Madison concerning Burr's activities that he called upon John Beckley to check up. In June Beckley reported that Albert Gallatin and David Rittenhouse were working for Burr in Pennsylvania, Robert Livingston for him in New York, and Congressmen Blount, Brown, and Cocke in Kentucky and Tennessee. "North Carolina and Georgia you know to be fixed," added Beckley; and by "fixed" he must have meant told to drop Burr, for in Georgia no votes were cast for him, and in North Carolina five Republicans wasted their second votes.[10]

[9] Higginson to Hamilton, December 9, 1796, *Hamilton Papers*, LC, *op. cit.*

[10] Beckley to Madison, June 20, 1796, *Madison Papers*, NYPL; The astronomer David Rittenhouse had been named to the Republican electoral ticket before his death in the summer of 1796. Mifflin at first agreed to take his place, but at the last moment declined. Beckley to William Irvine,

What right the Jeffersonians had to be shouting "Cataline" at Burr when he refused to hand the presidency over to Jefferson in 1800 appears doubtful. He had been betrayed in 1796, and apparently by orders from the top. John Taylor, planter, political philosopher, and close friend to Jefferson and Madison was chosen an elector in 1796. A few weeks after the election he disclosed to Senator Henry Tazewell that he had been "compelled reluctantly to sacrifice Burr."[11] Who there was in the Virginia organization besides Jefferson and Madison who could have "compelled" Taylor to vote against his own wishes it is difficult to see.

Perhaps personalities clashed when Burr met with Jefferson in 1795 at Monticello, but it is clear that the basic cause for Southern desertion of Burr was mistrust of his loyalties and political beliefs. He was known to be confidential with the none too savory Jonathan Dayton of New Jersey, half Federalist, half Republican; and at the very time that Burr was en route to Monticello leaders of both parties in New York were considering him as Clinton's successor in the governorship.[12] It is a fair assumption that Madison and Jefferson knew of this last fact, for their sources of information from New York were excellent. Their obvious fear of him was built upon something more substantial than unfounded rumor.

It is worth mentioning that President Adams wished to commission Burr a brigadier general in 1798, one of the few Republican politicians he considered for high rank. Either Adams was thinking of Burr's anger over the election of 1796 or he recognized that Burr had never been a party stalwart. Dayton was also on the list.

In 1800 Albert Gallatin asked his wife, the daughter of

September 22, 1796, *Irvine Papers*, Historical Society of Pennsylvania, XIII, No. 113.

[11] H. H. Simms, *Life of John Taylor* (Richmond, 1932), 64.

[12] J. B. Hammond, *Political Parties in New York*, I, 90.

James Nicholson, one of Burr's lieutenants in the new Tammany organization, to find out just how deeply the wound of 1796 had gone. "Papa has answered your question about the candidate for the Vice President [Burr]," she wrote. "Burr says he has no confidence in the Virginians; they once deceived him, and they are not to be trusted." [13] Aaron Burr managed to hide his feelings well, but the election of 1796 did not leave the Republican party without the serious danger of a future schism.

A week after the electoral colleges had met, John Beckley was sure that Jefferson had lost the presidency. "After all our exertions I fear Jefferson will fail altogether," he confided to General Irvine, "and that Adams and Pinckney will be, one of them President, the other Vice President." Returns from Massachusetts, Connecticut, New Jersey, Pennsylvania, Maryland, and Virginia showed Jefferson lagging behind Adams and Pinckney by sixteen and six votes respectively.[14]

Two days before Christmas, however, the two crucial states of New Hampshire and South Carolina reported in, and the word spread that Jefferson had moved ahead of Pinckney.[15] The refusal of New Hampshire's six electors to fall in with the Hamiltonian ticket had made the difference. Jefferson heard of it with relief, but his Pennsylvania friends remained downcast.[16] "John Adams has just saved his distance and Jefferson is Vice President and it is said will except [accept]," wrote George Wilson to William Irvine. "I say with Pope, 'What is right.' " [17]

When it became apparent that as a result of the sweep in Pennsylvania he might be chosen to office, Jefferson sent Madison instructions that four years later he could never have written: he made a candid plea for Adams's election. I

[13] May 7, 1800, Adams, *Albert Gallatin*, 243.

[14] December 16, 1796, *Irvine Papers*, XIII, No. 119.

[15] Gibbs, *Memoirs*, I, 414.

[16] Jefferson to Archibald Stuart, January 4, 1797, *Jefferson Papers*, LC.

[17] Philadelphia, January 4, 1797, *Irvine Papers*, XIII, No. 92.

had hoped that you might be the Republican candidate, he began. "There is nothing I so anxiously hope as that my name may come out either second or third . . . the last would leave me at home the whole year and the other two-thirds of it." Republicans had come through the election with greater success than he had anticipated, said Jefferson. "I have no expectation that the Eastern states will suffer themselves to be so much outwitted as to be made the tools for bringing in Pinckney instead of Adams."

Jefferson, with obvious sincerity, asked that Madison make his position clear about the election: he wanted Adams to be President and in the event of a tie, wanted Republicans in Congress to vote for Adams. "He has always been my senior," was Jefferson's simple explanation.[18]

Nothing could more conclusively demonstrate the importance of honor and friendship in the political relations of the eighteenth century. Nothing could more clearly demonstrate that the virulence of party feelings in the 1790's has been taken too often at its face value. The true bitterness of politics did not develop until 1798 when Jefferson began to take hold of his party with the determination to win the next election. In January, 1797, his confidence in Adams was strong enough to cause him to brush theories of government aside. How Adams would react to Jefferson's generosity was characteristic of the man. He could be warmhearted, forgiving, and so impulsive as to throw his party into a momentary panic.

The outcome of the election was a victory for the Federalists by a margin of three votes. Each of these votes has been located. Fisher Ames noted in passing through North Carolina that one elector was pledged to John Adams, and the single votes in Pennsylvania and Virginia were cast by men who had canvassed as Federalists. Thus John Adams was not

[18] December 17, 1796, *Jefferson Papers*, LC.

President by accident as many historians have concluded.[19] Jefferson received every electoral vote that was pledged to him, so far as can be discovered. Mr. Cousens (*Politics and Political Organizations*, p. 90) maintained that two electors, one a Federalist and one a Republican, made no choice; but the figures given in the *Annals* show that every vote was cast on both ballots.[20]

If there was any accident involved in Mr. Adams's election it is to be found in Maryland, where one elector cast a vote for each of the presidential candidates, or in Pennsylvania, where the Greene County returns might have given the Republicans a safe fifteen votes. There is no way of proving whether the Maryland elector was originally a Republican or a Federalist. The better guess is that he had been pledged to Adams, though William Vans Murray in suggesting this was naturally optimistic for the Federalists.[21] According to a report that Jefferson received in January the one Adams elector from Pennsylvania would not have been announced had the Greene County returns been unsnarled in time. Governor Mifflin, it was said, had decided to say nothing about the final results there when it was seen that Adams would win the election by one vote anyway. He added that Powell's vote from Virginia fortunately threw out the question of a disputed election regardless of Greene County.[22]

A sectional breakdown of the vote reveals the weakness of the Republican party in New England, New York, and New Jersey and the inability of the Federalists to penetrate the deep South and Southwest. It reveals that Pinckney lost the presidency because of New England's desertion of the Hamiltonian ticket, and that Senator Burr lost the votes that would

19 Even the cautious Edward Channing spoke of Adams as President "by accident." *History*, IV, 170.

20 See Appendix D.

21 *Supra*, pp. 161-162.

22 To T. M. Randolph, January 9, 1797, *Jefferson Papers*, LC.

have brought him within one or two votes of Pinckney's total because of the suspicions of Republican electors in the Southern states. Twenty-eight electoral votes were wasted on Republican candidates, all of them in states south of the Delaware. The Federalists threw away twenty votes, eighteen in New England and two in Southern states. Sectionalism reveals itself the most influential factor in the election and as a far more compelling force than party loyalty.

The fact that New England delivered twenty-one votes to Pinckney while the South, including Delaware, gave him but one less, suggests the strength of Hamilton's influence and the existence of a feeling that may be termed national party loyalty. On the other hand, Murray's plea for united action and Dayton's proposals so late in the campaign suggest that party development had not reached a very advanced stage. The confusion as to what other states would do expressed by Governor Wolcott in his letter to his son may have been the attempt to cover up actual design, but the large number of votes wasted in a section that was the stronghold of Federalism shows how loose party organization was and how easily the secondary leaders could cast aside the directions of the party's political chief.

Much the same is true of the Republicans. Their actions during the House appropriations fight were national in scope rather than regional just as the Federalist counterattack was. On the other hand, the fact that Madison, who was the party's chief spokesman on the national level, was doubtful concerning the wisdom of the attack against the treaty and completely in the dark so far as Adet's interference was concerned points to the freedom allowed secondary leaders such as John Beckley in influencing national strategy. One of the principal reasons that Republicans lacked unity was that Madison had withdrawn too far from party councils after the adjournment of Congress. His personal life seems to have taken precedence over his political life at the time. When offered the governorship of Virginia almost unanimously, he refused it. Dolly Madison and his estate thrust themselves between him and the direction of the campaign.[23]

Nevertheless, Madison's contribution to the strong showing made by the Republicans in 1796 was great. Largely through his efforts, Jefferson had been prevented from withdrawing; Madison had done his utmost to soften the blow that his colleagues in the House had aimed primarily at Washington in making their onslaught against the Jay treaty, and it was obviously bad politics to throw Washington's popularity into the election picture any further than was absolutely necessary. No Republican of his stature took over the direction of the national campaign in the decisive last three months. Possibly only Jefferson could have filled the breach, and he would say and do nothing for himself. Perhaps the freedom allowed to secondary party leaders benefited the Republicans momentarily. Jefferson or Madison would have discouraged using Pierre Adet in the campaign, and it is clear that the fears occasioned by his notes greatly helped the Republican cause in Pennsylvania.

In the final analysis, the outstanding cause for Republican failure to capture the executive department may be assigned to the Jay treaty strategy. Public anger against the administration was reversed in many areas as a result of the assault touched off by Edward Livingston. Had the situation been left alone the state elections of 1796 would have reflected public discontent. New York and Maryland were apparently ready to turn toward the Republican party until the Republicans in the House galvanized the Federalists into action. Federalists were able to turn once more to the popularity and prestige of Washington as a result of the Republican program. Both Washington and Hamilton saw the value of keeping the President before the public until the last minute and cleverly did so.

[23] Brant, *Madison*, 445.

It would be difficult to see how the Federalist party could have won the election by a wider margin. Perhaps in accepting the candidacy of Adams in the first place Hamilton and his friends made a mistake, but the step seems to have been unavoidable. According to eighteenth-century standards Adams had a claim to the office, he was on the scene, and he had tremendous popularity in New England. Fisher Ames, George Cabot, and Christopher Gore were great admirers of Hamilton, but they wanted Adams to be President nevertheless.

The worst blunder that Hamilton made was in championing Pinckney as a presidential candidate. It was in the long run a more fatal mistake than any that the Republicans committed, for it brought Adams into office fully prepared for a showdown with Hamilton and ready to split the party in the process. Adams was well aware that many prominent Federalists had preferred Pinckney to himself, and in the four years that followed he showed no sign of having forgiven or forgotten. Hamiltonians were not appointed to offices within his control, and the thorny problem that arose in 1798 over Hamilton's army appointment finally began the split within the Federalist party that allowed Jefferson his triumph of 1800

Hamilton badly miscalculated the sentiments of the Adams men when he thrust his hand-picked candidate unhesitatingly at them. Without his backing Pinckney would never have been a candidate, but with it Thomas Pinckney became the helpless instrument of party schism. Furthermore, the South Carolinian would have run a better race without the "letters eastward" that put Adams supporters on the defensive. This is the worst condemnation of Hamilton as a politician that can be made. As a political chief he showed up poorly in 1796.

Representative Goodrich of Connecticut denied that Hamilton had attempted to bring Pinckney in ahead of Adams but recognized that the belief had gained such credence as seriously to impair the party's strength. He saw in the anger of Southern Federalists over what they termed New England's desertion a sore point for the future. Like many of the Hamiltonians, he never stopped to think that the coin might be reversed. If the Southerners were angry with New England, he wrote to Governor Wolcott, imagine how Burr's friends must feel about Virginia political faith.[24] Pierre Adet was only trying to make a bad situation look bright when he consoled his government with the remark: "It is not without chagrin that Hamilton and his party see Adams arrive at the presidency. Pinckney was the man of their choice." [25] A few weeks later the Directory gave unmistakable proof of their disdain for the new administration.[26]

Hamilton's reaction to the outcome was one which showed that he took no part of the blame for Jefferson's election upon himself. At least he would not do so openly. New England, he told Rufus King, was responsible for Jefferson's election as Vice-President. According to Hamilton, the most important consequence of the election was the desertion of Burr by the Virginians.[27]

From where he sat Oliver Wolcott, Jr., viewed the election as a disaster. He feared Jefferson more as Vice-President than as President, he confided to his father, for Jefferson would be in an excellent position to undermine and divide the administration.[28] Young Wolcott was pessimistic over his future and had been thinking since June of the calamities that could befall his party and his country. "It is folly," he said, "to suppose that this government can be long adminis-

[24] December 17, 1796, Gibbs, *Memoirs*, I, 412-413.

[25] December 15, 1796, *Correspondence of French Ministers*, 978.

[26] J. Q. Adams, to Abigail Adams, The Hague, February 8, 1797, *Writings*, II, 110. Young Adams laid C. C. Pinckney's rebuff to the outcome of the election.

[27] To King, December 16, 1796, Hamilton, *Works* (Lodge ed.), X, 216-217.

[28] November 27, 1796, Gibbs, *Memoirs*, I, 402.

tered against the opposition which now exists—either the people must change their representatives or change their government." [29]

The strongest and most bitter Federalist reaction to the election results came from Fisher Ames, and he did not hesitate to place the blame where he thought it belonged. What difference would it make if Federalists did control the Executive and the Senate so long as Republicans held the House, he asked Hamilton. "The heads of Departments are mere clerks . . . committees already are the ministers . . . What we call a government is a phantom so long as the Democrats prevail in the House. We expect confidently that the House of Representatives will act out of its character—for if it should act according to it, we are lost. Our government will be a mere democracy which has never been long tolerated."

Ames warmed to his subject as he went on. We need a republican government, he said, but instead move steadily towards a democratic one. "We are broken to pieces. Some able man of the first order of abilities and possessing the rare union of qualities that will fit him to lead a party is wanting. For want of such a leader many who would do good are useless." Secondary leaders in the party, he went on, tended to break away unless the pressure against them exerted by the opposition was strong enough to force unity upon them. While our number increase, our internal weaknesses multiply. "They cannot believe that its fair outside conceals such alarming weakness," Ames concluded in a letter that must have stung Hamilton as no letter on record did.[30] Ames speaks too well for himself to make further comment necessary. It is perhaps a tribute to Hamilton's self-confidence that he left it among his papers.[31]

Whatever John Adams felt about the election he kept to

[29] To William Heth (Heath) of Virginia, June 19, 1796, *ibid.*, 362.

[30] January 26, 1797, *Hamilton Papers*, LC.

[31] This remarkable letter has never been used in a secondary work to this writer's knowledge.

himself at first. Only his wife shared his anger with him in the first days after the election. In a letter that Adams wrote to his wife just after the full impact of his narrow victory had hit him he spoke of what he hoped would be the growing unpopularity of Hamilton, Jay, and their friends. The maneuver to squeeze Pinckney in ahead of him, he declared, was reacting unfortunately upon them. For his part, he would do everything possible to destroy their influence and power. "There is an active spirit in the Union who will fill it with his politics wherever he is. He must be attended to, and not suffered to do too much." [32]

On February 8 Mr. Adams, as President of the Senate, announced the official results of the electoral balloting and took leave of the men he had presided over for the first eight years of national life. In doing so he thanked his colleagues for allowing him the "independence of judgment which they asserted for themselves," and declared that he had "never had the smallest misunderstanding with any member of the Senate . . . ," a rare tribute to the good manners of the early Senators or an indication of poor memory on Adams's part.[33]

Washington washed his hands of twenty years of public life on the third of March by remitting the fine of a smuggler and pardoning ten men who had been convicted of treason during the Whiskey Rebellion.[34] What he was thinking in the last days of his administration would be worth quoting at length, but Washington lived up to his own advice in the Farewell Address by doing and saying nothing that might commit his feelings in any way. William Giles threw the last diatribe at him from Congress. "There are a thousand men in the United States who were capable of filling the presidential chair as well as it has been filled heretofore," and Benjamin Bache, who had never wavered in his support of

[32] December 12, 1796, Adams, *Works*, I, 496. There is no evidence that Jay took any part in pushing Pinckney's candidacy.

[33] *Ibid.*, VIII, 526.

[34] Washington, *Writings*, XXXV, 417.

Jefferson, expressed a sigh of relief to have Washington out of the way.[35]

Perhaps here and there a few men stopped to marvel at what took place on inauguration day. William Smith of South Carolina dropped his party mask for a few moments and looked admiringly at the drama that he had been privileged to witness. "The change of the Executive here has been wrought with a facility and a calm which has astonished even those of us who always augured well of the government and the general good sense of our citizens. The machine has worked without a creak. On the 4th of March John Adams was quietly sworn into office, George Washington attending as a private citizen. A few days after he went quietly home to Mt. Vernon; his successor as quietly took his place. . . ."[36]

[35] Marshall, *Life of Washington,* V, 723-724; *Aurora,* March 5, 1797.

[36] William Smith to Rufus King, April 3, 1797, King, *Life and Correspondence,* II, 167.

10

Adams and Jefferson: Friendship and Politics

JOHN ADAMS CONSIDERED HIS REVOLUTIONARY SERVICES AS meriting him the confidence of his fellow citizens, but the degree of their confidence was expressed in the three-vote margin by which he had defeated Jefferson. The contrast between Washington's two victories and his own was too obvious for Adams or anyone else to miss. Historians have not failed to realize that the humiliation that the second President felt when he took office had a direct bearing on his subsequent actions. The authors of one standard history have concluded that "to make the dose more unpalatable, since Jefferson stood second in the poll, Adams found himself yoked for a four year term with his most redoubtable foe as Vice President." [1] Let this be our point of departure.

When he realized how close the election of 1796 was going to be, Jefferson called upon James Madison to exert his influence for the selection of his rival and to make it clear that he wanted it that way. Perhaps he honestly considered Adams his senior and therefore deserving of the office, but Jefferson was human, too. He feared the war clouds rising up from Paris, and if his words reflect his convictions, he had no desire to be caught in the downpour that would follow Washington's retirement. "The President is fortunate to get off just as the bubble is bursting, leaving others to hold the bag. Yet, as his departure will mark the moment when the

[1] C. A. and Mary Beard, *The Rise of American Civilization*, rev. ed. (New York, 1942), 373.

difficulties begin to work, you will see that they will be ascribed to the new administration, and that he will have his usual good fortune of reaping credit from the good acts of others and leaving to them that of his errors."[2] Jefferson's willingness to let Adams have the presidency thus had two sides to it, but the public heard rumors of one only.

The French Minister at Philadelphia noted to his foreign office that the Republicans were showing little fear of the new President. The anti-Federalists, he wrote, believe that John Adams has changed many of his convictions and that he will not serve the British faction. An aristocrat in theory, he is a republican in practice; he loves the British form of government but detests the British people. He added that the new administration would be easier to attack, because the new President did not have the popularity of the old.[3]

While Fisher Ames noticed a change in the Republican attitude towards Adams, he ascribed it to no change in Adams' opinion of them. He had heard about the friendly letters Jefferson was writing and considered them sheer hyprocrisy. Why shouldn't Jefferson appear friendly, he sneered in writing to his friend Gore, he will be responsible for nothing, can be blamed for nothing, and all the while can be cultivating popularity with his pious declarations. He will end it all by stealing the chair away from Adams.[4]

From all appearances it seemed that Mr. Adams was going to grasp the extended hand of friendship. Benjamin Rush knew both men well, and he thought so. Congratulations on missing the presidency, he wrote Jefferson. You have just escaped reaping the harvest that "the New York Administration" has sowed. "Mr. Adams does you justice upon all occasions" and views the Pinckney scheme "in its proper

[2] January 4, 1797, *Jefferson Papers*, LC.

[3] December 15, 1796, *Correspondence of French Ministers*, 978-979.

[4] To Christopher Gore, December 17, 1796; quoted in McMaster, *History*, II, 307.

light." [5] Stephen Higginson reported to Hamilton that a political witch hunt had commenced in Massachusetts as soon as election returns were in. The Adams men held Hamilton and Jay responsible for Jefferson's victory and had begun to seek out all who had championed Pinckney. Some said that Adams knew everything and would turn to Jefferson in his anger, he said. Higginson, who must have been feeling nervous about his Federal berth, concluded that the uproar might lead to a fatal division within the party.[6]

From New York Rufus King received word that the Republicans were acting as though they had won the election. Hamilton's friend Robert Troup wrote, "The anti-federalists appear at present to be well pleased . . . and are now fraternizing with Adams and his particular friends and endeavoring to raise an opinion that Hamilton and his friends wished to bring Pinckney forward in preference to him." [7]

It was hard for Hamilton to deny the allegations when Robert Harper quite honestly and publicly admitted them. In a letter to his constituents written on January 5 the South Carolina Congressman called Jefferson a man who was fit to be a college professor, perhaps, but never a chief magistrate. "I am one of those who would have preferred Major Pinckney to either, as . . . possessed, in a higher degree than either, of those qualities which fit a man for holding the reins of government." [8]

The editor of the Philadelphia *Aurora* kept the embarrassing situation before the public, too, contrasting Jefferson's good will with Hamilton's evil design. On January 8 Bache printed a story about the circulation of one of Jefferson's conciliation letters, and Representative Goodrich was fearful. "The democrats are besetting Mr. Adams with attention. Since his election has become ascertained, the scurrility in

[5] January 4, 1797; *Jefferson Papers*, LC.
[6] January 12, 1797; *Hamilton Papers*, LC.
[7] January 28, 1797; King, *Life and Correspondence*, II, 135.
[8] Elizabeth Donnan, ed., "Papers of James A. Bayard," 24-25.

Bache's paper has ceased, and it is said the democrats are recommending to him conciliation of parties."[9] Sedgwick was shown Jefferson's letter to Madison of December 17 in confidence. The Republicans were passing it around as proof that Adams' worst enemy was Hamilton rather than Jefferson.[10]

Justice Iredell, however, thought the talk was most encouraging. During the election both Adams and Jefferson had said commendable things about each other, he told his wife, and it was even said that Jefferson was delighted with the outcome. "It is hoped that great harmony will subsist between him [Adams] and Mr. Jefferson, and that the violence of party spirit may subside."[11] Finally, Hamilton could contain himself no longer. The talk sickened him—a "united and vigorous administration," indeed—and he unburdened himself to his good friend King. "If Mr. Adams has vanity, t'is plain a plot has been laid to take hold of it. We trust his real good sense and integrity will be a sufficient shield."[12]

John Dawson, elected in March to Madison's vacant seat in the House, was passing the word southward that good will and harmony prevailed in Philadelphia, at least in Mr. Adams' breast where it most counted. He wrote his friend Joseph Jones of Fredericksburg, Virginia, that Adams had changed many of the opinions that he had expressed in his *Defense of the Constitutions* and was ready to administer the government "as an independent republican." This information was relayed back to Madison, who was not so sure that all was well.[13]

The little Virginian had been on edge ever since November. Above all, he wanted Jefferson to accept the vice-pres-

[9] To Governor Wolcott, January 9, 1797; Gibbs, *Memoirs*, I, 417.

[10] Sedgwick to King, March 12, 1797; King, *Life and Correspondence*, II, 156-157.

[11] February 9, 1797; February 17, 1797, *Iredell*, II, 491-492, 493.

[12] February 15, 1797, Hamilton, *Works* (Lodge ed.), X, 238.

[13] Joseph Jones to Madison, February 5, 1797, *Madison Papers*, LC.

idency, but he was also afraid that his friend would make a false step in doing so. During December and January an important series of letters passed between Philadelphia and Monticello that reveal how delicate a situation had developed out of the display of friendship and good feeling on the part of Adams and Jefferson. To accept Mr. Adams' olive branch (Jefferson had already taken the first step in that direction) meant to endanger the life of the Republican organization that had developed out of the political conflicts of four years or more.

Adams, on the other hand, had everything to gain and nothing to lose by turning toward Jefferson. He was in the position to act, Jefferson merely to advise, so far as national policies were concerned. The reports from France were not encouraging, and the growing menace of war was ever in the background. The President-elect had not committed himself on the subject of the crisis with France, and he did not do so until May. If Jefferson, who was given to occasional outbursts of enthusiasm, were to allow his sincere wishes for the success of Adams' administration to draw him into a compact with Adams in January or February, he might suddenly find himself committed to a policy that his party could not follow in March or April.

The struggle between friendship and politics that took place in the opening weeks of 1797 reveals how closely bound up with France the Republican party had become. The outbreak of war at a time when the leader of the Republican party was being drawn into a position of publicly recognized friendship with the man who would have to conduct that war would have seriously compromised the Republican party; withdrawal would have been considered treasonable and not legitimate opposition. Madison and Jefferson did not see the full implications of an entente with Adams for several weeks.

Madison at first saw nothing but gain in accepting the

friendship and confidence of Adams. Early in December when he felt that the election might turn in any direction, he wrote Jefferson, "You *must* reconcile yourself to the secondary as well as the primary station, if that should be your lot," underlining the word "must." [14] A few days later he explained his reasons for being so insistent. "On the whole it seems *essential* that you should not refuse the station which is likely to be your lot." (Madison then went into code.) "There is reason to believe also that your neighborhood to Adams may have a valuable effect on his councils, particularly in relation to our external system. You know that his feelings will not enslave him to the example of his predecessor. It is certain that his censures of the paper system and the intrigues at New York for setting Pinckney above him have fixed an enmity with the British faction. Nor should it pass for nothing that the true interest of New England particularly requires reconciliation with France as the road to her commerce. Add to the whole that he is said to speak of you now in friendly terms and will no doubt be soothed by your acceptance of a place subordinate to him. . . . It must be confessed however that all these considerations are qualified by his political principles and prejudices." [15] Three weeks later Madison again pressed his friend to accept the vice-presidency. The election of Adams and your own acceptance, he declared, would be a great aid to the cause of republican government, just as the election of Pinckney would have been a definite repudiation of it.[16]

Jefferson had been silent under the demands of Madison, but on December 28 he sat down to write a letter that would have all but ended the matter. This famous letter was addressed to John Adams, but fortunately (for the future well-being of the Republican party) he gave it a second thought

[14] December 10, 1796, *Madison Papers*, LC.
[15] December 19, 1796, *Madison Papers*, LC.
[16] January 8, 1797, *ibid.*

and sent it to Madison for his perusal. Madison's eyes must have popped. In the letter Jefferson expressed his delight with Adams' victory, but warned him that he might yet be cheated "by a trick worthy the subtlety of your arch-friend of New York." As far as he was concerned, wrote Jefferson, he would "leave to others the sublime delights of riding out the storm, better pleased with sound sleep and a warm berth below, with the society of neighbors, friends, and fellow-laborers of the earth, than of spies and sycophants." [17]

The letter that enclosed the note to Adams showed that Jefferson sensed no uneasiness about the nature of his remarks to the President-elect; he had acted on a lucky hunch in mailing it first to Madison. The vice-presidency is the only office in the world that I cannot decide whether I want or not, he said. "Pride does not enter into the estimate. I can particularly have no feelings that would revolt at a secondary position to Mr. Adams." Again he repeated that Mr. Adams was his senior in every respect. "If Mr. Adams could be induced to administer the government on its true principles . . . it would be a worthy consideration whether it would not be for the public good to come to a good understanding with him as to his future elections. He is the only sure barrier against Hamilton's getting in." [18] This was precisely what Madison had been driving at in his letter of December 19.

This entire episode is so familiar as to be quickly sketched. Madison took the liberty of withholding the letter to Adams and gave Jefferson excellent reasons for doing so. There is no need further to emphasize your friendliness, he replied,

[17] This letter has been quoted many times. Brant, *Madison*, 446-447; Randall, *Jefferson*, II, 320-321. Randall notes that in writing it Jefferson was sacrificing no political theories and was not compromising his republicanism. The biographer believed that Adams' disgust with Hamilton's election scheme and his financial measures were well known to Jefferson and that he was only trying to break the solid federalism of New England by a possible compromise with the moderates.

[18] January 1, 1797, *Jefferson Papers*, LC.

Adams already knows of it; the tone of the letter is somewhat strained; Adams seems well aware of Hamilton's scheming; your allusion to "riding out the storm" may suggest that you consider him ambitious; your supporters may be angry after working so hard for your election; and, finally, you leave Adams in possession of a written testimonial of confidence that might prove embarrassing. Madison added that he regretted having to disapprove, because he knew Jefferson was sincere and that what he was doing was not "inconsistent with the duty and policy of cultivating Mr. Adams' favorable dispositions, and giving a fair start to his Executive career." [19] The plan to reach an understanding with Adams was not dropped then, but the manner of approaching it that Jefferson had taken was modified.

A few days after receiving Madison's objections, Jefferson began to pursue the same objective through a more subtle means. There was a change in attitude taking place in his mind. He had heard in the meantime from other sources at Philadelphia and must have breathed a sigh of relief that Madison had intervened. Washington had sent his message and the papers dealing with French relations to the Senate, and the prospect of peace appeared less encouraging than ever. The whole matter of hostilities now rested with Adams, wrote Jefferson to Madison. What if Adams had given his sanction "by a complimentary initiation into the business?" [20] His own role was clear: if he could, he would convince Adams that peace was essential.

Letters from Philadelphia spoke of Mr. Adams' warm expressions of friendship "and with satisfaction in the prospect of administering the government in concurrence with me," said Jefferson. Madison's reasoning, Washington's message, and something in the letters he had just received from the capital caused Jefferson at this point to shift his position from

[19] January 15, 1797, *Madison Papers*, LC.
[20] January 22, 1797, *ibid.*

that which had gradually been taking hold in the public mind and apparently in Adams'. "As to my participating in the administration, if by that he [Adams] meant the executive cabinet, both duty and inclination will shut that door to me. . . ." [21] Here was the loophole through which he might escape from the dilemma that mere expressions of friendship had produced. He might wish to take part in the administration of the government, but the Constitution forbade it. The Vice-President was assigned by the Constitution to a place in the legislative branch of the government, and since the theory upon which it was built was that of the separation of powers, participation in executive affairs was impossible.

The logic was watertight and would have to be recognized as such by the legalistic mind of the political philosopher Adams. Still, Jefferson could express his best wishes and hopes for the four years to come, work toward an entente with the new President, and prevent the outbreak of war—perhaps even draw the moderate Adams men still further from the arms of Hamilton and into the Republican fold.

Cleverly, as if from design, Jefferson began by clarifying his position to intimate friends and those who might present it to Adams as if it were their own observations. Madison was the first to hear it. On the same day he wrote his son-in-law expressing the identical sentiments: Adams is cordial and talks of administering the government with me. The Constitution strictly limits my duties to the legislative branch.[22] It would be healthy for the Virginians to hear this. They had just spent months in denouncing Adams as an aristocrat, and Jefferson was skillfully covering his tracks. The third letter he wrote on January 22 was addressed to Senator John Langdon of New Hampshire. He confined himself to an expression of friendship and gladness over the election

[21] *Ibid.*
[22] To T. M. Randolph, January 22, 1797, *Jefferson Papers*, LC.

results. "I assume this will be shown to Adams," he told Madison.[23]

In the meantime, all political conversations were becoming attuned to the news from Paris. Madison reported to Jefferson that the temper of the Federalists against France was rising and that they had thrown off the mask of peace now that the election was over. They were attempting to force Washington into one last denunciation of France, but how far they were succeeding with Adams, he could not see. "No further discovery has been made of the mind of the President-elect. I cannot prevail on myself to augur much that is consoling from him." [24]

Just before he left for the capital, Jefferson received from his friend the first hint of Adams' intentions. It was reliably reported that Mr. Adams would ask the advice of the Senate as to whether Washington's appointments were binding on his successor or not. This has implications, said Madison. Either he is still dreaming about the British constitution and regards his own administration as a continuation of the same reign, or else he is inviting the Senate (including Jefferson) to play a wider part in the administration of policy than it has heretofore.[25]

On his route to Philadelphia, Jefferson spent the night of February 21 as the guest of Madison's friend Joseph Jones at Fredericksburg. He found Jones aware of the talk of friendship with Adams and did his best to clarify his position. Jones's letter to Madison, written two or three days after his conversations with Jefferson, probably reflect much that Jefferson had said. Jones felt that the friendship of the two men was sincere but that Adams might still be "too much of an Angloman and will yield to predispositions." Many Vir-

[23] January 30, 1797, *ibid.*
[24] Philadelphia, January 29, 1797, *Madison Papers*, LC.
[25] February 11, 1797, *ibid.*

ginians were still suspicious of Adams, but there was the possibility that the truth about his politics was not known, he thought. Finally, Jones was hopeful that "the politicks of the states to which they (Jefferson and Adams) belong may be more assimilated and harmonized." [26] All these reflections were in keeping with what Jefferson and Madison had finally adopted as their policy toward Adams and the approach to be taken in winning his confidence.

The best proof of what had taken place in Virginia as a result of the advances that Jefferson and Adams had made toward renewing their friendship and of what Jefferson was thinking on the eve of his departure to meet Adams face to face is to be found among his notes marked "February 1797" in the Library of Congress. In his handwriting is a note saying in effect: what I knew could happen has happened—expressions of friendship and co-operation with Mr. Adams have been "rendered *mal a propos*" by circumstances at Philadelphia unknown to me. With this note is a laboriously written and much crossed out first draft of a letter to James Sullivan of Boston dated February 9, 1797, which shows how cautious Jefferson had suddenly found it expedient to become regarding his position in the new administration. He found it necessary, he told Sullivan, to reassert his reluctance to accept office again. His faith in the inherent republicanism of the American people was as firm as ever, the letter continued. He made a friendly inquiry as to the health of "my antient and respected friend, Mr. Samuel Adams," whose principles had remained "so pure" over the years, and the letter ended with the bald statement that this was his answer to the friends at Boston who had expressed "anxiety" over his willingness to accept office under a Federalist President. Meanwhile, what of Mr. Adams himself?

Mr. Adams had been pleased to find the Republicans

[26] February 23, 1797; February 24, 1797, *ibid.*

speaking cordially about his election, and in a letter to his wife written two weeks before Christmas he was pleased to quote William Giles of Virginia as saying: "The point is settled. The Vice President will be President. . . . The old man will make a good President, too. But we shall have to check him a little now and then. That will be all."[27] Giles was one of the most active Jeffersonians in the House and a close associate of Madison's. From his old friend Elbridge Gerry Adams received assurances of Jefferson's friendship and a condemnation of the way in which his own party had treated him. Gerry was an old friend of the family and had addressed his remarks to Abigail Adams. She replied that she and her husband had always been fond of Jefferson, though differing from him on such issues as Paine's "Rights of Man." No doubt, she agreed, Colonel Hamilton had his own plans for the election. "To what other motive can be ascribed the Machiavellian policy of placing at the head of the government a gentleman scarcely heard of beyond the state which gave him birth. . . ."[28]

The President-elect expressed fond hopes of closer ties with Jefferson in his own letters. It was no surprise to hear of the Republican leader's testimonials of friendship and confidence. They had shared many experiences during the dark days of the Revolution both at home and abroad, and he had never lost faith in the honor, integrity, and patriotism of his erring friend. His patronage of such characters as Freneau and Tom Paine, said Mr. Adams, had long "been a source . . . of anxiety to me. . . . But I hope and believe that his advancement and his situation in the Senate, an excellent school, will correct him. He will have too many friends about him to flatter him, but I have hope we can keep him

[27] December 12, 1796, Adams, *Works*, I, 495.

[28] December 31, 1796, James T. Austin, *The Life of Elbridge Gerry* (Boston, 1829), 144-145.

steady." [29] It was all a matter of education and proper guidance, then, and all would be fine, providing Mr. Jefferson chose to be re-educated.

In response to a second letter from Elbridge Gerry, who was most interested in the possibility of re-establishing the old alliance between Massachusetts and Virginia, Adams was more reticent. He was not going to reveal the schism within the party to anyone whose politics were of a doubtful color, and Gerry had yet to prove himself a convert to Mr. Adams' way of thinking. The talk of a plot to deprive me of the election is mistaken in a sense, he declared. "They were frightened into a belief that I should fail, and they, in their agony, thought it better to bring in Pinckney than Jefferson." [30] A few days later Adams received concrete evidence from a trusted friend at Albany that Hamilton had done his utmost to win the election for Pinckney,[31] but letters not addressed to Gerry leave little doubt that his mind had been made up on that score for weeks.

Just a few days before Jefferson arrived in Philadelphia for the inauguration, Adams sketched for Gerry the part that he hoped his Vice-President would play in the four years to come: "I feel no apprehension from Mr. Jefferson. The Cause of the irritation upon his Nerves, which broke out in some disagreeable Appearances a few years ago, is now removed as I believe"; a belief that Hamilton had been the principal cause of Jefferson's opposition to the administration: "I expect from his ancient friendship, his good Sense, and general good dispositions, a decorum of Conduct at least, if not as cordial and uniform a support as I have given my Predecessor, which is the Pride and boast of my life." [32]

[29] Adams to Tristam Dalton, January 19, 1797, Jefferson, *Writings* (Ford ed.), VIII, 272, Note 1.

[30] February 13, 1797, Adams, *Works*, VIII, 524.

[31] *Ibid.*, 524, Note 1.

[32] February 20, 1797; "Warren-Adams Letters," II, 331, Massachusetts Historical Society *Collections*, 72-73 (Boston, 1925), in response to an unpublished letter of Gerry's of January 30, 1797.

Considering the fact that Adams had played little part in making executive policy and had been drawn into cabinet discussion only two or three times in eight years, his final analysis of the part that Jefferson was to take is not greatly different from that which the new Vice-President had evolved for himself in the weeks between the election and the inauguration.

Adams and Jefferson had not seen each other or communicated since January, 1794, when Jefferson had left Philadelphia worn and exasperated from his continual tug of war with the triumphant Secretary of the Treasury. How they greeted each other, what their first words were, or how cordial the meeting appeared to outsiders, we do not know. There must have been considerable reminiscing along with much shifting of the feet. We do know that the initial meeting was friendly enough to promise the renewal of what had once been a warm comradeship for, to the delight of some and the consternation of others, they soon took rooms in the same boarding house. One Justice remarked to another, "I am much pleased that Mr. Adams and Mr. Jefferson lodge together. The thing carries conciliation and healing with it, and may have a happy effect on parties. Indeed, my dear sir, it is high time we should be done with Parties." [33]

On March 4 the President *pro tempore* of the Senate, Federalist William Bingham of Pennsylvania, administered the oath of office to Thomas Jefferson during a brief ceremony in the Senate chamber. In his short acceptance speech, Jefferson paid tribute to the man whose office he now filled and who had been called to higher functions.

"These have been justly confided to the eminent character . . . whose talents and integrity have been known and revered by me through a long course of years, have been the foundation of a cordial and uninterrupted friendship between us. . . ."

[33] William Paterson to James Iredell, March 7, 1797, *Iredell*, II, 495.

Leaving Bingham and company to mull over these words, Jefferson led the way into the chamber of the House of Representatives where the President would be sworn into office. Amidst a rustle of excitement and admiration, the stately Washington, followed by his secretaries and the district marshall, made his way to the speaker's platform where Adams and the Speaker of the House were already seated with other high officials. As Adams stepped up to deliver his inaugural message, the audience prepared itself to listen. Mr. Adams was known to favor lengthy orations, had considerable reputation as an orator, and had had no opportunity to exercise his talents in some years. His address was far more simple and brief than was to be expected. The emphasis that the stolid New Englander had put into his inaugural was on the content and not the decoration. He came directly to the point when he took up the subject of political principles.

In the interest of national unity he felt it necessary to make his stand perfectly clear: he did not favor a permanent Executive or Senate and saw no necessity of changing the Constitution of the United States in any way except "such as the people themselves . . . should see and feel to be necessary or expedient. . . ."

In alluding to the subject of the Constitution, the new President was answering the many who had charged during the campaign that he would be unable to uphold in good faith a Constitution that he was supposed to consider deficient, and Adams was taking up a role that in the public mind he had dropped in the period after the Declaration of Independence—he was proclaiming with pride his own faith in republican government. Here were words that no Jeffersonian could disapprove or Federalist take open exception to. Over the years, he said, his respect for the Constitution had steadily increased. "What other form of Government, indeed, can so well deserve our esteem and love?"

Near the end of his speech the new Chief Executive took

up the matter of American relations with France. This was the crucial question about which all political matters would revolve and upon which the future of an entente between the Adams Federalists and the Jeffersonian Republicans would hang. "If a personal esteem for the French nation, formed in a residence of seven years, chiefly among them, and a sincere desire to preserve the friendship which has been so much for the honor and interest of both nations . . . can enable me to . . . comply with your wishes, it shall be my strenuous endeavor that this sagacious injunction [the neutrality proclamation] shall not be without effect." [34]

Chief Justice Ellsworth administered the oath, Adams repeated it after him, and the ceremony ended with Washington following—not without considerable bowing in deference to Mr. Adams—the second President out into the street. The crowd cheered, and the government had changed hands.

Reactions to the President's inaugural address varied according to party sympathies. Benjamin Bache of the *Aurora* was delighted. "How grateful to every republican to hear their new President so highly estimating 'institutions which spring from the hearts and judgements of an honest and enlightened people.' . . . Not less pleasing must it be to hear him place in a light bordering on ridicule, the 'diamonds, robes, and other ornaments and decorations' of royalty. . . . How will the anti-republicans foam at finding him also determined not to attempt or support any amendments to the constitution of the United States but in the mode prescribed therein. He has thought proper to announce . . . that he will 'love virtuous men of all parties and denominations.' . . . May he persevere in it uninfluenced by the menaces or machinations of artful and designing men. . . . Nor ought Mr. Jefferson's *extempore* speech to the Senate pass unnoticed. The terms in which he speaks of Mr. Adams . . . do

[34] *Annals*, 4th Congress, 2d Session, 1581-86. Adams' description and a copy of his address in Adams, *Works*, I, 505-506.

credit to his head and heart. How satisfactory . . . to know from Mr. Jefferson himself, that the strictest friendship subsists between the two first officers in government."[35]

Three days later the Republican editor was still praising John Adams. "It is universally admitted that Mr. Adams is a man of incorruptible integrity, and that the resources of his own mind are equal to the duties of his station. . . . He declared himself the friend of France and of peace, the admirer of republicanism, the enemy of party, and he avows his determination to let no political creed interfere in his appointments . . . how characteristic of a patriot."[36] And how quickly the tone of Bache's *Aurora* had changed.

At New York, Noah Webster, editor of one of Hamilton's favorite newssheets, found the President's first message a reflection of the false flattery being bestowed upon him through the wiles of the democrats. Bache took up the President's cause by pointing out that Webster was merely voicing the anger of his chief over the outcome of the election. The *Minerva*, said Bache, had been very favorable to Mr. Adams until it became known that Pinckney was the right candidate.[37] On March 20 the *Aurora* printed what it chose to regard as a complete exposé of the Pinckney election plot. Republicans were grasping with keen acumen the one issue that could be used to widen the rift throughout federalism. They would not let Adams forget.

On the other hand, the editor of the New York *Gazette and General Advertiser* had come up with evidence of French machinations in Jefferson's cause that he hoped might drive a wedge between the new President and Vice-President. A few days after the inauguration a long letter signed by a certain William Wilcocks was printed, detailing activ-

[35] March 11, 1797.
[36] March 14, 1797.
[37] *Aurora*, March 16, 1797. For a summary of press reaction to Mr. Adams' inaugural see J. B. McMaster, *History*, II, 308-311.

ities of French agents in the Western states in behalf of Mr. Jefferson's election.[38]

While the editors fought it out, private sentiments were being voiced in favor of the conciliation of parties. One of the most touching of these was that addressed by old Sam Adams to his distant cousin John. "I congratulate you as the first citizen of the United States–I may add of the World. I am, my dear Sir, notwithstanding I have been otherwise represented in party papers, Your Old and unvaried Friend, S. Adams." [39]

Elbridge Gerry, the man who showed most interest in the entente, was led to express himself in utter frankness to Jefferson a few days after the inaugural. I had desired your election as Vice-President from the beginning, he wrote, and said so at our electors' meeting. "As we were unanimously of opinion that Mr. Adams' pretensions to the chair were best, it was impossible to give you any votes without annulling an equal number for him; otherwise you would have had mine and I have reason to think several others for Vice President." Gerry added that the Constitution ought to be changed in that connection and mentioned his belief in a concerted attempt to deceive Adams during the election. He was looking forward to a truly neutral administration, but he wished to warn Mr. Jefferson of the efforts which would be made to separate him from Adams.[40]

Jefferson's reply to Gerry was a carefully prepared compound of frankness with caution. He wrote that he commended Gerry's attitude toward Mr. Adams and added that the President could not have hurt feelings because of his lack of interest in his own election. "I consider as a certainty that nothing will be left untried to alienate him from me. These machinations will proceed from the Hamiltonians who sur-

[38] March 9, 1797.
[39] April 17, 1797.
[40] March 27, 1797, *Jefferson Papers*, LC.

round him, and who are only a little less hostile to him than to me." He had fears, however, that Mr. Adams would not believe this. Jefferson concluded by pledging his efforts to the achievement of genuine neutrality; he could not, he pointed out, take part in executive consultations.[41]

Other New Englanders took a different view of the new situation. Governor Wolcott predicted that civil war would grow out of it with Federalists and Republicans fighting as Whigs and Tories had. It was Adams' own fault: he had asked for the adulation of "the French faction" by making advances first through his "unnecessary" compliments to France in the inaugural message. The old Governor still had confidence in Adams, however, but thought he was less able than he considered himself. He would need young Wolcott's "able counselling."[42]

Henry Knox was the only dyed-in-the-wool Federalist who could see a ray of hope in the opening weeks of the new administration. Whether he was speaking from his own heart or from the mind of his onetime chief in New York, it is impossible to tell. Soon after the inauguration he suggested to the President that it would be an excellent move to nominate Jefferson as Envoy to France. To preserve peace was an excellent aim, he said. What could please and flatter the French government more than to send their old friend Jefferson to treat with them? It would be welcomed by the majority of Federalists, would "delight" the Republicans, and would hold an advantage worth weighing. (Knox's reasoning was clever, perhaps too clever to have been hatched in his brain.) If Jefferson should go to France and the negotiation collapse, who could anyone blame? Certainly not the administration or the Federalist party. The Republicans would be in a most unfortunate position, compelled to fol-

[41] May 13, 1797, Austin, *Gerry*, 136-142.
[42] March 20, 1797; Gibbs, *Memoirs*, I, 476.

low and committed to the weakening of their own political forces.[43]

Here Knox suggested precisely what Madison and Jefferson had seen as the danger in too close an association with the confused administration that commenced in March, 1797.

If Adams' reply to Knox ever reached the desk of Alexander Hamilton, it must have brought a smile and a sigh of relief from him. The President by three votes had not allowed the Pinckney scheme to sink into the back of his mind—he called a nation who would allow such a trick to succeed "a sordid people"—but there was evidence that relations with Mr. Jefferson were not as friendly as appeared on the outside.

He had already thought of sending Jefferson, but his offer had been refused, he wrote. "It is a delicate thing for me to speak of the late election. . . . Had Mr. Jay or some other been in question, it might have less mortified my vanity. . . . But to see such a character as Jefferson, and much more, such an unknown as Pinckney, brought over my head, and trampling on the bellies of hundreds of other men infinitely his superior in talents, service, and reputation, filled me with apprehensions for the safety of us all." [44] Most of the invectives were aimed at Hamilton and his associates, but there was a tone of wounded pride in his remarks about Jefferson as well. What had gone wrong?

Both Adams and Jefferson have left explanations of the rift that developed. Unknown to the public, it had its beginnings at the very moment that the friendship appeared most solidly re-established. According to Adams it occurred on the day before the inauguration. He had approached Jefferson on the possibility of sending a high-ranking Republican to Paris to join General C. C. Pinckney and possibly to supersede him. Jefferson refused to go himself and seemed

[43] March 19, 1797, Adams, *Works,* VIII, 533-534.
[44] March 30, 1797, Adams, *Works,* VIII, 535-536.

so cool when the President suggested some other Republican that Adams felt rebuffed.[45]

Jefferson's version is slightly different. The day before the inauguration Adams called upon him at Madison's—where he had gone upon his arrival the day before—and had brought up the French negotiations. Adams, as Jefferson recalled it, ruled the Vice-President out as being unable to go because of his Senate duties, and mentioned Madison or Gerry for the post. Jefferson promised to interview Madison on the topic. Three days later the subject again came up after a dinner at Washington's home. Jefferson told Adams that Madison had declined the mission, whereupon the President, looking somewhat embarrassed, blurted out that it was just as well since objections to Madison's nomination had come up that he had never anticipated. Jefferson's guess was that the Cabinet, which met with Adams for the first time during the interval, had raised strong objections to Madison.[46]

On this point both men are in agreement. In one of his famous letters printed in the Boston *Patriot* in 1809, Adams explained that he had proposed nominating Mr. Madison only to have Oliver Wolcott exclaim, "Mr. President, we are willing to resign." [47]

Adams, looking back on the affair, wrote, "We parted as good friends as we had always lived; but we consulted very little together afterwards. Party violence soon rendered it impracticable, or at least useless. . . ." [48] Jefferson's account agreed that he was never again consulted on executive matters during the remainder of Adams' term.[49]

Despite the friction caused by the French mission there was still no outward indication that the entente was ended.

[45] *Ibid.*, I, 508.

[46] Jefferson, *Writings* (Ford ed.), I, 334-336 ("Anas").

[47] Adams, *Works*, IX, 286; Adams to Benjamin Rush, August 23, 1805, Biddle, *Old Family Letters*, I, 76-77.

[48] *Ibid.*, IX, 285.

[49] Jefferson, *op. cit.*, 336.

The accounts pointing to the first week in March as the decisive date were written years afterward. News from overseas was rapidly bringing about a crisis which was to make it apparent to all that friendship and politics were often unharmonious. Adams' letter to Knox was an indication of what was happening, and a note written to Elbridge Gerry thanking him for the suggestion of sending Jefferson to France and noting the Vice-President's refusal was a second; [50] but the President's proclamation of March 25 was a warning for all to see and interpret.

"Whereas an extraordinary occasion exists for convening congress and divers great and weighty problems claim their consideration . . ." Congress was called into session on May 15.[51] Jefferson continued to live at The Francis Hotel as Mr. Adams' neighbor, and at least one Federalist continued to see deception in it until early April; however, there was little to support his suspicions.[52]

Word had come from France that the Directory would regard all Americans serving on British ships as pirates and that the principle of free ships, free goods would no longer be considered a legitimate neutral policy. On May 16 the President submitted his first message to Congress, and to the Republicans it looked like a declaration of political war, as well as bad diplomacy.

The refusal of the French government to deal with Charles C. Pinckney as the new American Minister was announced, the French decree of March 2 aimed at American commerce was enclosed, but worst of all to the Republicans was the President's recommendation for the creation of a navy, coastal defenses against what he termed "sudden and predatory incursions," and the enlarging of both the artillery and cavalry branches of the army. Finally, as though expecting

[50] April 6, 1797, Adams, *Works,* VIII, 538.

[51] *Annals,* 5th Congress, 1st Session, 49.

[52] William Smith to Rufus King, April 3, 1797, King, *Life and Correspondence,* II, 167.

an invasion, Mr. Adams asked Congress to consider the establishment of a provisional army.[53]

Jefferson immediately wrote Madison that things had gone from bad to good to bad again. The year began with rumors about Pinckney's mistreatment, then we all happily agreed that peace was the thing, in keeping with Adams' inaugural remarks, and now this, he wrote. He enclosed a copy of the special message. There was great enthusiasm for defense in certain quarters, he said. The argument, spurious from his point of view, was that defense would aid negotiation; but how can negotiations be carried out after an address like this one? The rest of his report was equally gloomy. Beckley has been thrown out by a cheap trick—a vote was called for when many Republicans were absent—and the tone of the President's message was driving the wavering into the Federalist corner. "It is said that three from Virginia separate from their brethren," Jefferson finished.[54]

The Vice-President, rapidly assuming the role of party leader in Madison's stead, was less frank in a similar letter written that day to Thomas Bell of Charlottesville. The desire for peace was not so certain, he declared, but instead of saying that three Virginia Republicans had deserted the cause, he stated that elections in Virginia had been going badly and that the Republican forces lacked real leaders. To his son-in-law he merely expressed his contempt for the idea of talking about arming while trying to negotiate.[55]

From the top to the bottom, Republicans saw that their visions of an entente with Mr. Adams and his friends had been a forlorn hope. The healthy debate in the House occasioned by the President's surprising message was marked by William Giles' confession of a mistake in judgment: he had thought the President worthy of confidence, said Giles, but

[53] Richardson, *Messages*, 71-72; *Annals*, 5th Congress, 1st Session, 54-59.

[54] May 18, 1797; Jefferson, *Writings* (Ford ed.), VIII, 288-289.

[55] May 18, 1797, *Jefferson Papers*, LC; to T. M. Randolph, May 19, 1797; *ibid.*

the speech of May 15 had forced him to change his opinion.[56]

The editor of the *Aurora*, who had been running well ahead of the Republican pack in his expressions of glee over Mr. Adams' desertion of Hamilton, took up his party pen again. "From the temper which a great man shewed in his speech on Tuesday to a great assembly we are unavoidably led to believe that his men Timothy and Oliver have fed him upon pepperpot these three weeks past in order to bring his nerves to a proper anti-gallican tone. The effects which aromatics on high seasoned food produce upon a cold northern constitution every quack can tell." The day after, Bache hit home with a jibe that must have hurt. "Whatever may be said of the President by *three votes*, he has certainly one characteristic feature, that of dissimulation. From the time of his appointment untill the present moment he has completely deceived the people, who were led by his inaugural speech and other circumstances to believe . . . that he was under no *extraneous influence*." [57] The Republican organ thus announced the downfall of the brief conciliation movement. Parties seemed triumphant over all.

Just so that Federalists would not be left without ammunition with which to recommence the political war, fate ordained that Mr. Jefferson's commentary on George Washington [58] should appear at that moment. In his letter to the Italian sculptor and republican, Phillip Mazzei, the Vice-President had spoken of the potential enemy France as deserving of American sympathies and understanding. "She is their true mother country, since she has assured to them their liberty and independence." Then came the famous allusion to Washington as "Sampsons in the field and Solomons

[56] *Annals*, 5th Congress, 1st Session, 364.

[57] May 18, 19, 1797.

[58] Jefferson first saw his letter printed in the Bladensburg, Virginia, newspaper edition of May 9, 1797, while en route to Philadelphia for the special session. Randall, *Jefferson*, II, 361-362. Randall asserted that there is no proof that "Sampson" was Washington and that Washington never took it in that sense. The explanation is not convincing.

in the council . . . who have had their heads shorn by the harlot England."

On May 20 "Peter Porcupine" opened the assault upon Jefferson for his attack upon the good "Cincinnatus of the West." [59] Here was ample diet for Federalist fire-eaters: a Vice-President of the United States who demanded and pledged himself to support neutrality praising an enemy that called American seamen pirates and refused to treat with a bona fide American negotiator. Jefferson was silent.

To put the finishing touches on the burial of an ancient friendship, an Adams well-wisher mailed a copy of one of Jefferson's letters to the President. The contents dealt with his message to Congress and Jefferson's low opinion of it. Wrote Adams in reply to his informer, "It is evidence of a mind, soured, yet seeking for popularity, and eaten to a honeycomb with ambition, yet weak, confused, uninformed and ignorant. I have long been convinced that this ambition is so inconsiderate as to be capable of going to great lengths." [60] So far as he was concerned, also, the honeymoon was over. In fact, the long string of adjectives referring to his companion suggests that someone was holding a shotgun at the wedding.

A few days after the highly publicized coalition fell apart, Jefferson was ready to take a more open stand as leader of the opposition. Remembering that we are dealing with an age when men, who had long held a monopoly of political offices knew each other intimately regardless of party affiliations, it should not be too surprising to find that the man to whom he chose to announce his apostasy was none other than Thomas Pinckney, soon to take his seat as Senator from South Carolina on the Federalist side of the chamber.

[59] April 24, 1796, Jefferson, *Writings* (Ford ed.), VIII, 238.

[60] To Gen. Uriah Forrest of Georgetown, Md., June 20, 1797, Adams, *Works*, VIII, 546-547. Randall traced the letter to one written by Jefferson to Peregrine Fitzhugh, a relative of Forrest's. The original was dated June 4. Randall, *Jefferson*, II, 355-356; III, Appendix 15, 605 ff.

Jefferson began by lamenting the growth of parties, and went on to question the wisdom of the new President. "I do not think the speech and addresses of Congress as conciliatory as the preceding irritations on both sides would have rendered wise." He added the friendly note, "I shall be happy to hear from you at all times." [61] (Perhaps there was better basis for a bargain with South Carolina than with Massachusetts anyway.)

In keeping with his new policy of seeking friends regardless of past relations, Jefferson next turned to Aaron Burr, the man who had received one Virginia electoral vote. Mr. Adams, he wrote, is taking the most direct route to the destruction of the Republican party that can be imagined. If the United States should find itself at war with France or if Louisiana becomes a French colony, the party will be in mortal danger. He believed, he said, that the public could be convinced that war measures would undermine the republican character of their government. "If New York can be pushed into the Republican column, we might still hope for salvation." [62]

The rough draft of the letter shows how carefully and painstakingly this reopening of negotiations with Burr was prepared. Gone was the optimism of January when the Republican leader had told Madison, in the midst of their planning for an entente with Adams, "Let us cultivate Pennsylvania, and we need not fear the Universe." [63]

Aaron Burr was far too sagacious a politician to sulk. "The moment requires free communication among those who adhere to the principles of our revolution," read his acceptance of Jefferson's call to battle. He was deeply disappointed in Adams, he said, especially after the "professions of February and March. . . . The gauntlet I see is thrown.

[61] May 29, 1797, *Jefferson Papers*, LC.
[62] June 17, 1797, *Jefferson Papers*, LC.
[63] January 22, 1797, Jefferson, *Writings* (Ford ed.), 273.

. . ." He suggested that they could best talk over future plans in private and invited Jefferson to meet with him within a week.[64]

Other evidences of the rising tide of party feeling were the report given out by Attorney Charles Lee that no more Republicans would benefit by patronage and the President's subsequent nomination as envoys to France of John Marshall and Justice Francis Dana of Massachusetts, both stanch Federalists.[65] On June 21 word was received that Dana would not accept. As his replacement, Adams called upon his old friend Elbridge Gerry.

"A good exchange," wrote Jefferson to his son-in-law,[66] and he tried his utmost to insure Gerry's acceptance. Having failed to keep his own foot in the President's door, the Vice-President was delighted to find Gerry destined to play a leading role in the crucial French negotiations. Gerry was the last instrument through which to reach Adams, for he had no standing in the Federalist party, and above all he was personally liked and trusted by Adams. Furthermore, Gerry had already shown a desire to see the brief rapprochement take hold and was to be the last to give up the idea.

"It was with infinite joy to me," wrote Jefferson, "that you were yesterday announced to the Senate as envoy extraordinary." You must accept, he said, or a party appointment is sure to be made.[67] In reply the Massachusetts independent voiced his hopes that friendship might be revived. Mr. Adams, he said, did not regard the Vice-President with hostility nor did Adams give heed to the rumors that Jefferson hated him as an obstacle to his own career. The public welfare demanded that your friendship be renewed, as it was the only way to prevent foreign influence from taking hold

[64] June 21, 1797, *Jefferson Papers*, LC.

[65] Jefferson to Madison, May 29, 1797, Jefferson, *Writings* (Ford ed.), VIII, 296.

[66] To T. M. Randolph, June 22, 1797, *Jefferson Papers*, LC.

[67] June 21, 1797, *ibid.*

of the government again, Gerry wrote.[68] His own behavior at Paris during the coming months only tended to drive the two men further apart, however, and intensified the hostility of parties already marked at the time of his departure.

A set of notes that Jefferson made in the summer of 1797 set down clearly what he regarded as the causes of the disruption of his brief entente with Adams. The main cause was his disappointment over the President's handling of French negotiations. After promising to send Madison along with Pinckney and Gerry, he had first nominated a Hamiltonian sympathizer, Judge Dana, and included the worst enemy of the Virginians in their domestic squabbles, John Marshall. (Jefferson's intense dislike of Marshall has become famous.)

He added that the appointment of William Smith and William Vans Murray to diplomatic posts had not been consistent with Adams' protests against partisanship. Actually, Smith's appointment had been made by Washington, but Murray had taken an active part in Adams' campaign in Maryland.[69]

James Monroe, perhaps reflecting Jefferson's opinion, later testified that it was all Adams' fault that a rupture had taken place. "He would have none in his ranks but tried men, whose political creed corresponded with his own."[70] Representative John Dawson, also of Virginia, found himself unable to promise good results from a patronage request sent to him that summer and declared that Mr. Jefferson was just as doubtful. "He assures me that the President has not opened his lips to him on politicks since his appointment." The Vice-President had said that for him to present the request would only injure the man's chances.[71]

[68] July 6, 1797, *ibid.*

[69] *Jefferson Papers,* LC, filed under July, 1797.

[70] Monroe to Jefferson, February 19, 1798, Monroe, *Writings* (Hamilton ed.), III, 103.

[71] Dawson to Madison, June 4, 1797, *Madison Papers,* LC.

The war message, as the Republicans called it, was certainly an important turning point or at least the point of no return, but at the same time the Mazzei letter, which would have made close relations with Jefferson highly embarrassing if not impossible for Adams, had appeared.[72] Moving still further back, it would seem that insurmountable obstacles had arisen just when conditions had appeared most promising for a united administration. Both Adams and Jefferson testified to the opposition that the President had encountered from his advisors when he had suggested the name of Madison as a possible envoy to France. So often during his term of office John Adams was deceived and, from all appearances, bullied by the strange group of men surrounding him that we may take his first cabinet meeting as the turning point in the strange relationship that had developed out of the unexpected victory of both a Federalist and a Republican in the election of 1796. Behind the episode lay the threat of war and the overbearing behavior of the French Directory. War with France was the *bête noir* of Jefferson's political existence. He had feared it as the weak point in his contemplated entente with Adams, and when the choice between the future of his party and the future of his friendship presented itself he chose the former.

Four years later there were vague rumors that what had almost developed into a reality in 1797 was again taking shape. In the summer of 1800 Henry Lee warned the embittered President against Mr. Jefferson's protests of friendship. Adams was supposed to have cried out with feeling that Thomas Jefferson was a better friend than many whose displays of cordiality he had finally come to hate.[73] A Massachusetts Federalist said this to Rufus King in the late spring of 1800: "It is believed that there is a good understanding

[72] McMaster concluded that the Mazzei letter put the finishing touch on the already waning friendship. *History*, II, 324.

[73] Pickering, "Review," Section III.

between Jefferson and Mr. Adams, and they will make joint stock of their influence in the next election. . . ." [74] Perhaps the stories were based on fancy or fear, but there was strength enough in the brief and somewhat tragic rapprochement of 1797 to make men believe that a secret coalition was possible. If anything made it possible it was the elimination of the mediocre talents possessed by Timothy Pickering, Oliver Wolcott, and James McHenry, the alpha and omega of the misfortunes of President John Adams.

[74] King, *Life and Correspondence*, III, 249.

11

The Patronage Crisis and the Decline in Federal Status

IN MARCH, 1797, THE SECOND PRESIDENT TOOK OFFICE, BUT no one, with the possible exception of Mrs. Adams, would have ventured to say that John Adams had replaced General Washington. While even the warmest admirers of Mr. Jefferson admitted that in intellectual capacity and political experience the New Englander was second only to Jefferson as presidential timber, no one could say that the nation's future looked as secure as it had when Washington had first taken office. The Adams administration was born to trouble; Washington had begun his presidential career in a rare interval of peace.

Homer might have done justice to the life of Washington and the heroic age that he wonderfully epitomized. Sophocles would have more fitly dealt with the figure of Adams as President. Whereas Washington was elected with a full measure of public confidence, Adams was a three-vote electoral college choice. Washington's stature has benefited by his association with Jefferson, Hamilton, and the genuinely distinguished men who inaugurated the Federal system. Adams was destined to be associated with the second-rate talents of his cabinet members. Not until John Marshall took the State Department in 1800 did a man of first-rate abilities enter the executive service under Adams. History has carelessly dissociated Washington's name from both the foreign crisis and the personnel problem that Adams struggled through. Yet both arose in 1795 as results of the Jay treaty, the one directly and the other indirectly. By 1795 it had become apparent that no constitution, however devised, would act as a permanent panacea for the nation's political cleavage and economic problems.

In retrospect, it seems evident that the original impulse that had driven the American colonists to create a nation had played itself out. To Washington it was humiliating, puzzling, and angering that the nation's political leaders were unwilling to accept office by appointment.

On the first of January, 1795, Hamilton and Knox, the last of Washington's original advisory council, retired, and the rapidly aging President began searching for assistants who might add strength to an administration that had two full years to run. In August Edmund Randolph, also an original member of his official family and a long-time friend, had been forced to resign office in disgrace; and a few weeks later the promising young Attorney General, William Bradford, met an unexpected death. As the year slipped by it became embarrassingly clear that men of national political reputation were suddenly unwilling or unable to accept appointments to the President's cabinet.*

When John Adams entered the presidency he retained Washington's advisors, the four men who had been found as replacements for Edmund Randolph, Hamilton, Knox, and William Bradford. Timothy Pickering, Oliver Wolcott, Jr., James McHenry, and Charles Lee were names that the average voter in 1796 could scarcely have identified, and many wondered how they had found their ways into Washington's inner councils.

"Mr. Lee, the Attorney General . . . is arrived with his family," noted John Adams to his wife in February of 1796.

* See Appendix E, p. 414, for complete list of men who were offered cabinet posts by Washington.

"So is Mr. McHenry, the Secretary of War. The offices are once more filled. But how differently than when Jefferson, Hamilton, and Jay etc. were here!" The Vice-President acknowledged that greater unanimity might now be expected within the cabinet, for there was not one of the new men who was considered a potential presidential candidate. Nevertheless, it seemed shameful that Washington could persuade no one of outstanding rank to take the positions left vacant by the death of William Bradford and the resignation of Randolph.[1]

Jefferson displayed more sarcasm than concern over the appointments of Charles Lee and James McHenry to high office. In his opinion it was the President's own fault that he was in trouble over appointments. Almost half the available men in the Union had become ineligible because of Washington's growing political bias. The new men, together with Oliver Wolcott and Tim Pickering, commented Jefferson to James Monroe, "by their devotion to genuine republicanism will show to our citizens on what principles alone they can expect to rise." [2]

The Republican charge seemed to be well founded and was circulated widely after Jefferson's retirement and the fall of Edmund Randolph. Washington had sided more often with Hamilton than with Jefferson during the second administration, and the Republican leader had gradually found his point of view inconsistent with policies adopted by the administration.

As a general Washington had become used to the idea of the council of war. Strategy and tactics might be, and most sensibly ought to be, freely debated; but once a decision had been reached and the orders issued a general could not, by the very nature of his office, tolerate further dissension. Most of Washington's executive experience had been in the military

[1] February 8, 1796, Adams, *Letters to His Wife*, II, 195.
[2] March 2, 1796, Jefferson, *Writings* (Ford ed.), VIII, 222.

line. The council of war attitude seems to have been that which Washington adopted in his relations with his official family. Thus he was tolerant of the disagreements that Hamilton and Jefferson had fallen into, and he made serious efforts to restore harmony between them, but he was extremely intolerant in his attitude toward the newspaper war that his two principal secretaries carried on, and he had little patience with the activities of Freneau and Benjamin Bache. The idea of a loyal opposition in Congress was not entirely foreign to a former British colonial, but to oppose a matter when it had become law smacked of treason in Washington's estimation. The Whiskey Rebellion was quickly and effectively dealt with. To find that one of his inner councilors had become implicated in the fostering of it was more than General Washington could stand. Even though Randolph's conduct may have appeared no more than indiscreet, to use indiscretion in the discharge of duties seems more a crime to the soldier than to the civilian.[3]

Over the years of political battle Washington had grown to appreciate loyalty and devotion to settled policy highly. His appointments came to be drawn increasingly from the men known for their political beliefs as Federalists, and if they had served in the Revolution as comrades in arms their chances for Federal office were excellent.

The charges of political bias made against Washington by Jefferson and other prominent Republicans is well substantiated by the appointments made during Washington's last year of office. At the end of 1794 the President began to consider the problem presented by the forthcoming resignations of Hamilton and Knox, and in March, 1795, he drew up a list

[3] For a concise discussion of Washington's use of his powers by a man who saw the situation from the inside see Martin Van Buren's *Political Parties*, 73 ff. *The American Commonwealth*, Vol. I (London and New York, 1889), 37 ff. contains a summary of early Federal attitudes toward office. Bryce believed Washington to have made a sincere effort to remain above party disputes much as the British monarch does. Leonard L. White, *The Federalist*, 27, is instructive.

of names that he might consider for future Federal appointments. Following most of the names, Washington placed the initials of his three remaining original secretaries.[4]

Washington left no hint as to the meaning of the initials, but it is clear that he considered Hamilton, Knox, and Randolph as best informed regarding the political leanings of the men listed. Thus for the state of South Carolina he listed John and Edward Rutledge, Charles Cotesworth Pinckney, and Charles Pinckney. Hamilton's initials appear beside the first three names, those of Knox next to the Rutledge's, and those of Randolph beside Edward Rutledge. No one at that time appeared certain about Charles Pinckney's political convictions, and it is worth noting that he received no appointment and was not invited to consider one.

The Virginia list is more puzzling. The names of both Jefferson and Madison head it, but the remaining six men (Henry Lee, Patrick Henry, James Innes, Edmund Randolph, John Marshall, and Cyrus Griffin [5]) seem to have been more Federalist than Republican from what is known about them. Washington may have still hoped to use the abilities of Jefferson and Madison, perhaps for diplomatic appointments. Randolph, but for his connection with the Whiskey Rebellion, would seem to have been a logical choice for a Supreme Court appointment. Hamilton's name is connected with every name on the Virginia list except those of Griffin and Patrick Henry.

The list as a whole may be broken down into three categories: those who had already proved ardent administration spokesmen, those whose positions seemed to have been determined by expediency, and those who had yet to commit

[4] The use of Randolph's initials is not surprising when it is remembered that the Virginian was never considered by Jefferson or Madison as a bona fide anti-Federalist. Jefferson left frequent complaints about Randolph's lack of strong political convictions during the cabinet debates of 1792–93 in his "Anas."

[5] President of the Continental Congress, 1787–88.

themselves to the two newly arisen parties in the United States. Among those who may be placed under the first division are William S. Smith of New York; William Bradford, William Bingham, and Richard Peters of Pennsylvania; Henry Lee and John Marshall of Virginia; John Quincy Adams and Christopher Gore of Massachusetts; Judge William Patterson of New Jersey and former Governor Thomas Johnson of Maryland. McHenry's name with Hamilton's initials stands at the bottom of the Maryland group.

The above list reads like a roll call of the men to whom Washington appealed in his frantic search for administrative assistants during 1795.

The most outstanding public figures who fit into the second group are Edward Rutledge, Governor Thomas Mifflin of Pennsylvania, and Elbridge Gerry of Massachusetts. Most arresting are the names of Aaron Burr and George Clinton of New York and Charles Jarvis of Massachusetts.[6] Perhaps the President had access to information about them that historians have failed to uncover. The outcome of the presidential election of 1796 suggests that both Burr and Clinton were not on friendly terms with the dominant Virginia-New York-Pennsylvania clique that conducted that campaign for Jefferson. Here is further suggestion that the mistrust of Burr on the part of Republican leaders was not without foundation.

Washington's disheartening search for men with whom to replace Jefferson, Hamilton, and Knox had its antecedents in his struggle to win Jefferson five years earlier. Hamilton, Knox, and Randolph had willingly entered upon their duties,

[6] Washington's private list is to be found in the Fitzpatrick edition of his *Writings*, XXXIV, 168-169. A state-by-state survey of Federal patronage holders appears on pp. 165-167.

The frequency with which Hamilton's initials appear on this important list suggests the influence of Hamilton upon the President during the last few months of his administration. Van Buren's *Political Parties* (99-105), although unscholarly, contains a penetrating analysis of the subject of Hamilton-Washington relations.

but to win Jefferson from his genuine desire quietly to cultivate his fields at Monticello had demanded much patient entreaty. Finally Madison had succeeded in convincing him that sacrifices were essential to the launching of a successful Federal government. He stressed the fact that the State Department meant foreign affairs and little else.[7] Jefferson waited until February, 1790, and admitted to Madison that his acceptance was mailed with a reluctance "which has increased so as to oppress me extremely." [8]

Had he known that political warfare was to concern him so greatly while acting as the President's advisor, Jefferson would never have accepted. The price the Virginian paid for allowing himself to be thrust forward as the leader of the opposition party was a heavy one. When Thomas Adams of the Boston *Independent Chronicle* labeled the press attacks upon Jefferson as "slander" he was understating the case.[9]

Writing under the name "Metellus," Hamilton had begun his public condemnation of Jefferson's political views with a bold demand for his colleague's resignation. Readers of Fenno's *Gazette of the United States* were told that the only honorable course for the Secretary of State to pursue was that of an avowed opponent of the administration. Jefferson, it was asserted, was hiding behind his office.[10] Washington had already refused to accept Jefferson's first offer to retire and paid no attention to the "Metellus" letter.

When Jefferson's reluctance to remain in the cabinet became too marked to be ignored, the President proposed that he be named as Gouverneur Morris's successor at Paris. The offer, though as attractive as any Federal appointment from Jefferson's viewpoint, was declined. It was not the State De-

[7] Brant, *Madison,* 288.
[8] February 14, 1790, *Madison Papers,* NYPL.
[9] *Independent Chronicle,* October 18, 1792.
[10] *Gazette of the United States,* October 24, 1792; Lynch, *Fifty Years,* 27-28.

partment that he was leaving but all forms of government service, he told Washington.[11]

In the summer of 1793 the President and his Secretary spent an afternoon at Jefferson's country residence discussing the patronage situation. Washington began by suggesting James Madison as the best candidiate for Jefferson's office. The reply was that Madison had often expressed his repugnance at the idea of remaining much longer in public life. Eight men were brought up in the course of the afternoon, but there seemed doubts about each. John Jay was obvious, but he was satisfied with his station as Chief Justice. Senator King of New York, a close friend of Hamilton's was mentioned, but Jefferson declined expressing an opinion. Edward Rutledge and William Smith of South Carolina were connected in the public mind with the recent speculations in state bonds, thought Jefferson. Both considered Thomas Johnson of Maryland better for the Treasury Department than the State. Jefferson suggested Robert R. Livingston of New York, but to have two New Yorkers in his advisory council at the same time "would start a newspaper conflagration," commented Washington; and Hamilton's resignation could not yet be announced. Oliver Wolcott, Jr., was a clever man, but he knew little about him, said Jefferson of Hamilton's assistant in the Treasury Department; and his objection to the possibility of making Randolph his own successor was that his financial situation eliminated him as a man of independent views.

As Washington left he appeared deeply discouraged. It seemed, he said, that to find a man of reputation well versed in foreign affairs was almost impossible. It was like going to the gallows to have both Jefferson and Hamilton preparing to leave; he kept putting off the acceptance of their resignations but knew that he could not do so indefinitely. They

[11] Conversation with Washington recorded by Jefferson, February 20, 1793, *Jefferson Papers*, LC.

parted after Jefferson had explained his position fully. His office forced him to move in those circles where he was most hated, he was fed up with being misquoted in the papers, and he could not but feel that the administration would be more coherent and unified if he were out of the way. If Washington replied, Jefferson failed to note it.[12]

To James Madison, Jefferson fully unburdened himself of the sense of failure and frustration that had grown out of his quarrels with Hamilton and the dominant political faction. He had been in public life for twenty-four years, he said, ". . . worn down with labors from morning to night, and day to day; knowing them as fruitless to others as they are vexatious to myself, committed singly in desperate and eternal contest again a band who are systematically undermining the public liberty . . . in short, giving everything I love in exchange for everything I hate, and all this without a single gratification in profession or prospect . . . never let there be more between you and me on this subject." [13]

His friends, Madison and Monroe, attempted to postpone Jefferson's retirement, and it is significant that both appealed to him on the basis of the political consequences of the move. Your influence on the President, wrote Madison, late in the summer of 1793, will be a necessary and much needed counterweight to the current unpopularity of the French Minister, Citizen Genêt. Your successor, he argued, is bound to be one who will antagonize our relations with France. It would be of infinite value to the United States if Jefferson would stay in office until the end of the year.[14]

Monroe viewed the elimination of Jefferson from the President's councils much as Madison did, but he was more forthright about its effects upon the internal political situation. Your departure, he wrote after talking the matter over

[12] Jefferson's memorandum of the conversation of August 6, 1793; *Jefferson Papers*, LC.

[13] June 9, 1793; *Jefferson Papers*, LC.

[14] September 2, 1793; Madison, *Writings* (Hunt ed.), VI, 194-195.

with Madison, will have one virtue: that of leaving Hamilton completely exposed. He thought that as the situation then stood Hamilton had the advantage of overriding Jefferson's opinions and presenting administration measures as the product of all viewpoints within the cabinet. Other friends of his, however, considered Jefferson's presence a necessity if the United States was to retain character in foreign eyes as a republican government. His private feeling on the matter was that Jefferson's inside knowledge was a great asset to the opponents of the administration.[15]

The arguments of his friends persuaded Jefferson to remain in office until the end of the year, but he had asked Washington's leave to be absent for as much time as possible. With an eye to the future, he had arranged a compromise that he explained to Madison, "The President was to be absent 3 weeks, and after that I was to be absent 6 weeks. This got me rid of 9 weeks of the 13 and the remaining 4 Congress would be sitting. My view in this was precisely to avoid being at any more councils as much as possible, that I might not be committed in any thing further."[16]

On January 1, 1794, Washington accepted the first Secretary of State's resignation in a cordial note that praised Jefferson for his "integrity and talents." He was to discover that both integrity and talents were difficult to find in a man who would fill the vacant office and that Jefferson's experiences served as a warning to others who might otherwise have come to the aid of the Federal government in a period of deep embarrassment during which foreign relations were to dominate the political history of the new nation.[17]

The case of Jefferson has been examined in detail, because

[15] September 3, 1793, *Jefferson Papers*, LC.

[16] Jefferson to Madison, September 15, 1793, *ibid.*

[17] The words used by Jefferson in explaining his resignation seem preferable to inferences and speculations that might be based upon his conduct and that of Hamilton. Professor Bemis pointed to what he termed Hamilton's "outrageous interference" in State Department affairs as a primary

it exemplifies the problem of Federal office-holding so well and because Jefferson stood for a growing number of men seriously in doubt as to their ability to take a place in an administration whose policies seemed to sacrifice local liberties to centralized authority. To fill the office of Secretary of State Washington turned to Edmund Randolph. In August neither the President nor Jefferson had considered Randolph seriously, and not until one week before Jefferson's departure was the Attorney General invited to take the chief cabinet post.[18] While Washington's writings contain no record of a search for anyone else, undoubtedly the President had conducted a personal canvass during the fall among the politicians at the capital.

Edmund Randolph had years of distinguished service in the cause of American independence behind him when he entered the cabinet. At the beginning of the American Revolution he had split with his father on the independence issue. He had been recommended to serve as an aide to Washington by such distinguished Virginians as Jefferson, Richard Henry Lee, Patrick Henry, and Benjamin Harrison; and as a young man he had been elected to the convention of 1776 that drew up Virginia's first constitution. At the end of the war he had been governor, chosen over both R. H. Lee and Theodorick Bland, had been a delegate to the Annapolis convention, and in the Constitutional Convention had presented the important Virginia plan of union.

Though he had refused to sign the projected constitution because it was not republican enough in character, Randolph had come to its defense in the Virginia ratifying con-

---

cause. (S. F. Bemis, *American Secretaries of State,* II, "Thomas Jefferson," 29).

Beveridge (*John Marshall,* II, 96) concluded that it was to take the leadership of the incipient Republican party that Jefferson resigned when he did, French relations forcing it. Most generally accepted is the idea that he found his opinions increasingly overlooked and those of Hamilton increasingly accepted by Washington, hence his resignation.

[18] Washington, *Writings,* XXXIII, 216.

vention. There he had distinguished himself as Madison's ally against Patrick Henry and the strong antifederalist faction. When the Federal government was inaugurated Randolph was chosen Attorney General. Possessed of a fine analytical mind, he had much to recommend him as Jefferson's successor even though he lacked specific experience in foreign affairs.

It is impossible to place Randolph in the ranks of the Jeffersonians, because Jefferson himself could not have listed him as one of his supporters. "When he is with me he is a Whig," Jefferson wrote to Madison in a moment of petulance, "when with Hamilton a Tory, when with the President he is what he thinks will please him. . . . I have kept on terms of strict friendship with him hitherto that I might make some good of him, and because he has some good private qualities." [19]

Jefferson's notes frequently complain against the waverings of Randolph, and even when the final vote was taken on administration policies over which Hamilton and Jefferson had decisively split, Randolph's hand was raised as often against as for Jefferson's position.

As Secretary of State from January 1, 1794, to August 19, 1795, Randolph left no great mark upon the history of American diplomacy. Washington, often with Hamilton's aid, made his own decisions, and on the critical question of the Whiskey Rebellion in Pennsylvania Randolph added his support to that of the other three cabinet members in recommending strong action. The revelations of his connection with the opponents of the tax threw Randolph into disgrace with Washington, and the obloquy has never been lifted completely from his shoulders.

The suddenness of Randolph's resignation forced Washington to appoint Secretary of War Timothy Pickering as acting Secretary of State. No one, including Pickering him-

[19] August 11, 1793, *Jefferson Papers*, LC.

self, supposed that his function was anything more than that of a fill-in.

Justice William Paterson of the Supreme Court was first asked to take Randolph's post, but either he preferred the permanence of the bench to a political office or felt unqualified for the position; he refused the offer.[20] The next three men to whom Washington appealed, Thomas Johnson, C. C. Pinckney, and Patrick Henry, were Southerners. The list began and ended with a Northern man. Evidently Washington was more concerned about the man than the geographic location from which he came.

Governor Johnson, a Marylander who had served with distinction in both the first and second Continental Congresses, was very much in the President's confidence. He had been appointed a commissioner of the new District of Columbia, had been consulted on important administration decisions, and had the approval of both Jefferson and Hamilton as a man worthy to fill high office.[21] Johnson declined on grounds of age and health and sent a letter from the President addressed to General Pinckney on to Charleston as soon as he had reached his decision.[22] On grounds of personal consideration Pinckney, who had previously refused the war office, also declined the honor of becoming George Washington's chief administrative assistant.[23]

In the midst of his humiliating search, the President received a suggestion from Col. Edward Carrington of Richmond, which surprised him greatly. The idea that Patrick

20 Washington to Hamilton, October 29, 1795; *Writings*, XXXIV, 347. Tench Coxe ingratiated himself (or attempted to so) by suggesting Paterson to Washington through Col. Pickering. Coxe to Paterson, August 27, 1795; *Paterson Papers*, Bancroft Collection, New York Public Library.

21 Jefferson spoke with approval of Johnson during his conversation with Washington in August, 1793 (*supra*). Hamilton's initials appear next to Johnson's name on the patronage list drawn up by the President in March, 1795. See also above.

22 Washington, *Writings*, XXXIV, 285n; Steiner, *McHenry*, 161; Washington to Johnson, August 26, 1795; *Writings*, XXXIV, 287.

23 Washington, *Writings*, XXXIV, 285-286.

Henry, long considered an uncompromising opponent of the new system of government, might accept a Federal appointment was novel. John Marshall and Carrington had noted a gradual change in the old orator's political sentiments and thought the time ripe for sounding him out. "So much have the opposers of government held him up as their oracle, even since he ceased to respond to them," wrote Carrington, "that any event, demonstrating his active support to government could not but give the [Republican] party a severe shock." A flattering invitation to take the State Department might bring him over into the Federalist camp.[24]

Washington was wary but interested. After checking with Henry Lee he felt reassured and gave Carrington the authority to tender the appointment. He explained the grave difficulties he had experienced during the summer and agreed with his Richmond friends that the offer could do no harm, even though he anticipated Henry's refusal.[25] Carrington was invited to take the War Department over if it became necessary to name Pickering as permanent Secretary of State.

Henry's refusal was written immediately upon the receipt of Washington's letter, but it was friendly in tone and undoubtedly tended to draw him out of his political neutrality.[26] A few months later Hamilton and Rufus King felt confident enough of Henry's cordiality toward the administration to pursue him as a presidential candidate, and within four years he stood for election to the Virginia assembly as an avowed supporter of Mr. Adams' French policy. The news that he had been approached by the administration seemed incredible to Madison when he heard of it in December. "The offer of the Secretaryship of State to P. Henry

[24] No date (summer, 1795), T. A. Boyd, *Lighthorse Harry Lee* (New York, 1931), p. 237.

[25] October 9, 1795, Washington, *Writings*, XXXIV, 331-333.

[26] Carrington to Washington, *ibid.*, 333n; Henry to Washington, October 16, 1795, *ibid.*, 335n.

is a circumstance I should not have believed without the most unquestionable testimony," he wrote Jefferson [27]

The principal office in his advisory council had been vacant for more than two and a half months when Washington turned the problem over to Hamilton. "What am I to do for a Secretary of State?" He was reluctant to appoint a man with a recent voting record (a present member of either house), but Senator King would make an excellent choice, despite his well-known pro-British sympathies, he said. Hamilton was asked to suggest any qualified man for either the State Department or the Attorney Generalship. John Marshall had already refused to take the office left vacant by the sudden death of William Bradford. "In short," wrote Washington, "what with non-acceptance of some; the known dereliction of those who are most fit; [28] the exceptionable drawbacks from others; and a wish to make a geographical distribution of the great offices of the Administration, I find the selection of proper characters an arduous duty." [29]

Hamilton found the task of converting King impossible. Ever since King had taken his place in the Senate he had won the enthusiastic endorsement of leading administration supporters. When Randolph's resignation was first heard of Senator Gunn of Georgia concluded that his colleague from New York would be an outstanding candidiate for the position. At the end of August he had written, "If the President offers you the appointment of Secretary of State, I beg you to accept—have the goodness to recollect the situation of the Executive. Colonel Hamilton will take your place in the Senate and all will be well. If ever the Executive wanted aid, this is the moment." [30]

[27] December 6, 1795, *Madison Papers,* LC.

[28] Washington had in mind particularly Col. James Innes of Virginia. In the same letter he referred to Innes as too lazy to accept the Attorney General's office. *Writings,* XXXIV, 348.

[29] October 29, 1795, *ibid.,* XXIV, 347-349.

[30] August 22, 1795, *King Papers,* New York Public Library, Box 6, No. 43.

At the height of the Jay treaty furor Christopher Gore of the Essex Junto added his entreaties to those of Gunn. In Massachusetts it was already expected that King's nomination would be forthcoming from the President. "It is generally agreed that such is the critical situation of affairs that you would sacrifice your ease for your country's good." The liberties of American citizens, he declared, depended upon the soundness of the executive branch of the government.[31]

Rufus King, however, had been in public life since 1784 and was in no mood to continue. A diplomatic appointment proved attractive, but he had had his fill of politics.[32] Hamilton wrote the President with more than his usual candor. He said that King would definitely not accept and that to find a suitable man for the office would be almost impossible. "Smith (of South Carolina), though not of full size . . . has more real talent than the last incumbent . . . but he is . . . considered as tinctured with prejudice towards the British . . . besides it is very important that he should not be removed from the House of Representatives." [33]

Hamilton, who had but six weeks to remain in office, went on to name two of the four men who were to make up the cabinet of the next four years. As Attorney General he considered Henry Lee or his younger brother Charles Lee advisable, and to replace Henry Knox he lukewarmly endorsed James McHenry, previously unnamed. "McHenry you know would give no strength to the administration but he would not disgrace the office. . . . In fact a first rate character is not attainable. A second rate must be taken with good dis-

[31] September 13, 1795, *ibid.*, Box 6, No. 45.

[32] Lynn Montross, *The Reluctant Rebels* (New York, 1950), 361, 375-389, 398, 417.

[33] Apparently the belief that William L. Smith of South Carolina would be appointed Secretary of State was widespread. An obscure Pennsylvania Republican, Andrew Ellicott, wrote to General William Irvine, November 13, 1795, "William Smith of S. Carolina will be the next Secretary of State." *Irvine Papers*, Historical Society of Pennsylvania, XIII, 85.

positions and barely decent qualifications. . . . T'is a sad omen for the government." [34]

In Jefferson's case it was a sense of futility, the longing for private life, and political abuse that caused resignation from Washington's cabinet. Why should Hamilton have resigned from a post that he had made powerful, second only to that of the President and one from which he was able to wield a greater measure of power over American economic and political life than any other man of the day? It was certainly not out of a sense of futility that Alexander Hamilton withdrew from public life at the beginning of 1795.

Like Jefferson, Hamilton could complain of the unfair treatment that he had received at the hands of newspaper editors. As early as December, 1792, for example, Philip Freneau's Jeffersonian sheet had alleged that the Secretary of the Treasury favored a vigorous policy of war against the Indian tribes of the frontiers, because he was profiteering from army contracts. Hamilton easily met such a charge by asking whether the writer had any idea which department of the government let army contracts—General Knox was the man to see.[35]

Over and over again Hamilton was charged with embezzlement, the most famous attack being that of Representative William Giles of Virginia in the House. With the aid of Jefferson, who chose this method of striking back at "Metellus," a series of resolutions were prepared and placed before the House of Representatives in February, 1793. Using information supplied by House Clerk John Beckley, Jefferson had compiled a list of congressmen holding stocks or dealing in securities. So many appeared champions of Hamilton's financial schemes that Jefferson and Giles were certain that the source of the smoke was a fire fed in Hamilton's office. The

34 November 8, 1795, *Hamilton Papers,* LC.

35 Copy of Hamilton's "Anti-Defamer" article with explanatory notes in his handwriting, *Hamilton Papers,* LC.

last resolve was a point-blank demand for Hamilton's resignation. "Resolved: That the Secretary of the Treasury has been found guilty of maladministration in the duties of his office, and should, in the opinion of Congress, be removed from office by the President of the United States." [36]

The charges made by Giles made little impression upon Congress, only the most stalwart Republicans voting for them.[37] Evidently the Virginians hoped to undermine Hamilton's reputation. They could scarcely have counted on success in Congress, but it would nevertheless affect public opinion in a way harmful to Hamilton simply to point out that demands for an investigation of his department had been made. From Virginia Edward Carrington reported that the opposition was loudly trumpeting the corruption charge. In an effort to offset their campaign, Carrington had had the proceedings of Congress printed in the most influential Richmond papers, and at Hamilton's suggestion, he had sent the same material on to papers at Norfolk, Petersburg, Alexandria, and Winchester.[38]

In the summer of 1793 Hamilton was again informed that the antiadministration campaign in Virginia had been little affected by the truth. If the opposition fail to carry their charges at the next session, suggested Carrington in July, their influence here will fall considerably. "I have pressed this idea here, and trust it will be generally entertained." He went on to advise that Hamilton take up their challenge. "Should your persecutors not come forward at the next session with an impeachment, it is my opinion that you should call for one; it would ensure at once their destruction. . . . Your determination to continue in office and stem the storms

[36] Jefferson, *Writings* (Ford ed.), VI, 168-171.

[37] Political independents like Elbridge Gerry of Massachusetts voted against the Giles resolutions. Hamilton left a note to this effect, *Hamilton Papers*, LC.

[38] March 26, 1793, *Hamilton Papers*, LC.

which envy, malice, or ambition can generate . . . is that on which your salvation depends." [39]

Carrington was more useful as a lieutenant than as a strategist and often proved overly optimistic, but for once Hamilton took his advice. At the beginning of the short session of the winter of 1793–94 Hamilton invited an investigation of his department. Finally on February 24 Giles took up the challenge, calling for the appointment of a committee to look into the Treasury records. Representative Baldwin of Georgia, a staunch antiadministration man, headed the committee that died a natural death when the session closed a few days later.[40]

So far as the Republicans were concerned the only good that arose out of the Giles resolutions was a brief rift between Hamilton and the President and some venomous rumors. When Hamilton publicly asked the President for a declaration relating to foreign loans, Washington wrote so ambiguous a reply that it was taken up and printed as incriminating evidence against Hamilton.[41]

The first salvo against Hamilton's administration of the Treasury Department was a failure in the sense that Hamilton had emerged with his reputation for honesty unshaken, but it almost produced the result that was hoped for. On June 21, after the Giles resolution agitation had subsided, Washington received Hamilton's resignation. "Considerations, relative both to the public interest and to my own delicacy, have brought me after mature relection, to a resolution to resign . . . towards the close of the ensuing session of Congress." [42]

Washington succeeded in persuading Hamilton to put off

[39] July 2, 1793, *Hamilton Papers,* LC.

[40] Hamilton, *Republic,* VI, 13-15.

[41] Copy with marginal notes of Washington's letter to Hamilton, April 8, 1794, in *Jefferson Papers,* LC. Hamilton to Washington, April 14, 1794, *Hamilton Papers,* LC.

[42] Hamilton to Washington, June 21, 1793, *Hamilton Papers,* LC.

the step for a year and a half, but its imminence together with Jefferson's announced intentions produced in him the gloom of August that Jefferson has recorded. Rumors of the resignation (Jeffersonians called it a retreat) caused excited comment.

General Schuyler, Hamilton's father-in-law, noted that the usual causes assigned were that Hamilton wished to become Governor of New York and that the Treasury Department was hopelessly confused.[43] Jefferson was certain that Hamilton was getting out before the awful truth was discovered. To Monroe he wrote that Hamilton had arranged a convenient appointment as minister to England, "a more degrading measure could not have been proposed." Washington's true purpose, he thought, was that of "withdrawing H. from the disgrace and public execrations which sooner or later must fall on the man."[44]

While Jefferson, happily withdrawn from the political circles he had so disliked, continued to lament the "shameless corruption" of the first and second Congresses of the United States for their devotion to the Treasury Department and to urge support for his resolutions that Giles continued to talk about,[45] Federalists rallied around Hamilton. "Mr. Giles must feel very much mortified, and his constituents cannot be pleased at seeing him placed so far in the background," wrote Boston port collector Stephen Higginson.[46] Carrington gloried in the success of his own plan. The Republicans in Virginia were disgraced, at least temporarily.[47] William Heath, also a Virginian, hoped that Hamilton would not take the final failure of the attack as a signal for

[43] Schuyler to Hamilton, Albany, January 5, 1794, *ibid.*, Second Series.
[44] April 24, 1794, *Jefferson Papers*, LC.
[45] Jefferson to Edmund Randolph, February 3, 1794, *ibid.*
[46] To Hamilton, June 17, 1794, *Hamilton Papers*, LC.
[47] Carrington to Hamilton, June, 1794, Hamilton, *Republic*, VI, 34-35; July 9, 1794; *Hamilton Papers*, LC.

triumphant retirement.[48] All three men had been on the Federal payroll, the recipients of Treasury Department favors, and Jefferson would probably have said the same of the men who gathered in respectable taverns to toast the Secretary of the Treasury and American commerce.[49]

When Hamilton finally did resign on January 1, 1795, he had successfully staved off continuous attacks of twelve months' duration. His reputation was undamaged, and as far as Federalist leaders were concerned he had never appeared more successful. Close friends assured those who spoke of his immediate political plans that there were none, yet it seemed hard to believe. Madison was certain that the spring would witness a hot fight between Hamilton and Burr for the governorship of New York, and Carrington thought he had it figured out when he wrote, "I anticipate with pleasure, your appearance in the character of a Representative . . . ;[50] but William Bradford, temporarily Attorney General, probably came closest to divining Hamilton's future when he wrote, "You were made for a statesman, and politics will never be out of your head."[51] Bradford never lived to witness the course of Washington's administration through the last two years. If he had, he would have known how correct he was. Out of office, Hamilton was as influential in determining policy as he had been while an official advisor, and he seemed to have more time for Federalist party business.

Hamilton's opponent, Jefferson, seems seriously to have believed that the retirement was brought on by a sixth sense: Hamilton was getting out in time to escape the condemnation that would follow hard upon the inevitable financial

[48] Heath to Hamilton, July 6, 1794, Hamilton, *Republic, op. cit.;* also in *Hamilton Papers*, LC.

[49] Hamilton's note of a businessman's dinner in his honor in the summer of 1793, *ibid.*

[50] Madison to Monroe, December 4, 1794, *Madison Papers*, LC; Carrington to Hamilton, December 12, 1794, *Hamilton Papers*, LC.

[51] Bradford to Hamilton, July 2, 1795, *ibid.*

collapse of the American economy. John Quincy Adams, doubtless echoing his father's sentiments, ascribed it to ambition. "He had retired from the administration in 1795 because it presented no object of magnitude sufficient to satisfy his aspirations. . . ." [52] Others assumed it had been brought about because of future political plans, but John Marshall hit the nail on the head when he set down as the true cause of Hamilton's retirement his financial embarrassment.[53]

[52] J. Q. Adams, *Parties in the United States* (New York, 1941), 27.
[53] Marshall, *Life of Washington*, V, 607.

12

The President and His Secretaries

HAMILTON HAD NO FORMAL PLANS WHEN HE RETIRED IN 1795, because he could not afford them. His friend William Heath of Virginia understood Hamilton's personal problem and rejoiced for his sake that he had retired. Heath had found that two and a half years of government service was enough to ruin any man. "It is a mortifying reflection," he wrote, "that . . . the emoluments of office for the last 12 months have little more than defrayed the expense of it."[1] According to Henry Lee, Hamilton had spoken of taking up private law practice again as an absolute necessity. His entire savings account of £3,000 had been spent trying to make up the difference between salary and living expenses. His death, Hamilton was reputed to have said, would have made his family completely dependent upon his father-in-law's generosity.[2]

The problems of a public servant of the United States at the time of its founding were well set forth by Hamilton in a letter that he wrote to a distant cousin a few months after he had quit his cabinet post. "Public office in this country has few attractions. The pecuniary emolument is so inconsiderable as to amount to a sacrifice to any man who can employ his time to advantage in any liberal profession." In addition, he said, there was such political animosity as to destroy constructive use of authority, and party struggles had grad-

[1] Heath to Hamilton, July 6, 1794, *Hamilton Papers*, LC.
[2] Joseph Jones to Madison, December 26, 1794, *Madison Papers*, LC.

ually eliminated the desire for power with any anticipation of using it. Finally, fear of the Executive authority had produced such a crop of defamations and criticism that hope for future recognition seemed unfounded.[3]

According to eighteenth-century republican ideals devotion to the public good was enough to draw men into government service at a personal sacrifice. Jefferson often championed the cause of frugality in government, and he included Federal salaries in his catalogue of things to be frugal over despite his own experience. The President's salary of $25,000 was generally considered more than adequate, but it soon became apparent that $3,000 per annum was far too little to support a Secretary of State or a Supreme Court Justice. When both Washington and Adams made recommendations for increases in the Federal pay scale the democratic opposition quite illogically objected.[4] Rich men or second-raters continued to fill offices.

When one of the District of Columbia commissioners suggested to the President that higher recompense might allow him to give his full time to the business of creating a national capital, Washington agreed but could offer little comfort except to remind him that others shared his vexation. "With respect to your ideas of a future allowance, I am bold in assuring that, no fixed Sallery (*sic*) in the United States (however they have been reprobated for their extravagance)

[3] Hamilton to Alexander Hamilton of Scotland, May 2, 1797, Hamilton, *Works* (Hamilton ed.), VI, 243.

[4] The salaries of the principal officers set in 1790 were: President, $25,000; Vice-President, $5,000; Chief Justice, $4,000; Associate Justices, $3,500; Secretary of War, $3,000; and Attorney General, $1,500. *Annals*, 1st Congress, 1st Session, Appendix, 2233-38. On May 6, 1796, Representative Smith of Maryland put a resolution before the House calling for increases in salary for the secretaries of departments and their subordinates, but the resolution was immediately tabled. (*Connecticut Gazette*, May 19, 1796.) By a law of February, 1799, the salaries of the four secretaries were raised $1,500 each. Although strongly opposed by the Republicans the bill passed the House, 52-43. This pay scale was kept throughout Jefferson's two administrations. (Gibbs, *Memoirs*, II, 182.)

from the Chief Magistrate to the Doorkeeper of the House of Representatives is equal to One Thousand dollars clear of expenses." [5]

Jefferson left a note for Randolph declaring that he had discovered the annual expenses of the office of Secretary of State to be $9,661, almost three times the allowance granted by law.[6] Sensing that many potential public servants were holding back because of the expense of office, Jefferson stressed duty very highly. On the day before his retirement he wrote in this vein to Edward Rutledge, a man whom he continually urged to accept a Presidential appointment. It had been eighteen years since they had first met, he wrote, and he had spent sixteen of those years as a public servant. "I believe you are happier in the line you have chosen; but you have not yet proven to me that the performance of a certain tour of duty in any line which the public calls for can be rightfully declined." [7]

He again appealed to Rutledge at the end of 1795 after the South Carolinian had written of the necessity for the President to appoint men of first-rate abilities. "The present situation of the President, unable to get the offices filled, really calls with uncommon obligation upon those whom nature has fitted for them." [8] Rutledge was unmoved.

Evidently Jefferson considered that he had more than done his duty. When his successor in the State Department sought him to take the Spanish mission that Thomas Pinckney finally accepted, Jefferson answered that "no circumstances . . . will ever more tempt me to engage in anything public." [9] Such was the taste left in his mouth by a public career.

The worst victim of the public service was Edmund Ran-

[5] Washington to David Stuart, March 3, 1793, *Writings,* XXXII, 367.

[6] Note in the *Jefferson Papers,* LC.

[7] December 30, 1793, *ibid.*

[8] November 30, 1795, *ibid.*

[9] Randolph to Jefferson, August 28, 1794; Jefferson to Randolph, September 7, 1794; D. R. Anderson, "Jefferson," *American Secretaries of State* (Bemis ed.), 120-123.

dolph. At the time he took over Jefferson's duties he was almost bankrupt and on the point of retiring from the cabinet, but the offer that Washington made was apparently so flattering as to cause his acceptance. Perhaps he had hopes of living within his budget, but the system then in vogue hardly allowed it. The head of a department was held responsible for all financial losses that might be incurred in the transacting of its business, and when Randolph left the State Department a deficit of more than $50,000 was discovered and charged to him and to his heirs. In 1804 a court order forced Randolph to pay $53,000, and it was not until 1889 that his descendents succeeded in having Randolph's name erased from the Treasury Department's list of debtors.[10] Thus Edmund Randolph lost both his fortune and his reputation by accepting office under the Federal government.

While James McHenry thought over the amazing suggestion that he become Henry Knox's successor, his friend Representative Murray assured him of living in comfort, if not in ease. The salary, wrote Murray, was sufficient to maintain a modest establishment and was sure to be increased in the near future. He described the homes of Pickering and Wolcott as small but "neat." Each seemed able to live within his means.[11] Among Mr. Pickering's few earthly possession at the time of his death, however, was a copy of a note that he sent in answer to socialite William Bingham's invitation to dinner. "It is not easy for me," wrote the Secretary of State, "to offer an apology that has not truth for its basis. . . . Mrs. Pickering and I are constrained to forego many pleasures of society, because we cannot persuade ourselves to enter on a career of expenses which, being far beyond our income, would lead to ruin." [12] The Pickerings, it would seem, had

[10] W. C. Ford, *George Washington*, II, 224; D. R. Anderson, "Edmund Randolph," *American Secretaries of State* (Bemis ed.), II, 157-158.

[11] Murray to McHenry, January 28, 1796, Steiner, *McHenry*, 166-167.

[12] December 17, 1795, Upham, *Pickering*, III, 171.

viewed the financial ruin of Randolph and of General Knox with genuine alarm.

Governor Oliver Wolcott commiserated with his son during his term as Secretary of the Treasury for the pittance that was allowed to high officers of the Federal government as well as for the unjust criticism that was their constant diet. The importance of the responsibility held by the administrative officers would lead one to expect that they might build up a sizable fortune within a few years' time, he wrote, but such was not the case. He advised his son to resign his office in the event that Washington refused a third term.[13]

What was true on the level of high office was equally true with regard to port inspectors, district marshals, justices, and army officers. Concerning General St. Clair's reorganization of the United States Army, John Marshall wrote, ". . . the laws furnished such small inducements to engage in the service, that the highest military grades were declined by many to whom they were offered."[14] In 1798 Fisher Ames was appointed an Indian Commissioner to the Cherokees. He was forced to decline, because the pay would not support his family during his absence.[15]

The office of Attorney General, offering the salary of $1,500 per year, was a problem of special difficulty. The office lacked the prestige of the other three as the recompense plainly indicated, and only by holding out to John Marshall the possibility of combining its not too burdensome duties with a lucrative Philadelphia law practice did Washington believe it possible to win him over.[16] Marshall, like Patrick Henry, was eagerly sought in order to strengthen the Federalist party in Virginia. Marshall was offered the War Department and the Attorney Generalship, and Henry the

[13] July 4, 1796, Gibbs, *Memoirs,* I, 372.

[14] John Marshall, *Life of Washington,* V, 373.

[15] Ames to Oliver Wolcott, Jr., February 2, 1798, Gibbs, *Memoirs,* II, 12.

[16] Washington to Marshall, August 26, 1795, *Writings,* XXXIV, 287-288; Washington to Pickering, September 16, 1795, *ibid.,* 306.

nation's three highest offices—President, Secretary of State, and Chief Justice.

When President Adams' appointment as a minister extraordinary was tendered to him in 1797 Marshall accepted, because it was one of the few appointments from which he might emerge better off than when he took it up. His Richmond law practice in 1796 was bringing in more than $5,000 a year, but for eleven months' service as an envoy to France Marshall was paid the amazing sum of $19,963.[17] Marshall was supposed to have called the appointment "the greatest Godsend that could ever have befallen a man." [18] He, like Robert Morris and Henry Knox, had lost heavily in land speculations.

A Richmond Federalist holding the office of master in chancery complained that he had been steadily persecuted by political opponents and that his family could not live on his modest income.[19] In New Hampshire, Chief Justice Pickering of the State Supreme Court found his office both time-consuming and unrewarding. Senator King was asked to recommend him for a Federal bench appointment that would leave him more time for private practice.[20] Probably the worst sufferers were the important clerks in the executive departments. George Taylor, employed by the State Department, found his condition so intolerable that he had petitioned Congress for temporary aid in 1793. In 1795 the aid ended and Taylor was reduced to supporting a wife and family upon a yearly allowance of eight hundred dollars.[21]

Between 1789, when Washington and others high in political circles had been flooded with patronage requests, and 1795, the year of crisis in the government service, prices had

[17] Beveridge, *Marshall*, II, 201-202, 211, 372; Jefferson, *Writings* (Ford ed.), I, 355.

[18] Jefferson's *Anas*, March 21, 1800, *Writings* (Ford ed.), I, 355.

[19] J. W. Dunscomb to King, January 6, 1795, *King Papers*, New York Historical Society, Box 6.

[20] John Pickering to King, February 5, 1795, *ibid.*

[21] Taylor to Madison, January 30, 1796, *Madison Papers*, LC.

more than doubled. To live on what had been considered adequate when the laws were passed was impossible unless private income from investments or law practice could be depended upon. Others who accepted or continued to hold Federal appointments were reaching back into savings. Hamilton, who kept clear of investments for obvious reasons, and Randolph, who was unfortunate in land sales, were more hard hit than either Washington or Jefferson, who depended upon rents for the major portion of their incomes. Not one of the men who served under Washington and Adams in an advisory capacity left office without experiencing financial sacrifice, and it seems significant that when President Adams appointed a Secretary of the Navy in 1798 he chose a highly successful Maryland merchant. If there was a general decline in the efficiency of the government service (as the changeover in personnel would seem to indicate) it is little to be wondered at. Men who at first had sought small, part-time positions shunned them in 1795 and 1796; instead of demanding little time and adding to regular income, the less important offices were proving time-consuming and expensive to hold.[22]

The rise of political parties created a personnel barrier unforeseen at the time of the inauguration of the Federal government. By 1795 many men who had proved their executive or diplomatic capacities during the Revolution and Confed-

[22] Edward Carrington's case is not unique. In 1789 he petitioned Madison to help him get an appointment. He was more than grateful to be named a Federal marshal, and at least considered it possible that the small salary would supplement his regular income. Four months later he complained that "the compensation will not even feed a horse." Carrington to Madison, December 20, 1789, April 1, 1790, *Madison Papers,* New York Public Library.

The facts related above disagree in conclusion with the observations of Channing (*History*, IV, 49-61). The contrast between the reluctance of men to accept high office and the eagerness to receive an appointment to a lower office does not really stand up. It was true in the beginning, but within a few years there was difficulty in filling even the local offices with men of reputation.

eration period would not accept or be considered for appointment by Washington, who demanded a high standard of loyalty and conformity of his assistants. Since the Federalist party on the whole commanded the respect of men whose livelihood depended upon business and commerce rather than agriculture, we may, as a generalization, say that few outstanding political leaders south of the Delaware River were available for Federal office. The realization that this was true caused Washington to give a disproportionate share of the patronage to Southerners and to pursue such men as Patrick Henry, John Marshall and Charles Cotesworth Pinckney repeatedly with the highest offices at his disposal.

Many men who might have filled Federal positions with distinction refused to do so out of weariness with public life and the desire to remain in obscurity. Most of the men upon whom Washington called were veterans of the Revolution or former members of the Continental Congress. Washington, Jefferson, Hamilton, Knox, Jay, and even the rather youthful Madison all longed for retirement. Still others, such as Edward Rutledge and Sam Adams, preferred to confine themselves to state service. By the time Jefferson and Hamilton retired from public life the novelty of the Federal government had worn off. Madison withdrew from public service when he felt that the experiment had been successfully launched and would not return until he became convinced that radical measures threatened to alter the basic character of the American government.

So influential did the purely economic consideration appear from a survey of the writings of the men involved in the patronage crisis of 1794–95 that it has been stressed. The needs of their families caused Hamilton to resign and forced John Marshall to refuse appointments. There can be little doubt that men of first-rate abilities thought twice about accepting office after the experiences of the first cabinet members. A highly aristocratic republic might have been maintained had salaries from top to bottom of the Federal scale not been raised in the years following the Adams administration. As it was, even men of the most radical democratic sentiments were drawn from the wealthiest families. Only a severe political crisis such as the nation experienced in 1789 and in 1798–99 could add enough luster to Federal office to give the government service the prestige needed for it to compete on the open market for talent.

Until a new generation could ripen to maturity the nation was forced to accept the services of many men whose records clearly indicate a second order of abilities. It was the misfortune of John Adams to enter the presidency with such advisors and to carry on with them until his political reputation was damaged beyond repair.

The question has often been posed: why did Adams accept Washington's cabinet and why, after he had tested their capacities, did he not get rid of them? The answer seems abundantly clear. As Vice-President he was well aware of the struggle to find replacements for Jefferson, Hamilton, Knox, and Randolph, and it would seem that he willingly avoided the issue of the resignations of Washington's cabinet. How closely Adams had watched the situation is revealed by a letter written to his wife just after the reorganization of 1795. "Happy is the country to be rid of Randolph; but where shall be found good men and true to fill the offices of government? There seems to be a necessity of distributing the offices about the states in some proportion to their numbers; but in the southern part of the Union, false politics have struck their roots so deep, that it is very difficult to find gentlemen who are willing to accept of public trusts, and at the same time capable of discharging them. . . . The expenses of living at the seat of government are so exorbitant, so far beyond all proportions to the salaries, and the sure reward of integrity . . . is such obloquy, contempt, and insult, that no man of any feeling is willing to renounce his home, forsake his property for the sake of removing to Philadelphia, where he is almost sure of disgrace and ruin."[23]

Although Adams exaggerated somewhat, his estimate was based upon the truth, and inasmuch as the political climate had changed little in the succeeding twelve months we may accept this as his view of the patronage problem. The importance of the brief but promising entente with Jefferson is heightened in the light of the serious patronage problem. Had their friendship survived the strain of politics, a reservoir of personnel would have been available to the Adams administration that the closing years of Washington's administration had seen choked off. Throughout his four years of office Adams attempted to overstep the political party line in his appointments. His serious quarrel with Hamilton only increased a difficulty already alarming when he entered the presidency.

The four men who were to act as John Adams' principal advisors until 1800 were almost unknown to the public when appointed by Washington. Both Pickering and Wolcott were career men, the first in the nation's history, and the other two were individuals who would have remained unknown save for the dilemma of 1795.

Timothy Pickering had graduated from Harvard in 1763 and was admitted to the bar three years later. Finding law distasteful, he took up teaching and for a time acted as a choir director. His brief career during the Revolution as an officer in the Quartermaster Corps gained for him an appointment as Quartermaster General in 1780. When the office was abolished in 1785 Pickering and his expanding family moved to Philadelphia, where he failed as a businessman, a farmer, and a real estate agent.

When the Federal government was inaugurated, Pickering was appointed an Indian agent to the Iroquois. Good reports of his diligence reached Washington, and in 1791 he was

[23] January 7, 1796, Adams, *Works*, I, 483.

named Postmaster General at a salary of $1,500. At the time he held the post-office position his family added up to one wife and nine children. Almost out of mercy, the House of Representatives increased the salary to $2,400. When Washington failed to persuade Pinckney, Carrington, and John Marshall to fill Henry Knox's post, he hit upon the hard-working Postmaster.

Pickering has had many critics. His activities while acting supposedly under President Adams scarcely merit praise, and as a Secretary of State he proved unexceptional; but there was such integrity in the man that he never lacked friends, and each step of his upward climb was made possible by the recommendations of others. When Randolph suddenly resigned under heavy fire, Pickering was asked to act as temporary Secretary of State, a post for which he was as unsuited as any man Washington could have found. To his credit it must be said that he was perfectly willing to admit as much. When the long search for a permanent replacement proved as illusive as El Dorado the President asked him to continue in office.

An energetic administrator and a loyal servant so long as he respected his master, Pickering proved competent if nothing more. Washington acted as his own authority on foreign affairs with the advice of Hamilton. Although Hamilton was acquainted with Pickering as a subordinate, the post office being a subsidiary of the Treasury Department, the ties between the two were never as cordial as tradition has painted them. It was Wolcott who most strenuously urged Pickering's acceptance of the State Department, and in the last phase of the Jay treaty fight Pickering more than once showed an independence of view that Hamilton found disquieting. During Mr. Adams' administration Hamilton rarely approached Pickering directly. He much preferred the more pliable Wolcott or the worshipful McHenry to carry out his suggestions. Pickering was treated with a degree of deference that the other two never expected.[24]

Both McHenry and Oliver Wolcott, Jr., were Hamiltonian protégés. Wolcott, the more clever of the two, proved to be Hamilton's chief lieutenant during the election of 1796 and throughout the years of the Adams administration. He first entered government service as auditor for the Treasury Department, where he was directly under Hamilton's supervision. Although he proved capable of running his department without help in contrast to McHenry, who had to be instructed regularly on War Department business, Wolcott never moved far from Hamilton's direct sphere of influence. Washington was favorably impressed by the young man from Connecticut, and wrote in 1791 to Robert Morris that Wolcott's advancement from auditor to comptroller was made possible by his own merits.[25]

Hamilton viewed the Treasury Department as something akin to a private political club and made every effort to bring into it men who had shown by their intelligence and personal loyalty capabilities as political lieutenants. He not only recommended Wolcott as his successor, but he also attempted to place Edward Carrington there despite the President's suggestion that a man from the deep South be recommended.[26] So confident of Wolcott was Hamilton that when he began making plans for the election of 1796 he asked him to do some private research in State Department records. "It is very desirable, now that a free access to the files of the department (of State) can give the evidence, to examine them accurately; noting times, places, circumstances,

[24] An adequate biography of Pickering needs to be written. The only available study (C. W. Upham and Octavius Pickering, *Life of Timothy Pickering*, 4 vols., Boston, 1867–73) is highly biased and poorly written. The most recent and most scholarly treatment of Pickering's State Department career is that of H. J. Ford in the *American Secretaries of State and Their Diplomacy* (Bemis ed.), II, 168-244.

[25] June 16, 1791, Washington, *Writings*, XXXI, 298.

[26] Hamilton to Washington, January 26, 1795, *Hamilton Papers*, LC.

actors, etc. I want this very much for public use, in my opinion essential."

Hamilton singled out as information especially needed a copy of Jefferson's letter to Congress recommending "the transfer of the French debt to private money-lenders."[27] Had Hamilton been on intimate terms with Pickering he would not have had to bother to go through Wolcott for such an easily understood request.

McHenry's admiration for both Washington and Hamilton needs scant mention. He had served as an aide to the General during the Revolution and came under the spell of Hamilton while both were young men. Occasional questions regarding patronage requests from Marylanders were addressed by the President to his former lieutenant, and McHenry felt confident enough of Washington's esteem to ask directly for appointment to the special commission authorized to negotiate the release of Lafayette from a French prison.[28] No appointment was made, however, and it was only Hamilton's last-minute suggestion that brought McHenry into the Federal service at all.[29]

Washington was blunt in asking McHenry to take the office, admitting freely that he had already been turned down by C. C. Pinckney, Edward Carrington, and former Governor John E. Howard of Maryland. The acceptance showed how little enthusiasm McHenry had for the work he was asked to undertake. It was only out of personal attachment to the President in an hour of crisis, he wrote, that he was willing to come to Philadelphia.[30]

When he heard the news that Hamilton was retiring, McHenry wrote an oft-quoted letter in which he said, "Though

[27] October 30, 1795, Hamilton, *Works* (Lodge ed.), X, 128.

[28] Washington to McHenry, November 30, 1789, August 12, 1792, April 8, 1794, Washington, *Writings,* XXX, 470-472, XXXII, 110-111, XXXIII, 318-319.

[29] See below, p. 281.

[30] Washington to McHenry, January 20, 1796, *Writings,* XXXIV, 423-424; McHenry to Washington, January 26, 1796, Steiner, *McHenry,* 164.

not writing I have never ceased to love you, nor for a moment felt any abatement of my friendship." [31] It was several months later that Hamilton made the suggestion that McHenry be taken up.

The first formal meeting that President Adams had with his advisors was devoted to a discussion of how best to deal with the diplomatic crisis with France. The French government had refused to treat with Charles C. Pinckney when he arrived at Paris as James Monroe's successor, and the problem of avoiding war was one that haunted the Adams administration from start to finish. When the President submitted a series of questions on the problem to his secretaries, three of the four men turned immediately to Hamilton for suggestions. Charles Lee was as much indebted to Hamilton for his appointment as were McHenry and Wolcott, but he either did not know it or was not as impressed with the fact.

Hamilton's policy was one that would tend to unite the nation politically but would leave decision safely in the hands of administration supporters. He called for a three-man commission to be made up of Madison or Jefferson and two Federalists, Pinckney and George Cabot of Massachusetts. McHenry obediently agreed with the proposals and turned them over to Adams in his own handwriting but with almost no change in wording.[32] Both Wolcott and Pickering put up a fight. The French situation was playing into the hands of the Federalist party, and neither could see the sense of sacrificing anything to the Republicans.

The Secretary of State stood in a relationship to Hamilton that allowed him greater freedom of action than either Wolcott or McHenry. He owed everything to Washington and little to Hamilton so far as his rise to fame was concerned. His actions during 1796, when he had crossed swords with French Minister Adet, had won for him the enthusiastic en-

[31] February 17, 1795, *ibid.*
[32] Hamilton to McHenry, March 22, 1797, *Hamilton Papers*, LC.

dorsement of ultra-Federalists, and the record shows that the first political correspondence that passed between Hamilton and himself had been instigated by Pickering without any provocation from New York.[33] Wolcott had taken the trouble to assure Hamilton that Pickering's politics were of the right kind at the time Washington named Pickering Secretary of State,[34] and the manner in which the Federalist chief dealt with Pickering shows that he felt a certain degree of wariness necessary.

Both Wolcott, over whom Pickering exercised a considerable influence, and Pickering finally gave in on the idea of a commission without either being firmly convinced that a Republican ought to be named.[35] The episode illustrates the hold that Hamilton had over the cabinet and reveals McHenry as easily the most subservient. When Adams called for written answers to the questions he wished to raise in his speech to Congress of May 15 (the speech that put the finishing touch to his brief entente with Jefferson) James McHenry again turned to Hamilton and found Hamilton's answers so perfectly in agreement with his own views as to turn them over to the President with almost no change. This he admitted freely to Hamilton.[36]

Charles Lee, the only member of the President's cabinet who stood outside Hamilton's political orbit, is a man about whom very little is known. Like McHenry and Pickering he was a last-resort candidate for the office he held when John Adams entered upon his presidency. Washington had first

[33] Pickering to Hamilton, November 17, 1795, *Hamilton Papers,* LC, relating to possible candidates for the War Department.

[34] Wolcott to Hamilton, October 6, 1795, *ibid.*

[35] Hamilton's views and those of Adams were in almost exact agreement. Both understood that unity could not be completely sacrificed to politics with war a possibility. Hamilton to Pickering, March 29, 1797; Pickering to Hamilton, April 5, 1797; Hamilton to Wolcott, March 30, 1797; Hamilton to William Smith, April 5, 1797, *Hamilton Papers,* LC and Hamilton, *Works* (Lodge ed.), X, 246.

[36] McHenry to Hamilton, May 4, 1797, *Hamilton Papers,* LC; Hamilton to Wolcott, June 6, 1797, *ibid.*

considered Samuel Dexter and Christopher Gore of Massachusetts for the office, but Dexter had just been defeated for the House and Gore was known to have engaged in government bond speculations. Washington next looked southward for the right kind of man. What he had in mind he described to Pickering.

"I shall not, whilst I have the honor to Administer the government, bring a man into any office, of consequence . . . whose political tenets are adverse to the measures which the general government are pursuing; for this, in my opinion, would be a sort of political suicide." [37]

John Marshall and James Innes, both of Virginia, were correct in their political thinking; but Marshall could not afford the move, and Innes was considered too lazy finally to accept. On Carrington's recommendation the idea was dropped.[38] Henry Lee suggested that his younger brother might fill the bill, unless former Governor Howard of Maryland could be persuaded to come out of retirement. Lee was given authority to approach Howard, who refused, and then to present Washington's invitation to Charles Lee.[39]

The new Attorney General had outstanding legal abilities, and had already made a name for himself as a promising lawyer at the time he was appointed. His later career was distinguished. President Adams named him to the bench along with that notorious group that has become known to history as "The Midnight Judges," and he was chosen as defense attorney in both the Chase impeachment trial and the Burr conspiracy trial. He was also counsel in the celebrated Marbury *vs.* Madison case, but at the time he was named Attorney General he was a newcomer without reputation.[40]

[37] September 27, 1795, Washington, *Writings*, XXXIV, 315-316.

[38] Washington to Carrington, September 28, 1795, *ibid.*, 317-318.

[39] Boyd, *Lee*, 238; Washington to Charles Lee, November 19, 1795, *Writings*, XXXIV, 365.

[40] Dumas Malone and Allen Johnson, eds., *The Dictionary of American Biography*, XI, 101-102.

Lee had gotten no further in politics than the Virginia assembly to which he had been elected twice, 1793–94 and 1794–95. During his second term he had supported Marshall and his brother Henry Lee in their attempts to prevent the passage of the Virginia resolutions of 1795 that opened the presidential election and brought the Jay treaty before the nation as an election issue.[41] He and Benjamin Stoddert were to prove loyal Adams supporters, and for that reason alone they deserve mention since Mr. Adams' cabinet has been consistently referred to as a cabal aligned against him.

There was no precedent to follow regarding tenure, and John Adams found himself confronted with an embarrassing question when his election to succeed Washington was assured. British practice would have it that upon the succession of a new executive, ministers automatically tendered their resignations. The United States was a republic, however, and the heads of departments, not being members of Congress, were not ministers. Hamilton's attempt to plead before Congress for his financial measures had failed to establish a precedent during Washington's first administration. Even had Adams looked upon his position as analogous to that of a British monarch, the situation was complicated by the fact that only Wolcott submitted a resignation.[42] He did not accept it, and there is no indication that he was offended because Pickering, McHenry, and Lee did not. Doubtless the other three looked upon Wolcott's action as a trial balloon.

Charles Francis Adams, using his father's notes, accounted for Adams' acceptance of Washington's cabinet on the grounds that Mr. Adams had no desire to go through the lengthy and politically dangerous process of searching for

[41] Carrington wrote enthusiastically of Lee's speeches in favor of the administration during the Jay treaty debate in the Virginia assembly, Carrington to Washington, November 10, 1795, Beveridge, *Marshall*, II, 132.

[42] Wolcott's memorandum, Gibbs, *Memoirs*, I, 450; Adams, *Works*, I, 500-502.

new men.[43] Washington could do no better, and even Adams must have realized that a President by three votes would have little prospect of attracting better talent than that which was already available. He could not choose from among Jefferson's friends without alienating the entire hierarchy of the Federalist party, and if he were to dismiss Wolcott and Pickering he was bound to produce a rift with the Hamiltonians, the Wolcott faction in Connecticut, and the Massachusetts junto, who were especially fond of Pickering. His election showed that he was in no position to do the latter, and if the bipartisan administration that he at first dreamed of was to become a reality he could not very well push his friendship with the Southerners to the point of making them his closest advisors. By accepting Washington's official family he raised no hopes and disappointed none. The outcome of the election of 1796 committed Adams to retain the services of Hamilton's friends.

Aside from considerations of politics, Adams may have been guided by two other motives. He was on record as opposed to rotation in office as a principle of government. He had written to Jefferson in 1795 that the changes in the executive departments smacked of the pernicious rotation principle that would operate ". . . till all the ablest men in the Nation are voted out. . . . If public offices are to be made punishments, will a people be well served?" [44] Furthermore, he had taken the responsibility of casting his decisive vote against a bill that came before the Senate in 1789 allowing the President to remove the Secretary of State only with the consent of the Senate.

Many reproached Adams for his vote on the assumption that he would be the next President, but actually nothing could have been more consistent with the principles of government that he had been expounding since the days of the

[43] *Ibid.*

[44] February 5, 1795, *Jefferson Papers*, LC.

Confederation. Adams favored a strong executive who might play the role of mediator between the two houses of Congress, which he thought destined to be in eternal conflict, representing as they did the many and the few. It was more delicate to leave personnel alone and not to be reminded of past actions. President Adams was a man highly conscious of criticism and of the force of public opinion.[45] For a few days just before the inauguration it was rumored that the President-elect would consult the Senate as to whether Washington's appointments were binding upon his successor, but Adams never chose to do so.[46]

Finally, there is nothing to suggest that Mr. Adams personally disliked any of Washington's secretaries or that he foresaw any of the intrigue and disloyalty that characterized the internal history of his administration. The event that played into the hands of Wolcott and Pickering was the President's long absence from Philadelphia during the year 1798. It was brought about by Mrs. Adams' vaguely defined but apparently serious illness; her husband was deeply devoted and convinced that she lay close to death. His assumption that he could as well conduct the business of the executive by mail from Quincy as from Philadelphia proved erroneous; the department heads, in theory administrative assistants, took matters into their own hands and delayed carrying out his orders so long as to bring on the disastrous crisis in the Federalist party of 1799. Had Adams been on the scene questions over which tempers flared up for weeks could have been settled in a matter of hours.

The first collision between President and advisors took place just a few weeks after the inauguration. Adams asked their opinions of Elbridge Gerry as third man on the diplomatic mission to France. According to McHenry's account,

45 *Annals*, 1st Congress, 1st Session, 457 ff.; Adams, *Works*, I, 449-450; Mitchell, *New Letters*, 20-21; White, *Federalists*, 20-22.

46 Madison to Jefferson, February 11, 1797, Madison, *Writings* (Congress ed.), II, 117.

no one spoke for some moments. Finally he observed that from all he had ever known of Gerry a nomination more likely to ruin the mission could not be made. Pickering and Lee would not speak, and Wolcott said only that he doubted the wisdom of adding Mr. Gerry to Pinckney and Marshall.[47] There was no great explosion, and for several months the President seemed to be on the best of terms with his official family.

Hearing of Pickering's illness in the late summer of 1797 the President wrote, "Have a care of yourself. Your country cannot spare you at present." [48] Again, when the Secretary of State objected to the appointment of Benjamin Rush as Treasurer of the Mint, Adams wrote, "If you have any doubts, we will delay the appointment for further consideration." [49]

When the army was strengthened in 1798 during the war scare produced by the XYZ revelations, a bitter quarrel ensued over the appointment of general officers. Adams studiously avoided naming Hamilton Inspector General or dating his commission before that of Knox, Morgan, Gates, or Benjamin Lincoln. In cabinet meeting Pickering openly belittled Mr. Adams' favorites, calling Morgan sickly, Gates "an old woman," and Lincoln "always asleep." According to Pickering's notes, the President said nothing in reply.[50]

Washington was finally called in to settle the matter, and the President, knowing full well that his advisors had trumped him with Washington's tremendous popularity, submitted to putting Hamilton in virtual command of the army of the United States. In a fury, Adams (from Quincy) wrote McHenry that there had been too much intrigue in placing Hamilton first. McHenry denied it, said that he could no longer continue in office unless absolutely trusted,

[47] McHenry to Pickering, February 23, 1811, Steiner, *McHenry*, 224.
[48] September 4, 1797, Upham, *Pickering*, III, 456.
[49] September 18, 1798, *ibid.*, 457.
[50] *Ibid.*, 463.

and offered to resign. John Adams, the man who has so often been portrayed as touchy and sensitive to an extreme, answered that he had intended nothing personal. He had only meant to imply, he explained, that McHenry was overly impressed with the popularity of Hamilton among leading Federalists.[51]

From Wolcott, whom Adams knew to be intimate with Hamilton, the President accepted a policy statement relating to future negotiations with France that was inserted into his speech to Congress of December, 1798.[52] This high degree of confidence was shown just a few weeks after an angry exchange of letters with Wolcott over Hamilton's appointment. He told his Secretary of the Treasury that Washington had been set against him, that Hamilton's appointment as senior Major General was "the most responsible action" of his entire life, and that he knew far more than any of his cabinet ministers about public opinion.[53]

The story of the conflict within the Adams administration has been often told, but the record shows the President to have been a far more patient man than secondary sources have admitted. McHenry had proved himself utterly unable to cope with the expansion of his department by the time his offer of resignation was sent to Adams, yet Adams passed over his impertinence and refused to accept a resignation. He took no open offense when Pickering dissuaded a group of Senators from confirming the appointment of his son-in-law to high military rank.[54] Wolcott's evident devotion to the man whom Adams hated most was not held against him; on the contrary, he was rewarded with a bench appointment.

[51] Adams to McHenry, August 29, 1798, McHenry to Adams, September 6, 1798, Adams to McHenry, September 13, 1798, Steiner, *McHenry*, 338-339.

[52] Wolcott to Adams, November, 1798, Gibbs, *Memoirs*, II, 170-171.

[53] Adams to Wolcott, September 24, 1798, *Works*, VIII, 601-602.

[54] July, 1798, Upham, *Pickering*, III, 470.

Pickering was warmly thanked for his defense of the Executive written in answer to a series of resolutions passed by a hostile public meeting in Virginia in the fall of 1798.[55]

Finally, in the fall of 1799 Adams awoke to the fact that for almost an entire year his advisors had used every means at their disposal to put off the most decisive step that he had taken while President. In January 1799 the President asked Pickering to draw up a consular convention and treaty such as France might present to the United States, a clear indication that he was thinking in terms of peace with France. Pickering delayed and in the meantime pointed out the insulting insinuations in Gerry's published account of his mission to France. It was this account of the mission upon which Adams based his final decision to bring to an end the quasi war with France of 1798–99.[56] When the President requested that Gerry's defense of his conduct be printed, Pickering refused.[57] For almost eight months after Adams had nominated William Murray to act as minister plenipotentiary to France, the Hamiltonian secretaries continued to sow thorns in the path to reconciliation. Considered in the light of his relations with his advisors, Adams' reputation for impatience, hypersensitivity, and suspicion seems groundless. If anything, he was lenient to the point where it damaged himself and the government over which he presided.

Adams became well aware of the dangers of allowing his advisors so free a rein over executive affairs. Just a month after his sudden nomination of Murray, his friend Uriah Forrest urged him to return to the capital at once. His secretaries were in need of supervision and moderate men were beginning to fear that the President's continued absence was harmful to the cause of peace. "The people elected you to

[55] Adams to Pickering, October 15, 1798, Adams, *Works,* VIII, 605-606.

[56] Adams to Pickering, January 15, 1799; Pickering to Adams, January 18, 1799; Adams, *Works,* VIII, 621, 622.

[57] *Ibid.,* 616-617.

administer the government. They did not elect your officers. . . ." [58]

The President's answer was characteristic of both sides of his nature: Mrs. Adams was still too weak to be moved, the mails were running regularly between Philadelphia and Quincy.

Years after the Adams administration had passed, James McHenry explained what was the basic cause of the serious troubles that marked the presidency of John Adams. Mr. Adams had just published the view that the heads of departments were meant to be little more than clerks. Such a viewpoint was not what General Washington held, wrote McHenry to Timothy Pickering. "Three of the gentlemen who were heads of departments with Mr. Adams were also heads of departments with General Washington. These gentlemen could never for a moment depart from his maxims; they were the soul of their system; they could not tear them from their hearts, and retained their honor and their integrity." [59]

It was not the shadow of Jefferson and a youthful democratic movement that overhung the Adams administration: it was the majestic figure of George Washington.

[58] April 28, 1799, Adams, *Works,* VIII, 637-638.
[59] February 23, 1811, Lodge, *Cabot,* 208-209.

13

Political Consequences of the XYZ Papers

WASHINGTON'S INFLUENCE UPON THE INTERNAL HISTORY OF the Adams administration was equally great upon its foreign relations. Republican France, harboring transoceanic ambitions as great as her continental successes, had found Washington, the symbol of New World liberty, cold in response to her appeals for a new order of world politics. Americans who shared the enthusiasm of Jefferson for things French were disgusted with Washington's neutralism and became rapidly disheartened as the Adams administration showed signs of following the same fundamental policy.

Joel Barlow, an American devotee of the Revolution who studied American developments from Paris during the 1790's, set forth the history of Washington's treason for Jefferson in the spring of 1798 as the two nations stood poised for war. First, wrote Barlow, was the General's devotion to Gouverneur Morris; this notorious aristocrat had not only been American Minister to France by Washington's choice, but had also been commissioned by Washington to act as unofficial observer of European events after his dismissal from the diplomatic post. The President's secret commission to Morris had fallen into the hands of the Directory in 1795, and it had become their firm conviction that Morris had acted as liaison agent between Britain, Austria, and Prussia in arranging terms for the coalition against France. Thus the coalition's existence was blamed indirectly upon Washington.

Then, Barlow continued, James Monroe had been sent to Paris, a man whose actions and attitude had become "a counterweight to all the weight of resentment." But instead of keeping the popular Virginian at Paris the President had ordered him home in disgrace. This act of the President's and not, as many believed, the Jay treaty, had been regarded as conclusive evidence of the administration's animosity.

Toward Mr. Adams the French government looked with the same contempt as toward his predecessor, Barlow went on. "The French saw that the character of the new president would be a criterion by which the decided friendship or enmity of the United States for France could clearly be seen." And what was the outcome of the election of 1796, they asked? "The candidates were Adams and Jefferson; the one a reputed royalist . . . the other an eminent republican. . . . When the election of Adams was announced here it produced the order of the 2nd March (1797); which was meant to be little short of a declaration of war."

France had seen nothing in the new President's subsequent behavior to offset its hostility. His speech of May 15, 1797, had been bellicose; as envoys to make peace he sent one who had already been refused, a second known to be an opponent of the French party in America, and a third who was totally unknown. This seemed doubly offensive after it had been reliably reported that either Jefferson or Madison would be an envoy. These were the news items from the United States that had produced the serious crisis and not the provisions of a treaty with England, concluded Barlow.[1]

Thus, regardless of his intentions, John Adams was placed at the head of what became to all intents and purposes a wartime administration, and it was to be his primary task for three years to regain the position of neutrality that Washington, in contradiction to the French viewpoint, had

[1] Joel Barlow to Abraham Baldwin, March 4, 1798, to Jefferson, March 12, 1798, *Jefferson Papers*, LC.

proudly acclaimed in his valedictory to be the cornerstone of both his domestic and foreign policies. How was the United States, decidedly a third-rate power lacking manpower, money, and above all a navy, to force the most powerful military nation in the world possessing a sizable naval establishment into peaceful relations when she was obviously bent upon war? This was the fundamental question of John Adams' administration.

The threat of war with France had deep political repercussions in the United States. Nothing so easily demonstrated this as Adams' break with Jefferson, which became apparent after the President's May 15 speech in 1797. Adams had proclaimed his policy as one that sought peace but not at the price of national humiliation. At the same time he was unwilling to see the United States become an appendage to the British power. If the United States was to force France into a decent respect for her vital interests (and to a New England President this especially meant commercial interests), resistance just short of war would have to be shown, and Mr. Adams was not impressed with embargoes as instruments of force.

The possibility of war was brought very close by the announcement that General Pinckney, the new American Minister, had been refused recognition by the French government, and the President's address to a specially convened sitting of Congress in May had made war seem close in many minds. "The great theme of every man's inquiries is, are we going to war with France," wrote Fisher Ames a few days after the news of Pinckney's rebuff had been learned at Philadelphia. War was to be avoided but not at the price of honor, thought Ames.[2] Representative Tracy of Connecticut told Governor Wolcott in the midst of the excitement that the question of war was up to France. Should her latest elections turn out well, war could be avoided, he thought, but

[2] Ames to Governor Wolcott, March 24, 1797, Gibbs, *Memoirs*, I, 477.

". . . unless an alteration, either of man or measures, or both, takes place in France, we must have war with her." [3]

Members of the President's cabinet were not explicit about war, but they most certainly wanted no peace commission with Jefferson or Madison on it, despite the constant entreaties of Hamilton to the contrary.[4] "The U. States have the strongest motives to avoid war," he had written to James McHenry in April. "They may lose a great deal; they can gain nothing . . . France in declining to receive Mr. Pinckney, has not gone to the *ne plus ultra.* She has declined to receive a minister until grievances of which she complains are redressed." [5]

Hamilton had picked Representative Tracy of Connecticut to lay his plans for a bipartisan commission before Adams, knowing that Tracy stood high in the President's confidence. Tracy frankly admitted that it was Hamilton's plan, and Adams apparently recoiled.[6] Instead he would nominate Marshall and Dana of Massachusetts to join Pinckney, and in May he sent his nominations together with a request for defense appropriations to Congress. Only when Dana declined did Adams give his old friend Elbridge Gerry a place on what turned out to be a bipartisan peace commission.

With grim pleasure Pickering announced to Hamilton that neither Jefferson nor Madison would accept appointment, and William Smith frankly admitted to Hamilton that ". . . the idea does not seem to coincide with the opinions of any

[3] March 26, 1797, *ibid.*, 478.

[4] Hamilton to William Smith, April 10, 1797; Hamilton to McHenry, April 1797, Hamilton, *Works* (Lodge ed.), X, 256; Steiner, *McHenry*, 217; Hamilton, *Works*, VII, 724.

[5] April 1797, Steiner, *op. cit.*, 217.

[6] Hamilton, *Works* (Hamilton ed.), VII, 724; Gibbs, *Memoirs*, I, 483; Hamilton, *Public Conduct and Character of John Adams* (New York, 1800), 47; Adams, *Works*, IX, 288-289; Jefferson, *Writings* (Ford ed.), I, 344.

of your friends here."[7] The extremists seemed to have the upper hand from the beginning, though the appointment of Gerry dashed some cold water upon their good spirits. Cabot feared that the French would outwit the administration and its peace commissioners no matter what was done. His guess was that impossible terms for a new treaty would be advanced only to embarrass the administration when it was forced to turn them down. His hopes that Mr. Adams would sit tight soon were forgotten in his enthusiasm for the President's declaration of firmness of May 15.[8] The speech would "excite the most national feeling of anything that has been published since the French disease infected this country," he wrote Governor Wolcott. "After reading and considering it all Sunday afternoon, at my home, a large company of good men [i.e., Federalists] all agreed that it was in every particular exactly what they would have wished, and was expressed in a masterly and dignified style."[9]

The popularity that Adams was gaining among some men was not encouraged by Jefferson. "Nothing can establish firmly the republican principles of our government but an establishment of them in England," he complained despairingly. He was watching the foreign news, hoping that French military victories would force impending defense measures to die in committee rooms.[10] His friend John Dawson, who had taken Madison's seat in the House, had the same hopes. "The accounts from Europe abound with the brilliant successes of that wonderful man Buonaparte," he wrote Madison. "Nothing less than the arm of the omnipotent will prevent his storming heaven. His success may save us by restoring peace to Europe, without which I very much

[7] Pickering to Hamilton, April 29, 1797, Smith to Hamilton, May 1, 1797; *Hamilton Papers*, LC.

[8] Cabot to Governor Wolcott, April 17, 1797, Gibbs, *Memoirs*, 493.

[9] Cabot to Wolcott, Jr., May 24, 1797, *ibid.*, 536-537.

[10] Jefferson to Edmund Randolph, June 27, 1797, *Jefferson Papers*, LC.

fear we shall be engaged in a war in six months, such is the rage of many against France." [11]

There was little the Republicans could do beyond pinning their hopes on French arms; Federalists had control of both houses of Congress. Jefferson had depended upon a Republican majority in the lower house, but the news from France had turned what he called "our three renegades" [three Virginia members] over to the cause of war preparedness.[12] When a reply to the President's message was drawn up, Speaker Dayton had called for a resolution to the effect that France should be treated on an equal footing with other nations. The degree of jingoism already rampant could be seen, commented Jefferson, by the fact that Dayton's suggestion was grudgingly approved by only a five-vote margin.[13] Moderation was hardly appreciated by editor Peter Porcupine, who labeled Dayton ". . . a shallow, superficial fellow—a bawler to the galleries and unfit to play the cunning part he has undertaken." [14]

By the middle of June, Jefferson confided to Aaron Burr that the Republicans were losing strength in the legislature while the unexpected unity of the "Treaty party" continued. A Senate bill for the purchase or building of twelve frigates, the first step in the creation of the United States Navy, was passed 16 to 13, while a House fortifications bill passed by the margin of seven votes two days later. There was considerable desire "in both parties to shew our teeth to France," was the Vice-President's explanation of the phenomenon.[15]

Congress broke up at the end of June without laying the groundwork for an army, however, and Jefferson gave a

[11] June 4, 1797, *Madison Papers*, LC.

[12] Jefferson to Madison, June 8, 1707, *Jefferson Papers*, LC.

[13] To Madison, June 1, 1797, *ibid.*

[14] *Porcupine's Gazette*, June 3, 1797.

[15] Jefferson to Madison, June 15, 1797, to Burr, June 17, *Jefferson Papers*, LC.

momentary sigh of relief. A Senate bill for an army of fifteen thousand men had been narrowly defeated.[16]

The President could see little to hold him in Philadelphia for the yellow fever season and prepared to depart for Quincy. He was badly in need of rest, according to his wife, but John Marshall, stopping in for dinner before his departure for France, found the President much at ease. "I dined on Saturday in private with the President," wrote the envoy to his wife after his first meeting with John Adams, "whom I found a sensible, plain, candid, good tempered man and was consequently much pleased with him." Mrs. Wolcott, however, expressed anxiety at the thought of the President's departure in the midst of crisis.[17]

Two months on his Quincy farm helped fortify the President for the attack upon the executive that Republicans launched when Congress reconvened in the fall. In the House Albert Gallatin led a fight reminiscent of the Livingston resolution struggle of 1796. Again it was asserted that the House had the constitutional right to refuse appropriations for diplomatic expenses incurred by the President and the Senate, but the members of the second session showed themselves to be a majority of Federalists—the resolution was lost by four votes.[18] In the Senate Virginia's Senator Tazewell struck back at the President's leadership by introducing a proposal for a constitutional amendment that would allow impeachment by jury rather than by the Senate. Only Virginia's two senators and Andrew Jackson of Tennessee voted for it, however.[19]

The President's message of December 6 was as heated as that of the preceding May, and Madison placed the blame for the continued warlike atmosphere of the capital squarely

[16] Jefferson to Madison, June 22, 1797, *ibid.*

[17] Abigail Adams to her sister, July 6, 1797, *New Letters of Abigail Adams* (Mitchell ed.), 101-104; July 2, 1797, Beveridge, *Marshall,* II, 214.

[18] Hamilton, *Republic,* VII, 94-98.

[19] *Ibid.*, 98.

on Adams' shoulders. "Those who tolerate at present the fashionable sentiments will soon be ready to embrace them. . . . Let us hope that the tide of evil is nearly at its flood," he wrote Monroe,[20] whose printed defense of his conduct as minister to France Jefferson was at the same time helping to distribute.[21]

In this verbose production, "A View of the Conduct of the Executive . . ." Monroe attempted to prove that the Federalists had deliberately duped him during the Jay negotiations and had recalled him as a purely political matter.[22] Its length (the original edition running to well over two hundred pages) doomed Monroe's efforts at retaliation to obscurity. His handling of the printing and distribution of the political treatise marked one of Jefferson's first steps toward directing Republican party strategy.

The temper of Congress when it convened in November was tense and excited. Rumors of the peace mission's failure produced impatience, Federalists believing that France was not to be trusted and Republicans as firmly believing that the administration would cloud the truth. Looking about him at his colleagues in the House, Albert Gallatin concluded that the opposition would be something less than brilliant. The House as a whole lacked talent, and the best speakers—Harper, Dana, and Sewall—were all Federalists. His own cohorts lacked unity and doubted what attitude to take on the all-important issue of peace with France. His guess in the middle of December was that there would be no declaration of war unless the negotiations at Paris fell through.[23]

Men of Republican leanings were suddenly found to be no longer respectable. The Comptroller of the Treasury De-

20 December 17, 1797, *Madison Papers*, LC.

21 Jefferson to John Eppes, December 21, 1797, *Jefferson Papers*, LC. Jefferson announced shipping 300 copies via Bache to Richmond.

22 Monroe's argument with Washington's rebuttal to each point is printed in Washington, *Writings*, XXXVI, 194-237.

23 Gallatin to his wife, December 19, 1797, *Gallatin Papers*, New York Historical Society, I, 23.

partment, Tench Coxe, was suddenly and without specific provocation dismissed from his office by the President. He had been originally appointed with the blessing of Hamilton, but it was suspected that his politics were not in agreement with those of Oliver Wolcott.[24] Mrs. Adams confided to her sister that Coxe had bitten the hand that fed him and had written anti-Federalist pamphlets during the late election.[25] He was to turn up in 1799 as Republican organizer of the important gubernatorial contest in Pennsylvania.

Among the respectable men whose emotions were aroused by the gnawing anxiety of early 1798 was the usually placid ex-President. With scorn Washington described the Republican position as absurd. They were almost comical in their anxiety over usurpations of authority on Adams' part while at the same time applauding a nation that could tolerate a military *coup d'état* such as Bonaparte and his friends had just pulled off at Paris. They crow about the rights of man while lauding a despotism, he told John Marshall in a letter written just after the news of the revolution of 18 Fructidor had arrived.[26]

Charles Lee, hitherto businesslike and unheard from, occupied himself with pamphlets and newspaper articles answering Monroe's charges.[27] Even the head of a high-ranking businessman fell beneath the knife of partisanship. Gallatin noted that the president of the North American Insurance Company had been turned out by the board of directors on the grounds that he was "a disorganizing democrat." [28]

To his way of thinking it seemed that an organized conspiracy to kill off the opposition was in full swing, wrote Jef-

[24] Gallatin to his wife, January 16, 1798, *ibid.*, I, 25.

[25] Abigail Adams to her sister, February 5, 1798, *New Letters* (Mitchell ed.) 126-127.

[26] December 4, 1797, Washington, *Writings*, XXXVI, 94.

[27] Monroe to Jefferson, January 27, 1798, *Jefferson Papers*, LC.

[28] Gallatin to his wife, January 16, 1798, *Gallatin Papers*, New York Historical Society, I, 25.

ferson to Madison in February. First, Dayton had been bought off by offering him the War Department in case of war (at least that was the rumor), then Matthew Lyons of Vermont had been expelled just to be rid of his vote, and finally Senator Blount of Tennessee was being caught up on dubious charges of conspiring with a foreign power on the frontier. Such proceedings, said Jefferson, were a disgrace to the Federal government, and he had hopes that the people would come to lean more heavily on their state governments.[29]

The bitterness of party feeling was intensified in the winter of 1797–98 as rumors increased that the peace mission had failed. "The legislature is as much divided and the parties in it as much embittered against each other as it is possible to conceive," wrote Senator James Ross of Pennsylvania to Washington. Legislation was impossible. "One party or the other must obtain a decisive Victory before the machine of Government can move with efficacy." [30]

The President, following Washington's precedent, had in the meantime called upon his secretaries to provide him with written suggestions for dealing with the French crisis. Hamilton's reply to McHenry's routine request for help was cleverly calculated to catch public favor. Everything should be done to avoid a declaration of war, he said, because public opinion was set against it. A belligerent attitude and defense preparations would, on the other hand, build loyalty to the government while at the same time leaving the door open for negotiations. Hamilton specifically recommended the arming of merchant vessels, the construction of warships, increasing the army to twenty thousand men, and setting up machinery for a provisional army of thirty thousand additional troops. The temptation to seek an alliance with Great

[29] February 15, 1798, *Jefferson Papers,* LC.
[30] February, 1798, Washington, *Writings,* XXXVI, 164, Note 96.

Britain, he pointed out, would be great in some circles; the mutual self-interest of the two countries would lead to close co-operation without going through the formality.[31]

Cabinet discussions that followed led to the adoption of Hamilton's proposals as the administration policy with the exception of those items relating to an army. Naval measures made sense to Adams; a large regular army and a sizable reserve did not. The breach between the President and his Hamiltonian advisors over the military situation proved to be permanent and at the time provided material for resentment and hurt feelings that arose out of a Washington's birthday celebration.

President and Mrs. Adams were personally offended by Philadelphia socialites who sent out invitations to attend a festive ball celebrating the birthday of General Washington. "How could the President appear at their Ball and assembly, but in a secondary character . . . I do not know when my feelings of contempt have been more called forth," wrote the first lady to her sister.[32] The "Jacobins," as Mrs. Adams was fond of calling the opposition, were delighted. Although editor Bache crowed happily, the Adamses were touched with the politeness of the Vice-President in refusing to attend.[33]

Jefferson probably had his own reasons. At any rate he was pleased to see the division among his opponents caused by the celebration of the first President's birthday. "The late birthnight has certainly sown tares among the executive federalists," he wrote Madison. "It has removed the grain from the chaff. The sincerely Adamsites did not go. The Washingtonians went religiously. . . . Goodhue, Tracy, Sedgwick,

[31] Hamilton to McHenry, February 1, 1798, Steiner, *McHenry*, 291-295. McHenry presented Hamilton's scheme *in toto* to the President on February 15 over his own signature.

[32] February 15, 1798, *New Letters* (Mitchell ed.), 133.

[33] Abigail Adams to her sister, February 28, 1798, *ibid.*, 136-137.

and Co. (Adams supporters in Congress) did not attend: but the three secretaries and Attorney General did." [34]

James Monroe noted the political wrangling, lamented it, and blamed Adams for refusing to grasp the friendly hand that Jefferson had extended him in the opening weeks of the administration.[35] Mr. Jefferson himself was under abusive attack owing to the appearance and continued reprinting of his Mazzei letter and was so worried over it that he called for a conference with Madison and Monroe to find a way of meeting the criticism.[36]

Late in the fall, however, Republicans were afforded amusement over the embarrassment caused in Federalist circles by Hamilton's forced confession of adultery in the Reynolds case. No sooner had they stopped laughing than they found Jefferson ensnared in a public charge of libel by Luther Martin of Maryland. Jefferson had written and spoken of the "murder" of one of the Logan family by a certain Mr. Cresap, and Martin, who had married into the Cresap family, was angrily and relentlessly demanding a public apology or the proof.[37] Again Jefferson thought it best to be silent.

Members of the Essex Junto in Massachusetts were in disagreement with their friends in Philadelphia and New York who proposed a large army. Arming merchant vessels was one thing, but an army was not part of their thinking on the policy of defiance.[38] Pickering sent in his suggestions to the President for his speech of March 19, and found them in complete agreement with Hamilton's.[39] He and Adams quarreled about Gerry in the midst of top-level discussions. The

[34] March 2, 1798, *Jefferson Papers*, LC.
[35] February 19, 1798, Monroe, *Writings* (Hamilton ed.), III, 103.
[36] Jefferson to Madison, August 3, 1797, *Jefferson Papers*, LC.
[37] Gov. John Henry to Henry Tazewell, March 13, 1798, *ibid.*
[38] Jonathan White to H. G. Otis, February 19, 1798, Morison, *Otis*, I, 87.
[39] Hamilton to Pickering, March 17, 1798, Hamilton, *Works* (Lodge ed.), X, 276.

President hoped that Gerry could explain his prolonged stay in Paris after Marshall and Pinckney had left, but Pickering replied that the answer to that question could be deduced easily enough from the state of Mr. Gerry's politics before he left.[40]

Jefferson heard rumors of the failure of the mission and believed that the continued silence of the administration was a cover-up. "Their information if made public would check the disposition to arm," he wrote Madison. Still there was silence and the rumors continued. It was widely believed that several members of Congress had written letters to the Directory urging them not to receive the American mission. Letters to this effect had been intercepted by the British navy, Washington had heard.[41]

In Virginia there was wild talk of a slave insurrection. Only one state in the Union would aid Virginia, wrote Jefferson gloomily, and she would also have her hands full.[42] Bishop White of the Episcopal Church refused to drink a toast to Alexander Hamilton, and the President, always sensitive about family honor, became deeply involved in a squabble with Republicans over the appointment of his son John Quincy as special envoy to Prussia for the renewal of a commercial treaty.[43] British navigation acts of 1797, placed before Congress in February, demonstrated that the decrees of France were scarcely more intolerable than those of the supposed ally. "Eastern men are silent," commented Jefferson.[44] His friends hoped that England might fall to the might

[40] Jefferson, *Writings* (Ford ed.), I, 347; Morison, "Elbridge Gerry," *New England Quarterly*, II, January, 1929, 14; Adams, *Works*, IX, 284-289; Austin, *Gerry*, 157.

[41] Washington to Alexander White, March 25, 1798, *Writings*, XXXVI, 191.

[42] Jefferson to T. M. Randolph, February 22, 1798, *Jefferson Papers*, LC.

[43] James Callender to Jefferson, September 28, 1797, *Jefferson Papers*, LC; *Annals*, 5th Congress, 2d Session, 922; Abigail Adams to her sister, February 5, March 20, 1798, *New Letters* (Mitchell ed.), 127, 146-147.

[44] Jefferson to Madison, January 1, 1798, *Jefferson Papers*, LC.

of Napoleon, whose preparations for the invasion of Britain General Gates prophesied would bring on a struggle as crucial "as that of Antony and Caesar–the Empire of the World." [45]

Countless incidents pointed to mutual mistrust between Americans on the eve of the famed XYZ disclosures. The Vice-President was on edge, singling out his erstwhile confederates Cabell and Giles as noticably absent from their seats in the House while noting that "not one anti-republican is from his post." Absences and waverings in the face of rumors from Paris had turned what he had counted upon as a Republican majority in the House into a Federalist majority. The strictly party vote on the expulsion of Matthew Lyons, for example, was 52 to 44. At the beginning of February, Jefferson was informed that British spies were infiltrating the post-office service, his correspondent believing that a counterrevolution in Virginia was aimed at.[46]

And in New York a spirited gubernatorial campaign between John Jay and Chancellor Livingston was under way when President Adams finally revealed that the mission had been an utter failure. The blow was expected, but the official pronouncement of the collapse of negotiations together with President's call for further defense measures sent a tremor of excitement through the land.

Members of the Federalist debating society in Essex County, Massachusetts, were no longer in doubt about Adams or armaments. "Mr. Adams has immortalized himself in the Opinion of Yankees," wrote Jonathan Mason, Jr., to Harrison Otis, delegate from the society to Congress. "He seems to stand alone with the sentiments he set out with in 1763 and '75–and they do not appear impaired." Good men were reconciled to the thought of war, he added, but

[45] Gates to Jefferson, February 27, 1798, *ibid.*
[46] Arthur Campbell to Jefferson, February 2, 1798, *ibid.*

they were not as sure that civil war would necessarily follow as many were affirming.[47]

Pennsylvania Republicans were loath to accept the President's stern pessimism. A day after his message to Congress a resolution was introduced in the Pennsylvania legislature disapproving defense measures against what it termed "a people with whom our hearts and hands have so lately been united in friendship." The resolution failed, according to Jefferson, because Quaker members thought more of government war contracts than their religious convictions.[48]

For ten days Republicans attempted to scoff away the seriousness of the charge against France. There was some explanation that the administration feared to reveal, they said. On March 30 William B. Giles made the mistake of demanding that the papers relating to the negotiation be released by the President, and three days later the House officially made the request.[49]

Republicans were thunderstruck and Federalists jubilant at the record of French diplomacy. Impossible conditions for respectable negotiations had been made; Talleyrand's special agents (called "X," "Y," and "Z" in the dispatches) had suggested that bribe money for the Directors would smooth the way toward a peaceful settlement of differences. This was what the public and politicians alike would remember, though it was the demand for a sizable United States loan as the *sine qua non* of negotiations that Pinckney and Marshall had balked at.[50] Elbridge Gerry alone of the three had stayed on at Paris in hopes that the friendly attitude shown toward him by certain French officials might be used to the advantage of peace.

Within three days the Senate had voted to release the information to the public, and borne upward to a height of

[47] March 30, 1798, Morison, *Otis*, I, 93.
[48] Hamilton, *Republic*, VII, 108-109.
[49] Anderson, *Giles*, 59.
[50] Channing, *History*, IV, 186-187.

popularity that they had never before experienced, the Federalists turned with ill-concealed delight to the task of discrediting the Republican party. The Vice-President was their principal target and was almost immediately charged with being implicated in the French action. "A criminal correspondence with the French Directory" had been traced to his desk, he informed Madison on the day the papers were made public.[51]

Resolutions of the merchants and shippers of Philadelphia flooded in overnight condemning the French cause and its partisans, and the President's answer to a Lancaster, Pennsylvania, resolution that specifically mentioned Monroe as the man who had set up the situation was in complete agreement.[52] Two weeks after the release of the papers, Jefferson noted with alarm that Bache's *Aurora* was dangerously close to financial collapse. Subscriptions and advertising had fallen off badly.[53] Under the pressure of public and official condemnation Republican ranks thinned noticeably in Congress. Four Southern congressmen left precipitantly for home.[54] "The publick opinion here is changing very fast, and the people begin to see who have been their firm unshaken Friends . . . ," commented the wife of the President. "The common people say that if Jefferson had been our President, and Madison and Burr our Negotiators, we should all have been sold to the French." [55]

John Adams was busier each succeeding day answering the scores of petitions and resolutions of loyalty brought to his office. He was genuinely popular for the first time since the Federal government had been inaugurated, and he took maximum advantage of it. Typical of the resolutions that the

[51] April 5, 1798, Jefferson, *Writings* (Ford ed.), VIII, 400.

[52] Jefferson to Monroe, April 19, 1798, *ibid.*, 408; to Monroe, April 21, 1798, *Jefferson Papers*, LC.

[53] Jefferson to Madison, April 26, 1798, *Writings* (Ford ed.), VIII, 412.

[54] Jefferson to Monroe, April 19, 1798, *op. cit.*

[55] To her sister, April 13, 1798, *New Letters* (Mitchell ed.), 156.

President received was this one from the students of Princeton College.

"The students of the College of New Jersey," it began, "awfully impressed by the threatening clouds which obscure the political horizon . . . offer their feeble, though hearty concurrence in applauding your administration, and energy of government." [56] A long recitation of patriotic virtues and promises followed.

In his full-blown answer, the President besought the youth of the nation to apply themselves to the study of history, particularly the history of revolutions. In that study they would see that ". . . the good intended by fair characters from the beginning was defeated by Borgias and Catilines; that these fair characters themselves were inexperienced in freedom, and had very little reading in the science of government. . . ." He went on to ask, "If the choice of the people will not defend their rights and privileges, who will? To me there appears no means of averting the storm, and in my opinion we must all be ready to dedicate ourselves to fatigues and dangers." This prescription for a sound Republican education was printed in local newspapers for the benefit of all.[57]

The flow of presidential language spread far and wide over the nation during 1798, and observations of its effect varied according to political sentiments. Jefferson, of course, thought it ridiculous, and Madison wrote of it, "The answers of Mr. Adams to his addressors form the most grotesque scene in the tragi-comedy acted by the government." [58] Federalists, however, could not speak highly enough of the President's spirited leadership.

George Cabot of Massachusetts declared that he was impatient to express his admiration for the manner in which the President had awakened the country. "All men, whose

[56] Princeton University Library *MSS* (May 15, 1798).

[57] Reprint from the New Brunswick, N.J., *Advertiser*, May 29, 1798, *ibid.*

[58] Madison to Jefferson, June 10, 1798, *Madison Papers*, LC.

opinions I know, are unbounded in their applause of the manly, just, spirited, and instructive sentiments expressed by the President in his answers to the addresses."[59] And from a member of the Essex Junto, John Davis, came one of the most classical of tributes. "It is said of Pericles," he wrote Wolcott, "that he frequently repeated to himself, 'Remember Pericles, that you command free men. . . .' A greater and better man than Pericles seems to decide and act under the spirit of similar reflection . . . he will not be disappointed in the honorable opinion formed of his countrymen."[60]

While keeping the door open to diplomatic intercourse with France (Gerry, it should be carefully noted, was not repudiated by the President and his speeches were never concluded without mention of his willingness to settle differences on a respectable and honorable basis), the presidential addresses could not but have had a powerful effect upon diplomatic relations and could not but maintain the feeling of patriotic fervor that the XYZ disclosures had called into being. It was difficult to conceive how a government could be pursuing the cause of peace when its head referred to the enemy in such bombastic terms as those which he used in a reply to an address from the Society of Cincinnatus of South Carolina.

"As to the French," wrote Adams, "I know of no government ancient or modern that ever betrayed so universal and decided a contempt of the people of all nations, as the present rulers of France."[61]

While Federalists as a whole fell enthusiastically in line with the President, there was a desire among Hamilton's friends to thrust their favorite forward. Governor Jay of New York appointed Hamilton Senator from New York when Hobart resigned suddenly in April. Jefferson con-

[59] To Wolcott, Jr., June 9, 1798, Gibbs, *Memoirs,* II, 53.
[60] July 16, 1798, *ibid.,* 72-73.
[61] Adams, *Works,* IX, 223 (September 15, 1798).

cluded from the fact that Hobart's resignation came immediately after the adjournment of the state legislature that the step was predetermined.[62] Jay made the appointment without sounding Hamilton out first, however, and his friend's refusal was prompt. He could not afford the appointment, wrote Hamilton, but it might become necessary for him to make some sacrifice in the near future.[63] It was not the War Department that Hamilton was waiting for. At the end of April Robert Harper urged him to take McHenry's office. McHenry was apparently ready and willing to move aside and, astounding if true, Harper claimed that President Adams had assured him in private conversation of his willingness to make the appointment if Hamilton was sure of accepting. He ended his appeal to Hamilton with the statement that if the right war minister and the right general could be found, it would be possible to "put arms into the hands of all our friends." [64]

Possibly, though not probably, Adams had noted the fundamental agreement between his own views and those of the New York Federalist leader. Neither would speak directly of war, though each was an outspoken advocate of armaments. In a series of articles written during April, Hamilton had outlined an American policy just short of war with special emphasis on naval retaliation and defense.[65] Such was the President's policy, but it scarcely follows that coincidence of viewpoint would have led to so generous an offer. Harper was either stretching a point or Adams had momentarily allowed the patriotic sentiment expressed in his many addresses to override his political prejudices. Considering his later actions with regard to Hamilton's army rank, the second alternative appears highly unlikely.

[62] Jefferson to Madison, April 26, 1798, *Writings* (Ford ed.), VIII, 412-413.

[63] Jay to Hamilton, April 19, 1798, *Hamilton Papers*, LC; Hamilton to Jay, April 24, 1798, Hamilton, *Works*, X, 281 (Lodge ed.).

[64] April 27, 1798, *Hamilton Papers*, LC.

[65] Articles entitled "The Stand," *ibid.*

Hamilton was not supine in the midst of the XYZ enthusiasm despite his unwillingness to take an open part in political affairs. In May he urged General Washington to make a circuit through the opposition strongholds of the South when, as was anticipated, he was appointed to command the army. Such an excursion through North Carolina and Virginia, as Hamilton put it, would "throw the weight of your character into the scale of Government and revive an enthusiasm for your person that may be turned into right channels." [66]

Washington was not pleased with the suggestion. His reception in these areas was not so certain as Hamilton assumed, he wrote, and if it were enthusiastic there would be no need for such a health excursion; furthermore, his health had never been better. He could see no cause for the assumption that war was inevitable anyway, he concluded.[67] Hamilton quickly retracted his suggestion as "an undigested thought begotten by my anxiety." [68]

To Rufus King at London Hamilton urged that every effort be made to impress the British government with the harmful effect that continued British seizures were having in America. Upon his close friends in Congress he urged action, the passage of defense measures as quickly as possible: and to Wolcott he advised keeping the President's language as temperate as possible. A recent presidential address to the Governor of New Jersey he called "revolutionary." [69]

For the Secretary of State Hamilton also had advice and advice that could scarcely have been appreciated. In 1796 Hamilton had urged that Pickering control his temper and be more neutral in his writings, but the suggestions had been indirect. By the summer of 1798 his connections with Pickering had become more intimate, and he spoke his mind freely. Picker-

66 May 19, 1798, Hamilton, *Works* (Lodge ed.), X, 286-287.

67 May 27, 1798, Washington, *Writings*, XXXVI, 271-272.

68 June 2, 1798, Hamilton, *Works* (Lodge ed.), X, 287.

69 To Wolcott, June 5, 1798, *Hamilton Papers*, LC.

ing had drawn up a state paper with regard to France that Adams could not use because of the Secretary's intemperate language. Pickering had described the Directory's actions in the XYZ negotiations as a bold attempt to "fleece" the American people and as motivated by "avarice and lust for revenge." [70] President Adams wisely avoided the use of such extreme terms in his message to Congress on June 21 and in all his public statements showed that Mr. Pickering had moved down a path that he would not follow.

Pickering's writings, his diplomatic papers, were applauded in extremist circles, but as Hamilton could easily see, this playing to the galleries was forcing the President into a more independent conduct of foreign relations than suited Hamilton and his immediate circle. He therefore noted for Pickering's edification that the supposed friend and ally, Great Britain, had been equally tyrannical as France in past months and that there was no logical grounds upon which to defend the tough policy against France while not applying it against Britain. "I would mete the same measure to both of them," Hamilton wrote. "One of them will quickly court us, and by this course of conduct our citizens will be enthusiastically united to the government." [71]

Enthusiastic public support for the administration and its measures was, as Hamilton saw it, the point to be kept constantly in the foreground. Had Jefferson or Adams intercepted this letter they would probably have labeled it a forgery. Hamilton was an Anglophile but he was not a sentimentalist and was willing to suppress his admiration for English ways when his own ambitions seemed jeopardized by them. What he was driving at became clearer as the weeks progressed.

By the end of May, 1798, it had become abundantly clear

[70] S. F. Bemis, ed., *American Secretaries of State*, II, 230-231.

[71] Hamilton to Pickering, June 8, 1798, Hamilton, *Works* (Lodge ed.), X, 294.

that adherents of the President's policy of defiance toward France were in control of both houses of Congress. On May 24 Jefferson reported to his son-in-law that an alien control bill had passed its third reading in the House and that it was even more repressive than that which the Senate had been working on for more than two weeks. He further noted that ten of the fourteen absentee Congressmen were his own partisans and, worst of all, that the majority of petitions reaching the capital were highly bellicose. Only four of these petitions, he stated, had proclaimed a desire for peace, and these had come out of Republican strongholds in Maryland and Virginia.[72]

Within a month after the release of the diplomatic papers Congress had authorized the new navy to capture French vessels operating in American coastal waters, had empowered the President to raise a provisional army, and had abrogated all treaties with France. The alien acts were adopted, revenue bills that would provide $430,000 worth of ammunition and coastal defenses were approved, and further revenues for the purchase of more than a million dollars' worth of arms and supplies for the new army were provided by law.[73] The cost was unprecedented and the means revolutionary.

The Evaluation Act of July 9, 1798, better known as the "Window Tax," provided that a direct tax would be levied on the basis of land holdings, houses, and slaves at fifty cents per head. Although doubts were expressed over the advisability of a direct tax, it was considered an essential measure if the nine-million-dollar Federal budget was to be balanced.[74] Although a rider to the Evaluation Act declared that the assessment would be made in proportion to the population of the states, it was obvious that the greatest burden would

[72] Jefferson to T. M. Randolph, June 21, 1798, *Jefferson Papers*, LC.

[73] Washington, *Writings*, XXXVI, 279; *American Secretaries of State*, *op. cit.*, II, 233.

[74] R. G. Harper, to his constituents, July 23, 1798, Harper, *Works*, 269-274.

fall upon Southern farmers and planters. Many Republicans joined the Federalists in support of the bill, nevertheless.[75] The law abrogating the French treaties had passed the Senate by a vote of 14 to 5. More than a third of the members were absent, most of them Republicans.[76]

In June, Federalist supremacy seemed so complete that a declaration of war was widely anticipated and hotly debated. Those who wished for an early adjournment and who wished to avoid a war declaration at all costs were voted down in Federalist party caucus. Uriah Tracy, who was said to be especially intimate with the President, went as far as to urge postponement on the basis of keeping the war spirit alive.[77] The junior senator from New York, William North, was certain that war would be declared before the extremists would allow adjournment. "This it appears to me," he confided to Governor Jay, "there is no occasion for and no good will result from it." The Governor agreed and thought that when the public was ready for war everyone would know it.[78]

Moderate arguments in the Federalist party finally prevailed, and no war was declared; but the sedition act that Mrs. Adams had so long hoped for was pushed through both houses and signed by the President before the July adjournment. It was noted with amazement that even archdemocrat Joseph Varnum of Massachusetts was caught up in the prevailing spirit of national indignation and voted for the Sedition Act.[79]

[75] *Annals*, 5th Congress, 2d Session, Appendix, 3758-3763, 3778-3786.

[76] Jefferson to T. M. Randolph, *op. cit.*

[77] Jefferson to Madison, June 21, 1798, *Writings* (Ford ed.), VIII, 441.

[78] North to Jay, June 22, 1798, Jay to North, June 25, 1798, Jay, *Correspondence*, IV, 243.

[79] Abigail Adams to her sister, May 26, 1798, *New Letters*, 179; Warren, *Jacobins and Junto*, 99.

14

The Bête Noir of Federalism

THREE MONTHS AFTER HIS INAUGURATION JOHN ADAMS CALLED Congress together and in a solemn address recommended that measures for defense be immediately taken. Among the specific measures requested was that for a provisional army. He asked that officers be commissioned and arrangements for recruiting worked out, though he did not call for the establishment of a large professional army. Throughout the two years during which the possibility of war hung perilously close Adams made it clear that he put his faith in a strong navy and cared little for an army as an instrument of either defense or foreign policy. All he asked was that plans be made. His responsibility as President demanded that he take such a line so long as he believed war a possibility, and he was convinced that France could only be brought around to treat with American envoys on an even basis if it were made clear that Americans were prepared to fight rather than submit to further humiliation.

Federalists in Congress, both Adams men and Hamiltonians, far overstepped the arms limits laid down by the President, however. In 1799 Hamilton, as Inspector General and virtual commander of the army, attempted to recruit the twenty-thousand-man force allowed for by the laws of the Fifth Congress, and more than enough officers were commissioned to command the additional thirty thousand provisional troops that would be brought into service when and if the President saw fit to announce a full wartime emergency. Federalist leaders were convinced that an army was necessary, some because they considered war a likelihood and others because they anticipated a Southern rebellion. Hamilton and his intimate friends had private reasons for throwing themselves energetically into the work of creating a national army.

The Alien and Sedition Acts have so overshadowed the history of John Adams' administration that the vast significance of the army has been uniformly underestimated. The threat to freedom of speech contained in the Alien and Sedition Acts roused Jefferson and his friends to new enthusiasm for battle, but if the political history of Adams' administration is viewed from the Federalist point of view—from the viewpoint of the collapse of the Federalists rather than the rise of the Jeffersonians—the army reveals itself as the most significant single issue of that violent four-year period.

"The army," wrote John Quincy Adams, "was the first decisive symptom of a schism in the Federal Party itself, which accomplished its final overthrow and that of the administration." [1] When Adams broke the war crisis in February, 1799, by reopening negotiations with France, he put an abrupt end to the plans of the vindictive, militaristic faction that had seized control of the Federalist party. Adams believed that his action would be widely applauded and there is strong evidence to show that his chances for re-election were enhanced by the inauguration of the second peace mission rather than ruined by it, as Hamiltonians insisted. He gambled on the hope that the Hamiltonian wing of the party would be forced to follow his lead and accept a decision that circumstances made both necessary and expedient.

High-ranking Federalists welcomed the war crisis whether they believed it a bluff on the part of France or the prelude to actual hostilities. They had crept back into power in 1796 by too narrow a margin not to have seized upon the sudden

[1] J. Q. Adams, *Political Parties,* 25.

discomfiture of the Republicans without delight. The fence-sitters in Congress had swung over completely, and the public showed unmistakable signs of approving the administration's policy. A few powerful leaders wished to let no chance slip of destroying the opposition. Fisher Ames was consistently one of these.

Congress, he wrote to Timothy Pickering in June, 1798, lagged far behind the public in its enthusiasm for armament. The public demanded stronger defenses, and he was confident that they would welcome higher taxes in so worthy an understanding. But, warned Ames, the moment might soon pass when patriotism was stronger than the spirit of partisanship; the Jacobins were still alive. "They will soon rise from the mire, where they now lie, and attach themselves to any set of honest men, who in every question shall be for doing the least and latest. Thus a new party may be formed to paralyze and distract our measures. . . ." [2] Pickering's criticism that Adams had failed to take full advantage of the anger caused by the XYZ dispatches Ames brushed aside. The President, he wrote, is not to blame for half measures—Congress falters.[3]

There are men in every generation of political leaders who glory in national strength for its own sake and who tend to view party programs as crusades regardless of the direction in which they may be moving. Ames was such a man, and in 1798 it appeared that he and the champions of aristocracy had at last captured the new Federal government. Their advocacy of strong-arm methods had died in the Constitutional Convention only to emerge again at the time of the Whiskey Rebellion in western Pennsylvania.

"If the insurrection had not been crushed in the manner it was," wrote Madison in December, 1794, "I have no doubt that a formidable attempt would have been made to establish

[2] June 4, 1798, Ames, *Works,* I, 227.
[3] July 10, 1798, *ibid.,* 232.

the principle that a standing army was necessary for enforcing the laws. . . . Nor am I sure that the attempt would not have been made if the President could have been embarked in it, and particularly if the temper of New England had not been dreaded on this point." [4]

Again in 1796 they had shuddered at the thought of anarchy when in the closing weeks of the national election the influence of France was felt to be strong in the frontier territory. Cowards in Congress hesitated before a direct tax, Ames told Hamilton, because they feared popular resentment against it. "Our proceedings smell of anarchy. We rest our hopes on foolish and fanatical grounds . . . on human nature being different from what it is and better here than anywhere else. . . . Internal revenues demand systems and vigor. The collections must be watched and enforced. We want officers, courts, habits of acquiescence, in our country and the principles of Congress would hardly begin to form any of these." Passing on to the subject of a possible war with France, he was despairing. "The western country scarcely calls itself dependent on the Union. France is ready to hold Louisiana. The thread of connection is slender and that event I fear would break it. Yet we disband regiments!" [5]

Other prominent Federalists seemed less concerned over the possibility of anarchy and disunion than over the chances of Republican political domination. A few, including no less an influential man than Massachusetts Senator Theodore Sedgwick, willingly accepted the idea of war as preferable to that of being ejected from power. Sedgwick had served in the first four congresses, had been appointed by the Massachusetts legislature to the Senate in June, 1796, and was returned to the House at the end of his Senate term in 1799.[6] A man of high standing with both the Hamiltonians and the

[4] Madison to Monroe, December 4, 1794, *Madison Papers*, LC.
[5] Ames to Hamilton, January 26, 1797, *Hamilton Papers*, LC.
[6] Dumas Malone, ed., *Dictionary of American Biography*, XVI, 549-550.

Adams supporters from New England, Sedgwick was a well-established political figure in July, 1798, when he wrote Rufus King that it was necessary for Congress to declare war lest the Republicans recover the ground recently lost in the XYZ excitement.

We must declare war, he wrote, because the Republicans are certain to pose as the peace party and win favor by branding us as warmongers. It would be far better to take the step and face them with a *fait accompli.* He quoted Speaker Jonathan Dayton of New Jersey as saying that there was majority sentiment in favor of a declaration of war and that the vote could be rounded up by the Fourth of July.[7]

That same night the issue was argued out in a Federalist caucus attended by dependable party men from both Houses. While leaders urged such a move, the rank and file refused. A Virginia senator who knew of the caucus admitted to Jefferson that a declaration could be pushed through at any time the Federalists agreed. While Southern congressmen were leaving Philadelphia every day, Federalist chiefs were holding their partisans at their seats. The national holiday passed without the expected call for war, but the tension was scarcely relaxed by the passage of the Sedition Act ten days later.[8]

The most forthright and selfish demands for war came from New England Federalists. Stephen Higginson, who had just been appointed a government naval agent, placed the highest premium upon political survival. "Nothing but an open war can save us," he wrote to Oliver Wolcott, Jr., in July, "and the more inveterate and deadly it shall be, the better will be our chance for security in the future." [9] The blood of the nation was worth spilling for the sake of sound

[7] July 1, 1798, King, *Life and Correspondence*, II, 352-353.

[8] Henry Tazewell to Jefferson, July 5, 1798, *Jefferson Papers*, LC.

[9] July 11, 1798, Gibbs, *Memoirs*, II, 71; Higginson, *Life and Times of Stephen Higginson*, 187-215.

politics and possible fortunes, though undoubtedly Higginson considered himself a true patriot and a champion of sound political principles.

Old General Schuyler was highly distressed to hear that the latest rumor from Paris was of a pacific nature when he wrote Hamilton in August, "I hope the latter is unfounded for I feel that war with all its calamities, would be less injurious to my country than a peace which might be followed . . . with the reintroduction of the destructive principles which prevail in France." [10] From London George Cabot viewed the failure of Congress to take the final step as a national calamity. "It is unfortunate that Congress did not declare war," he wrote after learning that the Federalist caucus had ended in disagreement, "the danger from French artifice would have been much less. It is impossible to make the people feel or see distinctly that we have much more to fear from peace than war. . . . But war, open and declared, would not only deprive our external enemy of his best hopes, but would also extinguish the hopes of internal foes." [11]

Republican fears that their opponents desired war were not fabricated for electioneering purposes, nor were the worst suspicions as to the motives behind that desire unfounded. War would deal a death blow to Jefferson and his friends far more effectively than the most strenuously waged campaign for votes, and with surprising frankness Federalist leaders admittedly sought to deliver such a blow. Many sincerely believed that France had already begun to wage war without formally announcing it, and the desire to strike back was understandable. The editor of a small town New England newspaper, for example, printed a long list of French attacks upon American naval vessels for the winter of 1798 and then asked, "If the United States are not now in a state

[10] To Hamilton, August 6, 1798, *Hamilton Papers*, LC.

[11] Cabot to Oliver Wolcott, Jr., October 25, 1798, Gibbs, *Memoirs*, II, 109.

of war with France; in what state are they? Let the Loganites answer the question." [12]

As happens often in politics, men in high places acted during the war scare on the basis of their fears and not upon well-established facts. Many Federalists in 1798 were convinced that rebellion was about to commence in the South and in the western frontier areas of the nation close to Spanish colonial outposts.

The Secretary of State, who grasped at every opportunity of furthering the hatred for France and its American sympathizers, but who nonetheless was expected to know the most about French policy, went on record in the spring of 1798 that France was secretly fomenting a slave insurrection in the South. He had information that led him to believe that a French invasion would be launched by General Hédouville from Santo Domingo, he told Representative Harper of South Carolina. Specially hired Negro agents were rumored to be spreading arms among the slaves as a prelude to the French attack. Harrison Otis repeated the rumor in a pamphlet that was published in April.[13]

In western Pennsylvania a contributor of Fenno's *Gazette* noted the rise of a spirit of rebellion reminiscent of that which had called forth Federal troops in 1794. So strong had the spirit of sedition become, according to this observor, that a "Jacobin" governor could be easily elected "to raise the banner of opposition to the federal administration." [14]

When the Federalists called for a standing army and began to raise one it was assumed that the talk of a French invasion was nothing more than subterfuge to cover the actual design of using it in order to silence the opposition by powerfully enforcing the Sedition Act.

Historians have generally rejected this thesis. "This in-

[12] New London, *Connecticut Gazette*, January 16, 1799.

[13] Pickering to R. G. Harper, March 21, 1798, *Pickering-MSS*, Massachusetts Historical Society, X, 502, cited in Morison, *Otis*, I, 68, Note 11.

[14] *United States Gazette*, March 5, 1798.

dictment, that the regular and provisional armies were designed primarily to suppress democracy, and not to protect the country against France," wrote Professor Morison, "is not supported by the slightest evidence." Henry Adams believed that only because no French invasion of the United States took place could Republicans assert that the standing army was designed to crush the Republican party.[15]

Whether such an intention was foremost in the minds of such men as Hamilton, Pickering, Sedgwick, Tracy, and Cabot when they first urged the establishment of a sizable military machine it is difficult to prove, but there is conclusive evidence that they expected and hoped to use armed force against their political opponents. The most important man in the new army of 1798–99 was Hamilton, and Hamilton was a well-known advocate of military force as the backbone of law. His many champions and many of his severest critics alike have judged his attitude toward the war crisis from the famous declaration he made concerning the Sedition Act in 1798. "There are provisions in this bill which appear to me highly exceptionable," he wrote to Wolcott, "and such as, more than anything else may endanger a civil war. . . . Let us not establish a tyranny . . . if we push things to an extreme, we shall give to faction, body and solidity." [16]

On the basis of this statement Hamilton would appear to have been on the side of leniency and to have disapproved the idea of using force against civilians. Yet we must make an exception for civilians in rebellion. Hamilton believed that rebellion was on the point of breaking out, mentioning civil war at the same time that he cautioned Wolcott to use his influence against extreme measures. It was certainly with Hamilton in mind that Jefferson requested Madison to publish his notes on the Constitutional Convention, for Hamilton's speeches in 1787 leave no doubt that he favored the

[15] Morison, *Otis*, 102; Adams, *Albert Gallatin*, 103, 199, 211.
[16] June 29, 1798, *Hamilton Papers*, LC.

presence and use of standing armies to back up the courts of law.

According to Madison's notes, Hamilton had openly professed the belief that among "the great and essential principles necessary for the support of government" that might produce "an habitual attachment of the people" was "force," by which may be understood "a coercion of laws or coercion of arms." "A certain portion of military force is absolutely necessary in large communities."[17] So well known were Hamilton's sentiments that in the summer of 1792 Philip Freneau, then Jefferson's chief press lieutenant, attacked Hamilton because of his faith in standing armies as one of the mainstays of order and stability in government along with titles, permanent debts, and the necessary and proper clause of the Constitution.[18] Nothing in Hamilton's conduct during the Whiskey Rebellion suggests that his thinking had undergone any change whatsoever.

Hamilton's distrust of republican government and his fear that it could only end in disorder and despotism was abiding, as was his conviction that an aristocratic government was the most successful ever devised by men.

His reading of history had convinced Hamilton that disorder and rebellion were inherent in republican society and that through disorder monarchical government became established. Just after Hamilton's tragic death, Gouverneur Morris, one of the men who knew him best, described what he believed to have been Hamilton's attitude towards the army and war crisis of 1798.

"Our poor friend Hamilton bestrode his hobby to the great annoyance of his friends, and not without injury to himself. . . . He well knew that his favorite form (of government) was inadmissible, unless as the result of civil war; and I sus-

[17] Madison, *Writings* (Hunt ed.), III, 184-185.

[18] S. E. Forman, "The Political Activities of Philip Freneau," *Johns Hopkins University Studies*, XX, 514.

pect that his belief in that which he called 'an approaching crisis' arose from a conviction that the kind of government most suitable in his opinion, to this extensive country, could be established in no other way." [19]

Hamilton's reasons for taking up the task of organizing the army (and shouldering the work of the Secretary of War as well) with amazing energy and enthusiasm was based upon the firmest personal opinions and considerations. He believed that the President was wise in asking for preparedness and saw that to assume a bold attitude toward France would best insure successful negotiations. If Gouverneur Morris was correct, he felt at the same time that the final structure of the American government might well be determined by the outcome of a civil war that he considered imminent. The final proof of Hamilton's attitude toward military force and of the use that he thought might be made of it in 1799 rests upon letters written to Jonathan Dayton that year. They prove beyond the shadow of a doubt that his "Let us not establish a tyranny" statement is not an accurate or honest summary of his position.

"To preserve confidence in the Officers of the General Government, by preserving their reputations from . . . unfounded slanders," he wrote, "is essential to enable them to fulfill the ends of their appointment. It is therefore constitutional and politic to place their reputations under the guardianship of the courts of the United States. They ought not be left to the cold and reluctant protection of state courts.

"But what avail laws which are not executed? Renegade aliens conduct one or more incendiary presses in the United States. . . . Why are they not sent away? Vigour in the Executive are at least as necessary as in the legislative branch. If the President requires to be stimulated those who can approach him ought to do it."

[19] Cited in Randall, *Jefferson,* I, 580 ff. Martin Van Buren, *Political Parties,* 81.

First, he wrote, the government ought to be strengthened against change by a permanent army regardless of the state of foreign affairs. Second, he urged that an increase in the legal power of the Federal government over the states ought to be secured and the larger states reduced in size "so as to make state power more innocuous." Finally, Hamilton suggested strengthening the sedition laws, almost as though anticipating the Virginia and Kentucky resolutions.[20]

The common belief that Hamilton considered the Alien and Sedition Acts too extreme is absolutely false, and considering the fact that the largest states, particularly Virginia, were all Southern and Republican in political complexion there is excellent reason to conclude that Hamilton contemplated the necessity of using his military machine. Civil war would certainly have followed the attempt to realize his reactionary program. Dayton's mouth was closed by an appointment as Brigadier General in the provisional army, and there is no evidence that he ever revealed Hamilton's suggestions.

While President Adams finally concluded that Hamilton's sole purpose in organizing the army was to suppress possible domestic violence, Hamilton and his friends had still other dreams—dreams of conquest scarcely less grandiose than those of the Pizzaros.[21] In February, 1798, American Minister Rufus King informed the Secretary of State that the expected French invasion of Spain would lead to the immediate dismemberment of the Spanish colonial empire. The Venezuelan adventurer, Francisco Miranda, he pointed out, had been kept on the British payroll for just such an eventuality and was expected to lead a full-scale revolt with the assistance of the British navy. King, writing in cipher, promised to keep Pickering up to date on British plans inas-

[20] Hamilton to Jonathan Dayton, 1799, *Hamilton Papers*, LC; Hamilton, *Works* (Lodge ed.), VIII, 517-518.

[21] Adams, *Works*, I, 523-527.

much as the President was certain to be approached on the subject.[22]

What King and the Hamiltonian clique conjured up was a joint Anglo-American land and naval force meant to strike at Spanish armies from Louisiana, meeting with Miranda's insurgents somewhere in Central America. So confident and enthusiastic was King that he wrote General Pinckney of the plan while the latter was waiting in southern France after the failure of the first peace commission. If England fails to stop France from re-establishing her American empire, puppet republics are sure to be erected on our very doorstep, he argued. It seemed stupid, therefore, not to co-operate fully when Britain asked for help. King envisaged a new world order emerging as the result of successfully launching independent Spanish American states under the joint protection of the United States and Great Britain. Their independence, he concluded, "presents wealth and security to the U. States, and a new balance among nations." [23]

The American Minister pursued his dream in deadly earnest, daring Hamilton to be as audacious as the French, requesting Pickering to secure a full set of maps for the campaign, and offering to secure necessary military information for McHenry's use in the War Department.[24] George Cabot, then in England as a member of the Jay treaty commission, fell in completely with the project. Nelson's victory at the Battle of the Nile now ensures British supremacy on the seas, he wrote to King in December. "Indeed it has appeared to me evident that Great Britain, the United States, and Russia could triumph over all the powers and that the two former might even be enriched by the war." [25]

[22] King to Pickering, February 26, 1798, King, *Life and Correspondence*, II, 283-284.

[23] April 2, 1798, *King Papers*, New York Historical Society, Box 7, No. 66.

[24] King to Hamilton, July 7, 1798, to McHenry, December 8, 1798, *Life and Correspondence*, II, 361, 483.

[25] December 12, 1798, King, *Life and Correspondence*, II, 491.

Hamilton considered the project entirely possible and set the acquisition of the Floridas and Louisiana as the minimum price of American participation. When Washington commented that the only prize France could win in a war with the United States was Louisiana and the two Florida colonies of Spain, Hamilton replied, "I have long been in the habit of considering the acquisition of those countries as essential to the permanence of the Union." He likewise urged Pickering to allow no chance of buying the territories or of occupying them to go by.[26]

The intriguing frontier commander, Wilkinson, raised to the rank of Major General by Washington and Hamilton in 1798, willingly lent his aid to the cause by predicting a revolt on the frontier that was certain to demand the movement of troops southwestward.[27] The most promising prospects of success, however, were held out by the British government itself.

In a conversation with William Pitt, King was encouraged to believe that an Anglo-American agreement for the regulation of European trade might be in the offing, and for the defense of Charleston the guns and ammunition taken from a captured French naval vessel were graciously transferred to the American government by Britain. His Majesty's government, explained British Minister Liston, considered Charleston particularly vulnerable to French attack from the West Indies.[28] Anglo-American relations reached a degree of cordiality in 1798 not seen again until 1917 and scarcely imaginable before the XYZ blunder, despite what Republicans had said about the Jay treaty.

Hamilton, while interested, was well aware that the Span-

[26] Washington to Hamilton, January 26, 1799, *Hamilton Papers,* LC; Hamilton, *Republic,* VII, 210-212; to Pickering, March 27, 1798, *Hamilton Papers;* LC.

[27] James Wilkinson, to Hamilton, September 6, 1799, *Hamilton Papers,* L.C.

[28] Pickering to Washington, February 8, 1799, Washington, *Writings,* XXXVII, 132, Note 97; Liston to Pickering, September 10, 1798, Channing, *History,* IV, 198.

ish American expedition might never materialize and that events in Europe might cause the British government to drop the enterprise overnight. American forces should, he wrote to Harrison Otis, be prepared to take possession of the Spanish colonies on our borders, but even if French policy should change, our military measures would only serve to speed up any peaceful settlement France might wish to make.[29] Thus, Hamilton and his friends could claim to be working in the interest of peace while secretly planning for foreign conquest or the suppression of a Southern rebellion, or both. Among the Hamiltonians only Oliver Wolcott viewed the Spanish American design as unwarranted. He made no attempt to hide his opposition to it, stating to Jonathan Trumbull of Connecticut that he believed Spain's colonial power could as well be ended by a simple declaration that Britain and the United States would co-operate in defending their commerce in Spanish America as by an invasion.[30]

The Federalist party as a whole favored the President's recommendations for defense measures. Many openly demanded war, while most of the leaders were at least not opposed to it. Many Federalists feared and expected the outbreak of rebellion and championed an enlarged standing army as protection against the dismemberment of the Union, while behind their fears lay the desire to use force against political opposition. Again, the Federalists preferred to draw a very fine line between treason and legitimate opposition. Hamilton saw in the expected revolt an opportunity to establish the aristocratic type of government that he had always preferred and that he believed must arise out of the instability of republican societies. His dreams of military conquest and of intimate relations with Great Britain were in keeping with that order of government. His friends in the Federalist party

[29] A. B. Darling, *Our Rising Empire*, 325-327; to Otis, January 26, 1799, *Works* (Lodge ed.), X, 338.

[30] Wolcott to Trumbull, July 16, 1799, Gibbs, *Memoirs*, II, 246.

were persuaded that a standing army for internal use had become necessary for the protection of life and property and because they preferred to interpret what they saw and heard in the Southern states as certain evidence of preparation for civil war.

Even Washington in his old age had come to look with deep concern and distrust upon the nature of the Republican opposition. Writing to Lafayette in December, 1798, he declared, "A party exists in the United States . . . which oppose the Government in all its measures, and are Clogging its Wheels indirectly to change the nature of it, and to subvert the Constitution." [31]

President Adams almost alone did not share in his party's enthusiasm for the heavy military program of 1798. He had taken the lead in rousing the public to anger over French duplicity and had been the first to call for military and naval preparedness. Specifically, he had asked Congress to augment the size of the regular army, especially in the cavalry and artillery branches; he had approved the creation of a separate navy department to develop American sea power; and he had urged that American treaties with France be declared null and void. Adams did not ask for the Alien and Sedition Acts, direct taxes, new loans at high interest rates, or for a regular and provisional military force of fifty thousand men.[32] Although none of the measures of 1798 was passed over a presidential veto, the majority in Congress broke with the President over the question of defense. By emphasizing a large army rather than a navy they put themselves into an embarrassing situation. Of what use could a large infantry force be if a French invasion did not take place?

Obviously, the seizure of Canada was out of the question, and it was not clear that Spain's North American possessions

[31] December 25, 1798, Washington, *Writings*, XXXVII, 66.
[32] Adams, *Works*, I, 520-522.

were legitimate fields of operation. By refusing to play the President's game, the dominant faction in Congress allowed their opponents to charge that the army was meant for use against American citizens. Jefferson saw his opportunity and judiciously warned his friends against giving the Federalist high command any pretext for using the newly enlarged army. He much preferred to let the public come to its own conclusions on the matter.[33]

Hamilton, through Representative Tracy and the Secretary of War, urged the President to use his powers as Commander in Chief to direct congressional action, and when Adams refused to do so the Hamiltonians took matters into their own hands.[34] Adams was not consulted on such vital legislation as the Sedition Act or the direct tax, and he plainly resented it. When it appeared that he had lost direction of the defense program to Hamilton and his confreres, Adams sought to obstruct their designs as consistently as Pickering and McHenry purposefully delayed in carrying out his own.

"The army and navy must be attended to," wrote the Speaker of the House almost a year after the XYZ disclosures. "In regard to the former, the conduct of the Executive has been astoundingly dilatory. As yet not a single enlisting order has been issued."[35]

At the same time that Adams was instructing the new Secretary of the Navy, Benjamin Stoddert, to work as fast as possible in getting the new frigates afloat, he was reprimanding McHenry for being overly concerned over the army. When the Secretary of War wrote that both a strong army and a "commander of genius" were necessary for the nation's safety, Adams bluntly replied that the navy was his chief

[33] Jefferson to Madison, T. M. Randolph, Nicholas Lewis, January 30, 1799, *Jefferson Papers*, LC.

[34] Uriah Tracy to Hamilton, May 17, 1798, Hamilton to McHenry, May 17, 1798, *Hamilton Papers*, LC.

[35] To Rufus King, January 20, 1799, King, *Life and Correspondence*, II, 518.

concern. "A controversy between you and Mr. Stoddert," he barked, "would be easily answered by me." [36]

The debate within the party over the relative merits of a defensive army and an offensive navy was not barred from the cabinet. The new Navy Secretary naturally supported the President in opposing the military viewpoint that Pickering and McHenry supported in Hamilton's behalf. "I not only believe now, but always did, that a navy was the only national system of defense for this country," wrote Stoddert to Wolcott. "I believe a small army to be kept together to awe the Jacobins and to keep up appearances to France, a very proper thing." [37]

Oliver Wolcott, traditionally pictured as a Hamilton tool, strenuously opposed the army, and with astonishing adroitness was able to keep the President's favor and Hamilton's at the same time, despite his opposition to further recruiting. When Hamilton met with Washington, Pinckney, and the President's cabinet in December, 1798, Adams being conveniently absent, Wolcott warned them that the public would soon come to resent the army. He declared that "few officers ought to be appointed, and the expense of supporting idle men avoided as much as possible." His recommendation that military preparedness be limited to the collection of arms and the building of armories was overridden despite the fact that Washington, nominally the commanding general of the army, was fully convinced that a French invasion was beyond the realm of possibility.[38]

With an election but several months away, Adams, with the support of Wolcott, Stoddert, and the Attorney General, was still unable to end the hold that militarism had taken upon the minds of the Hamiltonians except by the most drastic action. Almost blindly the army faction refused

[36] Adams to Stoddert, May 19, 1799, Adams to McHenry, June 29, 1799, *Works,* VIII, 650-651, 662.

[37] November 27, 1798, Gibbs, *Memoirs,* II, 115.

[38] Wolcott to Ames, December 29, 1799, *ibid.,* 317.

to recognize the potency of the standing army issue in the hands of the Republicans. While Wolcott reflected the nation's changing mood his colleague, Mr. Pickering, refused to accept the warning of one of the party's most stalwart press defenders in his blunt statement that the American people did not want an army. It was in November, 1798, more than a year before the military organization was cashiered, that Noah Webster of the New York *Minerva* came out in favor of a navy rather than an army as the nation's most useful arm of defense.[39] The die-hards such as Cabot, Ames, Pickering, and Hamilton moved stubbornly on. The army may still be useful, wrote Ames to Wolcott in answer to the latter's objections to it. Without discussing the possibility of winning the election of 1800, Ames predicted Jefferson's victory and the outbreak of civil war that would surely follow.[40]

While doing his best to prepare the navy for what he regarded as its essential role for both defense and peace negotiations, the President gave no encouragement to the plans of the military clique. His attitude on this issue reflected a deep conviction. "The English have exhibited an amazing example of skill and intrepidity, perseverance and firmness at sea. We are a chip of that block, and we could do as we pleased, at least as we ought,, on the watery element, if it were not that we shall excite jealousy in the English navy. We must, however, stand for our right." [41]

Such was his attitude as he expressed it to his wife at the beginning of 1799. By not consulting the President on the legislation of 1798, Federalist congressional leaders had offended Adams, and by pursuing a military rather than a naval program, they had clearly angered him and opened a rift in the hitherto united ranks of the party. The act that made the split permanent, however, was the insistence on the part of

[39] Noted by Ames in a letter to Pickering, November 22, 1798, Ames, *Works*, I, 242.

[40] Ames to Wolcott, January, 1800, Gibbs, *Memoirs*, II, 320.

[41] January 1, 1799, Adams, *Letters to his Wife*, II, 259.

Washington, Pickering, and their followers that Hamilton be made second in command. Until the President's hand was forced in favor of Hamilton, disagreement arose over issues. There was as yet no personal animosity. Adams hated Hamilton and would never have dated his commission before those of his Revolutionary friends Knox, Morgan, and Lincoln had not Washington demanded it.

Adams made his original mistake in placing himself unreservedly in Washington's hands where military decisions were concerned. "I am at an immense loss whether to call out all the old Generals, or to appoint a young Sett," he confessed in June, 1798. "If the French come here we must learn to march with a quick step, and to Attack, for in that way only are they said to be vulnerable." He begged Washington's aid, even declaring that he would gladly step down to allow the ex-President to lead the nation in war if the Constitution would allow it and ended by asking for Washington's services in reorganizing the army.[42]

From this letter Washington quite correctly concluded that he had been given the right to place young officers in command if he saw fit.[43] Party leaders, Jay, Pickering, McHenry, Cabot, and Higginson among them, insisted that Hamilton was the right man for the great undertaking but ran immediately into Adams' opposition. New England, Adams declared, would never tolerate seeing Hamilton placed ahead of Henry Knox. Cabot, Jeremiah Wadsworth, and Washington all attempted to assuage Knox's indignation. Charles Cotesworth Pinckney, who had outranked Hamilton during the Revolution, gladly stepped aside in favor of the powerful Federalist chief, an action for which he was generously rewarded in 1800, but Knox refused to take any part in the building of the new army except as an aide-de-

[42] Adams to Washington, June 22, 1798, *John Adams Letters*, 1781–1826, Historical Society of Pennsylvania.

[43] Washington to Adams, July 4, 1798, Washington to McHenry, July 5, 1798, Washington, *Writings*, XXXVI, 312-315, 318-320.

camp to Washington. His humiliation was unfortunately shared by the President, for Washington let it be known that he wanted Hamilton and would insist on Hamilton. If the President persisted in blocking the appointment, Washington informed McHenry, their personal compact would be at an end. He had done his share by allowing his appointment as commander; it was up to Adams to fulfill the bargain by naming the men he wanted.[44]

Throughout the four-month wrangle over the Major Generals Adams had been at Quincy, where Knox and Lincoln were able to convince him that an intrigue was under way to bring Hamilton into a position of dominance in the administration.[45] Pickering and McHenry in their laudations of Hamilton added immeasurably to Adams's growing suspicion that the charge was true. Wolcott, despite his opposition to a large active force, joined Washington, Pickering, and McHenry in viewing Hamilton as the outstanding man to direct the work of creating an army.

In his letter to Washington outlining the strategy for pushing Adams into line Pickering revealed how deeply Washington had become implicated in the intrigue. The letter was secret and highly indicative of the attitude that the cabinet had allowed themselves to take with regard to their official functions. Even Stoddert joined his colleagues in supporting Hamilton.

It had been decided, wrote Pickering, to have Wolcott alone make the last appeal. "This is particularly the more eligible, seeing Mr. Wolcott cannot be suspected of intermeddling in the primary arrangement; having been absent in Connecticut . . . and may therefore be well supposed to step

[44] Washington to Adams, September 25, 1798, Washington to McHenry, October 1, 1798, Washington, *Writings*, XXXVI, 453-462, 476-477. Cabot to Pickering, September 29, 1798, *Hamilton Papers*, LC. Pickering to Washington, July 6, 1798, Washington, *Writings*, XXXVI, 324, Note 96. Jay to Pickering, July 10, 1798, *Hamilton Papers*, LC.

[45] Cabot to Pickering, September 29, 1798, *op. cit.* Cabot to Adams, September 29, 1798, *Hamilton Papers*, LC.

forward with an unbiased mind." He expressed his hope that the commanding general would not be wounded by the President's disregard for his wishes.[46]

The commissions were resubmitted, and Adams drank a very bitter cup. "The sun begins to shine," wrote the exuberant McHenry to his idol Hamilton when the President returned the commissions properly dated.[47] Within a few months Hamilton moved into Adams' cabinet as confidently and effectively as he had into Washington's during 1795. McHenry, utterly confused by his department's duties, turned his office over to Hamilton in everything but name. In April, 1799, Hamilton as much as told him to let him take on the burden of running the department.[48] Meanwhile his advice on all matters of state was channeled into the President's office via three of the President's five-man cabinet.

So far as Adams was concerned a provisional army could have been used very effectively in promoting the political strength of his own administration. Commissions would be sought and expected by many men of political importance, among them Republicans as well as Federalists. It was Adams' plan to unite the nation by commissioning outstanding Republican party leaders with the added hope that some of the more independent-minded might be won away from the Jeffersonian fold. There were men within the Republican ranks who might easily have welcomed a third political alignment between the extremes of Southern Republicanism and Eastern Hamiltonianism.

In 1805 John Adams admitted to Benjamin Rush that he had had hopes of using Madison's talents when the administration first opened but that the "ministers, whom Washington's appointment made my masters" showed open hostility

[46] September 18, 1798, *Hamilton Papers*, LC.

[47] October 5, 1798, *ibid.*

[48] Hamilton to McHenry, April 8, 1799, Hamilton to Wolcott, April 8, 1799, *ibid.*

to the idea.[49] When the war scare of 1798 swept the nation Adams again sought to return to the bipartisan policy with which he had opened his administration. Like Jefferson, he recognized the middle states as holding the balance of power in national politics and attempted to woo Pennsylvania and New York Republicans with high appointments.

The unceremonious way in which Aaron Burr's pretensions for the vice-presidency had been dropped by the Virginians in 1796 left hopes of winning him over, and President Adams included his name on the list of Brigadier Generals for appointment to the provisional army. Peter Muhlenberg of Pennsylvania, whose brother Frederick had been roughly handled by the Republicans for his vote on the Jay treaty appropriations, offered his services to the President in the summer of 1798 and was likewise proposed by Adams for a general's commission, but as in the case of Burr the Hamiltonians would have none of it.[50]

With the election of 1800 clearly in mind Adams wrote in his diary that he had hopes of conciliating the opposition by appointing Muhlenberg and Burr to high ranks. "But I soon found myself shackled. The heads of departments were exclusive patriots. I could not name a man who was not devoted to Hamilton without kindling a fire. . . . I soon found that if I had not the previous consent of the heads of departments, and the approbation of Mr. Hamilton, I ran the utmost risk of a dead negative in the Senate." Temporary safe majorities, he concluded, made the Federalists presumptuous and vindicative.[51]

What Adams wished to do was to appoint officers to the ranks to which their former services and revolutionary stand-

[49] Adams to Rush, August 23, 1805, Biddle, *Old Family Letters*, I, 76-77. From this statement has come the widely accepted opinion that Adams was somehow committed to accept Washington's secretaries. This seems unfounded from the evidence concerning the patronage presented in Chapter XI.

[50] Adams to Rush, September 30, 1805, *ibid.*, 84-85.

[51] Adams, *Works*, IX, 301-302.

ing would entitle them. "Gates, Schuyler, Lincoln, Knox, Clintons, Pinckneys, Sumpters, Muhlenbergs, who you will. But not one of my Ministers, not one Senator, not one Representative and what was more than all, Washington who was Viceroy over me, nor Hamilton who was Viceroy over all, would have heard the proposition with Patience. Old men with Knowledge and Experience are more worthy of Trust than Boys with their Ignorance and Vanity." [52]

Unfortunately for so ambitious a political dream, Adams had already asked of Washington whether it might not be wise to select younger men for the new type of warfare that France had introduced to the battlefields of Europe. Furthermore, to raise an army Adams had felt Washington's prestige a necessity and to bring the aged general out of his retirement he had found it equally necessary to allow him the right of approving all higher officers prior to commission.

For a provisional army even the Hamiltonians might have seen the wisdom of including some of their political opponents but, for an army that they seriously contemplated using, only Federalists were viewed as reliable. Everything depended upon the contemplated role of the army, and there were two views on the matter. Adams lamented the stupidity of the Hamiltonians and placed much of the blame for the outcome of the election of 1800 upon them for refusing to bring Burr and the Muhlenbergs into the administration camp.[53]

The only politician of formerly suspect opinions to win the approval of the Hamiltonians was Jonathan Dayton of New Jersey, but Dayton had seen the handwriting on the wall early and was an arden Francophobe at the time of his appointment as a Brigadier General. Even so, Dayton was first commissioned a Colonel but was raised in rank the day

[52] Adams to Richard Rush, August 11, 1813, *3rd Administration MSS*, Gratz Collection, Case 2, Box 15, Historical Society of Pennsylvania.

[53] Adams to Benjamin Rush, September 30, 1805, *Old Family Letters*, *op. cit.*

after his original nomination. Adams, said the *Aurora,* claimed that a mistake had been made, but the truth was that Dayton had been a Republican once and needed chastising.[54]

"Gentlemen of the first families, fortunes, and expectations" were eagerly accepted by Washington and Hamilton. Washington was delighted to appoint Robert Harper an aide-de-camp, and he drew up a list of appointees that included forty-nine good Federalists and not a single Republican.[55] The President's son-in-law, William S. Smith, was flatly turned down by the Senate for confirmation as Adjutant General. Pickering made no secret of his own low opinion of Colonel Smith and won the President's wrath for his lobbying against him.[56]

Federalists not only rewarded themselves and their friends with commissions in the army, but they also believed that they were doing the nation a service in allowing politics to be the principal qualification for appointments. Our main concern, wrote Representative Goodrich of Connecticut to Oliver Wolcott, is to mind our own business abroad and "take care of own Jacobins. . . . Some of our friends suspect a concert to get as many as they can into the army. Be that as it may, everyone of them ought to be rejected, and men only of fair property, employed in the higher and most confidential grades." [57] Goodrich was almost liberal: his fellow Federalists were not sold on the idea of minding their own business abroad nor of appointing "Jacobins" to the lowest grades. There was general agreement, however, that the Republicans might need looking after.

The army raised in 1798 and 1799 was the principal cause of the split in the Federalist party that revealed itself blatantly when Adams suddenly announced his intention to accept the peace feelers from Paris. There can be no doubt

[54] Nov. 5, 1798.

[55] Washington, *Writings,* XXXVI, 333-334, 382, 393-395.

[56] Pickering to Jay, July 20, 1798, *Hamilton Papers,* LC.

[57] August 12, 1798, Gibbs, *Memoirs,* II, 105.

that the party was already badly divided at the time of that startling announcement in February, 1799. In refusing to consult the President over the legislation of 1798, in changing the character of the defense measures which he had called for, in pushing Hamilton to the position of acting commander of the army, in refusing to recognize the necessity and the political expediency of giving key Republicans positions of trust in the military organization, and in the very act of raising a large standing army the Hamiltonians had played into the hands of the Republicans and had alienated the President with his large personal following. They shortsightedly viewed the Federalist party as their factional instrument, dismissing the popularity of the President with the rank and file as of secondary importance while placing their hopes for 1800 on a civil war that Jefferson wisely cautioned his followers against giving them any pretext for starting.

The only Federalist of any significance who seemed to fully comprehend the wisdom of Adam's leadership was John Marshall. Looked upon as one of the brighter lights of the party in 1796, he was branded as a political trimmer in 1799 for his refusal to accept the French peace suggestions as false and for publicly condemning the Alien and Sedition Acts during his campaign for the House in 1798.[58]

Marshall has "degraded himself by a mean and paltry electioneering trick," wrote Sedwick to Pickering; and Fisher Ames went so far as to label him a "moderate" and a man who had sold himself to "the base opposers of the law." [59] Adams offered him the seat on the Supreme Court bench left vacant by the death of James Wilson, but the Virginia Federalist preferred the active arena and accepted Washington's plea that he stand for the House of Representatives.[60] His actions during 1799 point to him as an Adams champion and

[58] Beveridge, *Marshall*, II, 389.

[59] Sedgwick to Pickering, October 23, 1798, Ames to Gore, December 18, 1798, *Marshall*, II, 391, Ames, *Works*, I, 245-247.

[60] Beveridge, Marshall, II, 387.

a man who saw eye to eye with the President on both domestic issues and foreign policy. Hamiltonians came to view the President's display of friendship for Marshall with almost as much alarm as his championship of Elbridge Gerry.

Elbridge Gerry returned to the United States in the fall of 1798 as an avowed exponent of peace with France and as such was shunned by every respectable member of the Essex circle. The resentment and chagrin that Adams had at first felt towards Gerry gradually softened. He had appointed him to the peace commission over the protests of his secretaries and felt their apparent triumph over him deeply.[61] By October Gerry's social visits to the Adams home at Quincy had the local Federalist chieftains worried. It seemed to them that Gerry had somehow cast a spell over the President and that his insidious propaganda might have damaging results to the all-important Federalist war program.

Samuel Sewall was at first delegated to call upon Adams to express the anxiety of his political friends over his apparent intimacy with a Francophile, but realizing that Sewall had never been anything but hostile towards Gerry, the Essex leaders delegated newcomer Harrision Otis for the diplomatic task. It failed to impress Adams that Gerry was viewed as a suspicious character. He had known it and felt it somewhat himself before hearing the full story that Gerry had to relate. Wolcott, whom the Federalist leaders rightly regarded as trusted by Adams, was then instructed to inform the President how "the friends of Government" felt towards the obnoxious Mr. Gerry.[62]

Adams could not take the warnings of Wolcott, Otis, and their friends as the basis for his actions, because he was convinced that peace could soon be arranged without humiliation to either nation and because peace was his avowed aim. The

[61] Abigail Adams to her sister, June 13, 1798, *New Letters*, 192-193.

[62] Cabot to Wolcott, October 25, 1798, October 10, 1798, Gibbs, *Memoirs*, II, 109-110.

President could not avoid nominating William Vans Murray as envoy to France in February, 1799, if he was an honest man. Too many forces were at work that pointed to peace as the only sane and honorable path for him to follow. His policy, despite the machinations of the Hamiltonians, had proved successful, and for very excellent reasons he believed that peace might prove as great a political blessing in 1799 as the threat of war had been in 1797 and 1798. John Adams was a patriot, but he was also a far more astute politician than most historians have given him credit for being. When he saw an opportunity to benefit the nation and the political fortunes of John Adams he quite naturally seized upon it.

15

A Just and Politic Peace

THE BEGINNING AND THE END OF JOHN ADAMS' POLITICAL career are marked by two great decisions. In 1776 he was foremost among the handful of radicals who openly called for independence and a declaration of war against Great Britain, while in 1799 he dramatically broke with the Hamiltonians, lost their support for the presidency in 1800, and made peace with France. Historians in general have had far greater regard for Adams the revolutionary radical than for Adams the President and peace-maker.

John Adams' nomination of a new peace envoy in February, 1799, brought the wrath of the Hamiltonian faction down upon him, because it put an end to their dreams of political preponderance and military glory. It seemed to the Hamiltonians that Adams had deliberately cut them off from his thinking on this important decision and had committed political suicide by allowing the Republicans to come out of their eclipse to campaign actively for Jefferson's election in 1800. It has seemed as simple as this to most historians since.

The standard pro-Hamiltonian viewpoint is that Adams had little reason to reopen negotiations at the moment he did. The French government had not made a direct approach or any announcement concerning the XYZ affair that expressed regret or willingness to make amends. Talleyrand, in an injured tone, had stated that the American envoys had been taken in by a band of thieves and had left France before checking with his office on the standing of the three agents known as "X," "Y," and "Z." The Federalist high command asked how France had fulfilled the President's own requirement: that negotiations would not be resumed until France gave certain assurances that American diplomats would be received as the representatives of a great, free, and independent nation. According to them, Adams had killed the spirit of patriotic loyalty and the spirit of resentment against France that had sent the Republicans into disgrace and rocketed the Federalists to their peak of popularity.

"The military preparations of the autumn of 1798 had aroused the martial spirit of the land," wrote the pro-Hamiltonian chronicler of Adams' administration. "The bravest, the ablest, the most honored of our citizens were enrolled among the followers of the national banner." Just as the wave was reaching its crest, as Gibbs saw it, a bitterly resentful President insanely threw Hamilton and his followers down and made peace with France.[1]

It was not Adams' purpose simply to destroy Hamilton's power. He admittedly wished to be President for a second term, but President without being under obligation to a faction within his party that had shown itself to be antirepublican and militaristic when the French crisis had allowed it to reveal its true nature in 1798. The Hamiltonian interpretation may be attacked on several political grounds.

In the first place, the martial spirit that had been so strong in the spring and early summer of 1798 was seen to be rapidly dying by the beginning of 1799; and in the second place, the "bravest, ablest, and most honored" citizens who volunteered their services for defense were in the great majority of cases applicants for commissions, and troops had not been raised. There was ample evidence to show that France was willing to negotiate on an honorable basis when Adams made his nomination of Murray as envoy to Paris, and equally strong indications that the American people would welcome peace

[1] Gibbs, *Memoirs,* II, 184; Upham, *Pickering,* III, 438.

and gratefully support the man who called a halt to standing armies, direct taxes, and unnecessary spending. Adams prided himself on his knowledge of diplomacy and on his ability to sense the direction of public opinion. Public opinion unmistakably showed itself to be weary of Federalist war measures.

In January, 1799, a petition to the President was drawn up by the citizens of York County, Pennsylvania, a strongly Federalist section of that state, that is typical of many. "While we are warmly attached to the Union," the petitioners stated, "we cannot but express our concern at several acts passed in the two last Sessions of Congress: the law for erecting a standing army, the Sedition and Alien Laws, the Stamp Act, the Direct tax on land, and great increase in Revenue officers." [2]

In the South the debate over the Federalist program of 1798 had become so violent that Republicans and Federalists alike charged their opponents with plotting a civil war. While the North Carolina legislature expressed its willingness to support "all the constitutional measures of our federal government," there were doubts expressed about the constitutionality of much that the Federal government had done.[3] The Virginians were standing on the brink of a civil war of their own if words belied intentions. Madison's famed resolutions were the center of a stormy debate at Richmond during December. "The result of adopting the resolutions proposed," cried a Federalist speaker, "would be insurrection, confusion and anarchy." The Alien and Sedition Acts were defended as the bulwarks of law and order, bulwarks against what were described as "horrid scenes of desolution." [4]

With equal fervor William Giles, long-time opponent of Federalist measures and officers, branded the administration's

[2] *Aurora,* January 22, 1799.
[3] Adopted December 24, 1798, *Connecticut Gazette,* April 10, 1799.
[4] Anderson, *Giles,* 65.

defense measures but a pretense to cover the lust for power exhibited in a navy, a standing army, and the Alien and Sedition Acts.[5] Virginia would co-operate to preserve the Union and would oppose foreign intervention from any quarter, read the preamble to the Virginia Resolutions; and the Assembly went on record as resentful of attacks on United States shipping, and upon American citizens, but "Resolved, nevertheless, that our security from invasion and the force of our militia render a standing army unnecessary."[6]

Straight through the month of January the debate at Richmond continued. "So insatiable is a love of power that it has resorted to a distinction between the freedom and licentiousness of the press for the purpose of subverting the third amendment to the Constitution . . . ," declared the triumphant Republican majority in a resolve adopted on the twenty-third. Certain measures of the Federal government, they asserted, proved that a monarchical system destructive of the liberty of the states was aimed at. "In armies and navies, which will . . . enlist the tendency of man to pay homage to his fellow creature who can feed or honor him; and . . . employ the principle of fear, by punishing imaginary insurrections, under the pretense of preventative justice," proof was seen. A financial system favoring the wealthy, heavy patronage, and "a mode of construing the Constitution as will rapidly remove every restraint upon federal power" were all listed as causes for fear of the central authority.[7]

By the end of 1798 Virginians widely believed that Hamilton's army would be marched against them, but they passed their resolutions nonetheless. The scurrilous pamphleteer, James T. Callender, then under Jefferson's patronage, noted the appearance of the yellow fever at Philadelphia with the

[5] *Ibid.*, 66-67.
[6] Madison, *Writings* (Hunt ed.), VI, 332.
[7] *Ibid.*, VI, 332-340.

comment that it was "justly deserved by all the male adults," and might prove "a happy check to a much worse one; the Black Cockade Fever—I mean the fever, that under pretense of defending us from a *foreign* war, aims at provoking a *civil* one." [8]

As far back as June, James Monroe had taken up the question of meeting military violence with countermeasures in his correspondence with Jefferson. The talk of civil war was in the air, he wrote, but he could not see that the Republican party would gain by declaring itself ready to fight back if civil war was the object of the Federalists; [9] and Jefferson, according to his biographer, "believed that the 'crisis' of the Constitution had come—that statutes and decisions had in essential particulars subverted it—that armies were organizing to crush opposition and make that subversion complete." [10]

Instead of losing strength in the spring elections of 1798 the Republicans in Virginia appeared more firmly in power than ever before. Washington made his famous plea to Patrick Henry to sacrifice his comfort for a return to the political arena. Henry's avowed determination to lead a crusade against internal dissension, wrote Washington as he read the reports from the state house at Richmond, would be "a bulwark against such dangerous sentiments." [11] The four years of wooing seemed about to bear fruit. Henry was willing to enter the state legislature, but he was too feeble for the trip to Philadelphia as a member of Congress. "My Children would blush to know that you and their Father were Contemporarys, and that when you asked him to throw in his Mite for the public Happiness he refused." [12]

The Federalist cry that Republicans were charging others with what they themselves were plotting was strongly rein-

[8] Callender to Jefferson, October 26, 1798, *Jefferson Papers*, LC.
[9] Monroe to Jefferson, June 1798, *ibid.*
[10] Randall, *Jefferson*, II, 451.
[11] Washington, *Writings*, XXXVII, 87-90.
[12] February 12, 1799, *ibid.*, XXXVII, 90, Note 48.

forced when John Nicholas, formerly one of Jefferson's most loyal lieutenants in the House of Representatives and brother of Wilson Carey Nicholas, who carried the Kentucky Resolutions to Kentucky, dropped his Republican party loyalties and charged the Virginians with planning a civil war. In the midst of the debate on the Virginia Resolutions John Nicholas suddenly deserted his former associates and attacked the resolves as the prelude to a disunion movement; the legislators were buying arms and storing them in the Richmond state arsenal for use against the Federal government, he maintained.[13] Hamilton's assertions that civil war was in the offing could have received no more valuable support than this, coming from the quarter it did.

Many of the men who had been most instrumental in creating the Federal government seemed convinced that the great crisis of the Constitution had come. Fortunately, the growth of peace sentiment in Paris kept pace with the desperation of the Hamiltonians for a showdown. Despite denials of their authenticity the peace rumors from France were persistent and convincing. By the fall of 1798, less than eight months after the President had released the XYZ papers, there were definite indications of a sudden change in French policy. The question of peace has fallen squarely into the President's lap, wrote Monroe to Jefferson in November. The reports of French willingness to reopen negotiations were too well known to be branded as duplicity any longer. How stupid of the Administration not to see its way out of the present dilemma, he declared. Adams could go before the public completely vindicated by stating that the switch in French policy had been caused by his own firmness.[14]

John Marshall may well have suggested such a course to Adams when he arrived at Philadelphia in June. According to Chancellor Livingston, who had driven with the American

[13] Koch, *Jefferson and Madison*, 194.

[14] November 16, 1798, Monroe, *Writings* (Hamilton ed.), III, 149-152.

negotiator from New York, Marshall was set against hasty action, declaring that he had sensed no general war spirit against the United States in France. Although met outside the city by Pickering and a cavalry escort and subsequently lionized at fetes held in his honor, Marshall's moderate language had little effect upon congressional leaders. The war measures were just then in the process of being enacted.[15]

Some Federalists had no desire to take heed of the news from Europe that followed on the heels of the initial rebuff. Marshall was promptly forgotten and was not drawn into the army or into consultation on legislative matters, but General Pinckney won the distinction of being the Hamiltonian candidate in 1800 by identifying himself completely with the policy of defiance and militarism.

Elbridge Gerry's reports from Paris went unheeded and were scoffed at by Federalists. He had had private talks with Talleyrand that he had tried to conceal from General Pinckney, exclaimed McHenry. Pickering sent him a reprimand a few days after Marshall's return that would prevent his doing further mischief, confided the Secretary of War to General Washington.[16] Republicans naturally took up Gerry's patriotic and pacific mission as the only worthwhile activity being carried on by the administration. A week before Federalists presented the Sedition Act to the President for his signature, Edward Livingston rose in the House to introduce a resolution requesting Adams to authorize Gerry to negotiate a new treaty with Talleyrand. Senator Mason of Virginia was revolted at the reception given this wholesome suggestion. The resolution was "indecently scoffed at . . . called infamous, scandalous . . . and even treason," he told Jefferson.[17]

Rufus King at London watched Gerry's escapades with

[15] Jefferson to Madison, June 21, 1798, *Jefferson Papers*, LC.
[16] June 26, 1798, Washington, *Writings*, XXXVI, 298, Note 82.
[17] S. T. Mason to Jefferson, July 6, 1798, *Jefferson Papers*, LC.

astonishment. His refusal to leave France when the other envoys did and his replies to Talleyrand's notes "place him in a more degraded light than I ever believed it possible that he or any other American could be exhibited," wrote King to Hamilton.[18] In Boston the Federalist conclave was planning the most frigid reception for Mr. Gerry.[19]

Despite the contrast between his own reception and that which Marshall had received, Gerry was apparently undaunted. He went straight to Adams and presented his conviction that France wanted peace as soon as possible.[20] The President had found Gerry's refusal to leave Paris personally embarrassing and in August had admitted to George Cabot that the best that could be said was that Gerry could do little harm to the administration as long as the public was well aware of the administration's firmness toward France.[21] When Gerry met Adams at Quincy in October he must have been unusually convincing; the President did not shut himself off from his old-time friend nor appear to repudiate him any further than to remain silent on his activities. When he spoke on the subject of French relations in December it was to hint at the possibility of peace, and two months later Murray was nominated as special envoy.

When the Essex Junto found to their amazement that Adams was allowing Gerry to be his personal guest and to be closeted with him in long conversations, Otis was again delegated to call at Braintree to warn Adams of the obvious plot to ensnare him.[22]

Less than a week after Elbridge Gerry first drew up his carriage in front of the Adams homestead at Quincy, the President sent an astonishing request to Pickering. He asked him to present two questions to the cabinet for discussion;

[18] July 14, 1798, *Hamilton Papers*, LC.
[19] Higginson to Wolcott, September 11, 1798, Gibbs, *Memoirs*, II, 107.
[20] Adams, *Works*, I, 532-533, VIII, 677-680.
[21] Cabot to King, August 18, 1798, King, *Life and Correspondence*, II, 397.
[22] Morison, *Otis*, I, 153-154.

first, would it be expedient to call for a declaration of war in his address to Congress in December, and second, would it be wise to name a new envoy to France provided some definite assurance were given that he would be decently received. In connection with the last question he even went so far as to submit a list of names from whom the new envoy might be selected—Senator Richard Stockton of New Jersey, Senator James Ross of Pennsylvania, Supreme Court Justice Patterson, or William Vans Murray of Maryland, who was already at the Hague.[23]

Murray's letters, describing his conversations with French officials in Holland, had been sent on by Pickering and had arrived at Quincy within three or four days of Gerry's arrival. In his first letter, dated July 1, Murray declared that the Directory was highly concerned over the possibility of an Anglo-American naval agreement. A maritime alliance was more than they had bargained for.[24] Self-interest as the mainspring of political action made sense to Adams, and in returning Murray's dispatches to the State Department the President wrote, "The first has made a great impression on me." [25]

The reaction in high Federalist circles was one of consternation. Pickering refused to confine the discussion to the President's official advisors, and placed it before the army high command when Pinckney, Hamilton, and Washington arrived at Trenton (the temporary capital during the yellow fever epidemic) in early November. The draft decided upon and presented by Wolcott for the President's use in preparing his State of the Union message stated that the United States would negotiate only if France sent an envoy to assure the President of its sincere intentions first.

If the cabinet wording had been adopted it would have

[23] Adams to Pickering, October 20, 1798, Adams, *Works*, VIII, 609.
[24] *Ibid.*, I, 532-533.
[25] Adams to McHenry, October 29, 1798, VIII, 614-615.

meant that the French government must publicly acknowledge its error and submit to the humiliation of fulfilling American demands for the reopening of negotiations exactly as the United States requested before the machinery could even start moving. Unless faced by economic or military collapse, no government could be expected to submit to such a procedure. In his message of December 8 Adams stated that he would nominate a new minister when he had received definite assurances that that Minister would be received. The manner by which he might receive such assurances was not prescribed, and Pickering, blaming Gerry for the President's stand on the issue, ordered Cabot to watch every move that Elbridge Gerry made and to "have his derelictions minuted for future use." [26] All that Cabot could report, however, was that Gerry was loudly condemning the action of the French government and upholding the President's firm policy. He was seen to be particularly cordial with General Knox and the other disaffected Federalists who had looked upon Hamilton's elevation with misgivings.[27]

It was a hypocritical game in Cabot's eyes and one that would leave Gerry with powerful friends no matter what happened. He applauds the President and the wisdom of defense measures in front of the Federalists here, reported Cabot; but in the company of democrats Gerry insists that France desires peace and ought to be encouraged in its change of policy. In public he was heard to praise no one but Adams,[28] and his personal loyalty to the President was becoming the source of Pickering's worst display of intransigence since Colonel Smith's nomination as Adjutant General of the Army. Mr. Pickering and the President are deadlocked on the question of how to treat Gerry in public, wrote George Cabot to Rufus King in mid-November.

[26] Pickering to Cabot, October 20, 1798, Lodge, *Cabot,* 174.
[27] Cabot to Pickering, October 31, 1798, *ibid.,* 175-176.
[28] Cabot to Pickering, November 24, 1798, *ibid.,* 185.

"Gerry since his return has declared pretty explicitly his approbation of our National Measures and his desire to see them persisted in and supported." Adams was thought to look upon his old friend as a firm patriot, one who had erred a bit, perhaps, but Pickering wanted nothing to do with him or his reports from Talleyrand.[29]

Federalist fears that Gerry would line up solidly with Jefferson were confounded. Not only would he not criticize the administration's handling of the French crisis, he four times rejected overtures from the Massachusetts Republicans to be their candidate for Governor and "refused to attend their caucuses as below the proper dignity of a gentleman."[30] Nonetheless, William Duane of the *Aurora* managed to acquire a copy of his notes on the July conversations with the French foreign minister and printed them on the front page of his antiadministration newspaper in November.[31]

Adams' speech at the opening of the short session of Congress in December stirred new hopes among the Republicans. "By the enclosed speech you will sense that the tone of the president is much changed, and that we may still hope for peace," wrote Representative Dawson to Madison. "What has produced this, or how far he is sincere we cannot yet determine." To Jefferson, commenting on the speech almost a month later, it smelled of Hamiltonian deviousness. "The President's speech, so unlike himself in point of moderation, is supposed to have been written by the military conclave, and particularly Hamilton." He noted, however, that Adams' promise to release Gerry's entire correspondence had not been fulfilled. The assumption was that it would show France to be conciliatory. "Therefore it is supposed

[29] November 16, 1798, King, *Life and Correspondence*, II, 468-469.

[30] S. E. Morison, "Elbridge Gerry, Gentleman-Democrat," *New England Quarterly*, II, January 1929, 29. Morison's article is the most scholarly piece of work yet done on Gerry. See also Lyon, "The Directory and the United States," *American Historical Review*, XLIII, 1938, 524 ff.

[31] November 1, 1798. It seems possible that Adams acquiesced, considering their intimacy.

that they will get their war measures well taken before they will produce this damper. . . . In the meantime the raising of the army is to go on. . . ." [32]

Madison was as mistaken as Jefferson in supposing that Adams and the so-called "military conclave," Hamilton, C. C. Pinckney, Pickering, Wolcott, and McHenry were in concert over the policy announced by the President's address of December 8. Adams had changed the vital wording on the question of recognizing French advances, and the promise to publish Gerry's correspondence was made over the most violent protests on Pickering's part. The House in answer approved the peaceful attitude adopted by France, but the Senate maintained its hostile and threatening attitude. If after all that our government has done to assure France of its sincerity she still refuses to arbitrate, said the Senate reply, such action "ought to be regarded as designed to separate the people from their government and to bring about by intrigue that which open force could not effect." [33]

What the House had to say added up to an obvious attempt to sound reasonable and fair to the public, commented Madison, but in the Senate's remarks he saw "the genius of that subtle partizan of England who has contributed so much to the public misfortunes. It is not difficult to see how Adams could be made a puppet through the instrumentality of the creatures around him, nor how the Senate could be managed by similar artifaces." The upper house was going to goad France into a war that it did not want to declare, thought Madison.[34]

Despite what was taking shape in his mind, the talks with Gerry, the news of Dr. Logan's solitary mission, and the late communiques from William Vans Murray, the President seemed as far from a determined peace policy when he for-

[32] Dawson to Madison, December 9, 1798, *Madison Papers,* LC; Jefferson to Madison, January 3, 1799, *Writings* (Ford ed.), IX, 3.

[33] Gibbs, *Memoirs,* II, 174-175.

[34] Madison to Jefferson, December 29, 1798, *Madison Papers,* LC.

mally accepted the Senate's reply to his address as he had before the speech had been given. "I have seen no real evidence of any change of system or disposition in the French Republic towards the United States." He asked the Senate to consider whether some means ought not to be taken for preventing the intrusion of unauthorized persons into the foreign affairs of the nation, a public repudiation of George Logan's well-intentioned peace expedition.[35]

Just what kind of a game Adams was playing it is almost impossible to ascertain. Perhaps he was building the war faction up for a bigger letdown, or perhaps he was drawing an extremely fine line between "real evidence" and satisfactory evidence, for by his own admission the decision for peace that he announced by nominating a new envoy to France on February 18 was based upon information that he had already received and studied; Gerry's report, which he declared had thrown Pickering into a rage, and Logan's testimony that what Gerry had to relate was absolutely reliable.[36]

Unlike Washington, who received Dr. Logan in November with more than his usual degree of coolness, Adams considered Logan sincere and, like Gerry, misguided rather than treacherous.[37] Logan's letter to his wife, written just before his departure for America, had been given front-page billing in the *Aurora*, which called it "a cruel blow to ambitious hopes, to the candidates for contracts, commissions, and commissaryships."

What Logan had written reinforced what both Murray and Gerry had mentioned as most influential upon the French government; American commerce and naval operations, if turned against France, would be intolerable when

[35] Gibbs, *Memoirs*, II, 175; Adams, *Works*, IX, 134.

[36] Adams to William Cunningham, March 20, 1809, *Adams-Cunningham Correspondence*, 105-106.

[37] Washington's notes of an interview with Logan on the night of November 13, 1798, Washington, *Writings*, XXXVII, 18-20.

added to the weight of Britain's naval superiority. "All American ships in the harbours of France have been released," wrote Logan in September. "All American prisoners have been set at liberty; and the most positive assurances have been made that France is ready to enter on a treaty for the amicable accommodation of all matters in dispute." [38]

What Adams knew when he made his dramatic nomination of a new French peace mission was that the Commanding General had given him his tacit approval before the step was taken. Had the military clique known that Washington had forwarded to Adams a letter from the notorious Joel Barlow with the notation that he (Washington) believed the letter written with the approval of the Directory and that the American people were "very desirous of peace," there would have been less uproar and invective thrown at the President. Washington had sent the letter in confidence, however.[39] Knowing that Washington would not add his immense weight to the disapproval that was certain to arise from party leaders, Adams had little to fear so long as the public approved, and that public opinion would stand with him and against the Hamiltonians Adams was convinced.

"I have long been anxious to know the real complexion of Gerry's report," wrote Madison to Jefferson a week before Adams released the information. "Several symptoms concur with your information that it does not favor the position which our Government wishes to take. . . . If truth shall be found to have been suppressed in order to trick the public into a war or an army, it will be one of the most daring experiments that has been made on the apathy of the people." [40]

Jefferson and Madison did not see, until the gauntlet was thrown down by the President, that administration policy

[38] *Aurora*, November 10, 1798.
[39] Adams to William Cunningham, March 20, 1809, *op. cit.*
[40] January 25, 1799, *Madison Papers*, LC.

was not moving toward war and that the Federalist party was deeply rent by disunion from within. On February 2 Adams released the Gerry notes of his conversations with Talleyrand and other prominent French leaders, and two weeks later Murray was unceremoniously nominated special envoy to Paris. Pickering in a towering rage wished to make it clear that he had had no part in shaping the President's decision. He expressed his disgust to Washington that Adams looked upon Talleyrand's sincerity as genuine, and the Secretary of State could not understand how Adams could send the communications to Congress without censuring Gerry. He felt called upon, he wrote, to keep the record straight by sending him his own report on the correspondence as it was originally worded before Adams had taken the liberty of changing it.[41]

The "real evidence" that Adams was waiting for came in the form of a letter from Talleyrand to the French chargé at the Hague, M. Pichon, which Murray had forwarded and which had arrived late in January.[42] There was a second convincing source that the President could not doubt but concerning which he could not make public mention. In the fall his son, John Quincy, had reported from Europe that the official French attitude had undergone a decided change in favor of peace. The Directory had been amazed at the American response to the XYZ affair and had paused in their determination to attack our shipping over the arming of our merchant vessels, wrote the President's son. Throughout the fall and winter his letters to his father expressed the same note. French policy would tend to follow American policy; firmness would be met by conciliation. Not until April did he express his conviction that the administration's tough policy had won a complete victory. "French policy with regard to neutral navigation in general, and to the

[41] February 2, 1799, Washington, *Writings*, XXXVII, 126, Note 90.
[42] Adams to Cunningham, *op. cit.*

United States in particular, has undergone an essential change." To Rufus King he wrote that Talleyrand was entirely sincere and saw French interests as demanding reconciliation with America.[43]

King, who was in close touch with diplomatic events on the continent, was as convinced as John Quincy Adams that France had been outmaneuvered, and he repeatedly warned the Hamiltonians that they must alter their policies. Their cry of treason was meant for public consumption—the President's decision for peace should have been no surprise to them if they had bothered to read King's letters.

In September he had written Hamilton that a change in the Directory's American policy might be anticipated. Logan's advances were accepted and his expressions believed, he noted, and most indicative was the fact that their embargo against neutral shipping had been raised.[44] A week later he again wrote Hamilton that on good authority he knew that France would talk conciliation, receive an American envoy, and probably break with the United States again after the election of 1800. Assuming that Adams would accept French advances, he declared, "You will have no war. France will propose to renew the negotiations laid down in the President's instructions to the Envoys (Marshall, Pinckney, and Gerry)." [45]

Likewise, at the beginning of October Murray had written his friend McHenry that war was not in the offing. "Be firm and persevering, my dear minister, and France will recoil, we shall triumph and once more establish the law of nations." [46] More than a week before Murray's nomination was made Robert Harper, in a letter to his constituents, accepted the idea that peace would result from the advances

[43] September 25, 1798, to Rufus King, April 15, 1799, J. Q. Adams, *Writings*, II, 367, 372, 402, 410.
[44] September 17, 1798, *Hamilton Papers*, LC.
[45] September 23, 1798, *ibid.*, II, 424; *Hamilton Papers*, LC.
[46] Harper to Constituents, February 10, 1799, *Bayard Papers*, 78.

being made to Murray through French diplomatic agents in Holland. "It is the President's intention to meet this advance, and to omit no opportunity that may offer of settling the dispute on safe and honorable terms; but Congress . . . has resolved not to be the dupe of her artifaces . . . nor to relax . . . from its measures of defense till justice is done for the past."[47]

An old friend of Harrison Otis at Paris wrote in August that Gerry's talks with Talleyrand were to be relied upon and that Logan's testimony had helped greatly in making the situation in the United States clear to the Directory. French policy would become conciliatory because the extent of damage done to American shipping in the West Indies had not been realized, because of the strong reaction against France in the United States, and because of the representations of Gerry, Logan, DuPont, and Volney (each one of whom had Jefferson's blessing, and in the case of all but Volney, letters of credence from Jefferson).[48] It seems inconceivable that this information could have been kept from other Federalists in Otis' immediate circle.

By the time Adams made his decision for reinstituting a settlement the leaders of the Federalist party were well aware that the step was possible, and if the President were to live up to his public promise, impossible to avoid. Their cry of betrayal came as the result of an expectation that Adams would delay until the election of 1800 had passed. How they expected to win that election except by repression or by renewing the crisis through some act on their own part it seems impossible to fathom. The news that France had changed its policy and was willing to negotiate was not their private possession. It was perfectly apparent to the public that the talk of war was a hoax, and behind the President's dramatic decision was the certain knowledge that public

[47] October 2, 1798, Steiner, *McHenry*, 344.

[48] Richard Codman to Otis, August 26, 1798, Morison, *Otis*, I, 168-169.

opinion would condemn the President and the party that continued to build and spend for war when war was no longer probable. John Adams acted as an honest public servant and as a wiser politician than any of the leaders of the Hamiltonian faction.

The Philadelphia *Aurora* refused to be silenced by the Sedition Act and its pages published every item of news from France that might bring public opinion over to the side of peace. "The President promised three weeks ago a communication respecting our affairs with France," commented the Republican editor on January 3. "Why is it kept back so long? Is he afraid of inflaming the nation against the French Republic? Or does he apprehend that the correspondence . . . would give the lie to many of the federalist echoes?" The query was repeated on the fifth, sixth, seventh, and eighth of the month. When the Talleyrand-Gerry letters were released to Congress on January 18, Duane printed them in full a few days later.

Other notices from Paris were brought to public attention, letters from Americans in Europe being printed from January 24 through January 28. "The war hawks are down in the mouth most completely by Mr. Gerry's communication . . ." which "have occasioned a considerable reaction of public opinion," wrote a Boston correspondent to a Federalist congressman. "If you will not declare war, wind up public sentiment by some strong measures or vivid speeches."[49] The letter may have been fictitious, but it served Duane's purposes well enough.

On the last day of January the *Aurora* carried the news that a bill declaring war had been drawn up and was being held in readiness in case the situation demanded it, and to further discredit the righteousness of the Federalist cause Duane had but to produce the figures comparing shipping losses at the hands of French and British war vessels. On

[49] *Aurora*, January 28, 1799.

February 1 the *Aurora* printed the Insurance Company of North America's figures for the last six months of 1798; American damages at the hands of British vessels equaled $280,000 and at the hands of French privateers only $260,000.

Even Pickering was chagrined at the poor showing of the nation's erstwhile ally. "The injuries we sustained by such captures and partial condemnation [by the British cruisers in the West Indies] are very considerable," he wrote to Rufus King. He acknowledged that the *Aurora's* figures were reliable and hoped that King might be able to make an effective appeal to the British government.[50] George Cabot, also writing King a few days before President Adams nominated Murray, admitted that British attacks were a source of angry puzzlement. The spirit of the nation falls off "visibly," he admitted.[51]

Less than one week before Adams acted to end the stalemate with France, news reached Philadelphia that French officials in the West Indies had been ordered to release all American vessels. An hour after the word spread through the halls of Congress the Senate passed a bill authorizing retaliation on French naval attacks. Only two dissenting votes were recorded by the clerk, wrote Jefferson scornfully.[52]

In addition to the pressure of the evidence evincing a desire for peace on France's part, and in addition to the fact that it was becoming increasingly difficult to differentiate between the potential enemy and the supposed ally, the administration was being pushed into a corner by the sizable business group that had profited by trade with France and particularly with the French West Indies. While many might hope to profit from a war with France, wrote George Cabot to Pickering, there are others who desire free intercourse with the French colonial possessions. This had become espe-

[50] February 5, 1799, King, *Life and Correspondence*, II, 535

[51] February 7, 1799, *ibid.*, 536.

[52] Jefferson to T. M. Randolph, February 12, 1799, *Jefferson Papers*, LC.

cially true in the last months of 1798 as shortages in the Indies sent the price of provisions rocketing upward. The millers and merchants of "the great flour cities" were among the most persistent advocates of peace, noted the Massachusetts Federalist.[53]

Adams might easily have rested his case for an immediate peace settlement upon the grounds of diplomatic satisfaction and economic expediency, but the political pressure upon the Chief Executive to end the quasi war with France was such that he could not afford to overlook it much longer than he did with any hope of seeing himself re-elected in 1800. His actions in 1799 promised political benefits both for himself and for the nation, because the passage of the Virginia Resolutions heralded a civil war in Federalist opinion, and the dominant faction within the party was prepared and willing to crush Southern opposition with armed might. Historians have long noted that Adams split his party wide open by his sudden peace move, but they have failed entirely to realize that it was politically intelligent, nevertheless. If New York is excepted, the figures show that John Adams received a greater electoral vote in 1800 than he did in 1796. He appears to have been a more popular man in 1800 than in 1796, and the reason for it is obvious, as was his bitter disappointment at Jefferson's victory; the rank and file of the Federalist party as well as the voters at large thought more highly of his successful peace decision than have the historians. It saved the nation from Hamiltonian militarism and prevented the outbreak of civil war.

[53] February 21, 1799, Lodge, *Cabot*, 220.

16

Politics and Peace, 1799

BY THE END OF 1798 THE SOUTHERN REPUBLICANS HAD BEcome convinced that nothing stood in the way of a peaceful settlement with France except the desire to maintain political supremacy on the part of their opponents. They looked upon the army and the Sedition Act as the engines of their own destruction, and, convinced at last that both would be turned against them, they began to arm in self-defense.

William Branch Giles, who had been an active participant in the Virginia debates of 1798, explained the attitude that his party took toward the Federalist war program in a speech that he delivered while Governor of Virginia in 1827. "Her representatives on the floor were threatened with arms—with incarceration. . . . They went earnestly and systematically to work. The first measure they then adopted was to pass a law to protect them in freedom of debate. . . . They then determined to arm the militia, to make provision to purchase 5000 stands of arms. . . . To defray the expenses of these measures, they raised the whole taxes of the state twenty-five per cent. . . . These were measures truly worthy of Virginia." [1]

Despite the fact that his own state had authorized Governor Jay to borrow $200,000 from the Bank of New York for the purchase of arms and the construction of harbor de-

[1] Anderson, *Giles*, 70. Acts of the Virginia Assembly of December 28, 1798, guaranteeing the rights of habeus corpus, and of January 23, 1799, the Armory Law. See also Gaillard Hunt, *James Madison*, 262.

fenses in the summer of 1798, Hamilton greeted the news of Virginia's military preparations as evidence of a civil war plot. Commenting on the passage of the Virginia Resolutions and the defense measures adopted in a letter to Jonathan Dayton, he said, "It is stated . . . that the opposition party in Virginia, the headquarters of the faction, have followed up the hostile declarations which are to be found in the resolutions of their General Assembly by an actual preparation of the means of supporting them by force—that they have taken measures to put the militia on a more efficient footing, are preparing considerable arsenals and magazines, and (what is an unequivocal proof how much they are in earnest) have gone so far as to lay new taxes on their citizens." Hamilton went on to outline his plans for the future security of the nation: to build Federal roads and canals through the South, to strengthen the powers of the Federal courts over the states, to use the Sedition Act with vigor, and to divide the larger states. "The subdivision of the great states is indispensable to the security of the General Government and with it, the Union." [2]

The Hamiltonian program was placed in the hands of the new Speaker of the House as well as the old Speaker. Theodore Sedgwick received advice for immediate action that paralleled in tendency the master blueprint that Dayton got. He advocated a legislative program for the sixth congress that would combat what he insisted was the rising tide of rebellion. First, Hamilton asked that a special committee of Congress consider the Virginia Resolutions and display "with calm dignity united with pathos the full evidence which they afford of a regular conspiracy to overturn the government." Second, Hamilton wanted both the Alien acts and the Sedition Act strengthened, and thirdly, he asked

[2] Hamilton to Dayton, January 1799, *Hamilton Papers*, LC and Hamilton, *Works* (Lodge ed.), X, 329-336. Jay to King, September 30, 1798, ordering the purchase of 3,000 muskets in Europe, King, *Life and Correspondence*, II, 475.

that a pamphlet be written containing a report of the southern conspiracy and the resultant need for stronger legislation against sedition that "should find its way into every house in Virginia." These provisions would publicize and dramatize the issue. The heart of his program was contained in the last and fourth recommendation.

Provisions for speeding up the recruiting service were vitally needed, said Hamilton. The militia of loyal states could not be counted on to restrain "a refractory and powerful state. . . . When a clever [?] force has been collected, let them be drawn toward Virginia, for which there is an obvious pretext [that of strengthening border defenses in the Mississippi Valley], then let measures be taken to act upon the laws and put Virginia to the test of resistance." [3]

Hamilton's letters, written at the moment when it was becoming perfectly clear that a settlement with France was finally possible, proves that the Federal army was intended primarily for domestic purposes and that Hamilton was even willing to foment a large-scale rebellion in the South. Albert Gallatin noted that the Federalist leaders were almost at the point of making their plans public. "They avow a design of keeping up a standing army for domestic purposes, for since the French fleet is destroyed [the Battle of the Nile occurred August 1, 1798] they cannot even affect to believe that there is any danger of French invasion. General Washington, Hamilton, and Pinckney are in town. In their presence and at the table of Governor Mifflin, Hamilton declared that a standing army was necessary, that the aspect of Virginia was threatening, and that . . . the ferment in the Western counties of Pennsylvania was greater than previous to the insurrection of 1794." [4]

Justice Iredell, a Southerner and a man of moderate views,

[3] Hamilton to Theodore Sedgwick, February 2, 1799, *Hamilton Papers*, LC, *Works* (Lodge ed.), X, 340-342.

[4] Gallatin to his wife, Henry Adams, *Gallatin*, 223.

looked upon the Federal government's preparations as fully justified. "The General Assembly of Virginia are pursuing steps which lead directly to civil war . . .," he wrote after a visit to Richmond in January,[5] and a friend of Attorney General Charles Lee enclosed a Republican pamphlet that attempted to justify the Virginia Resolutions as proof that the Republicans were preparing for rebellion.[6] Hamilton's friend William Heth of Richmond wrote that he expected to be among the first to be seized if civil war broke out. An act that would allow state courts to intervene for the protection of persons arrested for sedition under the Federal act had recently been proposed in the Virginia legislature, and the transfer of funds originally intended for the building of a state penitentiary to arms purchases added up to rebellion in his estimation.[7]

While the rumors and armaments continued to mount, John Nicholas' letter announcing his defection from the Republican party was being circulated in the state's newspapers. In the letter Nicholas expressed his conviction that the party's leaders intended to start a rebellion.[8] No less a figure than Governor Davie of North Carolina was convinced that Virginia would secede or fight. The plan was to secede with Pennsylvania with the expectation that North Carolina, Kentucky, South Carolina, and Georgia would soon follow, he asserted.[9] Although authorities on Virginia history during this period have proved that the Virginia high command had no intention of beginning an armed rebellion,[10] the impor-

[5] James Iredell to his wife, January 24, 1799, Iredell, *Life and Correspondence*, II, 543.

[6] B. Reeder to Charles Lee, March 22, 1799, *Hamilton Papers*, LC.

[7] Heth to Hamilton, January 18, 1799, *ibid.*

[8] Richmond *Argus*, March 29, 31, 1799. A. Koch and H. Ammon, "The Virginia and Kentucky Resolutions," *William and Mary Quarterly*, 3d Ser., V, No. 2, 163.

[9] Davie to Iredell, Iredell, *op. cit.*, 577 (June 17, 1799.)

[10] A. Koch and H. Ammon, "The Virginia and Kentucky Resolutions," *op. cit.*, P. G. Davidson, "Virginia and the Alien and Sedition Laws," *American Historical Review*, XXXVI, 1931, 336-342.

tant point was that the charges that Hamilton and his friends were making were believed. Men would act upon them, just as the Republicans, believing that the administration had intended to suppress them from the beginning of the French crisis, took steps to be prepared for Federal action. When the rebellion that Hamilton had been anticipating did break out it was far from Richmond and far from civil war proportions.

In March a group of angry Pennsylvania Germans led by a minor militia officer named Fries organized themselves into a rescue party in order to reclaim some of their more spirited brethren, who had defied the much-hated tax collectors. Federal marshals were prevented from imprisoning the men, many windows were broken in protest against the so-called "Window Tax," and General William McPherson's Pennsylvania "Blues" were rushed to the scene.[11] The affair proved disappointingly easy to break up for those who had seen in the Pennsylvania squabble the beginnings of the expected Republican revolt. Hamilton mistakingly anticipated the need for Federal intervention and warned McHenry against "magnifying a riot into an insurrection, by employing in the first instance inadequate force." "Wherever the Government appears in arms," he cautioned, "it ought to appear like a Hercules, and inspire respect by the display of strength." [12]

The years 1799 and 1800 passed without civil war, because Adams was able to put an end to the threat of militarism in the Federalist ranks and because Jefferson and Madison carefully warned their followers against taking an openly defiant attitude that might invite intervention.[13] Certainly there was pressure enough upon the President to act quickly and decisively in meeting the threat of civil war and for bypassing the niceties of diplomatic protocol. If the election of 1800

[11] McPherson to Hamilton, March 25, 1799, *Hamilton Papers*, LC.

[12] Hamilton to McHenry, March 18, 1799, *ibid.*

[13] *Supra*, Chapter XIV, Jefferson to Madison, August 23, 1799, *Jefferson Papers*, LC; Koch and Ammon, *op. cit.*, 165–166.

was to be free of military influence, and if Jefferson was to be prevented from running away with it, it was clearly necessary that the Federalist legislative program of 1798 be wiped away; by the end of the year Adams could see that his party's mistakes were turning Jefferson into a martyr and the Republican party into the party of common-sense politics.

Adams seems never to have viewed the Alien and Sedition Acts as violent or even unnecessary legislation, but undeniably they had proved a political headache. Adams' approval of John Marshall, who came out openly against the laws, shows that he had come to see the folly of passing them and his own mistake in signing them. The greatest of Federalist sins, however, was the standing army and the expensive war program that they had undertaken. Few historians have agreed with John Bach McMaster, whose study of newspaper sources led him to the conclusion that the Alien and Sedition Acts have been overemphasized as causes for the collapse of the Federalist party.[14] The attention given to the army and taxation as political issues by Republican politicians confirms his conclusion fully.

It seemed to Jefferson that the Federalist expense account as it emerged in June 1798 was aimed at crushing the agrarian economy of the South. "Of the two millions of Dollars now to be raised by a tax on lands, houses, and slaves, Virginia is to furnish between three and 400,000," he noted to his friend Archibald Stuart. This was but the beginning and but half of what it would cost to raise the provisional army, which in turn was but one tenth of the annual military budget.[15] By the end of the year the Federalists were aiming at a standing army of thirty thousand, which would cost more than twice that figure during the year 1799, and plans were under way to finance the upkeep of a separate volun-

[14] McMaster, *History*, II, 417.

[15] June 8, 1798, Jefferson, *Writings* (Ford ed.), VIII, 438.

teer force of about ten thousand men. Jefferson, in stating the figures to Madison, added that Pickering had called the state militias worthless unless regular troops were to be stationed throughout the states and was speaking of the fifty-thousand-man force as the ultimate objective.[16]

The Federal budget for the period from 1796 to 1800 reflects the burdensome cost of maintaining a heavy military establishment by an agrarian nation of four million people. In 1796 Congress approved a total budget of $5.8 millions and increased the figure by only $200,000 in 1797. For the year 1798, however, the cost of maintaining the Federal government had risen to nearly $8 millions.[17] The cost of government had nearly doubled during the Adams administration. Jefferson reported to Madison that the cost of the proposed military and naval establishment for 1799 was $11.5 millions alone, and urged his friend to make use of this fact by publishing his notes from the Constitutional Convention relative to taxation and armed forces.[18]

President Adams viewed the mounting expense of government with alarm, and in his letters to the Boston *Patriot* of 1809 commented that the fifty thousand troops that Hamilton demanded "would have raised a rebellion in every state in the Union. The very idea of the expense of it would have turned President, Senate, and House out of doors." [19] His unwillingness to issue recruiting orders stemmed from a knowledge that the army had cost the administration much of the popularity that the XYZ dispatches had given it. Speaker Sedgwick was delegated by the Hamiltonians to urge the Chief Executive into action but found him unmovable. Adams told him that if Congress demanded an army he would give it to them, but he declared, "It was

[16] February 5, 1799, *Jefferson Papers*, LC.

[17] C. A. Beard, *Economic Origins*, 355.

[18] January 16, 1799, *Jefferson Papers*, LC.

[19] Adams, *Works*, IX, 290-291. Adams disclaimed any connection with the Sedition Act, though he admitted the need for it.

making the government more unpopular than all these other acts."

The people had been patient over taxes "liberally laid on," said Adams, but "their patience will not last always." He was well aware that he had been left with almost no authority in military affairs. Sedgwick, reporting the conversation to Hamilton, believed that Adams had McHenry in mind when he spoke of being left in the dark and suggested that bringing a new man of real talents—"talents of that peculiar kind which gives an ascendency without its being perceived"—into the cabinet might help matters. Carrington, whom Hamilton had apparently mentioned previously, was not the man, Sedgwick thought.[20]

Adams was particularly fearful of the consequences of Federalist militarism, because New England more than any other section was reacting most violently against it. Jefferson noted that whereas the Alien and Sedition Acts were working in the Southern states "as powerful sedatives of the XYZ inflammation," the Eastern states were comparatively unmoved by them.[21] A Connecticut newspaper editor, jailed for sedition in Litchfield County and who was therefore sensitive to the free speech issue, testified to Jefferson that the Republican attack against government spending was proving the most effective campaign appeal in his state. "My acquaintances all agree that the rancor of party against those so called republicans has cooled since the eight per cent premium for the loan," he wrote. A list of Connecticut assemblymen with political sympathies noted was enclosed. The incarcerated Mr. Ogden was diligently directing the distribution of Gallatin's pamphlet on foreign intercourse from his cell.[22]

Professor Morse's study of Federalism in New England led him to conclude that heavy war taxes were the greatest

[20] February 7, 1799, *Hamilton Papers*, LC.
[21] Jefferson to Gerry, January 26, 1799, *Jefferson Papers*, LC.
[22] J. C. Ogden to Jefferson, February 7, 1799, *ibid.*

cause of the party's fall from favor in Massachusetts, far greater than the Alien and Sedition Acts.[23] Both Jefferson and Madison had anticipated such consequences when the Fifth Congress had first swung into action on military measures in the spring of 1798, and in January 1799 James T. Callender's biting attack on Federal extravagance and corruption, "Sedgwick and Company, or A Key to the Six Per Cent Cabinet," produced under Jefferson's patronage, first appeared.[24]

One of the Essex Junto confirmed Jefferson's predictions relative to the effect of the tax collector almost exactly when he wrote Rufus King, "In the New England States the alien and sedition acts make less noise than the land tax. Its novelty and immediate application to the purse-strings excite soft but general murmurs." [25] The same was true in New York where Aaron Burr was directing the Republican counterattack from his seat in the state legislature. He was unwilling to push the Virginia and Kentucky Resolutions to a vote, he wrote Jefferson, because they were certain to fail of approval in both houses. His recommendation was to sit tight and let the Federalists dig their own graves without any outside help. Even the most extreme Federalists were beginning to question the necessity for a huge army, navy, and tax program.[26] The Stamp Act of 1798 was the most generally hated enactment of the Fifth Congress in New York because of its odious name, according to a prominent state historian.[27]

Fisher Ames' brother, an ardent Massachusetts democrat, recorded in his diary the effect of arms and taxes upon Massachusetts sentiment. "House and land tax of Congress goes on heavily, causing great uneasiness. Some refuse and then to

[23] A. D. Morse, *Federalist Party in New England*, 176.
[24] *Jefferson Papers*, LC.
[25] Joseph Hale to King, January 15, 1799, King, *Life and Correspondence*, II, 508.
[26] Burr to Jefferson, Albany, February 3, 1799, *Jefferson Papers*, LC.
[27] Hammond, *Political Parties In New York*, I, 119.

avoid the penalty have to conform. . . . Silent indignation hath not yet exploded—tho' hard threatened. I fear civil war must be the result of Government measures." [28] Massachusetts Republicans were seen to be gaining strength rapidly in the spring elections of 1799 and had "availed themselves greatly of those momentary discontents which follow the promulgation of a new tax," according to George Cabot, who sent the word on to Wolcott at Philadelphia.[29] Jefferson himself attributed the political gains of late 1798 in Pennsylvania, Massachusetts, and Vermont primarily to the tax collector.[30]

The diary of a contemporary Pennsylvania Federalist paid tribute to the dire effects of taxation upon the Federalist party in the pivotal Keystone state. "A Provisional army was voted, volunteer corps invited, ships of war equipped, and as a part of the system of defense the alien and sedition acts were enacted. But the most volcanic ground of all was yet to be trodden. . . . It has been well said, that a disorderly people will suffer a robbery with more patience than an impost. . . . The simple, well-meaning Federalists . . . therefore, with no small degree of self-complacency . . . passed a law for a direct tax. . . . This tax on real property was the fatal blow to federalism in Pennsylvania." [31]

The political picture in Pennsylvania changed rapidly during the year 1798. With the publication of the XYZ dispatches Pennsylvania Republican ranks were split between the advocates of a bipartisan policy and those who wished to remain in open opposition. Jefferson's admission that all was not well in Pennsylvania, however, was coupled with the prophecy that what he termed "This disease of the im-

[28] Warren, *Jacobins and Junto*, 123.

[29] Cabot to Wolcott, May 2, 1799, Gibbs, *Memoirs*, II, 239.

[30] Jefferson to Monroe, January 3, 1799; to Madison, January 3, 1799, *Jefferson Papers*, LC.

[31] Alexander Graydon, *Memoirs of a Life Chiefly Passed in Pennsylvania*, Harrisburg, 1811, 407-409.

agination" would soon pass. "Indeed," he wrote to his friend John Taylor, "the doctor is now on his way to cure it, in the guise of a tax gatherer." [32]

In less than six weeks he could report to Madison that in both Massachusetts and Pennsylvania the tide had begun to change.[33] It changed so radically that the fall of 1799 the Republican state ticket headed by Judge Thomas McKean swept the state solidly into the Republican fold for the first time. Taylor's retort that the tax-gathering doctor could do just as he pleased so long as he had an army to protect him proved wrong.[34]

The platform upon which Judge McKean had defeated Senator James Ross in the gubernatorial contest was one of opposition to every defense measure that the Federalists had taken: the excise, the land tax, the standing army, and the Alien and Sedition Acts.[35] Local issues played very little part in the contest; the army and increased Federal taxation seemed to be the paramount issues. At Philadelphia Republicans established a temporary journal called "Cannibal's Progress," to record offenses against civilians committed by Federal troops stationed throughout the state.[36] In April a Lancaster newspaper editor who ventured to criticize the insolent behavior of a group of cavalry troops stationed nearby was seized in his office, dragged into the street, and prepared for a public whipping before officers intervened to prevent it.[37] A month later the most notorious of the Republican editors, William Duane of the *Aurora*, was beaten by another group of young cavalry soldiers for his constant flow of sarcasm directed toward the army.[38] Such incidents,

32 November 26, 1798, *Jefferson Papers*, LC.
33 January 3, 1799, Jefferson, *Writings* (Ford ed.), IX, 3.
34 Taylor to Jefferson, February 15, 1799, *Jefferson Papers*, LC.
35 Newlin, *Brackenridge*, 223.
36 Gibbs, *Memoirs*, II, 166.
37 *Aurora*, April 14, 27, 1799.
38 *Ibid.*, May 16, 1799.

together with the Fries Rebellion, showed Pennsylvania to be deeply roused against government measures.

A Washington County address to Albert Gallatin printed by the *Aurora* in the fall of 1798 listed as causes for general alarm four Federal measures: the Stamp Act because it "alienated the affections of the people from the government," the Salt Tax because it hit the poor severely, the Alien Act unconstitutional and unjust, and the Sedition Act "impolitic, unjust, and unconstitutional." [39] Duane found Americans worse off than the French before the Revolution because they were saddled with both a land tax and a salt tax, and on February 4 he came out openly for the abolition of both the army and the taxes since there was no longer a need for them.

Instead of heeding such warnings the Federalists went on to pass the most notorious money bill of all. "Our government is opening a new loan at 8 percent which does not seem to be relished," wrote Hamilton's friend Troup to Rufus King in January. "It is universally thought that the money will be subscribed in less than half an hour." [40]

Such were the issues as presented by the Republicans in the winter of 1798–99. On the one hand, standing armies, heavy taxes, threat to liberty, and on the other the abolition of all of them and a return to the principles of the Revolution. In Massachusetts, Vermont, Connecticut, New Jersey, Pennsylvania, Maryland, Virginia, and North Carolina there were signs of a turn away from the ardent nationalism of the XYZ explosion. Matthew Lyon was returned to Congress from Vermont, Sedgwick's plan to alter election districts in Massachusetts for the benefit of his party failed, North Carolina Federalists recaptured the governorship by an extremely narrow margin, and Washington found the situation so desperate for the government as to forsake his retirement from

[39] *Ibid.*, November 10, 1798.

[40] January 23, 1799, King, *Life and Correspondence*, II, 523.

politics and urged John Marshall, Patrick Henry, and Henry Lee to re-enter the public arena.[41]

The Federalist war program, based upon a momentary outburst of public indignation against France, had recoiled, threatening to leave them stranded in the wake of a Republican upsurge.

The key to the situation was the army, and from Adams' point of view it made far more sense to destroy it himself than to sit back while the Republicans took full credit for doing so after 1800. Two days after the President took the step that sealed the fate of Federalist militarism, the nomination of William Murray, the *Aurora* spoke of the move as the deathblow to the army and devoted a full page and a half to Josiah Quincy's 1774 address on the evils of standing armies.[42] Among the scores of resolutions and addresses sent to Congress by alarmed voters throughout the Union in the winter of 1798–99 the army was inevitably listed with the Sedition Act and heavy taxes as evidence of harmful Federal measures.[43] Hamilton's army proved the bête noir of Federalism, because over it the great personal antagonisms arose that split the party and because it proved to be the most hated and feared creation of the Federalists. It demanded heavy taxes, could not defend its own existence, and gave substance to the Republican charge that political freedom was in danger. It had become odious and, what was almost worse from Adams' point of view, it had become ridiculous. The Hamiltonians blamed him for it.

"The zeal and enthusiasm which were excited by the pub-

[41] Washington to Bushrod Washington, August 22, October 24, 1798, Washington to Pickering, October 15, 1798, *Writings*, XXXVI, 420, 494-495, 519; S. T. Mason to Jefferson, July 6, 1798, Henry Tazewell to Jefferson, July 5, 1798, S. T. Mason to Jefferson, November 23, 1798, B. H. Latrobe to Jefferson, *Jefferson Papers*, LC. September 22, 1798.

[42] *Aurora*, February 20, 1799.

[43] *Ibid.*, February 11, 12, 13, 21, 1799. Most of the resolutions came from the Philadelphia vicinity, but on February 21 one from Rutland County, Vermont, was printed.

lication of the Dispatches . . . are evaporated. It is now no more," wrote Washington to Hamilton a few days after Murray's nomination. Oddly enough, he explained the public attitude by pointing to the failure of the recruiting service and not as the result of the President's peace overtures.[44] From the very beginning of its existence the army of 1798 was destined to be something short of glorious. Two of the three men most instrumental in creating it, Adams and McHenry, did more to hinder it than to aid it. Only Hamilton as Inspector General brought both knowledge and enthusiasm to the task of finding and disciplining an army.

Three months after the first plans for military expansion had been laid Washington and Hamilton had come to the conclusion that McHenry was no administrator. Washington regretted ever appointing him but excused it on the grounds that he had had no choice.[45] His complaints and Hamilton's made McHenry's life miserable for two years. In August 1798 Washington, the titular commanding general, did not know whether there was a Quartermaster General or not. Hamilton urged Sedgwick to encourage the President and his Secretary of War to appoint some regimental officers—nothing could be accomplished until that was done. Two months have passed since the law establishing the recruiting service was approved and absolutely nothing has been done, wrote Washington angrily to McHenry in September, and furthermore none of his questions had been answered.[46]

By the end of January 1799 little improvement in the administration of the army could be seen by the Speaker of the House, who described the progress of the army as "feeble . . . taken with that gradation and hesitation which showed a want of system . . . of spirit and vigor." It was too late now

[44] Mt. Vernon, February 25, 1799, Washington, *Writings*, XXXVII, 137-138.

[45] Washington to Hamilton, August 9, 1798, *ibid.*, XXXVI, 394.

[46] Washington to McHenry, August 10, 1798, *ibid.*, 403, Hamilton to Sedgwick, August 29, 1798, Hamilton Papers, LC.

to make up for the time lost, he wrote. The timid members of Congress had missed the opportunity to declare war, take New Orleans, and avoid both "diplomatic seduction" and the Alien and Sedition Acts.[47] According to Sedgwick, the game was up a month before the President reopened negotiations with France.

By May 1799 Hamilton was able to report to Washington that recruiting had at last begun. The mortifying delay he attributed to the President's lack of interest, McHenry's bungling, and to Wolcott's opposition. "It is well understood that the Secretary of the Treasury is not convinced of its [the army's] utility." [48]

The prospects for recruiting when it did begin were not good, however. New England Federalists who supported the war program grew cautious when it came to raising troops in their section of the country. "The eastern men say (perhaps for fear of taxing themselves for the Southern States who will receive the greater benefits) that their militia is well armed and wants not assistance. . . . They want no further laws on the subject and if they did, the States individually have, if not full, a concurrent power with Congress to do what is necessary," wrote Senator North of New York to Governor Jay in June 1798.[49]

Southern political leaders, according to one of Hamilton's Virginia recruiting officers, were making every effort to convince the class of men from whom an army could be made that the army had no function except to increase the power of the Executive over the state governments. Men were not volunteering for service, and the only remedy that the Virginia Colonel could see was a declaration of war by France.[50]

[47] Sedgwick to R. King, January 20, 1799, King, *Life and Correspondence*, II, 514-515.

[48] May 3, 1799, *Hamilton Papers*, LC.

[49] June 6, 1798, Jay, *Correspondence*, IV, 242.

[50] Col. Wm. Bentley to Hamilton, May 3, 1799, *Hamilton Papers*, LC.

Adams did not entirely harm himself by his months spent at Quincy. When in August 1798 the question of calling officers to active duty came up he could only be reached through an exchange of letters that took two weeks. He made it plain that he saw no necessity for paying officers until their services were absolutely required. Hamilton bitterly complained that Adams could not be convinced that officers were needed before an enemy landed. There was a great difference between speculating on government and running one, he commented.[51] Hamilton's recruiting regulations were placed in the President's hands in December but Adams seemed in no hurry officially to sanction them.[52] January passed without any action on his part, and not until he had released Gerry's correspondence and decided on the peace mission—the act that would kill what little enthusiasm remained—did he allow recruiting to begin. McHenry pressed him to return the regulations just ten days before Murray's nomination and found that Adams had not even read them and was in no hurry to do so.[53] Three days before the blow fell, Hamilton notified Washington that recruiting could begin but would be delayed still further because of clothing shortages.[54]

Even after the mechanics of organization had been ironed out, officers found, and barracks constructed, the army of which Hamilton's friends have written such nostalgic accounts was a source of ridicule. Washington found many of his friends disgusted because congressmen had talked McHenry into canceling some appointments in favor of personal friends. The list that he had drawn up with Hamilton and Pinckney was torn apart out of political preferment.[55] When

[51] To Sedgwick, August 29, 1798, Hamilton, *Works* (Lodge ed.), X, 318, 321.

[52] Steiner, *McHenry*, 368.

[53] February 8, 1799, *Hamilton Papers*, LC.

[54] February 15, 1799, *ibid.*

[55] March 25, 1799, Washington, *Writings*, XXXVII, 157-164.

HcHenry went to Adams for help he was told that no man of common sense would enlist for five dollars a month when he could easily make fifteen as a sailor or a day laborer. "If this nation sees a great army to maintain without an enemy to fight, there may arise an enthusiasm little foreseen," Adams was reported as saying. He could see less prospect of a French army in America than in heaven.[56]

Wolcott continued to begrudge the army every penny. There was too little clothing, no barracks in some areas, and men were no sooner secured than they deserted.[57] Hamilton's papers are full of complaints from all parts of the Union coming from junior officers who found the worst element in every town the only material willing to enlist. Discipline was impossible to enforce; men refused to serve unless stationed near home where discipline problems mounted. Cannon and clothing were defective or too scanty, contractors used poor materials, and good engineers were almost nonexistent. On at least one occasion an officer reported that "in firing salutes part of the Works fell down." [58] Not until August 1799 was there any indication that the motley force assembled in the year after war enthusiasm had reached its peak was beginning to take shape.[59] Certainly one of the motives behind the deliberate procrastination of Pickering in drawing up the orders for the second peace mission was the desire to see the military organization on its feet.

The charge that Adams by his nomination of the second peace mission killed the martial spirit of the nation is correct, but the evidence shows that it was already dying months before his February announcement. In complaints against the President made at the time the Hamiltonians spoke only of his delays by holding up recruiting orders and of a generally

[56] McHenry to Washington, April, 1799, *ibid.*, 190, Note 44.
[57] McHenry to Hamilton, October 25, 1799, *Hamilton Papers*, LC.
[58] Note in *Hamilton Papers*, LC, winter of 1799.
[59] Washington to Pinckney, August 10, 1799, Washington, *Writings*, XXXVII, 326.

unco-operative attitude that Wolcott also shared. Later they charged that he had ruined a promising military organization, but there is no proof that the army was ever a well-functioning machine or had any prospect of being one. The Sedition Act was oppressive but it never succeeded in silencing the Republican press, and the news from France of a change in policy had been so widely spread that militarism had become loathsome rather than attractive less than six months after the XYZ papers had first stirred the nation.

The receipt of William Vans Murray's dispatches on January 31 containing Talleyrand's promise to receive a new American envoy, in the President's own words—"as the representative of a great, free, powerful, and independent nation"—decided the question in Adams' mind.[60] Gerry's important record was revealed three days later, and in less than three weeks Murray was nominated. "I cannot conceive how you could have avoided instituting a negotiation on the receipt of Mr. Murray's letter," wrote Stoddert in 1809 during the public debate between Adams and Pickering.[61]

Adams' popularity had been built upon the public belief that he had done nothing to justify French attacks upon American shipping. The standing army, the tax program, the Sedition Act, and the actions of Federal courts had already produced a revulsion of public feeling against the dominant party. To have overlooked an opportunity to destroy the causes of his party's loss of popularity would have been politically insane and would have hurt Adams personally. He avoided being classed with the war party finally by coming to his decision alone. No one could doubt that there was a rift between Adams and the Hamiltonians after February 18. The Hamiltonians showed surprise and condemned him openly. Adams clearly asked the voters to consider whether the Federalist party was not made up of two great

[60] Adams, *Works*, I, 541-542.
[61] Stoddert to Adams, October 12, 1809, Lodge, *Cabot*, 201-202.

factions—Hamiltonians and Adamsmen. Even the Republicans could not but applaud his decision and admit that they had been mistaken in ranking the President with the war enthusiasts.

Adams' action in 1799 was well calculated to retrieve the political fortunes that the Hamiltonians had squandered. He could be thanked and was thanked for ending the threat of internal oppression, for leaving the way open to a welcome reduction in taxes, and for silencing the reports of an impending civil war. His long absence from Philadelphia, from March to November of 1799, has often been pointed to as evidence of political ineptness. The Hamiltonians were left to delay the peace mission unguarded. As Mr. Haraszti has pointed out, it has puzzled historians ever since why Adams could not have been reading the correspondence of Frederick the Great and Voltaire at Philadelphia.[62] Yet his retreat from the capital just a few days after the nomination of Murray dramatized as nothing else could the split between Adams and the Hamiltonian faction. "The event of events was announced to the Senate yesterday," Jefferson wrote on February 19. "This has evidently been kept secret from the Feds of both Houses as appeared by their dismay." [63]

The election of 1800 was not far from his thoughts. "I have no idea that I shall be chosen President a second time," he wrote Mrs. Adams a few days after Murray's nomination.[64] It was certain that the Hamiltonians would desert him, but he wisely left them the alternative of following his leadership by maintaining Pickering and McHenry in office until 1800 was well advanced. Yet by avoiding their physical presence he made it plain that no *rapprochement* would be sought by him. Adams counted on the common sense of those Fed-

[62] Zoltan Haraszti, *John Adams and the Prophets of Progress* (Harvard University Press, 1952), 101.

[63] To Madison, February 19, 1799, *Madison Papers*, LC.

[64] February 22, 1799, Adams, *Works*, I, 544.

eralist leaders not blindly devoted to Hamilton to line up behind him, and he was not disappointed.

Adams attempted to leave the impression upon posterity that his peace decision cost him the presidency in 1800. "I will defend my missions to France, as long as I have an eye to direct my hand. . . . They were the most disinterested and meritorious actions of my life. . . . I desire no other inscription over my gravestone than: 'Here lies John Adams, who took upon himself the responsibility of the peace with France in the year 1800.' "[65] Most accounts of his administration have accepted the Hamiltonian line that the peace decision, inspired by patriotic motives and the desire to hurt Hamilton and his friends, broke the spell of Federalist popularity and sent the party to its ruin in 1800. Yet it has been here demonstrated that the popularity of the Federalists during the war crisis was extremely short-lived and that motives of political expediency existed that Adams would have been blind to have overlooked and not acted upon.

His own insistence, as Mr. Haraszti points out, that "the soundest statesmen of the ruling party in both houses" were pleased with his action; and his statement that the administration would have been turned out by a vote of two to one had peace not been instituted, suggests that his decision was not totally disinterested.[66] In fact, the question that arises out of the story of 1798 and 1799 is: How could Adams hope to win the election of 1800 without acting as he did? The choice that Adams made in February, 1799, was between peace and war, but it was equally a choice between the backing of Hamilton or the support of public opinion.

[65] Adams, *Works,* X, 113.

[66] *Ibid.,* 115, 118; Haraszti, *op. cit.,* 346, Notes 13, 14.

17

Independence

THE CRY THAT AROSE FROM THE THROATS OF FEDERALIST leaders in the spring of 1799 was a cry of betrayal. It seemed clear to most of them that Adams in nominating a peace envoy had also cleared the way for Jefferson's election in 1800. War with France would have sealed the fate of the Republican party permanently, and the threat of war with its attendant jingoism was enough to keep them in a position of supremacy at least until the next election had safely passed. Had Adams not shared in the party's popularity they might have understood, but he had been a genuinely popular President for the first two years of his administration, a fact that no one would have ventured to predict after his three-vote victory. It seemed that he had destroyed his own image. Those who were unwilling to diagnose his action as the result of sheer insanity maintained that he had resurrected the old scheme of a coalition with Jefferson, but the majority of the Hamiltonians had no answer at all. At Quincy he sat, seemingly oblivious to politics, and there he remained for the better part of a year. George Cabot, Hamiltonian envoy extraordinary, sought him out.

"The spirit of faction predominates over everything," Cabot concluded at the end of a lengthy interview. Adams was as bitter against Cabot's friends as they were against him. Once again Adams had launched into a defense of Elbridge Gerry and had insisted that he had never attempted to hide his desire for an honorable peace at the earliest opportunity.

Moreover, he seriously maintained that his action would prove politically wise. He had said, according to Cabot's account of their conversation, that his nomination of Murray as minister to France was intended to "silence the offensive remonstrants against Gerryism, to open a way for soothing Jacobin spirits, to provide for something like a support against the dictatorial temper of high-minded Federalists." [1]

Just two weeks after the startling nomination of Murray, the President confided still more of his thoughts on the question to Attorney General Charles Lee, one of the few Federalists who had immediately certified his approval. His peace move, wrote Adams, would prove once and for all who the true warmongers were. Too many Federalists, he said, have assumed that my election by three votes has made me a slave to party, but they now know they are mistaken. "If combinations of Senators, generals, and heads of departments shall be formed such as I cannot resist, and measures demanded of me that I cannot adopt, my remedy is plain and certain. I will try my own strength at resistance first, however." [2]

Adams' description of Murray's nomination as "the most disinterested, the most determined, and the most successful" act of his whole life [3] has obscured the fact that he was still a powerful political figure after the break with the Hamiltonians. While Pickering, Ames, Cabot, and Sedgwick hurried to be the first in denouncing what they considered the President's desertion of decent politics,[4] a few high-ranking Federalists such as John Marshall, Henry Lee, and Harrison Otis could be seen applauding in the background.

[1] Cabot to Christopher Gore, May 2, 1799, Lodge, *Cabot,* 231.

[2] March 29, 1799, Adams, *Works,* VIII, 629.

[3] Adams to William Cunningham, March 20, 1809, *Adams-Cunningham Correspondence,* 101.

[4] Sedgwick to Hamilton, February 19, 1799, *Hamilton Papers,* LC; Ames to Thomas Dwight, February 27, 1799, Ames, *Works,* I, 252; Pickering to King, March 6, 1799, King, *Life and Correspondence,* II, 549; Pickering to Hamilton, February 25, 1799, *Hamilton Papers,* LC.

Adams was the Federalist party's candidate for the Presidency in the following year, becauses the secondary leaders of the party refused to desert him, because Massachusetts was constant in its allegiance to him, and because a surprising number of party bigwigs finally chose Adams over Hamilton when the attempt to maneuver C. C. Pinckney into the presidency was begun by Hamilton.

Federalists in the Senate reasoned that if they could not defeat the Murray appointment they might at least use the threat of doing so to force Adams into appointing two more peace commissioners. They were fairly confident that one or both of the additional envoys would prove less enthusiastic over the prospect of peace than William Vans Murray seemed. Yet even among the five-man Senate committee that called upon Adams to press such demands there was division, and all were tried and true Hamiltonians. Secretary of State Pickering described both of Pennsylvania's Senators, Bingham and Ross, as undependable—Ross because he was cultivating popularity as candidate for Governor of Pennsylvania, and Bingham because he might hope to profit financially from certain commercial enterprises that the war crisis had interrupted.[5] Theodore Sedgwick, who acted as spokesman for the committee, admitted that there was no chance of persuading the Senate to defeat Murray's confirmation if Adams refused the commission suggestion. This would be his own answer to the problem, he told Hamilton, but the majority disagreed. Adams, wrote Sedgwick, showed no signs of comprehending public sentiment and had gone so far as to tell him "that his message would add to the federal energies of the legislature," that it would produce votes.[6]

In the eyes of his former friends, Harrison Otis of Massachusetts had committed political treason by warmly endorsing the President's peace decision. Having done so he voiced

[5] Pickering to Cabot, February 21, 1799, Lodge, *Cabot*, 221.
[6] Sedgwick to Hamilton, February 22, 1799, *Hamilton Papers*, LC.

slight misgivings to the Essex gentlemen who had sponsored his political career. "Well may you be in affliction for so gross a departure from principles and so gross a desertion of party," admonished Jonathan Mason of the Junto in reply, He solemnly warned Otis to guard against following a man who knew within himself that he had never been "the choice of the Federalists." Adams was a blind follower of Gerry in Mason's opinion, and he could be accounted a fool in believing that he could win public popularity by sacrificing honor for a humiliating surrender to France.[7]

Otis remained a heretic, however, while Pickering reported to Cabot that "the serpents of the *Aurora*" were "slavering Adams with their praise" and while Cabot in reply noted that both Federalist papers at Boston, the *Centinel* and the *Mercury*, had come out strongly behind the nomination. "Indignation, grief, and disgust are the only sentiments excited by the nomination of Mr. Murray in the breasts of well-informed, decided Federalists," declared Cabot. "The feeble see no harm while the temporizers, trimmers, and Federal hypocrites with Jacobin hearts rejoice in an opportunity to throw off the mask." He admitted, nevertheless, that the President's action had stunned Republicans and confused them.[8]

Foremost among the evil effects of Adams' sins was a noticeable decline in public enthusiasm for armies and war. To Cabot this was nothing short of tragic. "The incidents of active war would every day interest the feelings of the community and destroy that apathy which has been so dangerous. . . ." Robert Harper was inclined to believe that Mr. Adams' coach horses might perform a public service by carrying him into the first available ditch on the trip to

[7] February 27, 1799, Morison, *Otis*, I, 171-173.

[8] Pickering to Cabot, February 21, 1799, Lodge, *Cabot*, 221; Cabot to Pickering, March 7, 1799, *ibid.*, 224-225.

Quincy,[9] but by April of 1800 Harper was writing his constituents of the administration's great diplomatic victory in the quasi war with France; and as the Federalists bowed out in 1801 he was to praise warmly the Adams record: "Thus with France also peace. . . . This has been effected by the measures of the Federalists, who as soon as they saw the end attained for which these measures were adopted, gradually gave them up; beginning with such as involved the greatest expense to the nation. Thus the army was dissolved . . . thus the direct tax was abandoned. . . ." [10]

In the spring of 1799, however, Harper, along with the majority of the Hamiltonians, was damning the President. Their faithful press lieutenant, William Cobbet, when he first heard of Murray's nomination, branded the news nothing but a dirty rumor.[11] The small-town editor of the *Connecticut Gazette*, however, reflected what Adams believed public sentiment to be when he printed at the bottom of his third page: "The appointment of Mr. Murray as Minister Plenipotentiary to France has given general satisfaction." [12]

Federalist fears that peace would immediately benefit the Jeffersonians proved unfounded, and President Adams' contention that it would add strength to Federalist forces in Congress proved correspondingly correct. When the 6th Congress convened for its first session in December, 1799, Theodore Sedgwick of Massachusetts, acting the part of an administration spokesman while playing Iago to Adams,[13] was elected Speaker by a large majority over Jeffersonian

[9] To Wolcott, Jr., February 22, 1799, Gibbs, *Memoirs*, II, 183; reported by Jefferson, "Anas," January 24, 1800, *Writings* (Ford ed.), I, 352.

[10] April 7, 1800, March 5, 1801, *Bayard Papers*, 97; *Works*, 330.

[11] *Porcupine's Gazette*, February 19, 1799, reprinted in the *Aurora*, February 22, 1799.

[12] February 27, 1799.

[13] Sedgwick, Samuel Bayard of Delaware, and Harrison Otis were invited by the President to a private dinner just after the nomination of Murray, Adams assuming that all three were loyal supporters. Adams to Otis, February 19, 1823, Morison, *Otis*, I, 174-175.

Nathaniel Macon of North Carolina.[14] Federalists not only maintained their power in northern states, but greatly increased it throughout the South in elections held a few weeks after Adams' peace announcement.

"The election of April 1799 terminated more unfavorably to the republicans than had been anticipated," wrote Hammond of the outcome in New York State. "New York City, which for two years previous had elected republicans, this year elected federalists by the large majority of about nine hundred."[15]

Hamilton's New York friends were ecstatic over the outcome. "We have attained a glorious triumph . . . we have broken the democratic fetters," exclaimed Robert Troup in a report to Rufus King.[16] Their celebrations were somewhat dampened, however, by Burr's clever maneuver of sponsoring a resolution of gratitude to President Adams for his peace decision. Federalists in the legislature refused to endorse it, adding to the growing breach between Adamsmen and Hamiltonians. Governor Jay might have silenced one of the factions, but he remained neutral until the spring of 1800.[17]

In Massachusetts, where politicians were either friends or enemies of the President, the Federalists held the line by returning incumbent Increase Sumner to the governor's chair and by sending a large Federalist majority back to the legislature. The internal cleavage over national issues that state Federalist organizations everywhere experienced in 1799 did not show at the polls. Although the Republican ticket was supported by six thousand more voters than it had been in 1798, the total Federalist vote increased by more than seven thousand.[18]

[14] December 2, 1799; Sedgwick, 42; Macon, 27, *Connecticut Gazette,* December 11, 1799.

[15] J. B. Hammond, *Political Parties in New York,* I, 129.

[16] May 6, 1799, King, *Life and Correspondence,* III, 14.

[17] Hammond, *op. cit.,* 126-127; Parton, *Aaron Burr,* 238-239.

[18] Morse, *Federalist Party in Massachusetts,* 176-179; King, *op. cit.,* 14.

Boston's pro-administration *Columbian Centinel* warned Federalist leaders that a steady increase in the Republican vote might be expected unless Congress quickly cut heavy taxes that were turning hundreds of small farmers away from the party. The Essex Junto, however, continued to upbraid Otis and to view opposition to Fifth Congress legislation as evidence of weakness akin to treason.[19] Fisher Ames noted with his customary sarcasm that Adams supporters had joined the "Jacobins" in denouncing the army and demanding its dissolution.[20] Massachusetts bigwigs appeared deaf to the voice of public opinion.

The greatest political upheaval that spring occurred in Virginia and North Carolina, where more Federalists were elected than at any time since the birth of parties. Hamiltonian cries that Adams had crushed public enthusiasm by his February peace announcement seemed ridiculous. By the end of June Washington was certain that a sweeping change in Southern political sentiments was well underway. April elections had produced one Federalist Congressman from Georgia, a state that had known nothing but antifederalism for more than six years. Five of South Carolina's six Representatives in the new Congress were viewed as Federalist, seven of North Carolina's ten, and almost half the Virginia delegation. General Washington was convinced from reports he had received since the election that at least eight of Virginia's new congressmen were administration supporters and that three more had been defeated by a mere handful of votes.[21]

Although Washington's estimate of southern Federalist strength in the 6th Congress was overly optimistic, his enthusiasm was certainly well merited. Professor Dodd listed

[19] April 17, 1799, Morse, *op. cit.*; Cabot to King, April 26, 1799, King, *Life and Correspondence*, III, 9.

[20] Ames to Pickering, October 19, 1799, Ames, *Works*, I, 258.

[21] Washington to Jonathan Trumbull, June 25, 1799, *Writings*, XXXVII, 249.

only four of the Southerners as Federalists and found that the strength of the party remained substantially the same through the presidential election of 1800 when four Southern Federalist electors were chosen,[22] but John Beckley, who could scarcely have been mistaken, listed seven of the Virginia delegation alone as Federalists.[23] Hamilton's Richmond friend, William Heth, was so elated at the small-scale revolution that he jumped to the conclusion that the Republicans were rapidly dying. "We have obtained such an accession of numbers as well as of talents, that I think we may consider Jacobinism as completely overthrown in this state," he wrote Hamilton. Particularly gratifying to him was John Marshall's victory over William Giles in the city of Richmond. It was expected that Marshall and Henry Lee would prove towers of strength to the party.[24]

Simultaneously more than a third of the Virginia state legislature had fallen to the Federalists, and Washington considered Senator-elect John Tayloe so neutral in his politics as to warn Secretary of War McHenry against pressing him into military service lest his services in the Senate be lost.[25]

To Jefferson and his beleaguered forces the outcome was a distinct shock. "The Virginia congressional elections have astonished everyone," he wrote Tench Coxe, who was just commencing the Republican gubernatorial campaign in Pennsylvania. "They gave five certain federalists—three others on whom they can count. . . ." It was all the result of a series of peculiar circumstances, he stoutly maintained, and not an indication of new political sympathies sweeping the South, but nonetheless, he was worried.[26]

Pre-election jitters had induced state assemblymen to peti-

22 W. E. Dodd, *Nathaniel Macon,* 162.

23 Beckley to Wm. Irvine, May 10, 1799, *Irvine Papers,* Historical Society of Pennsylvania, XIV, No. 84.

24 May 11, 1799, *Hamilton Papers,* LC.

25 Washington to McHenry, May 5, 1799, *Writings,* XXXVII, 198.

26 May 21, 1799, Jefferson, *Writings* (Ford ed.), IX, 69; Simms, *John Taylor,* 94.

tion Madison in hopes of ending his retirement. Patrick Henry was expected to run for the House of Delegates, and Madison would be needed to counterbalance his prestige. "I am told," wrote Madison to Jefferson just as the canvass began, "that the parties will be precisely in equilibrio . . . except for one or two who switch from side to side." [27]

Both Madison and Henry won easily in their districts, but the anticipated renewal of an ancient parliamentary struggle between reason and oratory never came off. Henry's sudden death in June cut short what would have been one of the most remarkable comebacks in American political annals. Madison was badly needed, nonetheless, for the Republican plight had grown so desperate in the South that John Taylor began predicting the overthrow of the party. "I give up all for lost," he commented gloomily to Jefferson in the fall.[28] John Nicholas' defection and subsequent denunciation of alleged military plans against the Federal government, the failure of the Virginia and Kentucky resolutions to catch fire as an acceptable pattern for relief from future as well as present evils, and the success of administration supporters in 1799's elections made Jefferson's prospects for the presidency seem almost as barren as in 1798.[29]

So certain of losing ground were Virginia Republicans that Madison and Taylor pushed a new electoral bill through the state legislature as soon as the two houses convened in December. Under the new system electors would be chosen in district elections instead of by a general ticket vote.[30] Instead of allowing the freeholder a chance to select twenty-one presidential electors he was by virtue of the new law given the sovereign right of choosing one. Jeffersonians pre-

[27] December 29, 1799, Madison, *Writings* (Hunt ed.), VI, 343; Brant, *Madison*, 464-465.

[28] John Taylor to Creed Taylor, April 10, to Jefferson, October 14, 1799, Simms, *Taylor*, 94.

[29] Jefferson to Wilson C. Nicholas, September 5, 1799, *Writings* (Ford ed.), IX, 81.

[30] Simms, *John Taylor*, 96.

ferred to lose three or four seats in the college rather than to hazard the loss of perhaps a third.

Somehow, miraculously as far as Hamiltonians were concerned, the party had escaped disaster as the result of Mr. Adams' peace decision. A few gradually came to the conclusion that it had actually added new strength to the Federalist party. There was no great rush to Adams on the part of primary leaders in 1799, but a respectable and gradually increasing number slowly gave evidence of new respect for Adams' political capabilities. The gain had to be at Hamilton's expense.

It was nevertheless true that the only large political group that showed immediate enthusiasm for the peace decision was the Republican party. So loud was the outcry of anguish from Hamiltonians that even the pro-Adams secondary echelon remained silent, wondering if senatorial politics would succeed in blocking the move. The *Gazette of the United States* refused to say anything about the Murray nomination through February and March, and it was not until after the Senate's confirmation that Charles Lee forwarded to Adams John Marshall's endorsement of the policy.[31] By June George Cabot was beginning to fear Hamilton less and Adams more. The elections were a revelation to him after his dire predictions of doom. "The influence of the measure has indeed been *much less* pernicious than was feared, there having been great exertions everywhere to counteract it and the strange inconsistency of the President himself cooperated strongly to the same purpose," he told Rufus King. It now seemed that the greatest source of danger lay in the possibility that Adams might turn on those who had voiced opposition to his policies. He was noticeably cool in his relations with Pickering, Wolcott, and McHenry.[32]

[31] Charles Lee to Adams, March 14, 1799, *Vans Murray Papers*, LC; from Channing, *History*, IV, 203.

[32] June 2, 1799, King, *Life and Correspondence*, III, 27.

Instead of dismissing the three secretaries and urging Congress to scrap defense measures, Adams kept his cabinet and went on appointing officers to the provisional army. Such insane working at cross purposes was just one more of his anti-Hamilton, popularity-seeking stunts, according to Theodore Sedgwick, who complained that the President had done virtually nothing to raise a real army while busily signing dozens of commissions for his friends in the imaginary provisional army. Hamilton could not even begin to raise regiments in many sections of the country, because Adams would not sign commissions for active line officers.[33]

In May Otis began printing his pro-Adams "Envoy" articles in the Boston press, a step that marked his open break with the Essex circle; and Adams' old friends, Henry Knox and Benjamin Lincoln, began talking loudly of his responsibility to throw Pickering and McHenry out of office.[34]

While the Secretary of State, acting in conformity with a policy that he considered consistent with true Federalist principles and the nation's prestige, continued to block the departure of the peace commissioners, the President was receiving assurances that he had acted honorably and wisely. If the Essex Junto shunned him, at least Knox, Lincoln, and Gerry were with him. Governor Davie of North Carolina enthusiastically accepted a place on the diplomatic mission, and Henry Lee endorsed the move. Patrick Henry sent his congratulations, and at least two former Hamiltonian stalwarts from Massachusetts, Samuel Dexter and Harrison Otis, deserted their political cronies to espouse the President's peace policy.[35]

Furthermore, Adams could be certain of leadership in the new Congress that was bound to support him from John

[33] Sedgwick to Wolcott, Jr., May 8, 1799, Gibbs, *Memoirs*, II, 239; Sedgwick to King, July 26, 1799, King, *Life and Correspondence*, III, 70-71.

[34] Cabot to Pickering, May 2, 1799, to Wolcott, May 2, 1799, Lodge, *Cabot*, 229-230; Adams, *Works*, VIII, 626-628.

[35] Morison, *Otis*, I, 158-165; Adams, *Works*, I, 550, VIII, 626.

Marshall and Henry Lee as well as from Otis; and in the cabinet Benjamin Stoddert and Charles Lee remained steadfast. Oliver Wolcott was at least opposed to the recruiting of an army, though he disagreed openly with the suddenness with which Adams had acted in the French crisis. There was even a persistent rumor that a delegation of Maryland politicians had agreed to support him for re-election in return for the dismissal of Pickering and a speedy peace settlement.[36]

Republican attacks against the administration continued despite their delight with Adams for squaring off against the military faction. As Jefferson pointed out, there was plenty of target left at which to shoot: the direct tax and the army were still on the books for two more years. "Can such an army under Hamilton be disbanded even if the House of Representatives can be got willing to disband them?" he asked Edmund Pendleton. "I doubt it, and therefore, rest my hopes on their inability to raise anything but officers." [37]

Adams Federalists led an onslaught against the army's perpetuation as soon as the 6th Congress opened, but it was too late to have much effect upon Pennsylvania's gubernatorial election in November. During that revolutionary struggle parties seemed to turn themselves upside down and inside out. The Federalist candidate, Senator James Ross, was an outsider who had been chosen because of his popularity in the western counties where he had been associated somewhat mysteriously with the Whiskey Rebellion, while the Republican candidate was an eastern conservative, Justice Thomas McKean of the state Supreme Court. Federalists appealed to the radical vote while their democratic opponents made an obvious bid for the conservative vote. Former Treasury Department Auditor Tench Coxe, who had superseded John Beckley as Republican chairman in Pennsylvania, sounded

[36] Gibbs, *Memoirs*, II, 352-353.

[37] April 22, 1799, *Jefferson Papers*, LC; *Writings* (Ford ed.), IX, 65.

the keynote to Albert Gallatin in August. "It is of the utmost importance that early attention be paid to collecting solid and clear evidence of such objections to Mr. Ross as candid and good men, real friends to the order of society and to property may feel." [38]

Senator Ross was held up by the Republican strategists as the foe of vested interests in the east and as the friend of men of property in western counties. "We rely on the activity of all the men of property and influence in the Republican interest," read Alexander Dallas's unJeffersonian-sounding appeal to Cumberland County boss William Irvine.[39]

In a lively and closely watched campaign Judge McKean and Republican assembly candidates scored an easy victory. Internal troubles beset the Federalists. They were noticeably lacking in leadership on the local level, and the animosity felt by party regulars for Adams supporters was apparently not submerged for practical purposes as it had been in Massachusetts earlier in the year.[40] The standing army and militarism in general were as unpopular in Pennsylvania as in any state in the Union, and in urging the voters to elect Ross as a young man who could lead Pennsylvania militia against French invaders Federalist managers only aided McKean.[41]

The political barometer pointed unmistakably to a deep

[38] August 2, 1799, *Gallatin Papers*, New York Historical Society, Box 5, 1799, No. 30.

[39] June 14, 1799, *Irvine Papers*, Historical Society of Pennsylvania, XIV, 88. Dallas, who had been readmitted to the state organization in 1798, and Tench Coxe headed the Republican central committee. Apparently there was discontent among western party workers over McKean's selection. George Wilson of Mifflin County referred to McKean as a man who had been forced upon the party by easterners. Wilson to Irvine, April 25, 1799, *Irvine Papers*, XIV, 81.

[40] H. M. Tinkcom, "Political Behavior in Pennsylvania," 346-357. McKean received 38,036 and Ross 32,643 votes. Raymond Walters, *Alexander Dallas*, 90-91, accounts for the turnover by pointing to Federalist loss of the German counties, which had hitherto been evenly divided. The unpopularity of the "Window Tax" and the Alien and Sedition Acts made the difference in 1799.

[41] *Philadelphia Gazette*, August 20, 1799.

longing for peace and to a desire to be done with talk of subversion. Yet Hamiltonians persisted in their attempts to maintain the instruments of repression; army, heavy taxation, and the Alien and Sedition Acts. McHenry urged Hamilton to bring pressure to bear upon Oliver Wolcott for his continued opposition to army expenditures, Higginson encouraged Wolcott to keep the cabinet firmly against the departure of the peace commissioners, and George Cabot, as late as January, 1800, was criticizing Adams for shattering the French invasion hoax, the only threat that he felt could have kept anti-Republican sentiment alive.[42]

"Whatever may be the obstacles to an army," Cabot told the Secretary of the Treasury, "they ought to be overcome. The whole world is becoming military, and if we are wholly otherwise we shall be as sheep among wolves. Indeed we have wolves enough within our own fold to destroy us, if we cannot keep up our guards." [43] Even Jonathan Dayton, who could usually be trusted to read the writing on the wall to his own advantage, retained his hopes for a military career. "I am so intent upon serving immediately under *you*," he wrote Hamilton, "in the event of an important expedition, that I cannot avoid sometimes to feel as if I were now in service." [44]

In their perplexity Hamiltonian leaders turned once more to Washington as the only savior in sight. Gouverneur Morris and Governor Jonathan Trumbull of Connecticut pleaded with the General to forsake his private security once more for the good of the party. Not once, but twice, Trumbull braved Washington's disapproval. He would be called vain and ambitious in his dotage; the project was simply too rash, replied Washington to Trumbull's first draft notice.

[42] McHenry to Hamilton, June 26. *Hamilton Papers*, LC; Higginson to Wolcott, June 25, 1799, Gibbs, *Memoirs*, II, 245.

[43] January 16, 1800, Gibbs, *Memoirs*, II, 321-322.

[44] November 21, 1799, *Hamilton Papers*, LC.

Why did anyone think he could win more votes than Adams, he asked? A month later he firmly declined, and in doing so lectured Trumbull sternly about principles.

"The favorite today may have the curtain dropped on him tomorrow, while steadiness marks the conduct of the anti's [Republicans] . . . if principles instead of men are not the steady pursuit of the Federalists, their cause will soon be at an end. If these are pursued at the next election they will not divide. If they do divide on so important a point, it would be dangerous to trust them on any other. . . ." [45]

Washington's advice, so penetrating in its comprehension of party government and Federalist weaknesses, fell upon deaf ears. Pickering and McHenry, believing that they were performing a sacrificial service in defying and thwarting Adams, resorted to the most flagrant irregularities in their last days of Federal service. They seized upon Napoleon's grab for consular powers at Paris as good reason for suspending peace negotiations. Adams' continued absence alarmed both Washington and Stoddert. Oliver Ellsworth, one of the envoys, had adopted the Hamiltonian view of the peace effort from the beginning, Adams himself showed signs of uncertainty, and finally Pickering openly asked that the mission be postponed indefinitely. This was enough, and Navy Secretary Stoddert's second warning brought Adams in haste to the temporary capital at Trenton.[46] He gave the impression of being in no hurry about the departure of Ellsworth and Davie, and then suddenly he wheeled about and

[45] Washington to Trumbull, July 21, August 30, 1799, *Writings*, XXXVII, 312-313, 348-349; J. Q. Adams, *Political Parties*, 30. Wolcott, who knew of the design to draft Washington, refused to enter into it. He wrote Trumbull on July 16 that it seemed improper for him to take notice of it while serving under Adams and predicted "malign Circumstances" if it was persisted in. Gibbs, *Memoirs*, II, 246.

[46] Washington to McHenry, August 10, 1799, *Writings*, XXXVII, 328; Stoddert to Adams, August 29, Adams to Stoddert, September 4, Stoddert to Adams, September 13, 1799, Adams, *Works*, IX, 18-19; Pickering to Adams, September 24, 1799, *Works*, IX, 37.

on the morning of October 16 orders were issued for departure not later than November 1.[47]

The President's apparent hesitation was a blind to cover his true purpose of dispatching the commissioners in October regardless of the confusion at Paris. A month before his hurried trip from Quincy he had confided to George Cabot that his mind was absolutely made up on the question.[48] His handling of the peace mission from start to finish appears to have been aimed at throwing the military, domination-at-any-price faction off balance. Their disgust and resentment again dramatized his struggle for control within the party. "In most matters we are consulted and our ideas often adopted," wrote Pickering two weeks later, "but in this all important question, from first to last, we have been absolutely excluded." [49] The ministerial government that Hamilton and his friends so admired in Great Britain came closer to functioning between 1796 and 1800 than at any time in American history, but Adams' order of October 16 marked the end of its unglorious career.

In political circles the conclusion drawn was that Adams had taken a major step toward winning popular acclaim. John Marshall arrived at the capital in December and urged Southern congressmen to line up behind the peace program, maintaining that the measure was "sincere, honest, and politic." [50] No doubts could remain as to which side he had chosen in the intraparty struggle. Jedediah Morse of the Essex Junto believed, on the other hand, that Adams had sold out to the Jeffersonians and was convinced that Adams would receive Republican support for re-election, and Cabot ventured to predict Adams' appearance in the role of an Anglophobe. "Everything will be rendered odious that is

47 Adams, *Works*, IX, 39.

48 Cabot to King, September 23, 1799, King, *Life and Correspondence*, III, 110.

49 Pickering to Cabot, October 24, 1799, Lodge, *Cabot*, 249.

50 Wolcott to Ames, December 29, 1799, Gibbs, *Memoirs*, II, 314.

truly valuable; our army, public credit, etc., will be sacrificed to popularity." His friend Goodrich of Connecticut, however, conceded that the President's latest maneuver had dealt a necessary blow at the standing army that had gradually become "an exceptionable measure to good men," but Adams could easily have suggested less violent and harmful ways of conducting his pre-election campaign, remarked Goodrich.[51]

Whether the presidential foreign policy and the attack upon the Hamiltonian wing of the Federalist party would pay dividends at the polls remained a serious consideration for men such as Marshall and Otis, who had bolted the party to stand with Adams in his last months of office. In April, 1800, attention shifted from Philadelphia to Massachusetts, where the regular party organization faced the task of defeating both Adamsite Elbridge Gerry and a Republican gubernatorial candidate. Though Adams claimed neutrality so far as the three candidates were concerned,[52] a dangerous sign in itself, Gerry made no claim to neutrality in his views of national affairs. He was already known to have inspired the President's crucial peace policy, and in his campaign statements he completely endorsed the Adams record. According to Speaker Sedgwick, he went so far as to present himself as "the personal and confidential friend of the President."[53]

A record turnout of more than forty thousand voters gave Republican candidate Gill but two thousand votes and split the remaining thirty-eight thousand between Gerry and Federalist candidate and incumbent Caleb Strong. Strong's victory by two hundred votes was a tremendous blow to the

[51] Morse to Wolcott, November 8, 1799, Gibbs, *Memoirs*, II, 287; Cabot to Wolcott, October 16, 1799, *ibid.*, 284; Goodrich to Wolcott, November 18, 1799, *ibid.*, 288.

[52] Pickering to Cabot, May 7, 1800, King, *Life and Correspondence*, III, 233.

[53] Joseph Hale to King, May 13, 1800; Christopher Gore to King, May 14, 1800, King, *op. cit.*, 240-243.

prestige of the Essex Junto and so startled Tench Coxe that he immediately pressed Jefferson to replace Aaron Burr on the national ticket with Elbridge Gerry.[54]

Gerry's unexpected strength in the Massachusetts gubernatorial contest of 1800 proved a turning point in the struggle between Adams and Hamilton. Simultaneously with the blow that fell upon the regulars in New England came the Republican victory in New York State, which guaranteed Jefferson and Burr twelve electoral votes where before they had had none. Pennsylvania had already slipped from Federalist control in the fall of 1799, and of the three middle Atlantic states that had been so overwhelmingly Federalist in 1798, only New Jersey remained certain. Wary of the kind of last-minute maneuvering that had brought Jefferson so close to victory in 1796, Federalist leaders faced the question of standing by Adams or of making a second attempt to elect a Pinckney President. Theophilus Parsons, grand old man of the Essex Junto, and John Jay reached their conclusions together.

In answer to Jay's question about thirty thousand wayward votes, Parsons was in no doubt: the answer was that Gerry had made a strong appeal to the independent voters of both parties. Gerry, wrote Parsons, was considered a Federalist, because he had strongly supported Adams and was understood to be his trusted friend. Others were equally convinced that he was an anti-Federalist, because he had opposed the adoption of the Constitution in 1788 and because he had worked unceasingly for peace with France. Mr. Gerry was known to be "opposed to war, to a standing army, to a funding system, and attached to the agricultural interest. . . . An attention to the votes for Senators, will clearly evince the fact that a great part of the electors for Mr. Gerry were Federalists. . . . I believe at this time the

[54] Coxe to Jefferson, May 4, 1800, *Jefferson Papers*, LC.

universal sentiment of the Federalists is to support Mr. Adams, with all the activity and perseverance such a measure deserves," concluded a leader of the most influential Federalist machine in the nation.[55]

The Gerry-Strong election was as accurate an indication of public feeling toward Adams as could be produced, and the independence movement that Adams and Gerry had headed since the latter's return to the United States in 1798 slowly gathered momentum in one last effort to block both Jefferson's triumph and Hamilton's ascendency.

In December a Federalist caucus of party bigwigs had agreed to support Adams for re-election, despite their personal antipathy toward him. There was violent opposition to the idea before agreement could be reached, however.[56] On January 10, Governor Richard Bassett of Delaware in his address to the state legislature pointedly referred to the success of the President's foreign policy and spoke of Adams as "tried, distinguished, and beloved."[57] Sedgwick, meanwhile, had come to the conclusion that the army would have to go. "Good men in New England, where tranquility generally prevails, cannot easily be led to understand for what purpose the Army can be necessary provided a peace be made with France," he declared.[58]

By May, with the recent Massachusetts election serving to warn them, a second caucus met at Philadelphia and reaffirmed the choice of Adams and Charles C. Pinckney as the party's candidates in the forthcoming national election. "It is true that the President's late conduct has endeared him to the great body of Federalists," admitted Sedgwick to King, "but it is equally true that it has created an entire separation

[55] May 5, 1800, Jay, *Correspondence*, IV, 268-269.

[56] John Dawson to Madison, December 12, 1799, *Madison Papers*, LC.

[57] James A. Bayard, to Bassett, January 25, 1800, *Bayard Papers*, 94.

[58] Sedgwick to King, December 12, 1799, King, *Life and Correspondence*, III, 154-155.

between him and those whom he theretofore deemed his best friends. . . ." [59]

Adams preferred the majority of his party's minor leaders to the influential former "friends" and accentuated the division by dismissing McHenry and Pickering, a step that Knox and Otis had been urging for months and that the two secretaries had expected since November, 1799.[60]

Ever since the nomination of Murray, Adams had begun to denounce Hamilton freely, and a few weeks after the departure of the peace envoys he bluntly told Wolcott that it was his intention to create a third political party by drawing support from the independent-minded men of the other two.[61] His previous actions had been a challenge to the military faction, but the dismissal of Pickering and McHenry was a declaration of war. Those who began to talk in terms of three political parties in the United States, particularly after Gerry's campaign in Massachusetts, were only recognizing a fact made perfectly clear by the exit of Hamilton's henchmen from the cabinet. By keeping them in office long after he had become convinced of their devotion to Hamilton and his military designs, Adams had shown a willingness to conciliate. He had shown by his promises to make peace when France showed a willingness to meet him halfway and by his refusal to issue recruiting orders that he was earnestly opposed to war and to domestic bullying.

Out of the tangle of his foreign policy and personal relationships emerges a new John Adams—a man keenly aware of the demands of democratic politics and able to hold the majority of his party against the dictates of almost the entire

[59] May 11, 1800, King, *op. cit.*, 238.

[60] McHenry to Washington, November 2, 1799, *Hamilton Papers*, LC; Wolcott to Ames, December 29, 1799, Gibbs, *Memoirs*, II, 314-315; Cabot to King, January 20, 1800, King, *op. cit.*, 182-183; Sedgwick to Pickering, December 22, 1799, Morison, *Otis*, I, 182-183; Cabot to Wolcott, May 2, 1799, Gibbs, II, 239.

[61] Cabot to King, April 26, 1799, King, *Life and Correspondence*, III, 8; Wolcott to Ames, December 29, 1799, Gibbs, *Memoirs*, II, 313-315.

Hamiltonian wing. Adams was convinced that the public and the secondary leaders of the Federalist party would approve his policy of peace and that the party stood to gain by carrying them out. None of his announcements was made without what appears to have been careful consideration as to its probable effects upon public opinion. At no time did Adams appear to hurt his chances for re-election by appealing to the public rather than to Hamilton and his friends. Certainly his re-election would have been assured had he followed the Hamiltonian line: it would have wiped out the opposition as the military program with its important corollary, the Sedition Act, was meant to do. To sacrifice both conscience and domestic peace for another term of office seemed too high a price, however.

Those who might maintain that he had lost electoral votes by alienating high-ranking Federalists overlook the nature of the electoral process. Two caucuses had agreed to support Adams and General Pinckney when the dismissal of Pickering and McHenry was announced, and it was obvious that Hamiltonians rested their hopes on equal support for both candidates in every state but South Carolina, which was expected to divide as it had done in 1796. The fact is that Hamilton and his friends were out beating the drum for the Federalist ticket in November, because that ticket was pledged to both men. They could not urge the public to vote only for Pinckney electors; there were none. The lesson of 1796 clearly taught the politicians of both parties to avoid wasting votes in the electoral colleges, and in 1800 both sides applied this lesson. No one paid any attention to Hamilton's last-minute plea for Pinckney, and he himself did not dare admit such a design openly. The real enemy for both factions of the party was Jefferson. Adams saw that he could kill Hamiltonian militarism and win votes from Jefferson by the same judicious use of his presidential powers. Finally, by their own admission, Hamiltonians knew they had little hope, because the rank and file of Federalist politicians agreed with Adams and not with them.

Adams attempted to present himself to the voters in 1800 as an independent or third party candidate. Cabot spoke of "two Federal parties" as represented in Congress; the first, loyal to Hamilton, continued to condemn the peace mission, and the second, led by Marshall and Otis, defended it and took immediate action toward ending the recruiting service as Adams had recommended in his message to Congress of December 3.[62] Duane of the *Aurora* noted that Federalists met in two separate caucuses just after the exit of McHenry and Pickering, the "Adamites" at Senator Bingham's home, and the "Pickeronians" at Jacob Read's.[63] Three days after noting this development the Republican editor listed the principal politicians in each of the three parties. John Marshall was listed as a "trimmer" between the Republicans and Adamites, Senator Livermore of New Hampshire as a "trimmer" between Adamites and Pickeronians, and Senator Gunn of Georgia was distinguished as the only "archtrimmer," who attempted to be all things to all men.[64]

April and May were hectic months in Philadelphia. The first session of the 6th Congress was scheduled to run only until May in order that the exodus to the new capital at Washington might be made, and Congress wasted little time on nonessentials. There were only a few weeks before adjournment, and the national election was never more than momentarily beneath the surface of most men's thinking.

The Republicans, whipped into shape by Jefferson him-

[62] Cabot to King, January 20, 1800, King, *Life and Correspondence*, III, 183-184; *Annals*, 6th Congress, 1st Session, 247-252; Jefferson to T. M. Randolph, January 13, 1800, *Jefferson Papers*, LC.

[63] *Aurora*, May 16, 1800.

[64] *Aurora*, May 19, 1800; the "Adamites" listed were Bingham, Dexter, Foster, Howard, Lawrence, Schureman, Wells, Latimer, and Green. Only two, Bingham and Dexter, are familiar; but the "Pickeronians"—Goodhue, Hillhouse, Chipman, Dayton, Lloyd, G. Morris, Payne, Ross, and Tracy—include six veteran legislators.

self, struck with new vigor at Adams' use of presidential authority in turning over to British officials an alleged pirate of doubtful nationality.[65] They made an abortive attempt to repeal the Alien and Sedition Acts and demanded the repeal of laws that created the standing army.[66]

Not to be outdone in the race for public approval, Adams supporters in Congress argued for the termination of recruiting and in co-operation with Republicans they passed legislation releasing officers and men from service in the additional volunteer army as of June 15, 1800.[67] They next took issue with Hamiltonians, who proposed an embargo against France, Henry Lee branding it "an act of the most degrading duplicity,"[68] and Harrison Otis sponsored a National Bankruptcy Act that would lessen legal pressures against debtors.[69] "They are, on the approach of an election, trying to court a little popularity," commented Jefferson dryly. If further proof was needed, he told Madison, a look at their over-all record during the Session would suffice. He noted that when Congress adjourned not "a single strong measure," or repressive measure, had been passed.[70]

From reports that the Boston newspapers printed Fisher Ames's brother could see nothing but electioneering in anything that either Congress or the President had done for

[65] A certain Thomas Nash, wanted for piracy by British naval agents, claimed American citizenship as Jonathan Robbins, born in Danbury, Conn. Adams checked with the Town Clerk at Danbury, who certified that no such name appeared in his files, and ordered the Federal District Court at Charleston to turn Nash over to British custody. A resolution of censure that Edward Livingston sponsored was defeated after John Marshall's speech in Adams' defense. The speech was considered his greatest. Gibbs, *Memoirs*, II, 338-339; Jefferson to Madison, March 4, 1800, *Madison Papers*, LC.

[66] *Annals*, 6th Congress, 1st Session, 522-527, 626; Morison, *Otis*, I, 177-179.

[67] Jefferson to T. M. Randolph, May 14, 1800, *Jefferson Papers*, LC; *Aurora*, June 19, 1800; Hamilton, *Republic*, VII, 367.

[68] Boyd, *Harry Lee*, 264.

[69] *Annals*, 6th Congress, 1st Session, 527, 626.

[70] Jefferson to Randolph, *op. cit.;* to Madison, May 12, 1800.

months. "J. Adams striving to retrieve popularity by disbanding army, etc.," he confided to his diary. "As election approaches Adams turns out Tim Pickering . . . disbands army and seems a while to retract from high-handed explosions against France and Democrats." [71]

Evidently Dr. Ames failed to note that while Congress moved toward the destruction of the standing army Adams was nominating a third Major General, Brookes of Massachusetts, to the provisional army. Jefferson caught the move, however, and saw it as another step toward packing the officer corps with personal friends of the President.[72]

When Adams pardoned the handful of men arrested during the Fries Rebellion in Pennsylvania the *Aurora* classified it as "a palliative intended to operate on the minds of the people at the next election." [73] Representative Bayard of Delaware was half convinced that Adams and Jefferson had come to a secret agreement, so unaccountable did the President's recent actions seem.[74]

While Jefferson gave himself up completely to the task of winning the presidency by collecting and mailing pamphlets to Burr and to Philip Nicholas of Virginia with instructions to use the Virginia Republican committee for placing them in the hands of every county chairman in the state, and by even taking the responsibility for finding John Beckley a new clerkship,[75] Adams took the stump in defense of his record, the first presidential candidate in history to carry his appeal directly to the people.

[71] Warren, *Jacobins and Junto*, 150. The editor dates this entry May 16, 1799, but since Pickering was not dismissed until May, 1800, we may assume an error on the year.

[72] Jefferson to Madison, April 4, 1800, *Jefferson Papers*, LC.

[73] May 30, 1800.

[74] J. A. Bayard to John Rutledge, June 8, 1800, *Bayard Papers*, 111-112.

[75] William Floyd to Jefferson, New York, March 15, 1800, Jefferson to P. N. Nicholas, April 7, 1800, *Jefferson Papers*, LC; Jefferson to Joseph Priestly, January 18, 1800, *Works* (Ford ed.), IX, 95; Thomas McKean to Jefferson, March 7, 1800, *Jefferson Papers*, LC.

Why must the President go fifty miles out of his way to make the trip to Washington, asked the *Aurora* in June? The editor noted that Adams had driven first to Lancaster, where he was seen to receive the plaudits of state officials and other curious onlookers, and from thence to Fredericks-town, Maryland, and on to Washington. After a brief survey Adams had started back again using still a third route since his original trip at the end of May. This time he stopped at both Annapolis and Baltimore, forty unnecessary miles.[76]

From June 11 to June 14 the citizens of Alexandria, Virginia, staged a great celebration in honor of the arrival of the Federal government on the Potomac's shores. The President as guest of honor took advantage of the occasion to display his oratorical powers. How prosperous the upper South had become since he had first visited the region in the dark days of the American Revolution, he declared. Men who had risked everything for independence might be proud of the wealth and happiness of the nation.[77]

In shorter speeches made to small-town audiences between Washington and Philadelphia, Adams was heard speaking constantly of his revolutionary days, of national independence as a worthy object then and now, speaking in defense of his peace program, and pointing out to his listeners that Great Britain once again threatened to use her naval power against neutral American shipping.[78] He would not have the public believe that he was partial to either France or England.

Traveling toward Quincy later in the month Adams paused

[76] *Aurora*, June 8, 1800.

[77] *Aurora*, June 18, 1800; Adams, *Works*, IX, 233.

[78] *Gazette of the United States*, June 12, 1800; Wolcott to Cabot, June 18, 1800, Cabot to Wolcott, June 20, Lodge, *Cabot*, 279-281. Rumors of a new crisis with Britain began to circulate in November, 1799, when it was learned that British cruisers had been authorized to stop U.S. war vessels and ships under their convoy. Ames to Pickering, November 5, 1799, November 23, 1799, Ames, *Works*, I, 264, 270-273.

again at Baltimore to encourage its citizens in voting for men "of integrity of heart," praised the city for its sound political principles as represented by the men elected to Congress and the state legislature, and moved on.[79] "The very affectionate reception and respectable addresses which have everywhere met our venerable and vigilant President has greatly increased the malignity of the Jacobins," commented the *Gazette of the United States*.[80]

The editor of the Jeffersonian *Aurora* noted, on the other hand, that disgruntled Federalists at Newark, New Jersey had arranged no affectionate receptions for Mr. Adams. He made the best of it and was to be seen "walking in the streets in the free and uninterrupted garb of a private citizen," and was reported "to drink punch with Democrats, and to talk of things ordinary and local." [81]

While the pro-Adams press aligned itself with the President in condemning British high-handedness on the seas, and while the Jeffersonian press delightedly circulated an eight-year-old letter that Adams had written concerning British factions and the connection of the Pinckney brothers with them,[82] Adams made his way toward Quincy. Fisher Ames doubted that Adams had convinced many Jeffersonians of his right to a second term by reminding a New London crowd of his distinguished revolutionary services. "He inveighs against the British faction and the Essex Junto like one possessed," Ames testified. The defiant Adams was heard to defend his refusal to issue recruiting orders for the regular army by saying that had Hamilton been allowed free rein it would have taken a second army to disband the first one. Before a large dinner gathering at Faneuil Hall in Boston the

[79] *Aurora*, June 19, 1800.
[80] June 18, 1800.
[81] *Aurora*, July 4, 1800.
[82] *Gazette of the United States*, July 1, 1800; Lodge, *Cabot*, 283.

President raised his glass "To the proscribed patriots Hancock and Sam Adams." [83]

Federalist leaders such as Cabot swore privately and conformed. "Good men," declared Cabot with reference to the Hamiltonians, "have suppressed their true feelings and come out behind the President." George Cabot believed that Adams would certainly get the entire Massachusetts electoral vote despite his references to British sympathies and the Essex Junto, but it seemed equally certain that General Pinckney would do as well on the second ballot.[84] The Boston *Commercial Gazette* asked its readers to support both the President and those candidates who had shown sympathy for his peace policy, all of which added greater weight than ever to the rumor that Adams and Jefferson were secret allies.[85]

When Henry Lee reported that Adams had exploded against the hypocrisy of Federalist leaders and had declared Jefferson a better friend than any of them, there was a general nodding of heads at Hamiltonian gatherings.[86]

By the summer of 1800 a full-scale rebellion against Hamiltonian leadership was underway. Former Governor Thomas Johnson of Maryland sent his best wishes to Adams earlier than most. He was growing more certain all the time that the peace policy would add weight to Federalist chances in November, and a second term would be unavoidable, he told Adams. In the meantime Robert Harper had ended his story of congressional wisdom and had begun a new saga entitled "The Glories of Four Years." Writing to his constituents about the Jeffersonian cry that it was time for a change he

[83] Ames to King, July 15, 1800, King, *Life and Correspondence*, III, 275-276; McMaster, *History*, II, 495.

[84] June 14, 1800, Lodge, *Cabot*, 274 (to Oliver Wolcott).

[85] Reprinted in the *Gazette of The United States*, May 10, 1800.

[86] Boyd, *Harry Lee*, 267; Pickering, "Review," Section III; Cabot to King, May 29, 1800, King, *Life and Correspondence*, III, 249.

asked, "After all, what do these persons expect to gain for the country by a change of administration. . . . What more could any administration have done?" Governor Jay, continuing his correspondence with Theophilus Parsons, praised Adams as a man who had been unduly criticized. "His attachment to the dictates of honour and good faith . . . is amiable and praiseworthy." [87]

Hamilton, despite his faults, had the virtue of extreme frankness. His many biographers have not failed to note his political blunders during the waning days of the 1800 campaign. They have faithfully admitted that he attempted to persuade Governor Jay to maneuver Burr's electoral victory out of existence by recalling the legislature for a last minute change in the electoral laws, and it is generally admitted that his famous pamphlet on the conduct and character of President Adams was a blunder of the highest magnitude. Hamilton's rash behavior in 1800 was produced by a realization that he had been deserted by the rank and file of his party and, what was more important, overlooked by some of those who had hitherto been most outspoken in his defense. Like many powerful political leaders, Hamilton was as deeply concerned over the loss of leadership that he faced within the party as he was over the prospect of losing a national election.

He admitted that he had been overruled to Charles Carroll while urging him to support General Pinckney. Even in New England, Hamilton insisted, "the greater number of strong-minded men" preferred Pinckney to Adams "yet in the body of that people there is a strong personal attachment to that gentleman, and most of the leaders of the second class

[87] Johnson to Adams, April 8, 1800, Adams, *Works*, IX, 48-49; Harper to constituents, May 15, *Bayard Papers*, 107; Jay to Parsons, July 1, 1800, Jay, *Correspondence*, IV, 275. Jay wrote before election day supporting Adams in a personal letter. Three weeks later Adams offered him the Chief Justiceship. Adams, *Works*, IX, 89-91.

are so anxious for his election that it will be difficult to convince them otherwise." [88]

Hamilton's last political junket through New England did little to restore his prestige. "Hamilton has paid us a visit," wrote Joseph Hale of the Essex Junto to Rufus King in July. "Electioneering topics were his principal theme. In his mode of handling them, he did not appear to be the great general which his talents designate him. As November approaches the feelings of parties are excited and displayed not in the most liberal manner by either of the three parties. I am decidedly for the re-election of Mr. Adams; and not withstanding the opinions of men of more weight and intelligence than myself to the contrary, I believe Mr. Adams will be the [successful] candidate." [89]

The electors meeting in December proved Hale a poor prophet, and if we are to believe the standard accounts of the electon of 1800, it was the unpopularity of John Adams that brought the Federalist party to grief.[90]

Adams was defeated, and from this fact a multitude of doubtful conclusions have been drawn. By far the most consequential of these is that the American people had spoken clearly in favor of the democratic way of life and had repudiated the aristocratic, militaristic, and undemocratic policies of Federalism.

While it would be a useless task to portray John Adams as the champion of the democratic faith, it would seem equally impossible to find out whether the American people were thinking in terms of democratic rights or not. If they voted for the man and not the party it would seem that in preferring Jefferson electors to Adams electors the American people chose a President who believed in democracy as

[88] July 1, 1800, K. M. Rowland, *Charles Carroll*, II, 237.

[89] July 11, 1800, King, *Life and Correspondence*, III, 264.

[90] E. M. Sait, *American Parties and Elections*, 4th ed. (New York, 1948), 212; J. A. Woodburn, *Political Parties and Party Problems*, 3d ed. (New York and London, 1924), 31.

a sound form of government instead of one who believed it to be an unstable form of government. Jefferson, however, did not make it clear at the time that he preferred democracy to republicanism, and Adams, for his part, never condemned republican government. He was in perfect agreement with Jefferson that government by consent was the only sane and acceptable government for Americans. There they parted company, but they had both shown devotion to this basic idea since the opening days of the American Revolution.

The Jeffersonians believed that Adams, in his obsession for the theory of checks and balances or, in his terminology, the theory of mixed government, had drifted toward monarchy and aristocracy. They repeatedly accused him of favoring such notions in his voluminous writings. Yet his lifelong interest was in portraying the dangers that arise to republican governments by removing legal checks upon the will to power of the ever-present aristocratic and monarchical elements in society.

The French crisis had given new impetus to the ambitions of the aristocratic faction that followed Hamilton and was clearly not satisfied with the political status they had reached under the Constitution. Through the courts and the use of military power they had hoped to silence the Republican party and to establish their own political supremacy for years to come.

While Adams had no quarrel with the Sedition Act and the use that might be made of the federal courts in enforcing the law, he was deeply and unmistakably opposed to militarism. So long as he used his presidential powers to proclaim the perfidious nature of French diplomacy, to warn his fellow citizens of the need for defense measures, and to win popularity for the Federalist party, the Hamiltonians had rejoiced in the name of Adams; but when he used his executive authority to make peace and to make a return to two-party government inevitable, they denounced him.

Aside from moral considerations, it seeemd that Adams had blundered badly in his handling of French negotiations and that the great schism within the Federalist party was the result of his political maladroitness. It is more reasonable to conclude that the split had been purposely widened and emphasized by the President during 1799 and 1800 after he had concluded that the Hamiltonians would not follow where he had led. It was upon the ability of the voters to understand the cause of this schism and credit him for it that Adams based his hopes for re-election.

It seems highly unlikely that the American electorate was choosing between the underlying political philosophies of Adams and Jefferson when it voted in November, 1800, though this would not have been the case had Adams refused to reveal so dramatically his disdain for the Hamiltonian faction. It seems more likely that the voters were concerned with the record: with the Alien and Sedition Acts, high taxes, the standing army, and the possibility of future peace. Jefferson's election promised better things for America, because he was known to be the antagonist of everything in Federalism that stood for repression; but by the fall of 1800 it was abundantly clear that Adams had risked his political life to stand against the military clique and the prolongation of undeclared war.

"What is the charm which attaches the East so much to Mr. Adams?" asked James A. Bayard of Hamilton a few weeks before election day.[91] Like Sedgwick, Cabot, and Wolcott, who had also been playing a hypocritical game with Adams, Bayard was unable to see that the President's integrity was deeply appreciated, his political troubles at least partially understood, and unable to believe that there might be more than one way of defeating Jefferson.

Federalist leaders were haunted with a fatalistic belief that a Republican triumph was inevitable. There was no need for

[91] August 11, 1800, *Bayard Papers*, 114-115.

it. When pressed to do so they could do battle with the Jeffersonians intelligently and triumphantly. Their resurgence against the Republican party's attacks against the Jay Treaty in 1796 is proof enough that the Federalist party could hold its own using the accepted weapons of political warfare. In the Spring of 1799, more than a year after the first great outburst of indignation against France, Federalism made its first and last successful showing in the South; and it was certainly not the use of either Sedition Act or army that produced this large Federalist vote in such states as North Carolina and Virginia. John Marshall and Henry Lee were elected to Congress at a time when, according to the pro-Jeffersonian accounts of the era, the Alien and Sedition Acts were kindling a flame of resentment against the administration. Why were they elected? Local conditions are always important and may well have played an important part in each of the Federalist victories of that spring canvass, but moderate men supporting the President were able to make sense out of the administration's record. Defense measures had forced France to make peace overtures, and Adams had accepted them as genuine.

Hamiltonians, on the other hand, had so completely convinced themselves that their own program of intimidation was the surest plan for political survival that they came to believe it the only possible plan. Their desire for certain victory led them to overlook the fact that they were the majority party and had a better-than-average chance of winning the election of 1800. Convinced as they were that a Republican victory in the United States would lead to the destruction of all that was good and decent in society, they accused their political opponents of being "Jacobins" and of attempting to subvert the Constitution. It is certain that the plans outlined by Hamilton in his letters to Sedgwick and Dayton in 1799 would have subverted the spirit of that framework far beyond anything that they imagined the Jeffersonians capable of.

The Federalist ticket was defeated in 1800, and from this fact many have concluded that Americans turned their backs upon the past and effected a peaceful revolution. If so, it was the kind of revolution carried out by the men who championed the ratification of the Constitution. Adams ran stronger in 1800 than in 1796 and appears to have been more popular than he had been four years previously.

In the five New England states he was again given a unanimous electoral vote, in the states south of the Delaware he was granted the same electoral vote as in 1796, Pennsylvania and New Jersey delivered six more votes to him, and only New York seemed to have undergone a revolution in political sympathies. This change was brought about by Aaron Burr's cleverness and hard work. By convincing Livingston, Clinton, and Gates to run for the assembly in the spring of 1800, Burr was able to present the people of New York with a ticket as difficult for Hamilton to defeat as was the electoral slate that John Beckley had presented to his Federalist opponents in the Pennsylvania contest of 1796. The margin of Republican victory was less than five hundred votes, nevertheless.[92] When the New York legislature met in the fall the Republican majority selected twelve men pledged to cast their electoral ballots for the Republican candidates, Jefferson and Burr.

While it has been noted that Hamilton had not thrown himself into the spring canvass with his customary vigor,[93] fatigue, preoccupation with his military duties, and the knowledge that he was beaten before he began account for this more satisfactorily than the possibility that he held back out of either apathy or hatred for Adams. His championship of General Pinckney's candidacy and his attempt to recon-

[92] C. A. Beard, *Economic Origins of Jeffersonian Democracy*, 382-387.
[93] Edward Channing, *History*, IV, 237.

vene the old legislature for a change in the electoral method rule out the plausibility of this idea.

The President's deliberate break with the Hamiltonian faction presented only one danger to his chances for re-election—the possibility that Hamilton might be successful in persuading a few Federalist electors to vote for Pinckney and waste their second ballots. Here Adams gambled, pitting his prestige against Hamilton's and counting on the experience of 1796 to weigh more heavily than factional resentment.

The election of 1800 was not a political and moral revolution because Adams had inaugurated the return to responsible government by his peace decision in February 1799. He had closed the wide gap between what the Republican party stood for and what his administration represented by destroying the foundation upon which militarism was being built and by dismissing Pickering, a man who had come to symbolize the fervent anti-Gallicism of the Federalist party.

The election of Jefferson promised that political liberty might be assured of a healthy environment within which to grow, but it did not end the threat to liberty in America of that era. John Adams must be credited with having destroyed the instrument of repression and the influence of its champions months before the election took place. His struggle for independence in 1799 and 1800 was no less significant or remarkable than that in which he had taken a leading part during 1775 and 1776. In a very real sense, Adams' bold conduct allowed Jefferson to say with plausibility, "We are all republicans—we are all federalists."

In many respects Adams was a fitting successor to George Washington: his policies were aimed at preserving national neutrality, though they were carried out with a dramatic touch lacking in Washington's administrations. The balanced view of politics and of human nature that guided John

Adams and the majority of Federalists who followed him was aptly summarized by John Jay in 1796 in a statement which suggests that Federalism was moderate rather than reactionary and not so out of tune with its changing world as Jeffersonian opponents have charged.

"As to political reformation in Europe or elsewhere, I confess that . . . I do not amuse myself with dreams about an age of reason. I am content that little men should be as free as big ones and have and enjoy the same rights, but nothing strikes me as more absurd than projects to stretch little men into big ones, or shrink big men into little ones. . . . We must take men and measures as they are, and act accordingly." [94]

[94] Jay to William Vaughan, May 26, 1796, Jay, *Correspondence*, IV, 216-217.

Appendixes

APPENDIX A

METHODS BY WHICH ELECTORS WERE CHOSEN
1796

1. By legislature: 10 * states casting an electoral vote of		73
	New Hampshire, 6; Vermont, 4; Connecticut, 9; New York, 12; New Jersey, 7; Delaware, 3; North Carolina, 12; South Carolina, 8; Tennessee, 3; Massachusetts, 9.	
2. In districts: 4 * states casting an electoral vote of		42
	Maryland, 10; Virginia, 21; Kentucky, 4; Massachusetts, 7.	
3. By general ticket: 2 states with an electoral vote of		19
	Pennsylvania, 15; Georgia, 4.	
4. By town meeting: Rhode Island casting an electoral vote of		4
	Total	138

* The Massachusetts Constitution of 1781, largely drafted by John Adams, carried the prevailing theory of checks and balances over even into the electoral system. Recognizing two basic divisions in all societies, rich and poor, Adams aimed at preventing control of the electoral machinery by either economic group. The aristocratic or wealthy party was given a proportionate influence in choosing electors through its control of the upper house of the legislature and the democratic or poor party through its control of the lower house and direct elections. This, basically, was the reasoning behind the Massachusetts combination method. See Correa M. Walsh, *The Political Science of John Adams* (New York, 1915), for an analysis of Adams' political philosophy. His own *Works*, especially vol. VI, pp. 280 ff., and vol. IX, 570 ff., are but little more verbose than the commentary.

For a brief discussion of the strong and weak points of the electoral process used in early national times see John Bach McMaster, *History*, II, 306-307. McMaster's figures are in error in two respects. Georgia chose her electors by general ticket and not by means of the legislature. (U. B. Phillips, *Georgia and State Rights*, Washington, 1902, p. 91). Newspaper sources reporting the Virginia returns show that electors were chosen in district contests and not by general ticket as McMaster states. In 1800 Virginia switched.

APPENDIX B

PRESIDENTIAL ELECTORS
1796

Vermont: Elijah Dewey, Elisha Sheldon, J. Bridgman, Oliver Gallup

Massachusetts: Thos. Dawes, Samuel Phillips, E. Bacon, Ebenezer Mattoon, Joseph Allen, Stephen Longfellow, Nathaniel Wells, D. Ressiter, E. Hunt, Wm. Sever, Elijah Man, Elbridge Gerry, Samuel Holten, Thomas Rice, E. H. Robbins, Increase Sumner

Connecticut: Oliver Wolcott, Sr., Jeremiah Wadsworth, Eliezar Goodrich, Elias Perkins, J. Sturges, J. Trumbull, Heman Swift, Wm. Swift, Jesse Root

Rhode Island: Arthur Fenner, Samuel Potter, Wm. Green, George Champlin

New York: Lewis Morris, R. Thorn, Abijah Hammond, Johannes Miller, Jr., P. Cantinejun, R. Van Renssalaer, Abraham Ten Broeck, J. Honeywood, Charles Newkirk, Peter Smith, Wm. Root, A. VanVaghten

New Jersey: William Colfax, Aaron Ogden, Wm. Nielson, Elisha Lawrence, Caleb Newbold, J. Blackwood, Jonathan Rhea

Delaware: R. Basset, T. Robinson, Isaac Cooper

Maryland: J. Plater, Francis Deakins, George Murdock, J. Flynn, Gabriel Duvall, J. Aacher, J. Gilpin, J. Roberts, J. Eccleston, J. Done

Virginia: D. C. Brent, Leven Powell, Josiah Reddick, John Mason, Robt. Walker, Geo. Markham, Nathaniel Wilkinson, M. Hunter, W. C. Nicholas, Benj. Temple, C. Jones, David Saunders, Wm. Terry, Peter Johnston, John Taylor of Caroline, Wm. Madison, Wm. Nimmo, Archibald Stuart, Robt. Crocker, J. Brown, John Bowyer

APPENDIX C

PENNSYLVANIA ELECTORAL COLLEGE CANDIDATES, 1796

Successful candidates for the Pennsylvania electoral college are denoted by an asterisk.

Thomas McKean (Rep.)*	Philadelphia, city and county
Israel Whelen (Fed.)	
Jacob Morgan (Rep.)*	
Samuel Miles (Rep. and Fed.)*	
James Hanna (Rep.)*	Bucks County
Henry Wynkoop (Fed.)	
Jonas Hartsell (Rep.)*	Northampton County
John Arndt (Fed.)	
Joseph Heister (Rep.)*	Berks County
Valentine Eckhart (Fed.)	
Thomas Bull (Fed.)	Chester County
John Whitehill (Rep.)*	Lancaster County
Robert Coleman (Fed.)*	
William Maclay (Rep.)*	Dauphin County
J. Carson (Fed.)	
William Wilson (Fed.)	Northumberland County
William Irvine (Rep.)*	Cumberland County
Samuel Postlewaite (Fed.)	
Jacob Hay (Fed.)	York County
Benjamin Elliot (Fed.)	Huntingdon County
John Smilie (Rep.)*	Fayette County
Ephriam Douglas (Fed.)	
J. Woods (Fed.)	Allegheny County
James Edgar (Rep.)	Washington County
Thomas Stokely (Fed.)	

Abraham Smith (Rep.)*	Franklin County
William Brown (Rep.)*	Mifflin County
J. Piper (Rep.)*	Bedford County
Peter Muhlenberg (Rep.)*	Montgomery County

SOURCES: The Republicans are taken from a list included in John Beckley's letter of September 22, 1796 to General William Irvine, *Irvine Papers,* Historical Society of Pennsylvania, XIII, no. 113. The Federalist or so called "Federal and Republican" ticket was printed in *Claypoole's American Daily Advertiser,* November 4, 1796. Samuel Miles was finally settled upon as Governor Mifflin's replacement on the Republican ticket. Miles had already been selected as a Federalist electoral college candidate. He was elected on both and cast his two ballots for Jefferson and Burr according to *Claypoole's American Daily Advertiser,* November 25, 1796. No last-minute change, however, gave Adams his single electoral vote from Pennsylvania. Robert Coleman of Lancaster County, a strong Federalist district, gave Adams his vote and had been an avowed Adams supporter throughout the campaign. The same was true of the single Adams elector in the state of Virginia, Leven Powell, and apparently the unidentified Adams elector from North Carolina had also been an open Federalist.

APPENDIX D

ELECTORAL VOTES

1796

John Adams: 71 votes		Thomas Jefferson: 68 votes
a. New England, 39		a. New England, 0
New Hampshire	6	
Vermont	4	
Massachusetts	16	
Connecticut	9	
Rhode Island	4	

b. Middle States, 23
New York 12
New Jersey 7
Pennsylvania 1
Delaware 3

c. Upper South, 9
Maryland 7
Virginia 1
North Carolina 1

d. Lower South, 0
South Carolina
Georgia

e. West, 0
Kentucky
Tennessee

b. Middle States, 14
New York 0
New Jersey 0
Pennsylvania 14
Delaware 0

c. Upper South, 35
Maryland 4
Virginia 20
North Carolina 11

d. Lower South, 12
South Carolina 8
Georgia 4

e. West, 7
Kentucky 4
Tennessee 3

Thomas Pinckney: 59 votes

a. New England, 21
New Hampshire 0
Vermont 4
Massachusetts 13
Connecticut 4
Rhode Island 0

b. Middle States, 24
New York 12
New Jersey 7
Pennsylvania 2
Delaware 3

c. Upper South, 6
Maryland 4
Virginia 1
North Carolina 1

d. Lower South, 8
South Carolina 8
Georgia 0

e. West, 0

Aaron Burr: 30 votes

a. New England, 0

b. Middle States, 13
New York 0
New Jersey 0
Pennsylvania 13
Delaware 0

c. Upper South, 10
Maryland 3
Virginia 1
North Carolina 6

d. Lower South, 0
South Carolina
Georgia

e. West, 7

VOTES WASTED BY FEDERALIST ELECTORS, 20

Rhode Island	Oliver Ellsworth	4
Massachusetts	Oliver Ellsworth	1
New Hampshire	Oliver Ellsworth	6
Connecticut	John Jay	5
Massachusetts	Samuel Johnston	2
Maryland	John Henry	2

VOTES WASTED BY REPUBLICAN ELECTORS, 28

Virginia	Samuel Adams	15
Virginia	George Clinton	3
Georgia	George Clinton	4
North Carolina	C. C. Pinckney	1
North Carolina	James Iredell	3
North Carolina	Geo. Washington	1
Virginia	Geo. Washington	1

SOURCE: *Annals*, 4th Congress, 2d Session, 1543-44.

APPENDIX E

CANDIDATES PROPOSED BY WASHINGTON FOR THE SECOND CABINET, 1794–1796

	STATE	WAR
1.	William Paterson New Jersey	C. C. Pinckney South Carolina
2.	C. C. Pinckney South Carolina	Timothy Pickering Massachusetts, Pennsylvania
3.	Thomas Johnson Maryland	John E. Howard Maryland
4.	Patrick Henry Virginia	Edward Carrington Virginia
5.	Rufus King New York	James McHenry Maryland

STATE

6. Timothy Pickering
Massachusetts, Pennsylvania

WAR

TREASURY

1. Oliver Wolcott, Jr.
Connecticut

ATTORNEY GENERAL

John Marshall
Virginia

James Innes
Virginia

Charles Lee
Virginia

This list applies only to men to whom Washington actually sent formal invitations.

Bibliography

UNPUBLISHED MANUSCRIPTS

Library of Congress

Alexander Hamilton Papers, 1st and 2d Series.
Thomas Jefferson Papers.
James Madison Papers.

Historical Society of Pennsylvania

John Adams Letters, 1781–1829.
Benjamin Smith Barton Papers, 1778–1813.
Lewis Beebe Journals, 1776–1801.
Col. Elias Boudinot Papers, 1716–1828.
Aaron Burr Correspondence and Papers, 1774–1833, Gratz Collections.
Matthew Carey Correspondence, 1784–1839, Edward Carey Gardiner Collection.
Chester County Papers, 1684–1847.
Alexander Dallas Papers, 1791–1880.
Thomas Fitzsimons Papers, 1793–1800.
American Government MSS., 1785–1892, Gratz Collections.
William Irvine Papers, 1768–1834.
Thomas McKean Papers, 1759–1847.
Peters MSS., 1792–1807.
Read MSS., 1716–1872.
Thomas Rodney, Journal, 1796–1797.
Rutledge Papers.
Third Administration MSS., Gratz Collections.

New York Historical Society

Albert Gallatin Papers.
John Jay Papers.
Rufus King Papers.
Robert Troup Papers.

New York Public Library

Miscellaneous Papers of Alexander Hamilton, 1775–1803.
James Madison Papers.
James Monroe Papers.
William Patterson Papers, Bancroft Collection.

Princeton University Library

Bache Papers.
Phineas Bond-Richard Stockton Correspondence, 1795–1804.
Elias Boudinot Collection, Correspondence, 1758–1828.
Bradford Papers.
Aaron Burr Correspondence, 1792–1828.
Phillip Freneau-James Madison Correspondence, 1791–1815.

Individual letters:

John Adams to C. J. Ingersoll, July 17, 1812.
Thomas Bradford to Timothy Pickering, n.d.
Elbridge Gerry to his wife, September 18, 1797.
Alexander Hamilton to James McHenry, January, 1799.
Charles C. Pinckney to A. W. White, November, 1798.
Samuel Stanhope Smith to Jonathan Dayton, December, 1801.

PUBLISHED MANUSCRIPTS:

Abigail Adams, *Letters of Mrs. Adams, the Wife of John Adams*, ed. Charles F. Adams, 3d ed., Boston, 1841.

———, *New Letters of Abigail Adams, 1788–1801*, ed. Stewart Mitchell, Boston, 1947.

John Adams, *John Adams-William Cunningham Correspondence, 1803–1812*, Boston, 1823.

———, "John Adams-Mercy Warren Correspondence, July-August, 1807," Massachusetts Historical Society, *Collections*, Ser. 5, vol. IV, 315-511, Boston, 1878.

———, *Correspondence of John Adams and Thomas Jefferson, 1812–1825*, ed. Paul Wilstach, Indianapolis, 1925.

———, *Familiar Letters of John Adams and his Wife*, ed. C. F. Adams, Boston, 1875.

———, *Correspondence of John Adams with Benjamin Waterhouse, 1784–1822*, ed. W. C. Ford, Boston, 1927.

———, *Letters of John Adams to his Wife*, ed. C. F. Adams, Boston, 1841, 2 vols.

———, *The Works of John Adams,* ed. with a *Life* by C. F. Adams, 10 vols., Boston, 1850–1856.

———, "Warren-Adams Letters" (John Adams, Sam Adams, James Warren), Massachusetts Historical Society, *Collections,* vols. 72, 73, Boston, 1925.

———, *Selected Writings of John and John Quincy Adams,* ed. A. Koch and Wm. Peden, New York, 1946.

John Quincy Adams, *Memoirs of John Quincy Adams, 1795–1848,* ed. C. F. Adams, 12 vols., Philadelphia, 1874–1877.

———, *The Writings of John Quincy Adams,* ed. W. C. Ford, 7 vols., New York, 1913.

Samuel Adams, *Writings of Samuel Adams,* ed. H. A. Cushing, 4 vols., New York, 1904–8.

Fisher Ames, *Works of Fisher Ames,* ed. Seth Ames, 2 vols., Boston, 1854.

James A. Bayard, "Papers of James A. Bayard," ed. Elizabeth Donnan, American Historical Association, *Report,* 1913, vol. II, Washington, 1915.

Alexander Biddle, edited for, *Old Family Letters* (John Adams, Thomas Jefferson), 2 vols., Philadelphia, 1892.

Aaron Burr, *Correspondence of Aaron Burr with his Daughter, Theodosia,* ed. Mark Van Doren, New York, 1929.

———, *Memoirs of Aaron Burr,* ed. M. L. Davis, 2 vols., New York, 1858.

———, *Private Journal of Aaron Burr during his Residence of Four Years in Europe,* ed. M. L. Davis, 2 vols., New York, 1858.

———, *Private Journal of Aaron Burr,* ed. W. H. Sampson, Rochester, N. Y., 1903.

Charles Carroll, *Unpublished Letters of Charles Carroll of Carrollton,* ed. T. M. Field, New York, 1902.

William Cobbett, *Cobbett's Political Works,* ed. James P. Cobbett, 6 vols., London, 1837.

Phillip M. Freneau, *Letters on Various Interesting and Important Subjects,* ed. H. H. Clark, New York, 1943.

Albert Gallatin, *Writings of Albert Gallatin,* ed. Henry Adams, 3 vols., Philadelphia, 1879.

Alexander Graydon, *Memoirs of a Life chiefly passed in Pennsylvania,* Harrisburg, 1811.

Alexander Hamilton, *Works of Alexander Hamilton,* ed. J. C. Hamilton, 7 vols., New York, 1851.

———, *Works of Alexander Hamilton*, ed. Henry Cabot Lodge, 12 vols., New York, 1903.

Robert Goodloe Harper, *Select Works of Robert Goodloe Harper*, ed. C. W. Sommerville, Baltimore, 1814.

Patrick Henry, *Life, Correspondence, and Speeches*, ed. W. W. Henry, 3 vols., New York, 1891.

Stephen Higginson, "Letters of Stephen Higginson, 1783–1804," American Historical Association, *Report*, vol. I, 1896.

John Jay, *Correspondence and Public Papers of John Jay*, ed. H. P. Johnston, 4 vols., New York and London, 1890–93.

Thomas Jefferson, *Writings of Thomas Jefferson*, ed. P. L. Ford, 10 vols., New York, 1905.

———, *Writings of Thomas Jefferson*, ed. A. A. Lipscomb, 20 vols., Washington, 1903.

Rufus King, *Life and Correspondence of Rufus King*, ed. C. R. King, 6 vols., New York, 1894–1900.

James Madison, *Writings of James Madison*, ed. Gaillard Hunt, 9 vols., New York, 1900–1910.

———, *Letters and Other Writings of James Madison*, 4 vols., Congress edition, Philadelphia, 1865.

John Marshall, *An Autobiographical Sketch*, ed. J. S. Adams, University of Michigan Press, 1937.

Bernard Mayo, ed., "Instruction to the British Ministers to the United States, 1791–1812," American Historical Association, *Report*, 1936, vol. III, Washington, 1941.

Gouverneur Morris, *Diary and Letters of Gouverneur Morris*, ed. Anne C. Morris, 2 vols., London, 1889.

J. D. Richardson, ed., *Messages and Papers of the Presidents*, 20 vols., New York, 1897.

Benjamin Rush, *The Letters of Benjamin Rush*, ed. L. H. Butterfield, 2 vols., American Philosophical Society, 1951.

William L. Smith, "Letters of William Loughton Smith," *South Carolina Historical and Genealogical Magazine*, April, 1924–January, 1925.

Jared Sparks, ed., *Correspondence of the American Revolution*, 4 vols., Boston, 1853.

Richard Stockton, "Letters from Richard Stockton to John Rutherford in 1798," New Jersey Historical Society, *Proceedings*, 2d Series, vol. 3, Newark, 1874.

William Sullivan, *Familiar Letters on Public Characters and Public Events*, Boston, 1834.

Frederick J. Turner, ed., "Correspondence of the French Ministers to the United States, 1791–1797," American Historical Association, *Report*, 1913, vol. II, Washington, 1904.

George Washington, *The Writings of George Washington*, ed. J. C. Fitzpatrick, 38 vols., Washington, 1939–44.

———, *The Diaries of George Washington, 1748–1799*, ed. J. C. Fitzpatrick, 4 vols., Boston and New York, 1925.

John Cleves Symmes, *The Correspondence of John Cleves Symmes*, ed. B. W. Bond, Jr., New York, 1926.

Samuel Blachley Webb, *Correspondence and Journals of Samuel Blachley Webb*, ed. W. C. Ford, 3 vols., New York, 1894.

———, *Annals of Congress (Debates and Proceedings of the Congress of the United States)*, 1st–18th Congresses, 42 vols., Washington, 1834–1856.

NEWSPAPERS AND PAMPHLETS:

Argus, New York.

Aurora and General Advertiser, Philadelphia.

Claypoole's American Daily Advertiser, Philadelphia.

Columbian Mirror, Alexandria, Virginia.

Columbian Museum, Savannah, George.

Connecticut Gazette, New London, Connecticut.

Gazette of the United States, Philadelphia.

Greenleaf's New York Journal, New York.

Independent Chronicle, Boston.

Maryland Gazette, Annapolis, Maryland.

Benjamin F. Bache, "Remarks occasioned by the Late Conduct of Mr. Washington as President of the U. S." Philadelphia, 1797.

———, "Truth Will Out: the foul charges of the Tories against the Editor of the Aurora Repelled," Philadelphia, 1798.

John James Beckley, "Address to the People of the United States; with an Epitome and Vindication of the Public Life of Thomas Jefferson," Philadelphia, 1800.

James Cheetham, "An Answer to Alexander Hamilton's Letter concerning the Public Conduct and Character of John Adams," New York, 1800.

———, "A Narrative of the Suppression by Col. Burr of the History of the Administration of John Adams . . . with Strictures on the Conduct of John Adams and on the Character of Gen. C. C. Pinckney," New York, 1802.

William Cobbett, "A New Year's Gift to the Democrats, or Observations on . . . 'A Vindication of Mr. Randolph's Resignation'" (by Peter Porcupine), Philadelphia, 1796.

Tench Coxe, "The Federalist: a reply to William L. Smith's 'The Pretensions of Thomas Jefferson to the Presidency,'" Philadelphia, 1796.

———, "A View of the United States of America," Philadelphia, 1794.

William Findley, "History of the Insurrection in the Four Western Counties of Pennsylvania," Philadelphia, 1796.

Alexander Hamilton, "Letter from Alexander Hamilton concerning the Public Conduct and Character of John Adams, Esq., President of the United States," New York, 1800.

———, "Observations on Certain Documents contained in No. V and VI of 'The History of the United States for the Year 1796,'" Philadelphia, 1800.

Robert G. Harper, "Address . . . Containing his Reasons for Approving the Treaty . . . with Great Britain," Philadelphia, 1795.

———, "Observations on the Dispute between the United States and France," Philadelphia, 1797.

———, "Short Account of the Principal Proceedings of Congress in the Late Session," Philadelphia, 1798.

James Madison, "Letters of Helvidius," Philadelphia, 1796.

James Monroe, "A View of the Conduct of the Executive in the Foreign Affairs of the United States, during the Years 1794–1796," Philadelphia, 1797.

Timothy Pickering, "A Review of the Correspondence between the Hon. John Adams, late President of the United States, and the late William Cunningham, esq.," Salem, Mass., 1824.

Charles C. Pinckney, "The American Remembrancer" (speeches relating to the Jay treaty), Philadelphia, 1795.

Edmund Randolph, "A Vindication of Mr. Randolph's Resignation," Philadelphia, 1795.

William L. Smith, "The Pretensions of Thomas Jefferson to the Presidency Examined; and the late Charges against John Adams Refuted" (assisted by Oliver Wolcott, Jr.), Philadelphia, 1796.

Noah Webster, "The Prompter; A Commentary on Common Sayings and Subjects," Philadelphia, 1796.

John Wood, "A History of the Administration of John Adams," New York, 1802.

SECONDARY SOURCES:

American Political History and Problems of American Politics:

John Q. Adams, *Parties in the United States*, New York, 1941.

Extremely critical of President Jefferson. "The administration of Mr. Jefferson was professedly an administration of reform . . . he in truth reformed nothing" (p. 33). Discerning on the reasons for the collapse of the Federalists.

Charles A. Beard, *The American Party Battle*, New York, 1928.

———, *Economic Origins of Jeffersonian Democracy*, New York, 1915.

Beard explains the collapse of the Federalists as due to their short-sightedness in passing enough unpopular legislation—Sedition Act, direct taxes, Jay Treaty—to swing the balance of power against themselves.

Charles A. and Mary Beard, *The Rise of American Civilization*, revised edition, New York, 1942.

Samuel F. Bemis, ed., *The American Secretaries of State and Their Diplomacy*, vol. II, New York, 1927.

———, *Jay's Treaty*, New York, 1923.

The author concludes that it was remarkable that Britain would sign any kind of a treaty with a weak power and that considering U.S. dependence upon British commerce, Jay was not so great a failure after all.

Samuel F. Bemis, *Pinckney's Treaty*, Johns Hopkins University Press, 1926. Confined entirely to a study of Spanish American relations, 1783–1796.

Andrew J. Bethea, *The Contribution of Charles Pinckney to the Formation of the American Union*, Richmond, 1937.

Beverly W. Bond, *The Monroe Mission to France, 1794–1796*, Johns Hopkins University Press, 1907.

Claude G. Bowers, *Jefferson and Hamilton*, Boston and New York, 1925.

Unfortunately, still a standard interpretation of the politics of the 1790's. Highly imaginative, biased in Jefferson's favor, and erroneous in detail. Bowers vastly overrates the political consciousness of the average man in this era by taking Bache's editorials at face value, a mistake made by no one living at the time. Bowers is one of those who has established the legend that Jefferson's brain was behind every Republican party maneuver from 1792 to 1800, but he can cite little to prove it.

Clarence S. Brigham, *History and Bibliography of American Newspapers, 1690–1820*, 2 vols., Worcester, Mass., 1947.

Edward Channing, *A History of the United States*, vol. IV, New York, 1917.

Joseph Charles, *The Origins of the American Party System*, Williamsburg, 1956.

Gilbert Chinard, *The Commonplace Book of Thomas Jefferson*, Johns Hopkins University Press, 1926.

———, *The Literary Bible of Thomas Jefferson*, Johns Hopkins University Press, 1928.

Moncure D. Conway, *Omitted Chapters of History Disclosed in the Life and Papers of Edmund Randolph*, New York and London, 1888.

Randolph, according to the author, was the victim of Fauchet's mistrust, Pickering's hatred, and Wolcott's pro-British bias.

Theodore W. Cousens, *Politics and Political Organizations*, New York, 1942.

Merle Curti, *The Growth of American Thought*, New York and London, 1943.

Curti maintains that Adams is a far more reliable exponent of Federalism than Hamilton, because Adams was more balanced in his thinking. Federalism was the result of the reaction in America against the Enlightenment.

Arthur B. Darling, *Our Rising Empire, 1763–1803*, Yale University Press, 1940.

This is one of the few recent books to accept the idea that Federalism had hidden within it a large dose of militarism. Darling views Adams as an intelligent and discerning diplomatist during the French crisis.

Manning J. Dauer, *The Adams Federalists*, Johns Hopkins University Press, 1953. A scholarly analysis of Federalist failure during the Adams administration.

John Davis, *Travels of Four Years and a Half in the United States of America, 1798–1802*, New York, 1902.

Louise B. Dunbar, *A Study of Monarchical Tendencies in the United States, 1776–1801*, University of Illinois Studies in the Social Sciences, vol. X, no. 1, 1922.

Henry J. Ford, *Washington and His Colleagues*, Yale University Press, 1918, Chronicles of American Series, vol. XIV.

George Gibbs, *Memoirs of the Administrations of Washington and*

John Adams, edited from the Papers of Oliver Wolcott, 2 vols., New York, 1846.

As a history of the 1790's Gibbs' work is ludicrous, but as a source collection of the letters of the chief Federalists it is invaluable. This is probably the most important collection of published letters on the Federalist side.

Hugh B. Grigsby, *History of the Virginia Federal Convention of 1788* (Collections of The Virginia Historical Society), new series, IX, X, Richmond, 1890.

John C. Hamilton, *History of the Republic of the United States of America as traced in the Writings of Alexander Hamilton*, 6 vols., 2d ed., Philadelphia, 1864.

A more partisan defense of Hamilton than Hamilton himself would have written. Adams, Jefferson, and Burr were the agents of America's doom according to the author. Valuable source material.

Zoltan Haraszti, *John Adams and the Prophets of Progress*, Harvard University Press, 1952.

Mr. Adams argued with the European philosophes and emerged one of the outstanding philosophes of the age of Enlightenment, in the editor's opinion.

Homer C. Hockett, *Western Influences on Political Parties to 1825*, Ohio State University Press, 1917.

Constant struggles, chiefly economic, between Piedmont and seaboard shaped our first political parties.

Richard Hofstadter, *The American Political Tradition and the Men Who Made It*, New York, 1949.

According to Hofstadter, the differences between Federalists and Republicans were mostly campaign noise and "boiled down to a very modest minimum when Jefferson took office" (p. ix).

Isaac Jenkinson, *Aaron Burr, His Personal Political Relations with Thomas Jefferson and Alexander Hamilton*, Richmond, Indiana, 1902.

Merrill Jensen, *The New Nation*, New York, 1950.

Adams was the hero of the French negotiations at the end of the Revolutionary War as Jensen sees it. Adams a strong nationalist and as such, a good Federalist.

Allen Johnson, *Jefferson and His Colleagues; a Chronicle of the Virginia Dynasty*, Yale University Press, 1921.

Adrienne Koch, *Jefferson and Madison, the Great Collaboration*, New York, 1950.

This recent study covers the same ground as does Irving Brant in the third volume of his James Madison biography but nowhere nearly as well. A well-written account of a great friendship and partnership.

Henry B. Learned, *The President's Cabinet*, Yale University Press, 1912.

Eugene P. Link, *Democratic-Republican Societies, 1790–1800*, Columbia University Press, 1942.

Extremely valuable.

Henry Cabot Lodge, *Historical and Political Essays* (Madison and Gouverneur Morris), Boston and New York, 1892.

George D. Luetscher, *Early Political Machinery in the United States*, Philadelphia, 1903.

This is a valuable study, scholarly and concise. The author believed that the Federalists lost power because, unlike the Jeffersonians, they did not build their organization on the firm foundation of local politics but depended instead upon Federal officeholders to carry national tickets and policies. The work concentrates upon Pennsylvania and Delaware. He overlooks the fact that New York, Massachusetts, New Jersey and Connecticut had strong local organizations and that Washington and Hamilton both attempted to build up local machines in Maryland and Virginia without success. Adams in his appointments would seem to have been equally alerted to the problem.

William O. Lynch, *Fifty Years of Party Warfare, 1789–1834*, Indianapolis, 1931.

Weak on the early period up to 1800.

Charles H. McIlwain, Roy F. Nichols, and Roscoe Pound, *Federalism as a Democratic Process*, Rutgers University Press, 1942.

Three suggestive and mature essays on the nature of the Federal compact and the political problems with which it uniquely confronted the nation.

John Bach McMaster, *A History of the American People from the Revolution to the Civil War*, vol. II, New York, 1895.

McMaster's treatment of the 1790's is based primarily upon newspaper sources so far as politics is concerned (see especially pp. 321-356). On the whole, favorable to the Federalists.

Charles E. Merriam, *The American Party System*, New York, 1923.

John C. Miller, *Crisis in Freedom; the Alien and Sedition Acts*, Boston, 1951.

This was the best study of the subject until the appearance

of Smith's, *Freedom's Fetters* in 1956. Miller, however, places undue emphasis upon the Sedition Act as the issue that brought Jefferson to power. He mentions the army and direct taxes as important considerations but underestimates their significance in splitting the Federalist party and antagonizing New England. Jefferson's testimony is clear on this point: he believed a standing army and direct taxes the vital campaign issues of 1798 to 1800 and acted accordingly.

Meade Minnigerode, *Jefferson, Friend of France*, New York, 1928.

———, *Presidential Years, 1787–1860*, New York and London, 1928.

Overestimates the power of Hamilton in directing the political destinies of the Federalist party.

Lynn Montross, *Reluctant Rebels*, New York, 1950.

Gustavus Myers, *History of Tammany Hall*, New York, 1917.

Allan Nevins, *American States during and after the American Revolution, 1775–1789*, New York, 1925.

Excellent discussion of Adams' political philosophy.

Samuel P. Orth, *Five American Politicians: Burr, D. Clinton, Clay, Van Buren, Douglas*, Cleveland, 1906.

Victor H. Paltsits, *Washington's Farewell Address*, New York, 1925.

G. H. Payne, *History of Journalism in the United States*, New York, 1920.

John H. Powell, *Bring Out Your Dead*, University of Pennsylvania Press, 1950.

A marvelously drawn picture of a city caught in the grip of the yellow fever.

Wesley E. Rich, *The History of the U.S. Post Office*, Harvard University Press, 1924, Harvard Economic Studies, vol. XXVII.

Edward M. Sait, *American Parties and Elections*, 4th ed., New York, 1948.

James Schouler, *History of the United States of America*, rev. ed., 6 vols., New York, 1894.

Norman J. Small, *Some Presidential Interpretations of the Presidency*, Johns Hopkins University Press, 1932, Johns Hopkins University Studies in History and Political Science.

James Morton Smith, *Freedom's Fetters*, Cornell University Press, 1956.

The most scholarly analysis of the Alien and Sedition Acts to appear.

Edward Stanwood, *A History of the Presidency, 1788 to 1897*, Boston, 1898.

Kenneth Unbreit, *Founding Fathers*, New York, 1941.

Martin Van Buren, *Inquiry into the Origin and Course of Political Parties in the United States*, ed. S. T. Van Buren, New York, 1867.

A keen analysis of the growth of parties from the colonial period, a growth that Van Buren recognized as continuous.

Herman Von Holst, *Constitutional and Political History of the United States*, vol. I, Chicago, 1889.

Correa M. Walsh, *The Political Science of John Adams*, New York, 1915.

This detailed study of Adams' often misunderstood political philosophy is poorly written and overly scholarly. There are more concise and readable expositions of his ideas in both Allan Nevins, *American States during and after the Revolution*, pp. 121-179, and in *John Adams and the Prophets of Progress*, chap. III.

Charles Warren, ed., *Jacobins and Junto, the Diary of Dr. Nathaniel Ames*, Harvard University Press, 1931.

Fisher Ames and his brother violently differed on political matters. Nathaniel wasted no words in defense of Massachusetts Federalists.

Arthur P. Whitaker, *The Mississippi Question, 1795–1803*, New York, 1934.

Professor Whitaker views the French crisis of 1798 and 1799 as a Hamiltonian pretext to seize the Spanish borderlands.

Leonard D. White, *The Federalists, a Study in Administrative History*, New York, 1948.

An excellent study of administrative problems. Especially useful in the preparation of Chapters IX and X.

Woodrow Wilson, *A History of the American People*, vol. III, "The Founding of the Government," New York and London, 1903.

Wilson presents the view that many of the founding fathers looked upon the Federal government as an unpromising experiment and much preferred state positions. Wilson is, therefore, more sympathetic with the Federalists than his own political philosophy would lead us to suspect.

James A. Woodburn, *Political Parties and Party Problems in the United States*, 3d ed., New York and London, 1924.

Woodburn did not believe the Federalists and Anti-Federalists to be the first American parties, because important leaders such as Madison and Henry so quickly changed their allegiance to them. Adams is portrayed as a most unpopular President.

Sectional and Local Politics, 1789–1800:

James T. Adams, *New England in the Republic, 1776–1860*, Boston, 1926.

Based upon earlier secondary sources.

DeAlva S. Alexander, *A Political History of the State of New York*, 3 vols., New York, 1906–1909.

Charles H. Ambler, *Sectionalism in Virginia, 1776–1861*, Chicago, 1910.

Chapter III deals with the period from 1790 to 1816 and is important in describing the reasons for unrest and Federalism in the Shenandoah Valley while Jeffersonians dominated the State.

Walter R. Fee, *Transition from Aristocracy to Democracy in New Jersey, 1789–1829*, Somerville, N. J., 1933.

Dixon R. Fox, *Decline of Aristocracy in the Politics of New York*, Columbia University Studies in History, Economics, and Public Law, vol. LXXXVI, no. 198, New York, 1919.

An exceptionally clear description of the defeat of aristocratic eighteenth-century political mores from 1801 to 1840.

Jabez D. Hammond, *History of Political Parties in the State of New York from 1788 to 1840*, 2 vols., Albany, 1842.

An early classic in state politics, unfortunately out of print. Lacking in footnotes, much of what Hammond says must be taken at face value.

Irving S. Kull, *et al.*, *New Jersey, a History*, 4 vols., New York, 1931.

Francis B. Lee, *New Jersey, Colony and State*, 4 vols., New York, 1902.

Robert M. McElroy, *Kentucky in the Nation's History*, New York, 1909.

This is one of the better state histories, but it is very sketchy on the early period and touches only the high points.

John W. Moore, *History of North Carolina*, Raleigh, 1880.

Forrest Morgan, *et al.*, *Connecticut, as a Colony and as a State*, 4 vols., Hartford, 1904.

Descendants of Connecticut Federalists would seem to have sponsored the publication of this work. The anti-Jeffersonian, antidemocratic bias is evident.

Anson E. Morse, *Federalist Party in Massachusetts to 1800*, Princeton University Press, 1909.

An exceptionally valuable study. Professor Morse concluded years before Turner's thesis gained recognition that the frontier did not necessarily inculcate a democratic political philosophy. For the most part, New England frontiersmen were Federalists and conservative during the early national period. Shays's Rebellion seems to have turned the farmers against radicalism and the fact that the Republican movement, when it did take hold, was centered in the larger towns of the seaboard, seems to have kept the frontier loyal to the Federalist party.

William A. Robinson, *Jeffersonian Democracy in New England*, Yale University Press, 1916.

There was not much evidence of Jeffersonian democracy in New England until after 1798. The cause of its sudden development, according to Robinson, was the unpopularity of the war measures of the 5th Congress, the direct tax, and the standing army. Robinson did not find the Alien and Sedition Acts of much importance in New England.

John T. Scharf, *History of Delaware*, 2 vols., Philadelphia, 1888.

John T. Scharf and Thompson Wescott, *History of Philadelphia, 1609–1884*, 3 vols., Philadelphia, 1884.

Yates Snowden, et al., *History of South Carolina*, 5 vols., Chicago and New York, 1920.

A better than average state history, poorly arranged.

R. J. Taylor, *Western Massachusetts in the Revolution*, Brown University Press, 1954.

H. M. Tinkcom, "Political Behavior in Pennsylvania, 1790–1801," University of Pennsylvania Doctoral Dissertation, 1948.

A close analysis of political events and their underlying causes in Pennsylvania. The author was greatly impressed by the skill and hard work that went into the Republican campaign of 1796. The fact that Federalists took too much for granted and did not worry about getting out the vote is emphasized. The important gubernatorial contest of 1799, McKean vs. Ross, is well analyzed, a contest that ended Federalist domination of the state government once and for all.

Secondary sources: biographical

James T. Adams, *The Adams Family*, Boston, 1930

———, *The Living Jefferson*, New York, 1936.

Readable and, as a short, one-volume life, sound scholarship. Adams accepted the idea that the Federal army of 1798–1799 was meant for repression.

Henry Adams, *The Life of Albert Gallatin*, Philadelphia and London, 1880.

This biography could almost be placed among primary sources, so filled is it with quotations from Gallatin's papers. The period dealing with the 1790's is disappointing, because Gallatin's connections with state politics are passed over in silence. The book is far below the standards of his history in style.

Dice R. Anderson, *William Branch Giles: a Study in the Politics of Virginia and the Nation, 1790–1830*, Nenasha, Wisconsin, 1914.

Valuable for excerpts from Giles's papers and sounder on Virginia politics than on national.

James T. Austin, *The Life of Elbridge Gerry*, Boston, 1829.

Gerry held the key to much that occurred in Adams' administration, and a detailed biography of him is certainly needed. It would explain much that is taken for granted. Obviously the Essex Junto was powerful in Massachusetts, but it is also clear that there was a strong core of pro-Adams sentiment entirely dissociated from the dominant Hamiltonian clique. Who these men were and how they organized themselves in 1796 and especially in 1800 remains a mystery. Gerry remained steadfast to Adams and was extremely powerful in local politics. His papers, now in private hands, would reveal much about the great peace decision of 1799 and its political undertones. This early work is fragmentary but contains several extremely valuable letters.

William Barton, *Memoirs of the Life of David Rittenhouse*, Philadelphia, 1813.

Nothing on his political affiliations.

Albert J. Beveridge, *Life of John Marshall*, 4 vols., Boston and New York, 1916–19.

While Beveridge's biography has always been held up as one of the best in our historical literature, it is nonetheless highly biased against the Jeffersonians. Marshall's role in the Virginia Federalist organization is exaggerated: there was a long period during which he was well out of its activities.

Elias Boudinot, *The Life, Public Services, Addresses, and Letters of Elias Boudinot*, ed. J. J. Boudinot, 2 vols., Boston and New York, 1896.

This library of Boudinot papers contains very little political information but gives biographical data on several important men about whom our information is scant; William Bradford, Samuel Bayard (of Delaware), and Senator Richard Stockton.

Catherine Drinker Bowen, *John Adams and the American Revolution*, Boston, 1950.

Thomas A. Boyd, *Light-horse Harry Lee*, New York, 1931.

Henry Lee was a fascinating and tragic figure in our early history. He deserves a more detailed and painstaking study than this.

Irving Brant, *James Madison, Father of the Constitution, 1787–1800*, New York, 1950.

This work has been extremely useful. Brant traces Madison's connection with the Republican party accurately and intelligently. His claim that Madison made a far greater contribution to the organization of the Republican national party than historians have hitherto recognized seems fully justified. Too much credit for work that Madison and other leaders inaugurated and carried out has been granted to Jefferson, according to the author. Jefferson's retirement from politics from 1794 to 1797 was real and not apparent. The crucial test of the early party was the Jay Treaty fight, and Jefferson took almost no part in it. Madison was House majority leader. Brant's biography promises to be one of our best and should add up to a revealing portrait of the early Jeffersonians or Madisonians.

Noah Brooks, *Henry Knox*, New York and London, 1900.

William G. Brown, *The Life of Oliver Ellsworth*, New York, 1905.

Lacking in background—Ellsworth lived, worked, and thought in too much of a political vacuum according to this otherwise adequate biography.

Edward H. Brush, *Rufus King and His Times*, New York, 1926.

No sources cited, written almost entirely from King's papers.

Mellen Chamberlain, *John Adams, Statesman of the American Revolution, with other essays*, Boston and New York, 1899.

Adams was a patriot but no politician, according to this abbreviated version of his life. The author concentrates on his revolutionary activities.

Gilbert Chinard, *Honest John Adams*, Boston, 1933.

An excellent study in many respects. Dr. Chinard has attempted to understand the man and not his politics. Adams, he maintains, was a genuine conservative, with the instincts and virtues of the agrarian, and also a man with the deepest sense of independence. The chapters dealing with Adams's political philosophy and European experience are excellent.

———, *Thomas Jefferson, Apostle of Americanism*, Boston, 1929.

A well-written and thoughtful presentation of Mr. Jefferson as one of America's most representative figures as well as one of her most distinguished. This work is weak on Jefferson as a political leader and is based too much on his papers and published works.

William P. Cresson, *James Monroe*, University of North Carolina Press, 1946.

George M. Dallas, *Life and Writings of Alexander J. Dallas*, Philadelphia, 1871.

William E. Dodd, *Life of Nathaniel Macon*, Raleigh, N. C., 1903.

Excellent material on early North Carolina political history.

Francis S. Drake, *Life and Correspondence of Henry Knox*, Boston, 1873.

Bernard Fay, *The Two Franklins, Fathers of American Democracy*, Boston, 1933.

Poorly documented, popular account of the lives of Benjamin Franklin and Benjamin Franklin Bache.

John C. Fitzpatrick, *George Washington*, Indianapolis, 1933.

Valuable for little-known sidelights on the career of Washington. Fitzpatrick certainly knew our first President well.

Edward Ford, *David Rittenhouse, Astronomer-Patriot*, University of Pennsylvania Press, 1946.

Henry J. Ford, *Alexander Hamilton*, New York, 1920.

Hopelessly biased in Hamilton's favor. Every situation where doubts might be entertained over Hamilton's wisdom or patriotism is decided as Hamilton might have seen it. Ford pictures Hamilton standing up for Henry Knox's right to outrank him in 1798.

Paul L. Ford, *The True George Washington*, Philadelphia, 1897.

An attempt to let Washington speak for himself and to "humanize" the august figure. Not entirely successful.

Worthington C. Ford, *George Washington*, 2 vols., New York, 1900.

Unfortunately, this valuable work is only to be found in rare book rooms. In many respects it is the best history of Washington's life and times that has yet been completed. Ford attributed much of Jefferson's political opposition to Jefferson's exaggerated fears of royalty in America. Ford suggests that

Jefferson often saw what he wanted to see and not what was the truth of the situation.

Samuel E. Forman, *The Political Activities of Philip Freneau*, Johns Hopkins University. Studies in Historical and Political Science, Johns Hopkins University Press, 1902.

Daniel C. Gilman, *James Monroe*, Boston, 1898.

Allan M. Hamilton, *The Intimate Life of Alexander Hamilton*, New York, 1910.

John C. Hamilton, *Life of Alexander Hamilton*, 2 vols., New York, 1840.

William B. Hatcher, *Edward Livingston*, Louisiana State University Press, 1940.

A well-deserved study of one of the more important Jeffersonians; brief on Livingston's early career.

Charles D. Hazen, *Contemporary American Opinion of the French Revolution*, Johns Hopkins University Press, 1897.

Valuable for the intellectual side of Jeffersonianism.

Thomas W. Higginson, *The Life and Times of Stephen Higginson*, Boston, 1907.

As a biography this is second-rate, but the few letters reproduced are valuable. Spotty.

Helen Hill, *George Mason*, Harvard University Press, 1938.

Charles H. Hunt, *Life of Edward Livingston*, New York, 1864.

Gaillard Hunt, *Life of James Madison*, New York, 1902.

William Jay, *The Life of John Jay*, New York, 1833.

Biased, spotty, and outdated. The author refused to admit the truth of Hamilton's suggestion for changing the electoral laws in 1800 after Burr's ticket had carried the state.

Lewis G. Leary, *That Rascal Freneau*, Rutgers University Press, 1941.

A good biography, well written and scholarly. Little information on Freneau's party activities, however.

Henry Cabot Lodge, *Alexander Hamilton*, Boston and New York, 1910.

———, *Life and Letters of George Cabot*, Boston, 1877.

The letters published here are an extremely valuable source of information regarding the Massachusetts Federalist organization in the 1790's.

David G. Loth, *Alexander Hamilton, Portrait of a Prodigy*, New York, 1939.

Very little new light was shed on Hamilton's career in this

rather recent study. Loth portrays an absurd relationship between Washington and Hamilton: Washington is pictured as taking secret pleasure from Hamilton's outbursts of ego and disrespect.

———, *Chief Justice; John Marshall and the Growth of the American Republic*, New York, 1949.

Albert Beveridge's older biography is still to be preferred for scholarship. Loth writes well.

Dumas Malone and Allen Johnson, editors, *The Dictionary of American Biography*, 20 volumes.

Dumas Malone, *Jefferson and His Time*, Boston, 1948.

Excellent, but not meant as a history of Jefferson's political activities.

John Marshall, *Life of George Washington*, 5 vols., Philadelphia, 1807.

The fifth volume of this edition covers the years 1783 to 1799 and is more a constitutional history of the United States than a life of Washington.

James F. McLaughlin, *Matthew Lyon*, New York, 1900.

Valuable for sources, but a new biography on this ridiculous New England democrat would be worthwhile. The attempt on the part of historians loyal to the Jeffersonian ideals to portray Lyon as a diamond in the rough seems absurd. It was the zeal of Federalist judges that made him an important figure and not anything that he himself did. His salivary encounter with Congressman Griswold is a possible exception.

Griffin J. McRee, *Life and Correspondence of James Iredell*, 2 vols., New York, 1857–58.

An extremely worthwhile source of information on Federalist measures and men. Iredell was a devout Federalist but not so violent and cynical in his thinking as many. His comments on political matters are usually colored but rarely vindictive. He was one of the few Federalists who viewed the brief Adams-Jefferson Entente of 1797 with pleasure.

John C. Miller, *Sam Adams, Pioneer in Propaganda*, Boston, 1936.

A lively and valuable one-volume biography of the man who early in our history learned and taught the methods of modern electioneering.

Frank Monaghan, *John Jay*, New York and Indianapolis, 1935.

Samuel E. Morison, *Life and Letters of Harrison Gray Otis, Federalist*, 2 vols., Boston and New York, 1913.

This is an outstanding work in several respects. It may not

represent great historical writing, but the letters and biography are excellently written and chosen. Otis, as one of the few Hamiltonians who swung over to Adams in 1799, was a key figure in the last crucial years of Federalist control. He represents both the healthy and the unhealthy elements of the party, a man somewhat uncomfortable in what was rapidly becoming a democratic society.

John T. Morse, *John Adams*, American Statesmen Series, Boston, 1884.

Morse well understood Adams as a political figure. "He was not in the modern sense of the phrase . . . a party man; he acted beneath no sense of allegiance, in obedience to no bond of political fellowship. . . . Certainly he had not the hearty or undivided support of any party" (p. 250).

Eugene Tenbroeck Mudge, *The Social Philosophy of John Taylor of Caroline*, Columbia University Press, 1939.

Taylor deserves attention by modern scholars both as a philosopher and a political advisor of Jefferson. Mudge has paraphrased his works and added about one hundred letters to the result. He did not fit Taylor's thought into an intellectual climate or appear to study the corresponding ideas of Taylor's contemporaries. The author correctly recognized John Adams as Taylor's best American antagonist, but he did not familiarize himself with Adams' works. He thus speaks of Adams' *defense of the Constitution of Government of the U.S.* and not of the *Defense of the Constitutions of Government* of all the states of the Union.

Curtis P. Nettels, *George Washington and American Independence*, Boston, 1951.

Professor Nettels has dared to say that George Washington understood and practiced the art of politics with considerable skill, a point of view that my own studies have led me heartily to endorse. By his acts as commander of the army in 1775 and 1776 the General made the act of declaring independence all the more inescapable, and he did so, says Nettels, fully understanding the implications of his actions. Though the author does not specifically state that he has set out to make Washington appear human and comprehensible, he has taken an important step toward doing just that.

Claude M. Newlin, *Life and Writings of Hugh Henry Brackenridge*, Princeton University Press, 1932.

Brackenridge played an important part in both the Whiskey

Rebellion and the Jay Treaty fight in western Pennsylvania. Newlin sheds considerable new light on his activities in connection with both.

Albert J. Nock, *Jefferson*, New York, 1926.

Reliable, good for an accurate description of his many-sided interests and activities.

Saul K. Padover, *Jefferson*, New York, 1942.

An interpretation of Jefferson's political career as a great crusade for human liberties by a modern liberal.

James Parton, *The Life and Times of Aaron Burr*, New York, 1858.

This, one of our earliest biographies, is excellent in style and useful for facts; unfortunately, no sources are cited.

George Pellew, *John Jay*, Boston and New York, 1891.

Henry S. Randall, *The Life of Thomas Jefferson*, 3 vols., New York, 1863.

Monumental in its day, Randall's work leaves much to be desired for objectivity. Jefferson's moral halo was untarnished by political expediency, according to his great biographer. He prints Jefferson's famous "riding out the storm" letter that Madison vetoed, but he omits the section of Jefferson's explanatory letter to Madison in which the Republican candidate mentioned writing similar sentiments to Senator Langdon of New Hampshire with the belief that it would reach Adams in due course. The appendexes are excellent.

Theodore Roosevelt, *Gouverneur Morris*, Boston, 1898.

Kate M. Rowland, *The Life of Charles Carroll of Carrollton with his Correspondence and Public Papers*, 2 vols., New York and London, 1898.

One of the better memoirs editions to appear on the 100th anniversary of the establishment of the Federal government. The correspondence is disappointing for the last years of the Maryland Signer. Little politics.

———, *The Life of George Mason, 1725–1792*, 2 vols., New York and London, 1892.

Richard Rush, *Washington in Domestic Life*, Philadelphia, 1857.

Sentimental laudations of the first President's home life.

Nathan Schachner, *Aaron Burr*, New York, 1937.

Mr. Schachner's biographies are accurate and well written for the layman.

———, *Alexander Hamilton*, New York and London, 1946.

Based too much on Federalist MSS.

Henry H. Simms, *Life of John Taylor*, Richmond, 1932.

Chaps. IV through VI, dealing with his political work in the 1790's, are instructive. Valuable quotations from Taylor's letters.

Ellen H. Smith, *Charles Carroll of Carrollton*, Harvard University Press, 1942.

A thoroughly delightful book; well written, amusing, and honest.

Ernest W. Spaulding, *His Excellency George Clinton, Critic of the Constitution*, New York, 1938.

Bernard C. Steiner, *Life and Correspondence of James McHenry*, Cleveland, 1907.

A valuable source of documents and letters from Federalists of the 1780's and 1790's. McHenry's adoration of both Washington and Hamilton must be kept in mind constantly.

Nathaniel W. Stephenson and Waldo H. Dunn, *George Washington*, 2 vols., New York, 1940.

Strongly biased against Jefferson and the Republican party.

Arthur Stryon, *The Last of the Cocked Hats*, University of Oklahoma Press, 1945. The life of James Monroe.

The background of this book is "eternity," the theme is the struggle for agrarian democracy of which Shays's Rebellion was an early flare-up, and the author's approach is indicated by his belief that "democracy cannot tolerate leaders, only representatives." He dedicates it to Franklin Roosevelt. Unscholarly.

C. W. Upham and Octavius Pickering, *The Life and Times of Timothy Pickering*, 4 vols., Boston, 1867–73.

This defense of Secretary of State Pickering's career in the Adams cabinet is based almost entirely on Mr. Pickering's papers. Much of what Pickering was involved in is missing. For example, there is no intimation that a violent disagreement over Gerry's appointment to the peace mission in 1798 existed in the Executive Department. Valuable when Pickering is allowed to speak for himself from his letters.

Raymond Walters, Jr., *Alexander James Dallas*, University of Pennsylvania Press, 1943.

Especially valuable for Pennsylvania politics. Unfortunately Beckley and his friends read Dallas out of the party as a "trimmer" after the 1796 election.

Samuel H. Wandell and Meade Minnigerode, *Aaron Burr*, 2 vols., New York and London, 1925.

The authors claim to present a new interpretation based on new sources, Princeton University library, New York Public

Library, and New York Historical Society. Rather extravagant claims are made for Senator Burr as the leader of northern Republicanism at the expense of Livingston, Jefferson, *et al.*

Harry R. Warfel, *Noah Webster*, New York, 1936.

The author champions Webster as the most fair of contemporary editors. A Federalist in his sympathies, Webster chose freely between Adams and Hamilton during Adams' turbulent administration.

Bird Wilson, *Memoir of the Life of the Rt. Rev. William White*, Philadelphia, 1839.

Bishop White knew many political leaders well, most of them Federalists. His memoirs are intelligent and provide an interesting portrayal of social life in the national capital up to 1800. Few Republicans seem to have attended divine services.

Secondary sources: articles

Douglas Adair, "The Tenth Federalist Revisited," *William and Mary Quarterly*, January, 1951, 48-68.

Harry Ammon and Adrienne Koch, "The Virginia and Kentucky Resolutions; an episode in Jefferson's and Madison's Defense of Civil Liberties," *William and Mary Quarterly*, April, 1948, 145-176.

The best account of the authorship and purposes of the famed resolutions.

F. M. Anderson, "Enforcement of the Alien and Sedition Acts," American Historical Society, *Report*, 1912, 113-127.

———, "Contemporary Opinion of the Virginia and Kentucky Resolutions," *American Historical Review*, XXXVI, 336 ff.

Samuel F. Bemis, "The London Mission of Thomas Pinckney, 1792–1796," *American Historical Review*, January, 1923.

———, "The Letters of Stephen Higginson, 1783–1804," American Historical Association, *Report*, 1896, vol. I.

Frederick J. Brown, "A Sketch of the Life of Dr. James McHenry," *Fund Publication No. 10*, Maryland Historical Society, Baltimore, 1877.

Lyman H. Butterfield, "The Dream of Benjamin Rush; the Reconciliation of Jefferson and Adams," *Yale Review*, XL, No. 2, 1951.

Manning J. Daur, "The Two John Nicholases," *American Historical Review*, XLV, January, 1940, 338-353.

A possible blackmail story concerning Washington and Jefferson that has yet to be cleared up.

P. G. Davidson, "Virginia and the Alien and Sedition Acts," *American Historical Review*, XXXVI, 336 ff.

Huntley Dupre, "The Kentucky Gazette Reports the French Revolution," *Mississippi Valley Historical Review*, XXVI, 1939, 163-180.

Bernard Fay, "Early Party Machinery in the United States," *Pennsylvania Magazine of History and Biography*, LX, 1936, 375-390.

Carl R. Fish, "Removal of Officials by the Presidents of the United States," American Historical Association, *Report*, 1899, I. Washington, 1899, 67-86.

Homer C. Hockett, "Federalism and the West," *Essays in American History, dedicated to F. J. Turner*, 113-135.

J. A. James, "French Diplomacy and American Politics, 1794–1795," American Historical Association, *Report*, 1911, I, 153-163.

E. W. Lyon, "The French Directory and the United States," *American Historical Review*, XLIII, 1938, 514-532.

Philip M. Marsh, "Randolph and Hamilton," *Pennsylvania Magazine of History and Biography*, LXXII, July, 1948, 247-252.

———, "Philip Freneau and His Circle," *Pennsylvania Magazine of History and Biography*, LXIII, 1939, 37-59.

———, "John Beckley, Mystery Man of the Early Jeffersonians," *Pennsylvania Magazine of History and Biography*, LXXII, January, 1948, 54-69.

Samuel E. Morison, "Elbridge Gerry, Gentleman Democrat," *New England Quarterly*, II, January, 1929, 6-33.

Anson D. Morse, "The Politics of John Adams," *American Historical Review*, IV, 292 ff.

Ulrich B. Phillips, "The South Carolina Federalists," *American Historical Review*, XIV, July, 1909, 731-743.

———, "Georgia and States Rights," *Report of the American Historical Review, 1901*, Vol. II, Washington, 1902.

Robert E. Reeser, "Rufus King and the Federalist Party," UCLA Doctoral Dissertation, 1948–49.

William A. Schaper, "Sectionalism and Representation in South Carolina," American Historical Association, *Report*, 1900, Washington, 1901.

F. J. Turner, "Documents on the Blount Conspiracy, 1795–1797," *American Historical Review*, X, 274-606.

H. S. Turner, ed., "Memoirs of Benjamin Stoddert," Columbia Historical Society, *Records*, XX, Washington, 1917.

Index